FEELING
AND FORM

Susanne K. Langer

FEELING AND FORM

A THEORY OF ART

DEVELOPED FROM *Philosophy in a New Key*

CHARLES SCRIBNER'S SONS   NEW YORK

ISBN 0-684-15538-9

To the happy memory
of
ERNST CASSIRER

INTRODUCTION

In *Philosophy in a New Key* it was said that the theory of symbolism there developed should lead to a critique of art as serious and far-reaching as the critique of science that stems from the analysis of discursive symbolism. *Feeling and Form* purports to fulfill that promise, to be that critique of art.

Since this philosophy of art rests squarely on the above-mentioned semantic theory, the present book cannot but presuppose the reader's acquaintance with the previous one; it is, in fact, in the nature of a sequel. I would rather have made it quite independent, but its own subject matter is so large—despite the sketchy form it has sometimes taken—that to repeat the relevant or even the most essential contents of the earlier book would have necessitated two volumes, the first of which would, of course, have practically duplicated the work which already exists. So I must beg the reader to regard *Feeling and Form* as, in effect, Volume II of the study in symbolism that began with *Philosophy in a New Key*.

A book, like a human being, cannot do everything; it cannot answer in a few hundred pages all the questions which the Elephant's Child in his 'satiable curiosity might choose to ask. So I may as well state at once what it does not attempt to do. It does not offer criteria for judging "masterpieces," nor even successful as against unsuccessful lesser works —pictures, poems, musical pieces, dances, or any other. It does not set up canons of taste. It does not predict what is possible or impossible in the confines of any art, what materials may be used in it, what subjects will be found congenial to it, etc. It will not help anyone to an artistic conception, nor teach him how to carry one out in any medium. All such norms and rulings seem to me to lie outside of the philosopher's province. The business of philosophy is to unravel and organize concepts, to give definite and satisfactory meanings to the terms we use in talking about any subject (in this case art); it is, as Charles Peirce said, "to make our ideas clear."

Neither does this book coordinate theories of art with metaphysical perspectives, "world hypotheses" as Stephen Pepper calls them. That aim is not outside of philosophy, but beyond the scope of my present philosophical study. In the limits I have set myself, I can develop only one theory of art, and have not constructed the "world hypothesis" that might embrace it—let alone compare such a vast conceptual system with any alternative one.

There are, furthermore, limitations I have to accept simply in the interest of keeping my own ideas and their presentation manageable. The first of these is, not to take issue explicitly with the many theories, classical or current, that contradict my own at crucial points. Were I to follow out every refutation of other doctrines which my line of argument implies, that line would be lost in a tangle of controversy. Consequently I have avoided polemics as much as possible (though, of course, not altogether), and presented for discussion mainly those of my colleagues' and forerunners' ideas on which I can build, directing criticism against what seem to me their limitations or mistakes. As often as possible, moreover, I have relegated comparative materials to the footnotes. That makes for many annotations (especially in the chapters on poetry, fiction, and drama, subjects that are traditionally studied by scholars, so that their critical literature is enormous), but it allows the text to proceed, unencumbered by any arabesques of eclectic learning, as directly as possible with the development of its own large theme. The footnotes have thus become more than just references by chapter and verse, and are intended for the general reader as well as the special student; I have, therefore, departed from the strict custom of leaving quotations from foreign authors in their original languages, and have translated all such passages into English, in the notes as in the text. Wherever, therefore, no translator of a work with a foreign title is named, the translation is my own.

Finally, nothing in this book is exhaustively treated. Every subject in it demands further analysis, research, invention. That is because it is essentially an exploratory work, which—as Whitehead once said of William James's pragmatism—"chiefly starts a lot of hares for people to chase."

What *Feeling and Form* does undertake to do, is to specify the meanings of the words: expression, creation, symbol, import, intuition, vitality, and organic form, in such a way that we may understand, in terms of them, the nature of art and its relation to feeling, the relative autonomy of the several arts and their fundamental unity in "Art" itself, the functions of subject matter and medium, the epistemological problems of artistic "communication" and "truth." A great many other problems—for instance, whether performance is "creation," "recreation," or "mere craftsmanship," whether drama is "literature" or not, why the dance often reaches the zenith of its development in the primitive stage of a culture when other arts are just dawning on its ethnic horizon, to mention but a few—develop from the central ones and, like them, take answerable form. The main purpose of the book, therefore, may be described as the construction of an intellectual framework for philosophical studies, general or detailed, relating to art.

There are certain difficulties peculiar to this undertaking, some of which are of a practical, some of a semantical nature. In the first place, philosophy of art should, I believe, begin in the studio, not the gallery, auditorium, or library. Just as the philosophy of science required for its proper development the standpoint of the scientist, not of men like Comte, Buechner, Spencer, and Haeckel, who saw "science" as a whole, but without any conception of its real problems and working concepts, so the philosophy of art requires the standpoint of the artist to test the power of its concepts and prevent empty or naive generalizations. The philosopher must know the arts, so to speak, "from the inside." But no one can know all the arts in this way. This entails an arduous amount of non-academic study. His teachers, furthermore, are artists, and they speak their own language, which largely resists translation into the more careful, literal vocabulary of philosophy. This is likely to arouse his impatience. But it is, in fact, impossible to talk about art without adopting to some extent the language of the artists. The reason why they talk as they do is not entirely (though it is partly) that they are discursively untrained and popular in their speech; nor do they, misled by "bad speech habits," accept a "ghost in the machine" view of man, as Gilbert Ryle holds. Their vocabulary is metaphorical because it has to be plastic and powerful to let them speak their serious and often difficult thoughts. They cannot see art as "merely" this-or-that easily comprehensible phenomenon; they are too interested in it to make concessions to language. The critic who despises their poetic speech is all too likely to be superficial in his examination of it, and to impute to them ideas they do not hold rather than to discover what they really think and know.

But to learn the language of the studios is not enough; his business as a philosopher, after all, is to use what he learns, to construct theory, not a "working myth." And when he addresses his own colleagues he runs into a new semantic difficulty: instead of interpreting artists' metaphors, he now has to battle with the vagaries of professional usage. Words that he employs in all sobriety and exactness may be used in entirely different senses by writers as serious as he. Consider, for instance, a word around which this whole book is built: "symbol." Cecil Day Lewis, in his excellent book *The Poetic Image,* means by it always what I have called an "assigned symbol," a sign with a literal meaning fixed by convention; Collingwood goes still further and limits the term to *deliberately chosen* signs, such as the symbols of symbolic logic. Then he stretches the term "language" to cover everything I would call "symbols," includ-cluding religious icons, rites, and works of art.[1] Albert Cook, on the other hand, opposes "symbol" to "concept"; by the latter he means what Day Lewis means by "symbol," *plus* everything that he (Cook) condemns as "mechanical," such as the comedy of Rabelais. He speaks of "symbol's infinite suggestiveness."[2] Evidently "symbol" means something vaguely honorific, but I do not know what. David Daiches has still another usage, and indeed a definition: "As used here." he says in *A Study of Literature,* "it ['symbol'] simply means an expression which suggests more than it says."[3] But shortly afterwards he restricts its sense very radically: "A symbol is something in which sensitive men recognize their potential fate . . ."[4] Here the meaning of "symbol" may or may not be the same one that Mr. Cook has in mind.

All the poor philosopher can do is to define his words and trust the reader to bear their definition in mind. Often, however, the reader is not ready to accept a definition—especially if it is in any way unusual—until he sees what the author intends by it, why the word should be so defined; and that may be late in the course of the book. My own definition of "symbol" occurs, for just that reason, in chapter 20; and as that is really very late, perhaps I had better state it here, with the promise that the

---

[1] A fairly full discussion of Collingwood's work is given below, in chap. 20.
[2] *The Dark Voyage and the Golden Mean,* p. 173.
[3] *Ibid.,* p. 36.   [4] *Loc. cit., infra.*

book will elucidate and justify it: A symbol is any device whereby we are enabled to make an abstraction.

Almost all the key words in a philosophical discourse suffer from the wide range of meanings which they have had in previous literature. Thus Eisenstein, in *The Film Sense,* uses "representation" for what one usually calls "image," and "image" for something not necessarily concrete—what I would call an "impression." Yet his word "image" has something in common with Day Lewis's "poetic image"; furthermore there is this to be said for it—both men know, and let us know, what they mean by it.

A more difficult term, and an all-important one in this book, is "illusion." It is commonly confused with "delusion," wherefore the mention of it in connection with art usually evokes instant protests, as though one had suggested that art is a "mere delusion." But illusion as it occurs in art has nothing to do with delusion, not even with self-deception or pretense.

Besides the difficulties presented to art theory in general by the good and bad odors of words, which interfere with their strict meanings, and by the variety of even their defined meanings in the literature, each art has its special incubus of natural misconceptions. Music suffers more than any other art from the fact that it has marked somatic effects, which are all too often taken for its essential virtue. The affliction of literature is its relation to fact, propositional truth; of the drama, its nearness to moral questions; of dance, the personal element, the sensual interest; of painting and sculpture, the pseudo-problem of "imitation"; of architecture, the obvious fact of its utility. I have battled against all these bogeys as best I could; in the end, however, I hope it may be not direct refutations, but the theory itself, the whole systematic idea that will dispel special as well as general prejudices.

Toward the end of the book one might well expect that the ideas developed in relation to some art taken in isolation would be generalized and carried over to the other arts. Often the reader will be able to do this, and wonder why I neglected it. The reason is that when I do bring the arts into relation, and demonstrate their fundamental unity, it will be systematically done; that is another book.

Nothing in this essay, therefore, is finished, nor could art theory ever be finished. There may be new arts in the future; there may surely be new modes of any art; our own age has seen the birth of the motion picture, which is not only in a new medium, but is a new mode (see the Appendix, "A Note on the Film"). But as *Philosophy in a New Key* was a promise of a philosophy of art, this book, I fondly hope, is a beginning of something capable of indefinite continuation.

It would probably not be even a beginning—would not be at all—without the constant support of several friends who have aided me. For nearly four years I enjoyed, through the sponsorship of Columbia University, the help of the Rockefeller Foundation, that lightened my teaching load so I could devote myself to research, and gave me also, part of the time, an invaluable assistant. I thank both the Foundation and the University most heartily. The thanks I owe to that assistant, Eugene T. Gadol, cannot easily be rendered; besides putting his special knowledge of the theater at my disposal, he has been associated with the work almost constantly, and indeed has been my right hand. Furthermore, I want to express my special gratitude to Helen Sewell, who has given me the artist's view on many things, and has read and reread the script; in the light of her trenchant and frank criticism, chapter 5 was almost completely rewritten, and the faults that it retains are due to the fact that she did not write it. I am also indebted to Katrina Fischer for the research assistance she gave me with chapter 18, and to my sister, Ilse Dunbar, for help with the many translations from French and German sources; to Alice Dunbar for a sculptor's advices, and for her last-minute help in preparing the script for the press; and to Kurt Appelbaum for reading almost the whole work and giving me the benefit of a musician's very well-reasoned reflections. My debt to several of my former students is, I think, sufficiently clear in the text. But I must add a word in appreciation of the co-operative spirit with which the staff of Charles Scribner's Sons, especially Mr. Burroughs Mitchell, made this volume take shape according to my hopes.

A book that goes into the world with such a heavy load of gratitude is almost a community venture. I hope the community of artists, art lovers, and scholars will receive it with continued interest, and keep it alive by serious criticism.

S. K. L.

Hurley, N. Y., 1952

CONTENTS

The Art Symbol

Chapter one

THE MEASURE OF IDEAS

Philosophy is a fabric of ideas. It is not, like science, a body of general propositions expressing discovered facts, nor is it a collection of "moral truths" learned by some other means than factual discovery. Philosophy is a stocktaking of the ideas in terms of which one expresses facts and laws, beliefs and maxims and hypotheses—in short, it is the study of the conceptual framework in which all our propositions, true or false, are made. It deals primarily with meanings—with the sense of what we say. If the terms of our discourse are incompatible or confused, the whole intellectual venture to which they belong is invalid; then our alleged beliefs are not false, but spurious.

The usual sign of confusion in our basic ideas on any topic is the persistence of rival doctrines, all many times refuted yet not abandoned. In a system of thought that is fundamentally clear, even if not entirely so, new theories usually make old ones obsolete. In a field where the basic concepts are not clear, conflicting outlooks and terminologies continue, side by side, to recruit adherents.

This is notoriously the case in the domain of art criticism. All considered judgment rests, of course, on theoretical foundations of some sort; but the greatest experts in this field cannot really develop an interesting theory to account for their findings. Philosophical reflections on art constitute a large and fascinating literature, ranging from learned treatises to pure belles-lettres—essays, aphorisms, memoirs, even poetry. In this accumulated lore a wealth of doctrines has been laid down, some of them the flower of a long tradition, others quite new, genial insights, unsystematic but profound, and all of them in mixed profusion that obscures their natural connections with each other and with the history and actual life of the creative arts.

Yet the arts themselves exhibit a striking unity and logic, and seem to present a fair field for systematic thought. Why the confusion? Why the disconnected theories, the constantly alleged danger of losing touch with reality, the many philosophical beginnings that still fail to grow into organic intellectual structures? A truly enlightening theory of art should rise upon important artistic insights and evolve naturally from phase to phase, as the great edifices of thought—mathematics, logic, the sciences, theology, law, history—grow from perennial roots to further and further reaches of their own implications. Why is there no such systematic theory of art?

The reason is, I think, that the central issues in the appreciation and understanding of art, however clear they may be in practice, have not been philosophically sifted and recognized for what they are. A systematic discipline becomes organized only as its key problems are formulated; and often those problems, the solution of which would require and beget a powerful terminology and a principle of operation, are obscured by the incursion of *obvious* questions, immediately proposed by common sense, and regarded as "basic" because of their obviousness. Such questions are: What are the materials of art? Which is more important, form or content? What is Beauty? What are the canons of composition? How does a great work of art affect the beholder? Many of them have been mooted for hundreds of years, but when we make up our minds about the answers, theory goes no further. We have taken a stand, and we stand there.

All these questions are legitimate enough, and the purpose of a philosophy of art is to answer them. But as starting points of theory they are baneful, because they are products of "common sense," and consequently foist the vocabulary and the whole conceptual framework of common sense on our thinking. And with that instrument we cannot think beyond the commonplace.

There are certain misconceptions about philosophical thinking that have arisen, oddly enough, from the very concern of modern philosophers with method—from the acceptance of principles and ideals that sound impeccable as we avow them in conferences and symposia. One of these principles is that philosophy *deals with general notions*. This dictum is repeated in almost every introductory text, and voiced in one connection or another at every philosophical congress. The accent is always on the "general notions"; but the interesting point is that we profess to deal with them, and that this dealing is philosophy.

The immediate effect of the principle is to make people start their researches with attention to generalities: beauty, value, culture, and so forth. Such concepts, however, have no systematic virtue; they are not terms of description, as scientific concepts, e.g. mass, time, location, etc., are. They have no unit, and cannot be combined in definite proportions. They are "abstract qualities" like the elementary notions of Greek nature philosophy—wetness and dryness, heat and cold, lightness and heaviness. And just as no physics ever resulted from the classification of things by those attributes, so no art theory emerges from the contemplation of "aesthetic values." The desire to deal with general ideas from the outset, because that is supposed to be the business of philosophers, leads one into what may be termed "the fallacy of obvious abstraction": the abstraction and schematization of properties most obvious to common sense, traditionally recognized and embodied in the "material mode" of language.

Instead of constantly reiterating that philosophy deals with general ideas, or treats of "things in general," one should consider what it *does* in relation to general notions. Properly, I think, it constructs them. Out of what? Out of the more specific ones that we use in formulating our special and particularized knowledge—practical, scientific, social, or purely sensuous knowledge. Its work is a constant process of generalization. That process requires logical technique, imagination, and ingenuity; it is not achieved by beginning with generalities such as: "Art is expression," or "beauty is harmony." Propositions of this sort should occur at the end of a philosophical inquiry, not at its commencement. At the end, they are summaries of explicit and organized ideas that give them meaning; but as points of departure they prejudge too much and furnish no terms for their own elucidation.

Another unhappy product of our professional self-criticism is the dogma that philosophy can never really attain its goal, a completely synthetic vision of life. It can only approximate to success. Now even if there be such an ideal limit to our progressive understanding (and it may be doubted, for such a synoptic insight savors of an "illegitimate totality"), it does not offer any measure of actual achievement. On the contrary: when everybody is duly impressed with the impossibility of really meeting a challenge, we can claim too much indulgence; any failure may be excused as a "mere approximation." Consequently there is, today, practically no standard of philosophical work. Professional journals are full of stale arguments that do not advance their topics in any way, and forums leave their profound questions exactly as unanswered and unanswerable as they were before. The sort of effort and ingenuity that goes into solving scientific or historical problems would immediately analyze and blast the questions, replace them with more leading and suggestive ones, and then invent means of finding real answers. When there is a premium on definitive answers, people spend a good deal of time and labor on intellectual devices for handling difficult issues. Scientists rarely talk about scientific method, but they often find most elaborate and devious ways of turning a question so as to make it accessible to *some* method of investigation that will yield a solution. It is the problem that dictates the approach. Philosophers, on the other hand, usually decide on an approach to philosophical problems in general, and then tackle the age-old chestnuts—so traditionally chewed over that they have capitalized names: the Problem of Being, the Problem of Evil, etc. —just as they were formulated by Plato or his master, Parmenides.

Philosophy, nevertheless, is a living venture, and philosophical questions are not by their nature insoluble. They are, indeed, radically different from scientific questions, because they concern the implications and other interrelations of ideas, not the order of physical events; their answers are interpretations instead of factual reports, and their function is to increase not our knowledge of nature, but our understanding of what we know. Actually, the growth of conception, which is the aim of philosophy, has a direct bearing on our ability to observe facts; for it is systematic conception that makes some facts important and others trivial. Linnaeus, pioneering in natural science with obvious qualitative abstractions, classified plants according to the colors of their flowers; a morphological conception of botany, which relates every part of a plant to the whole organism, and furthermore connects plant life with animal life in one biological scheme, makes the color of flowers an unimportant factor.

There is a philosophy of nature, gradually developed by men like Poincaré, Russell, Lenzen, Weyl, which underlies our natural science; and though it may fall far short of the "synoptic" ideal, such philosophical work as, for instance, Whitehead has done in this field clarifies our concepts of physical order, of organic existence, and of mentality and knowledge. Similarly, the philosophy of mathematics has made that ancient discipline a paragon of intellectual clearness and negotiability. The thinkers who built up those conceptual systems left all the rival doctrines of Being and Value and Mind alone, and started from quite special problems—the meaning of "simultaneity" in astronomical observations, or the meaning of $\sqrt{-2}$ in the number series, or of "dimensionless point" in physical measurement. Note that these are all philosophical issues—all questions of meaning; but because they are special questions, the meanings to be construed must satisfy definite and rather complex demands. The definition of cosmic "simultaneity," for instance, required a complete reconstruction of space and time notions. The interpretation of $\sqrt{-2}$ demanded a theory of mathematical series to justify the very convenient use of that puzzling symbol. The concept of a dimensionless point, or pure location, led to Whitehead's theory of "extensive abstraction"—a highly important philosophical notion.

Such ideas usually prove, in the end, to have general as well as particular application—that is, they are found to be capable of *generalization*, once they have been formulated in detail for their special purposes. The statement of those ideas in their special form implies a great many other propositions statable in the same terms, and suggests further definitions. And as the philosophical analysis of the basic concepts proceeds, the subject matter becomes more and more systematic; from the central focus of actual problems made clear, similar forms present themselves in all directions, until a whole cosmology, ontology, or epistemology may result. Such philosophy is built up by the principle of generalization. It is all of a piece, yet it cannot be summarized in the statement of one *belief*, and elected or spurned as "such-and-such-ism"; neither can it be simply "applied" to interpret experience as a whole. Principles of logical construction empower us to cope with experience, but they do not offer us constructions ready made.

Of course, "scientific method in philosophy" has been discussed ever since Bertrand Russell, as a young man, launched his vigorous attacks on traditional metaphysics. Yet scientific method is not the same thing as philosophic method. Hypothesis and experiment hold no place of honor in philosophy, as they do in science; facts and connections of facts are starting points for it instead of findings. The findings are ideas—the meaning of what we say, not only about natural facts, but about all matters of human interest whatever: art, religion, reason, absurdity, freedom, or the calculus. Only a framework of further meanings gives such general words any real value.

The building up of a theory—"the architecture of ideas," as Charles Peirce called it—involves more logical considerations than people usually realize when they discuss methodology. It is not enough to survey the field of study, break it up into what seem to be its simplest constituent elements, and describe it as a pattern of these "data." Such a pattern is orderly, like an alphabetical index wherein anything known can be located, but it furnishes no leads to things unknown. To construct a theory we must start with propositions that have *implications;* theoretical thought is the expanding of their import. Therefore not every true statement about science, art, life, or morals, is an "approach" to the systematic study of the topic in question; the statement must contain ideas that may be manipulated, defined, modified, and used in combinations; it must be interesting as well as true. This logical requirement might be called *the principle of fecundity.*

Consider, as a great example of constructive thinking, the reinterpretation of physical events which Newton advanced in his *Principia Mathematica,* under the perfectly correct name of "natural philosophy." Legend has it that the first fact he described in new terms was the fall of an apple. That an apple falls to earth was always a commonplace; but that the apple is *attracted* by the earth expresses a great idea. What makes it great is, in the first place, that it is capable of generalization. Of course we may generalize the "fall" of the apple, too, and say: "all things tend to fall to earth," but such a rule has exceptions. The moon does not fall down, neither do the clouds. But: "All masses attract each other," has no exception. "The apple is attracted by the earth" serves to describe exactly the same observation as "the apple falls," but is true even while the apple hangs, and remains so when it is rotting on the ground. Also, the same thing may be said of the moon, though the moon never "falls"—that is, never gets to the earth; and of the clouds that float indefinitely, and even of the sun.

The second characteristic that makes Newton's interpretation great is its fecundity; for the concept of "attraction" entails a *dynamic* element that was absent from all previous mathematical physics. The purely geometrical systems all required the assumption of some special agency outside the world to supply its motion. But attraction was a force, and therefore a source of motion within the physical system. Moreover, it could be measured, and its measure proved to be proportionate to the more familiar conditions of mass and distance. Almost as soon as "the new natural philosophy" was propounded, it gave rise to a science of physics.

Art criticism is not science, because it is not concerned with description and prediction of facts. Even if its premises were clear and coherent, its terms powerful, it would remain a philosophical discipline, for its whole aim is understanding. But the principles of generalization and fecundity are not, essentially, principles of science; they are principles of philosophical thinking, and it is only in so far as science is an intellectual formulation that it partakes of them. Perhaps that is why the protagonists of "scientific method" for philosophy have largely overlooked them. Only where real philosophical work has been done—e.g. in laying the foundations of science, jurisprudence, and mediaeval theology —have they been given tacit acceptance.

It is peculiarly in the vague unsystematic realms of thought that a single problem, doggedly pursued to its solution, may elicit a new logical vocabulary, i.e. a new set of ideas, reaching beyond the problem itself and forcing a more negotiable conception of the whole field. To bring such an issue into the center of our interest is to begin serious work on the subject in hand. This is what I propose to do with the philosophy of art. It seems to me that, amid all the speculation of aestheticians and the half-baked, yet significant studio talk of artists, one crucial issue is never fully faced, but is skirted with a sort of intellectual awe, or treated emotionally with no demand for meaning at all: that is the problem of artistic creation. Is an artist's work really a process of creation? What, actually, is created? Is there justification for the fairly popular notion that one should speak rather of *re-creating* than of creating things in art? Or is the whole idea of "creative work" a sentimentalism?

All these questions, and several more, present aspects of the same problem. The solution of that problem answers them all with equal definiteness. But it requires something of a reorientation among the familiar ideas of art criticism and philosophy. It demands a stricter treatment of the term "expression," and gives a single and unmysterious meaning to "intuition." Above all, it entails a special formulation of almost every major problem concerning art, notably that of the unity of the several arts, in face of the often denied, yet patent fact of their actual division; the paradox of abstraction in a mode supposed to be characterized by concreteness; the significance of style, the power of technique. Once you answer the question: "What does art create?" all the further questions of why and how, of personality, talent and genius, etc., seem to emerge in a new light from the central thesis. That means, simply, that the thesis *is* central, and that the problem which elicited it is fecund and ultimately general.

As the subject becomes organized, the ideas that have been advanced in the past take on a new significance; and one finds that an amazing amount of good work in this field has already been done. The literature of art theory, which looks so incoherent and so cluttered with hapless "approaches," is really rich in vital thoughts and valuable, scholarly findings.

One does not need to begin with a *tabula rasa* and work in defiance of schools; the seeds of philosophical theory, and often substantial roots of it, are everywhere. In a way, this complicates the task, just because the combined literatures of all the arts as well as a good deal of philosophy and psychology make such a vast intellectual background, and the important contributions to knowledge are so deeply buried, that real scholarship in such a wide and fertile domain is humanly unattainable. The grounding of any new theory that purports to start from art itself, where "art" takes in music, literature, and dance as well as plastic expression, is inevitably frail and haphazard. But a philosophy is not made by one person; the whole body of a discipline cannot be in anybody's ken. One can only gather enough for each immediate purpose —in this case, to substantiate the treatment of a highly important, yet special subject, the problem of artistic creation. If that treatment really opens a vista to art theory in general, the literature behind us (known or unknown to any particular thinker) and the issues still before us should take their proper forms and places in that perspective, wherever we encounter them in the progress of philosophical thought.

Chapter two

PARADOXES

For the past two hundred years—that is to say, since the days of Winckelmann and Herder—philosophers have continually pondered the significance and motivation of the arts. The problem of art has even been honored as a special department of philosophy under the name of "aesthetics," variously defined as "the science of the beautiful," "the theory or philosophy of taste," "the science of the fine arts," or lately (in Croce's phrase) "the science of expression." All these definitions are more or less askew. A philosophical interest in a particular subject matter, such as taste, or beauty, or even the great topic of "expression," does not establish a science; if "the beautiful" is the field of aesthetics, this field is wider than that of the fine arts; so is the realm of "expression." Taste, on the other hand, is only one phenomenon related to beauty (in art or elsewhere), and is just as much related to decorum and to fashion. Perhaps it is better not to map an unknown continent in advance, but simply to study whatever philosophical problems the arts present, and trust that any careful analysis and constructive handling of even quite special questions (e.g. "What is expressed in architecture?" "Is musical performance a creative act?" or "Is taste related to talent?") will soon show their interrelations and define the general field of their relevance.

Meanwhile, even in the vague or arbitrary confines of a pseudo-science, a great deal of thinking has been done, sometimes in close connection with general philosophy, sometimes as a theoretical excursion from criticism. In the course of such serious reflection on the arts, certain dominant ideas have emerged that constitute a sort of intellectual vocabulary of contemporary aesthetics. They are all at least indirectly related to each other, yet their relationships are anything but clear and simple, and are, in fact, often antinomous. Some of the dominant ideas themselves seem to entail logical difficulties.

In broadest outline, these ideas, which occur again and again in different guises and combinations, are: Taste, Emotion, Form, Representation, Immediacy, and Illusion.[1] Each of them is a strong *Leitmotiv* in philosophy of art, yet the theories grounded on them, respectively, have a peculiar way of either openly clashing with one another, or leaving at least one topic completely out of consideration. Thus theories of art as sensuous satisfaction, i.e. appeal to taste, have to traffic very carefully with emotion, and stringently draw the limits of representation. The many emotion-theories can make but a very minor issue of taste, and what is worse, of form. Those which make form paramount usually rule out any appeal to emotion, and often find representation a curse rather than an asset; those which build chiefly on the concept of representation do well with illusion, and even with emotion, but they cannot treat form as an independent value, and reduce the function of taste to a mere office of censorship. Immediacy, which is a metaphysical virtue of pure reality, or concrete individuality, entails the idea of *intuition* as a direct perception of all there is to know about a work of art. It fits well into theories of taste, and is at least compatible with most of the emotion-theories, and with the subtler treatments of representation; but not, as is commonly supposed, with the notion of art as form. The uniqueness of a form is logically impossible to establish. No form is *necessarily* unique, and short of that the character of uniqueness could not serve to bestow a metaphysical status on it. As for the motif of illusion, it is generally coupled with its opposite, reality, and serves rather to raise difficulties than to solve them. Often it is the bête noire to be explained away.

The general disorder of our intellectual stock in trade in the realm of aesthetics is further aggravated by the fact that there are two opposite perspectives from which every work of art may be viewed: that of its author and that of its spectators (or hearers, or readers, as the case may be). One perspective presents it as an expression, the other as an impres-

---

[1]Any anthology of aesthetics will provide examples; Melvin Rader's *A Modern Book of Aesthetics*, for instance, classifies theories as "Emotionalist Theories," "Theories of Form," etc.

sion. From the former standpoint one naturally asks: "What moves an artist to compose his work, what goes into it, what (if anything) does he mean by it?" From the latter, on the other hand, the immediate question is: "What do works of art do, or mean, to us?" This question is the more usual, even in serious theoretical thought, because more people are beholders of art than makers of it, and this counts for philosophers as well as for any unselected public. Most aestheticians can treat the problem of artistic impression more authoritatively than that of expression; when they talk about the moods and inspirations of artists, or speculate on the sources and motives of any particular work, they leave the straight and narrow path of intellectual conscience and often let a quite irresponsible fancy roam.

Yet theories of expression, though harder for a layman in the arts to handle, are more fertile than analytic studies of impression. Just as the most interesting philosophy of science has been developed to meet the logical problems of the laboratory, so the most vital issues in philosophy of art stem from the studio.

The dominant ideas occur in both types of theory, but they look different when viewed from such different standpoints. This circumstance adds to the apparent confusion of aesthetic notions. What, in the impressionist perspective, figures as taste, i.e. a pleasant or unpleasant reaction to sensory stimulation, appears from the opposite angle as the principle of selection, the so-called "ideal of beauty" which is supposed to guide an artist in his choice of colors, tones, words, etc. Emotion may be taken either as the effect of a work on the beholder, or as the source from which its author's conception arose, and the resultant theories will appear to treat the whole subject of emotion entirely differently (one will tend to the sort of laboratory psychology that seeks aesthetic principles in the tabulated reactions of school children, parents, graduate students, or radio audiences, the other to a psychoanalytic study of artists). The contemplation of form from the standpoint of impression yields such notions as Universal Law, Dynamic Symmetry, Significant Form; from that of expression it involves us in the problems of abstraction. Representation may be taken as Plato and Aristotle took it—that is, as the social function of the picture or statue, poem or drama—the function of directing the percipient's mind to something beyond the work of art, namely the represented object or action; or it may be taken as the artist's motive for creating the work—a record of things that fascinate him, persons or scenes he desires to immortalize. He may paint his mistress, his memory of Tahiti, or more subtly his state of mind. But for the beholder, the picture furnishes a lady, a glimpse of the South Seas, or a symbol of libido. Similarly, the problem of illusion is treated from the critic's point of view as a demand on our credulity, our willingness to "make-believe"; from the studio point of view it is treated as play, "escape," or the artist's dream.

This inventory is by no means exhaustive of the wealth of ideas to be found in contemporary aesthetics. But even such a cursory survey gives one a sense of tangled profusion and of the general incommensurability of the outstanding concepts with each other. One aesthetician speaks in terms of "Significant Form" and another in terms of dream. One says that the function of art is to record the contemporary scene, and another maintains that pure sounds in "certain combinations," or colors in harmonious spatial disposition, give him the "aesthetic emotion" that is both the aim and the criterion of art. One artist claims to paint his personal feelings, and the next one to express Pythagorean truths about the astronomical universe.

But this peculiar mutual irrelevance of the leading notions is not the only disconcerting feature of current art theory; a more radical difficulty is their inveterate tendency to paradox. Most of the dominant ideas, even taken all alone, carry with them some danger of self-defeat. As soon as we develop them we find ourselves with dialectical concepts on our hands. We have Significant Form that must not, at any price, be permitted to signify anything—illusion that is the highest truth—disciplined spontaneity—concrete ideal structures—impersonal feeling, "pleasure objectified"—and public dreaming.

These oddities are not simply to be dismissed as self-contradictions.[2] There is a difference between mere inconsistency and paradox. Inconsistent ideas generally disappear from circulation as soon as their fatal defects are revealed, and if they are to pass muster even for a while their

---

[2]Still less as imposture or solemn nonsense, such as Mr. Ducasse imputed to Clive Bell, in a vehement, not to say vitriolic, tirade against the notion of "Significant Form" (Appendix to *The Philosophy of Art*).

faults must be somewhat hidden. An absurd term or self-contradictory proposition that continues to function in serious, systematic thought, although its logical scandal is patent, is paradoxical. The inconsistent ideas involved in it conflict with each other because they are actually distorted. Properly formulated they would not be mutually contradictory. They are misconceived, and consequently their union is misconceived, but it is motivated by a sound sense of their importance and logical connection. The word "paradox" bespeaks this peculiar status; both contradictory elements are "doctrinal," i.e. they are really accepted and the conjunction of them is admitted, even though it is not understood.

Wherever the "rich mud of vague conceptions" that is the spawning ground of human reason yields a genuine paradox, such as "fictional truth" or "self-representing symbols" or "impersonal feelings," we are faced with a direct philosophical challenge. Paradox is a symptom of misconception; and coherent, systematic conception, i.e. the process of making sense out of experience, is philosophy. Therefore a paradoxical idea is not one to be discarded, but to be resolved. Where both elements of an obvious antinomy maintain their semblance of truth, their pragmatic virtue, and both can claim to originate in certain accepted premises, the cause of their conflict probably lies in those very premises themselves. It is original sin. The premises, in their turn, are often tacit presuppositions, so that the real challenge to the philosopher is to expose and analyze and correct *them*. If he succeeds, a new scheme of the dominant ideas will be found implicit, without the paradoxical concepts of the old perspective.

But such a philosophical procedure is very radical. Usually, therefore, an attempt is first made to reconcile the opposed ideas by treating them as "principles" in the classical sense, antithetical characters that may be possessed in varying proportions, opposite poles with a point of perfect balance between them. This scheme is so well established in philosophical thought—going back, as it does, at least to Empedocles—that even a layman has no difficulty with it. It is the scheme of ancient and mediaeval science: such and such measure of hot principle with such and such measure of cold principle achieves a given temperature, so and so much motion and so and so much rest yield a particular velocity, etc. Heat and cold, motion and rest, action and passion, life and death, are extremes that counteract each other in whatever phenomena they govern, but always in some characteristic proportion.

The most famous use of this polarity of opposite "principles" is Nietzsche's ranking of all art works between the extremes of pure feeling and pure form, and his classification of them as Dionysian or Apollonian according to the preponderance of one principle or the other. In fact, this treatment of a basic antithesis in art theory has absorbed a whole class of related "polarities": emotion–reason, freedom–restraint, personality–tradition, instinct-intellect, and so on. Curt Sachs' "great rhythm" between the poles of "ethos" and "pathos" is the same sort of adjustment to the familiar oppositions in art theory.

Yet the paradoxical character of aesthetics is not remedied by a resort to "polarity." The polarity of feeling and form is itself a problem; for the relation of the two "poles" is not really a "polar" one, i.e. a relation of positive and negative, since feeling and form are not logical complements. They are merely associated, respectively, with each other's negatives. Feeling is associated with spontaneity, spontaneity with informality or indifference to form, and thus (by slipshod thinking) with *absence* of form. On the other hand, form connotes formality, regulation, hence repression of feeling, and (by the same slipshodness) *absence* of feeling. The conception of polarity, intriguing though it be, is really an unfortunate metaphor whereby a logical muddle is raised to the dignity of a fundamental principle. Of course the alternation of "ethos" and "pathos" phases in the history of art is an observable fact, and must have some significance; but to treat it as the revelation of a dualistic "principle" (in the mediaeval sense), and think it explains the nature of art, is not to resolve a paradox but to accept it as ultimate.[3] Thereby one takes a final philosophical stand just where philosophical inquiry should begin.

Furthermore, the old division between the two perspectives, that of the artist and that of the beholder—art as expression against art as im-

---

[3]Sachs regards the parallelism of ethos–pathos fluctuations in the several arts as a proof that all the arts are one. The logic of this "proof" is obscure, since any outside influence might cause such a fluctuation, always simultaneously, in quite distinct fields; in fact, his own later observation that fashions in dress, manners, and morals follow the same rhythmic pattern makes his principle prove either nothing, or too much—namely, that such phenomena also are "Art" and really indistinguishable from painting, music or literature.

pression—is not bridged by acceptance of an eternal tug of war between the opposed "poles," prescribed form and emotional content. Even a spiritual "field of force" looks different according to the two different standpoints. For the artist, who is supposed to achieve self-expression in the face of technical dictates and taboos, the embattled forces are his emotions against the canons of intelligibility, composition, and perfection of forms. For the critic, who is to find sensuous beauty in the forms, to view them at a proper "psychical distance" and with mental equilibrium, while he is excited by them to empathic feelings, the "poles" are aesthetic quality versus emotional stimulation.

In a practical way, the two alternative perspectives themselves present us with a difficult option. Shall we judge a work of art as an utterance, giving vent to its author's feelings, or as a stimulus, producing sentiments in the spectator? Obviously any art object may be both; but it may be perfectly adequate as expression and not as an incentive to feeling, or contrariwise may leave the artist still frustrated and yet produce the strongest reactions in its beholders. If self-expression is the aim of art, then only the artist himself can judge the value of his products. If its purpose is to excite emotion, he should study his audience and let his psychological findings guide his work, as advertising agents do.

Both hypotheses sound unorthodox, to say the least; to speak bluntly, they are both silly. The relation of art to feeling is evidently something subtler than sheer catharsis or incitement. In fact, the most expert critics tend to discount both these subjective elements, and treat the emotive aspect of a work of art as something integral to it, something as objective as the physical form, color, sound pattern of verbal text itself.

But feeling that is not subjective presents a new paradox. There have been several attempts to describe, if not to explain, such a phenomenon. Santayana regarded beauty as "pleasure objectified"—the spectator's pleasure "projected" into the object that caused it. Just why and how the projection occurs is not clear; it is not imputation, for we do not impute enjoyment to the Parthenon, or think Dürer's crucified Christ, the Disciple and the swooning Mother below the cross, or the cross itself, is "having" our alleged pleasure in the picture. What the picture "has" is beauty, which *is* our projected, i.e. objectified, pleasure. But why is subjective pleasure not good enough? Why do we objectify it and project it into visual or auditory forms as "beauty," while we are content to feel it directly, as delight, in candy and perfumes and cushioned seats?

A more radical handling of feeling as something objective may be found in a little article by Otto Baensch, entitled "Kunst und Gefühl," which appeared in *Logos* in 1923. Here the paradox of "objective feelings" is frankly accepted as an undeniable, even though incomprehensible, fact. By this counsel of despair the problem is brought to such a head that its solution is imminent; the intellectual stage is set for it, the necessary exhibits are all there. Baensch himself comes so close to the logical vantage point from which the whole snarl of artistic "expression" appears suddenly to disentangle and arrange itself, and to resolve an astounding number of other paradoxes in the process, that the best introduction to what I consider the key idea (though he completely missed the solution) is, perhaps, to quote his pregnant little essay at some length.

"In the following meditation," he says at the outset, "I hope to prove that art, like science, is a mental activity whereby we bring certain contents of the world into the realm of objectively valid cognition; and that, furthermore, it is the particular office of art to do this with the world's emotional content. According to this view, therefore, the function of art is not to give the percipient any kind of pleasure, however noble, but to acquaint him with something he has not known before. Art, just like science, aims primarily to be 'understood'. . . . But since that of which it makes us aware is always of an emotive character it normally calls forth, more or less peremptorily, a reaction of pleasure or displeasure in the perceiving subject. This explains quite readily how the erroneous opinion has arisen that the percipient's delight and assent are the criteria of art.

"The mood of a landscape appears to us to be objectively given with it as one of its attributes, belonging to it just like any other attribute we perceive it to have. . . . We never think of regarding the landscape as a sentient being whose outward aspect 'expresses' the mood that it contains subjectively. The landscape does not express the mood, but *has* it; the mood surrounds, fills and permeates it, like the light that illumines it, or the odor it exhales; the mood belongs to our total impression of the landscape and can only be distinguished as one of its components by a process of abstraction."

Here we are supposed, then, to encounter as an actual content of the world a feeling that is not being felt. No subject is expressing it; it is just objectively there. Baensch is, indeed, so well aware of its distinct status that he saves it deftly from confusion with feelings that are symptomatically expressed.

"The mien and attitude of a sad person may 'express' sadness so that we seem to perceive directly, in the person's appearance, the sorrow that inwardly possesses him; yet the objective feeling that belongs to a picture of such a sad person need not itself be sadness." The picture, for instance, may be ludicrous; it may be in very light mood, even in high spirits. Therefore, the author points out, "The feeling that appears to be expressed in a representational painting may be the same as the objective feeling which inheres in the work itself, but by no means is this necessarily the case; so far from it, in fact, that the two will often stand in a relation of sharp contrast.

"There are, then, 'objective feelings' given to . . . our consciousness, feelings that exist quite objectively and apart from us, without being inward states of an animate being. It must be granted that these objective feelings do not occur in an independent state by themselves; they are always embedded and inherent in objects from which they cannot be actually separated, but only distinguished by abstraction: objective feelings are always dependent parts of objects."

His next notable observation is the similarity of such feelings to sense qualities, although they have no sensory character. "They certainly do not belong," he says, "to the form of the object, they are not relations, but belong to the content. . . . They share in the non-sensory character of relational forms, but have something in common with the sensory content too, namely the fact that they are temporal qualitative contents . . . whose variety and richness readily match the prodigality of the sensory field."

But that is as far as parallels with the familiar ingredients, form and content, relations and qualities, will go. How feelings can "inhere" in lifeless objects is a challenge to analytic thinking. His attempt to explain it is not entirely successful, yet so circumspect and well aimed that it certainly serves to clarify the issue even if not to decide it. Whenever objective feelings "inhere" in concrete objects, he says, "the manner of their inherence is such that the analogy with the status of sense qualities breaks down. For the latter stand *in* relations to each other, they are combined and composed, so as to produce, jointly, the appearance of the object. Non-sensory qualities, on the other hand, surround and permeate this whole structure in fluid omnipresence and cannot be brought into any explicit correlation with its component elements. They are contained in the sensory qualities as well as in the formal aspects, and despite all their own variety and contrasts they melt and mingle in a total impression that is very hard to analyze."

All feelings, Baensch maintains, are non-sensory qualities; subjective ones are contained in a Self, objective ones in impersonal things. The great difficulty is to think of them apart from any host, to conceive them as independent contents of the world. "Certainly," he says, "feelings as experienced qualities are not vague or indefinite at all but have a very concrete and particular character. But to conceptual treatment they are recalcitrant as soon as we try to go beyond the crudest general designations; there is no systematic scheme that is subtle enough in its logical operations to capture and convey their properties.

"Nothing, therefore, avails us in life and in scientific thought but to approach them indirectly, correlating them with the describable events, inside or outside ourselves, that contain and thus convey them; in the hope that anyone reminded of such events will thus be led somehow to experience the emotive qualities, too, that we wish to bring to his attention."[4]

Here the crucial problem obviously is to present feelings not to enjoyment (even in Alexander's sense), but to conception; not experience of feelings (which is presupposed in the appeal to memory), but *knowledge about them* is difficult to achieve. "Since they are non-sensory qualities, our apperception of them is also of a non-sensuous sort. . . . There is no apperception so blind as the non-sensuous apperception of feelings.

". . . How can we capture, hold and handle feelings so that their content may be made conceivable and presented to our consciousness in universal form, without being understood in the strict sense, i.e. by means of concepts? The answer is: We can do it by creating objects wherein the feelings we seek to hold are so definitely embodied that any

---

[4]"Kunst and Gefühl," *Logos*, II, pp. 5–6.

subject confronted with these objects, and emphatically disposed toward them, cannot but experience a non-sensuous apperception of the feelings in question. Such objects are called 'works of art,' and by 'art' we designate the activity that produces them.[5]

Almost every paragraph of Baensch's article is relevant to the theory I am about to propose and develop. One is tempted to go on quoting indefinitely, and I shall freely return to the task on further occasion. But the above will serve, perhaps, to show the horns of the dilemma to which philosophy of art has come, in all their guises: expression and impression, form and feeling, significance and sensation. Here, in the latest version, art works *contain* feelings, but do not feel them. We find the feelings there and react to the apperception of them with pleasure or displeasure, which are our own feelings, the ones we have at the time. But the status of the unfelt feelings that inhere in art objects is ontologically obscure, and their non-sensuous apperception in a work that is generally supposed to be given directly and entirely to sensuous perception is epistemologically just as difficult.

The answer, I think, waits upon an idea that is itself not foreign to aesthetic theory, but has never been used in its highest capacity and to its true purposes. It is the most powerful generative idea in humanistic thinking today, wherefore I have called it, elsewhere, the "new key" in philosophy. As Baensch has left the problem of feeling in art, that problem at least is ready for transposition into the new key which will bring it into unexpected harmonies. More than ready, in fact; the modulation is almost complete when he proposes that the function of art, like that of science, is to acquaint the beholder with something he has not known before. Here the idea of symbolic agency is so close to overt expression that it fairly shimmers between the lines. But its real office here has nothing to do with the iconographic functions usually assigned to symbols in art. The artistic symbol, *qua* artistic, negotiates insight, not reference; it does not rest upon convention, but motivates and dictates conventions. It is deeper than any semantic of accepted signs and their referents, more essential than any schema that may be heuristically read.

The many leading ideas in aesthetic theory that are current today, each seeking to thread a different path through the mysteries of artistic

[5]*Ibid.*, p. 14.

experience, and each constantly evading or perforce accepting some paradoxical post, really all converge on the same problem: What is "significance" in art? What, in other words, is meant by "Significant Form"?

The answer to this problem entails, I believe, the solution of all the related yet oddly incommensurable paradoxes, and most directly the one involved in Baensch's notion of objective feelings, non-sensuous qualities invisibly seen. And the proposal of this answer is our first gambit.

Chapter three

THE SYMBOL OF FEELING

In the book to which the present one is a sequel there is a chapter entitled "On Significance in Music." The theory of significance there developed is a special theory, which does not pretend to any further application than the one made of it in that original realm, namely music. Yet, the more one reflects on the significance of art generally, the more the music theory appears as a lead. And the hypothesis certainly suggests itself that the oft-asserted fundamental unity of the arts lies not so much in parallels between their respective elements or analogies among their techniques, as in the singleness of their characteristic import, the meaning of "significance" with respect to any and each of them. "Significant Form" (which really has significance) is the essence of every art; it is what we mean by calling anything "artistic."

If the proposed lead will not betray us, we have here a principle of analysis that may be applied within each separate art gender in explaining its peculiar choice and use of materials; a criterion of what is or is not relevant in judging works of art in any realm; a direct exhibition of the unity of all the arts (without necessitating a resort to "origins" in fragmentary, doubtful history, and still more questionable prehistory); and the making of a truly general theory of art as such, wherein the several arts may be distinguished as well as connected, and almost any philosophical problems they present—problems of their relative values, their special powers or limitations, their social function, their connection with dream and fantasy or with actuality, etc., etc.—may be tackled with some hope of decision. The proper way to construct a general theory is by generalization of a special one; and I believe the analysis of musical significance in *Philosophy in a New Key* is capable of such generalization, and of furnishing a valid theory of significance for the whole Parnassus.

The study of musical significance grew out of a prior philosophical reflection on the meaning of the very popular term "expression." In the literature of aesthetics this word holds a prominent place; or rather, it holds prominent places, for it is employed in more than one sense and consequently changes its meaning from one book to another, and sometimes even from passage to passage in a single work. Sometimes writers who are actually in close agreement use it in incompatible ways, and literally contradict each other's statements, yet actually do not become aware of this fact, because each will read the word as the other intended it, not as he really used it where it happens to occur. Thus Roger Fry tried to elucidate Clive Bell's famous but cryptic phrase, "Significant Form," by identifying it with Flaubert's "expression of the Idea"; and Bell probably subscribes fully to Fry's exegesis, as far as it goes (which, as Fry remarks, is unfortunately not very far, since the "Idea" is the next hurdle). Yet Bell himself, trying to explain his meaning, says: "It is useless to go to a picture gallery in search of expression; you must go in search of Significant Form." Of course Bell is thinking here of "expression" in an entirely different sense. Perhaps he means that you should not look for the artist's *self*-expression, i.e. for a record of his emotions. Yet this reading is doubtful, for elsewhere in the same book he says: "It seems to me possible, though by no means certain, that created form moves us so profoundly because it expresses the emotion of its creator." Now, is the emotion of the creator the "Idea" in Flaubert's sense, or is it not? Or does the same work have, perhaps, two different expressive functions? And what about the kind we must *not* look for in a picture gallery?

We may, of course, look for any kind of expression we like, and there is even a fair chance that, whatever it be, we shall find it. A work of art is often a spontaneous expression of feeling, i.e., a symptom of the artist's state of mind. If it represents human beings it is probably also a rendering of some sort of facial expression which suggests the feelings those beings are supposed to have. Moreover, it may be said to "express," in another sense, the life of the society from which it stems, namely to *indicate* customs, dress, behavior, and to reflect confusion or decorum, violence or peace. And besides all these things it is sure to express the unconscious wishes and nightmares of its author. All these things may be found in museums and galleries if we choose to note them.

But they may also be found in wastebaskets and in the margins of schoolbooks. This does not mean that someone has discarded a work of art, or produced one when he was bored with long division. It merely means that all drawings, utterances, gestures, or personal records of any sort express feelings, beliefs, social conditions, and interesting neuroses; "expression" in any of these senses is not peculiar to art, and consequently is not what makes for artistic value.

Artistic significance, or "expression of the Idea," is "expression" in still a different sense and, indeed, a radically different one. In all the contexts mentioned above, the art work or other object functioned as a *sign* that pointed to some matter of fact—how someone felt, what he believed, when and where he lived, or what bedeviled his dreams. But *expression of an idea*, even in ordinary usage, where the "idea" has no capital *I,* does not refer to the signific function, i.e. the indication of a fact by some natural symptom or invented signal. It usually refers to the prime purpose of language, which is discourse, the presentation of mere ideas. When we say that something is well expressed, we do not necessarily believe the expressed idea to refer to our present situation, or even to be true, but only to be given clearly and objectively for contemplation. Such "expression" is the function of symbols: articulation and presentation of *concepts.* Herein symbols differ radically from signals.[1] A signal is comprehended if it serves to make us notice the object or situation it bespeaks. A symbol is understood when we conceive the idea it presents.

The logical difference between signals and symbols is sufficiently explained, I think, in *Philosophy in a New Key* to require no repetition here, although much more could be said about it than that rather general little treatise undertook to say. Here, as there, I shall go on to a consequent of the logical studies, a theory of significance that points the contrast between the functions of art and of discourse, respectively; but this time with reference to all the arts, not only the non-verbal and essentially non-representative art of music.

----

[1] In *Philosophy in a New Key* (cited hereafter as *New Key*) the major distinction was drawn between "signs" and "symbols"; Charles W. Morris, in *Signs, Language and Behavior,* distinguishes between "signals" and "symbols." This seems to me a better use of words, since it leaves "sign" to cover both "signal" and "symbol," whereas my former usage left me without any generic term. I have, therefore, adopted his practice, despite the fact that it makes for a discrepancy in the terminology of two books that really belong together.

The theory of music, however, is our point of departure, wherefore it may be briefly recapitulated here as it finally stood in the earlier book:

The tonal structures we call "music" bear a close logical similarity to the forms of human feeling—forms of growth and of attenuation, flowing and stowing, conflict and resolution, speed, arrest, terrific excitement, calm, or subtle activation and dreamy lapses—not joy and sorrow perhaps, but the poignancy of either and both—the greatness and brevity and eternal passing of everything vitally felt. Such is the pattern, or logical form, of sentience; and the pattern of music is that same form worked out in pure, measured sound and silence. Music is a tonal analogue of emotive life.

Such formal analogy, or congruence of logical structures, is the prime requisite for the relation between a symbol and whatever it is to mean. The symbol and the object symbolized must have some common logical form.

But purely on the basis of formal analogy, there would be no telling which of two congruent structures was the symbol and which the meaning, since the relation of congruence, or formal likeness, is symmetrical, i.e. it works both ways. (If John looks so much like James that you can't tell him from James, then you can't tell James from John, either.) There must be a motive for choosing, as between two entities or two systems, one to be the symbol of the other. Usually the decisive reason is that one is easier to perceive and handle than the other. Now sounds are much easier to produce, combine, perceive, and identify, than feelings. Forms of sentience occur only in the course of nature, but musical forms may be invented and intoned at will. Their general pattern may be reincarnated again and again by repeated performance. The effect is actually never quite the same even though the physical repetition may be exact, as in recorded music, because the exact degree of one's familiarity with a passage affects the experience of it, and this factor can never be made permanent. Yet within a fairly wide range such variations are, happily, unimportant. To some musical forms even much less subtle changes are not really disturbing, for instance certain differences of instrumentation and even, within limits, of pitch or tempo. To others, they are fatal. But in the main, sound is a negotiable medium, capable of voluntary composition and repetition, whereas feeling is not; this trait recommends tonal structures for symbolic purposes.

Furthermore, a symbol is used to articulate ideas of something we wish to think about, and until we have a fairly adequate symbolism we cannot think about it. So *interest* always plays a major part in making one thing, or realm of things, the meaning of something else, the symbol or system of symbols.

Sound, as a sheer sensory factor in experience, may be soothing or exciting, pleasing or torturing; but so are the factors of taste, smell, and touch. Selecting and exploiting such somatic influences is self-indulgence, a very different thing from art. An enlightened society usually has some means, public or private, to support its artists, because their work is regarded as a spiritual triumph and a claim to greatness for the whole tribe. But mere epicures would hardly achieve such fame. Even chefs, perfumers, and upholsterers, who produce the means of sensory pleasure for others, are not rated as the torchbearers of culture and inspired creators. Only their own advertisements bestow such titles on them. If music, patterned sound, had no other office than to stimulate and soothe our nerves, pleasing our ears as well-combined foods please our palates, it might be highly popular, but never culturally important. Its historic development would be too trivial a subject to engage many people in its lifelong study, though a few desperate Ph.D. theses might be wrung from its anecdotal past under the rubric of "social history." And music conservatories would be properly rated exactly like cooking schools.

Our interest in music arises from its intimate relation to the all-important life of feeling, whatever that relation may be. After much debate on current theories, the conclusion reached in *Philosophy in a New Key* is that the function of music is not stimulation of feeling, but expression of it; and furthermore, not the symptomatic expression of feelings that beset the composer but a symbolic expression of the forms of sentience as he understands them. It bespeaks his imagination of feelings rather than his own emotional state, and expresses what he *knows about* the so-called "inner life"; and this may exceed his personal case, because music is a symbolic form to him through which he may learn as well as utter ideas of human sensibility.

There are many difficulties involved in the assumption that music is a symbol, because we are so deeply impressed with the paragon of symbolic form, namely language, that we naturally carry its characteristics over into our conceptions and expectations of any other mode. Yet music is not a kind of language. Its significance is really something different from what is traditionally and properly called "meaning." Perhaps the logicians and positivistic philosophers who have objected to the term "implicit meaning," on the ground that "meaning" properly so-called is always explicable, definable, and translatable, are prompted by a perfectly rational desire to keep so difficult a term free from any further entanglements and sources of confusion; and if this can be done without barring the concept itself which I have designated as "implicit meaning," it certainly seems the part of wisdom to accept their strictures.

Probably the readiest way to understand the precise nature of musical symbolization is to consider the characteristics of language and then, by comparison and contrast, note the different structure of music, and the consequent differences and similarities between the respective functions of those two logical forms. Because the prime purpose of language is discourse, the conceptual framework that has developed under its influence is known as "discursive reason." Usually, when one speaks of "reason" at all, one tacitly assumes its discursive pattern. But in a broader sense any appreciation of form, any awareness of patterns in experience, is "reason"; and discourse with all its refinements (e.g. mathematical symbolism, which is an extension of language) is only one possible pattern. For practical communication, scientific knowledge, and philosophical thought it is the only instrument we have. But on just that account there are whole domains of experience that philosophers deem "ineffable." If those domains appear to anyone the most important, that person is naturally inclined to condemn philosophy and science as barren and false. To such an evaluation one is entitled; not, however, to the claim of a better way to philosophical truth through instinct, intuition, feeling, or what have you. Intuition is the basic process of all understanding, just as operative in discursive thought as in clear sense perception and immediate judgment; there will be more to say about that presently. But it is no substitute for discursive logic in the making of any theory, contingent or transcendental.

The difference between discursive and non-discursive logical forms, their respective advantages and limitations, and their consequent symbolic uses have already been discussed in the previous book, but because the theory, there developed, of music as a symbolic form is our starting point here for a whole philosophy of art, the underlying semantic principles should perhaps be explicitly recalled first.

In language, which is the most amazing symbolic system humanity has invented, separate words are assigned to separately conceived items in experience on a basis of simple, one-to-one correlation. A word that is not composite (made of two or more independently meaningful vocables, such as "omni-potent," "com-posite") may be assigned to mean any object *taken as one*. We may even, by fiat, take a word like "omnipotent," and regarding it as one, assign it a connotation that is not composite, for instance by naming a race horse "Omnipotent." Thus Praisegod Barbon ("Barebones") was an indivisible being although his name is a composite word. He had a brother called "If-Christ-had-not-come-into-the-world-thou-wouldst-have-been-damned." The simple correlation between a name and its bearer held here between a whole sentence taken as one word and an object to which it was arbitrarily assigned. Any symbol that names something is "taken as one"; so is the object. A "crowd" is a lot of people, but *taken as a lot,* i.e. as one crowd.

So long as we correlate symbols and concepts in this simple fashion we are free to pair them as we like. A word or mark used arbitrarily to denote or connote something may be called an associative symbol, for its meaning depends entirely on association. As soon, however, as words taken to denote different things are used in combination, something is expressed by the way they are combined. The whole complex is a symbol, because the combination of words brings their connotations irresistibly together in a complex, too, and this complex of ideas is analogous to the word-complex. To anyone who knows the meanings of all the constituent words in the name of Praisegod's brother, the name is likely to sound absurd, because it is a sentence. The concepts associated with the words form a complex concept, the parts of which are related in a pattern analogous to the word-pattern. Word-meanings and grammatical forms, or rules for word-using, may be freely assigned; but once they are accepted, propositions emerge automatically as the meanings of sentences. One may say that the elements of propositions are *named* by words, but propositions themselves are *articulated* by sentences.

A complex symbol such as a sentence, or a map (whose outlines correspond formally to the vastly greater outlines of a country), or a graph (analogous, perhaps, to invisible conditions, the rise and fall of prices, the progress of an epidemic) is an *articulate form.* Its characteristic symbolic function is what I call *logical expression.* It expresses relations; and it may "mean"—connote or denote—any complex of elements that is of the same articulate form as the symbol, the form which the symbol "expresses."

Music, like language, is an articulate form. Its parts not only fuse together to yield a greater entity, but in so doing they maintain some degree of separate existence, and the sensuous character of each element is affected by its function in the complex whole. This means that the greater entity we call a composition is not merely produced by mixture, like a new color made by mixing paints, but is *articulated,* i.e. its internal structure is given to our perception.

Why, then, is it not a *language* of feeling, as it has often been called? Because its elements are not words—independent associative symbols with a reference fixed by convention. Only as an articulate form is it found to fit anything; and since there is no meaning assigned to any of its parts, it lacks one of the basic characteristics of language—fixed association, and therewith a single, unequivocal reference. We are always free to fill its subtle articulate forms with any meaning that fits them; that is, it may convey an idea of anything conceivable in its logical image. So, although we do receive it as a significant form, and comprehend the processes of life and sentience through its audible, dynamic pattern, it is not a language, because it has no vocabulary.

Perhaps, in the same spirit of strict nomenclature, one really should not refer to its content as "meaning," either. Just as music is only loosely and inexactly called a language, so its symbolic function is only loosely called meaning, because the factor of conventional reference is missing from it. In *Philosophy in a New Key* music was called an "unconsummated" symbol.[2] But meaning, in the usual sense recognized in semantics, includes the condition of conventional reference, or consummation of the symbolic relationship. Music has *import,* and this import is the pattern of sentience—the pattern of life itself, as it is felt and directly known.

---

[2]Harvard University Press edition, p. 240; New American Library (Mentor) edition, p. 195.

Let us therefore call the significance of music its "vital import" instead of "meaning," using "vital" not as a vague laudatory term, but as a qualifying adjective restricting the relevance of "import" to the dynamism of subjective experience.

So much, then, for the theory of music; music is "significant form," and its significance is that of a symbol, a highly articulated sensuous object, which by virtue of its dynamic structure can express the forms of vital experience which language is peculiarly unfit to convey. Feeling, life, motion and emotion constitute its import.

Here, in rough outline, is the special theory of music which may, I believe, be generalized to yield a theory of art as such. The basic concept is the articulate but non-discursive form having import without conventional reference, and therefore presenting itself not as a symbol in the ordinary sense, but as a "significant form," in which the factor of significance is not logically discriminated, but is felt as a quality rather than recognized as a function. If this basic concept be applicable to all products of what we call "the arts," i.e. if all works of art may be regarded as significant forms in exactly the same sense as musical works, then all the essential propositions in the theory of music may be extended to the other arts, for they all define or elucidate the nature of the symbol and its import.

That crucial generalization is already given by sheer circumstance: for the very term "significant form" was originally introduced in connection with other arts than music, in the development of another special theory; all that has so far been written about it was supposed to apply primarily, if not solely, to visual arts. Clive Bell, who coined the phrase, is an art critic, and (by his own testimony) not a musician. His own introduction of the term is given in the following words:

"Every one speaks of 'art,' making a mental classification by which he distinguishes the class 'works of art' from all other classes. What is the justification of this classification? . . . There must be some one quality without which a work of art cannot exist; possessing which, in the least degree, no work is altogether worthless. What is this quality? What quality is shared by all objects that provoke our aesthetic emotions? What quality is common to Santa Sophia and the Windows at Chartres, Mexican sculpture, a Persian bowl, Chinese carpets, Giotto's frescoes at Padua, and the masterpieces of Poussin, Piero della Francesca, and Cézanne? Only one answer seems possible—significant form. In each, lines and colours combined in a particular way, certain forms and relations of forms, stir our aesthetic emotions. These relations and combinations of lines and colours, these aesthetically moving forms, I call 'Significant Form'; and 'Significant Form' is the one quality common to all works of visual art."[3]

Bell is convinced that the business of aesthetics is to contemplate the aesthetic emotion and its object, the work of art, and that the reason why certain objects move us as they do lies beyond the confines of aesthetics.[4] If that were so, there would be little of interest to contemplate. It seems to me that the *reason* for our immediate recognition of "significant form" is the heart of the aesthetical problem; and Bell himself has given several hints of a solution, although his perfectly justified dread of heuristic theories of art kept him from following out his own observations. But, in the light of the music theory that culminates in the concept of "significant form," perhaps the hints in his art theory are enough.

"Before we feel an aesthetic emotion for a combination of forms," he says (only to withdraw hastily, even before the end of the paragraph, from any philosophical commitment) "do we not perceive intellectually the rightness and necessity of the combination? If we do, it would explain the fact that passing rapidly through a room we recognize a picture to be good, although we cannot say that it has provoked much emotion. We seem to have recognized intellectually the rightness of its forms without staying to fix our attention, and collect, as it were, their emotional significance. If this were so, it would be permissible to inquire whether it was the forms themselves or our perception of their rightness and necessity that caused aesthetic emotion."[5]

Certainly "rightness and necessity" are properties with philosophical implications, and the perception of them a more telling incident than an inexplicable emotion. To recognize that something is right and necessary is a rational act, no matter how spontaneous and immediate the recognition may be; it points to an intellectual principle in artistic judgment, and a rational basis for the feeling Bell calls "the aesthetic emotion."

---

[3] *Ibid.*, p. 8.   [4] *Ibid.*, p. 10.   [5] *Ibid.*, p. 26.

This emotion is, I think, a result of artistic perception, as he suggested in the passage quoted above; it is a personal reaction to the discovery of "rightness and necessity" in the sensuous forms that evoke it. Whenever we experience it we are in the presence of Art, i.e. of "significant form." He himself has identified it as the same experience in art appreciation and in pure musical hearing, although he says he has rarely achieved it musically. But if it is common to visual and tonal arts, and if indeed it bespeaks the artistic value of its object, it offers another point of support for the theory that significant form is the essence of all art.

That, however, is about all that it offers. Bell's assertion that every theory of art must begin with the contemplation of "the aesthetic emotion," and that, indeed, nothing else is really the business of aesthetics,[6] seems to me entirely wrong. To dwell on one's state of mind in the presence of a work does not further one's understanding of the work and its value. The question of what gives one the emotion is exactly the question of what makes the object artistic; and that, to my mind, is where philosophical art theory begins.

The same criticism applies to all theories that begin with an analysis of the "aesthetic attitude": they do not get beyond it. Schopenhauer, who is chiefly responsible for the notion of a completely desireless state of pure, sensuous discrimination as the proper attitude toward works of art, did not make it the starting point of his system, but a consequence. Why, then, has it been so insistently employed, especially of late, as the chief datum in artistic experience?

Probably under pressure of the psychologistic currents that have tended, for the last fifty years at least, to force all philosophical problems of art into the confines of behaviorism and pragmatism, where they find neither development nor solution, but are assigned to vague realms of "value" and "interest," in which nothing of great value or interest has yet been done. The existence of art is accounted for, its value admitted, and there's an end of it. But the issues that really challenge the aesthetician—e.g. the exact nature and degree of interrelation among the arts, the meaning of "essential" and "unessential," the problem of translatability, or transposability, of artistic ideas—either cannot arise in a

---

[6]See reference above, p. 33, note 4.

psychologistic context, or are answered, without real investigation, on the strength of some general premise that seems to cover them. The whole tenor of modern philosophy, especially in America, is uncongenial to serious speculation on the meaning and difficulty and seriousness of art works. Yet the pragmatic outlook, linked as it is with natural science, holds such sway over us that no academic discussion can resist its magnetic, orienting concepts; its basic psychologism underlies every doctrine that really looks respectable.

Now, the watchword of this established doctrine is "experience." If the leading philosophers publish assorted essays under such titles as *Freedom and Experience*,[7] or center their systematic discourse around *Experience and Nature*,[8] so that in their aesthetics, too, we are presented with *The Aesthetic Experience*[9] and *Art as Experience*,[10] it is natural enough that artists, who are amateurs in philosophy, try to treat their subject in the same vein, and write: *Experiencing American Pictures*,[11] or: *Dance—A Creative Art Experience*.[12] As far as possible, these writers who grope more or less for principles of intellectual analysis adopt the current terminology, and therewith they are committed to the prevailing fashion of thought.

Since this fashion has grown up under the mentorship of natural science, it brings with it not only the great ideals of empiricism, namely observation, analysis and verification, but also certain cherished hypotheses, primarily from the least perfect and successful of the sciences, psychology and sociology. The chief assumption that determines the entire procedure of pragmatic philosophy is that all human interests are direct or oblique manifestations of "drives" motivated by animal needs. This premise limits the class of admitted human interests to such as can, by one device or another, be interpreted in terms of animal psychology. An astonishingly great part of human behavior really does bear such interpretation without strain; and pragmatists, so far, do not admit that there is any point where the principle definitely fails, and its use falsifies our empirical findings.

The effect of the genetic premise on art theory is that aesthetic values

---

[7]*Essays in Honor of Horace M. Kallen* (1947).   [8]John Dewey (1925).
[9]Laurence Buermeyer (1924).   [10]John Dewey (1934).
[11]Ralph M. Pearson (1943).   [12]Margaret H'Doubler (1940).

must be treated either as direct satisfactions, i.e. pleasures, or as instrumental values, that is to say, means to fulfillment of biological needs.
It is either a leisure interest, like sports and hobbies, or it is valuable
for getting on with the world's work—strengthening morale, integrating
social groups, or venting dangerous repressed feelings in a harmless emotional catharsis. But in either case, artistic experience is not essentially
different from ordinary physical, practical, and social experience.[13]

The true connoisseurs of art, however, feel at once that to treat great
art as a source of experiences not essentially different from the experiences of daily life—a stimulus to one's active feelings, and perhaps a
means of communication between persons or groups, promoting mutual
appreciation—is to miss the very essence of it, the thing that makes art
as important as science or even religion, yet sets it apart as an autonomous, creative function of a typically human mind. If, then, they feel
constrained by the prevailing academic tradition to analyze their experience, attitude, response, or enjoyment, they can only begin by saying
that aesthetic experience is different from any other, the attitude toward
works of art is a highly special one, the characteristic response is an
entirely separate emotion, something more than common enjoyment—
not related to the pleasures or displeasures furnished by one's actual surroundings, and therefore disturbed by them rather than integrated with
the contemporary scene.

This conviction does not spring from a sentimental concern for the

---

[13]Cf. John Dewey, *Art as Experience,* p. 10: ". . . the forces that create the
gulf between producer and consumer in modern society operate to create also a
chasm between ordinary and esthetic experience. Finally we have, as a record of this
chasm, accepted as if it were normal, the philosophies of art that locate it in a
region inhabited by no other creature, and that emphasize beyond all reason the
merely contemplative character of the esthetic."

Also I. A. Richards, *Principles of Literary Criticism,* pp. 16–17: "When we look
at a picture, read a poem, or listen to music, we are not doing something quite
unlike what we were doing on our way to the Gallery or when we dressed in the
morning. The fashion in which the experience is caused in us is different, and as a
rule the experience is more complex and, if we are successful, more unified. But our
activity is not of a fundamentally different type."

Laurence Buermeyer, in *The Aesthetic Experience,* p. 79, follows his account
of artistic expression with the statement: "This does not mean, once more, that
what the artist has to say is different in kind from what is to be said in actual
life, or that the realm of art is in any essential respect divorced from the realm
of reality."

glamor and dignity of the arts, as Mr. Dewey suggests;[14] it arises from the fact that when people in whom appreciation for some art—be it painting, music, drama, or what not—is spontaneous and pronounced, are induced by a psychologistic fashion to reflect on their attitude toward the works they appreciate, they find it not at all comparable with the attitude they have toward a new automobile, a beloved creature, or a glorious morning. They feel a different emotion, and in a different way. Since art is viewed as a special kind of "experience," inaccessible to those who cannot enter into the proper spirit, a veritable cult of the "aesthetic attitude" has grown up among patrons of the art gallery and the concert hall.

But the aesthetic attitude, which is supposed to beget the art experience in the presence of suitable objects (what makes them suitable seems to be a minor question, relegated to a time when "science" shall be ready to answer it), is hard to achieve, harder to maintain, and rarely complete. H. S. Langfeld, who wrote a whole book about it, described it as an attitude "that for most individuals has to be cultivated if it is to exist at all in midst of the opposing and therefore disturbing influences which are always present."[15] And David Prall, in his excellent *Aesthetic Analysis*, observes: "Even a young musical fanatic at a concert of his favorite music has some slight attention left for the comfort of his body and his posture, some vague sense of the direction of exits, a degree of attention most easily raised into prominence by any interference with his comfort by his neighbor's movements, or accidental noises coming from elsewhere, whether these indicate the danger of fire or some milder reason for taking action. Complete aesthetic absorption, strictly relevant to one object, is at least rare; the world as exclusively aesthetic surface is seldom if ever the sole object of our attention."[16]

Few listeners or spectators, in fact, ever quite attain the state which Roger Fry described, in *Vision and Design*, as "disinterested intensity

---

[14]Speaking of the separation of art from life "that many theorists and critics pride themselves upon holding and even elaborating," he attributes it to the desire to keep art "spiritual," and says in explanation: "For many persons an aura of mingled awe and unreality encompasses the 'spiritual' and the 'ideal' while 'matter' has become . . . something to be explained away or apologized for." John Dewey, *op. cit.*, p. 6.

[15]*The Aesthetic Attitude*, p. 65.   [16]*Aesthetic Analysis*, pp. 7–8.

of contemplation"[17]—the only state in which one may really perceive a work of art, and experience the aesthetic emotion. Most people are too busy or too lazy to uncouple their minds from all their usual interests before looking at a picture or a vase. That explains, presumably, what he remarked somewhat earlier in the same essay: "In proportion as art becomes purer the number of people to whom it appeals gets less. It cuts out all the romantic overtones which are the usual bait by which men are induced to accept a work of art. It appeals only to the aesthetic sensibility, and that in most men is comparatively weak."[18]

If the groundwork of all genuine art experience is really such a sophisticated, rare, and artificial attitude, it is something of a miracle that the world recognizes works of art as public treasures at all. And that primitive peoples, from the cave dwellers of Altamira to the early Greeks, should quite unmistakably have known what was beautiful, becomes a sheer absurdity.

There is that, at least, to be said for the pragmatists: they recognize the art interest as something natural and robust, not a precarious hothouse flower reserved for the very cultured and initiate. But the small compass of possible human interests permitted by their biological premises blinds them to the fact that a very spontaneous, even primitive activity may none the less be peculiarly human, and may require long study in its own terms before its relations to the rest of our behavior become clear. To say, as I. A. Richards does, that if we knew more about the nervous system and its responses to "certain stimuli" (note that "certain," when applied to hypothetical data, means "uncertain," since the data cannot be exactly designated) we would find that "the unpredictable and miraculous differences . . . in the total responses which slight changes in the arrangement of stimuli produce, can be fully accounted for in terms of the sensitiveness of the nervous system; and the mysteries of 'forms' are merely a consequence of our present ignorance of the detail of its action,"[19] is not only an absurd pretension (for how do we know what facts we would find and what their implications would prove to be, before we have found them?), but an empty hypothesis, because there is no elementary success that indicates the direction in which neurological aesthetics could develop. If a theoretical beginning

---

[17]*Vision and Design*, p. 29.   [18]*Ibid.*, p. 15.   [19]*Op. cit.*, p. 172.

existed, one could imagine an extension of the same procedure to describe artistic experience in terms of conditioned reflexes, rudimentary impulses, or perhaps cerebral vibrations; but so far the data furnished by galvanometers and encephalographs have not borne on artistic problems, even to the extent of explaining the simple, obvious difference of effect between a major scale and its parallel minor. The proposition that if we knew the facts we would find them to be thus and thus is merely an article of innocent, pseudo-scientific faith.

The psychological approach, dictated by the general empiricist trend in philosophy, has not brought us within range of any genuine problems of art. So, instead of studying the "slight changes of stimuli" which cause "unpredictable and miraculous changes" in our nervous responses, we might do better to look upon the art object as something in its own right, with properties independent of our prepared reactions—properties which command our reactions, and make art the autonomous and essential factor that it is in every human culture.

The concept of significant form as an articulate expression of feeling, reflecting the verbally ineffable and therefore unknown forms of sentience, offers at least a starting point for such inquiries. All articulation is difficult, exacting, and ingenious; the making of a symbol requires craftsmanship as truly as the making of a convenient bowl or an efficient paddle, and the techniques of expression are even more important social traditions than the skills of self-preservation, which an intelligent being can evolve by himself, at least in rudimentary ways, to meet a given situation. The fundamental technique of expression—language—is something we all have to learn by example and practice, i.e. by conscious or unconscious training.[20] People whose speech training has been very casual are less sensitive to what is exact and fitting for the expression of an idea than those of cultivated habit; not only with regard to arbitrary rules of usage, but in respect of logical *rightness and necessity* of expression, i.e. saying what they mean and not something else. Similarly, I believe, all making of expressive form is a craft. Therefore the normal evolution of art is in close association with practical skills—building, ceramics, weaving, carving, and magical practices of which the average

---

[20]Cf. *New Key*, Chap. v, "Language."

civilized person no longer knows the importance;[21] and therefore, also, sensitivity to the rightness and necessity of visual or musical forms is apt to be more pronounced and sure in persons of some artistic training than in those who have only a bowing acquaintance with the arts. Technique is the means to the creation of expressive form, the symbol of sentience; the art process is the application of some human skill to this essential purpose.

At this point I will make bold to offer a definition of art, which serves to distinguish a "work of art" from anything else in the world, and at the same time to show why, and how, a utilitarian object may be *also* a work of art; and how a work of so-called "pure" art may fail of its purpose and be simply bad, just as a shoe that cannot be worn is simply bad by failing of its purpose. It serves, moreover, to establish the relation of art to physical skill, or making, on the one hand, and to feeling and expression on the other. Here is the tentative definition, on which the following chapters are built: Art is the creation of forms symbolic of human feeling.

The word "creation" is introduced here with full awareness of its problematical character. There is a definite reason to say a craftsman *produces* goods, but *creates* a thing of beauty; a builder *erects* a house, but *creates* an edifice if the house is a real work of architecture, however modest. An artifact as such is merely a combination of material parts, or a modification of a natural object to suit human purposes. It is not a creation, but an arrangement of given factors. A work of art, on the other hand, is more than an "arrangement" of given things—even qualitative things. Something emerges from the arrangement of tones or colors, which was not there before, and this, rather than the arranged material, is the symbol of sentience.

The making of this expressive form is the creative process that enlists a man's utmost technical skill in the service of his utmost conceptual power, imagination. Not the invention of new original turns, nor the adoption of novel themes, merits the word "creative," but the making of any work symbolic of feeling, even in the most canonical context and

---

[21]Yet a pervasive magical interest has probably been the natural tie between practical fitness and expressiveness in primitive artifacts. See *New Key*, chap. ix, "The Genesis of Artistic Import."

manner. A thousand people may have used every device and convention of it before. A Greek vase was almost always a creation, although its form was traditional and its decoration deviated but little from that of its numberless forerunners. The creative principle, nonetheless, was probably active in it from the first throw of the clay.

To expound that principle, and develop it in each autonomous realm of art, is the only way to justify the definition, which really is a philosophical theory of art in miniature.

PART II

The Making of the Symbol

THE MAKING
OF THE SYMBOL

Chapter four

SEMBLANCE

It is a curious fact that people who spend their lives in closest contact with the arts—artists, to whom the appreciation of beauty is certainly a continual and "immediate" experience—do not assume and cultivate the "aesthetic attitude." To them, the artistic value of a work is its most obvious property. They see it naturally and constantly; they do not have to make themselves, first, unaware of the rest of the world. Practical awareness may be there, in a secondary position, as it is for anyone who is engrossed in interesting talk or happenings; if it becomes too insistent to be ignored, they may become quite furious. But normally, the lure of the object is greater than the distractions that compete with it. It is not the percipient who discounts the surroundings, but the work of art which, if it is successful, detaches itself from the rest of the world; he merely sees it as it is presented to him.

Every real work of art has a tendency to appear thus dissociated from its mundane environment. The most immediate impression it creates is one of "otherness" from reality—the impression of an illusion enfolding the thing, action, statement, or flow of sound that constitutes the work. Even where the element of representation is absent, where nothing is imitated or feigned—in a lovely textile, a pot, a building, a sonata—this air of illusion, of being a sheer image, exists as forcibly as in the most deceptive picture or the most plausible narrative. Where an expert in the particular art in question perceives immediately a "rightness and necessity" of forms, the unversed but sensitive spectator perceives only a peculiar air of "otherness," which has been variously described as "strangeness," "semblance," "illusion," "transparency," "autonomy," or "self-sufficiency."

This detachment from actuality, the "otherness" that gives even a bona fide product like a building or a vase some aura of illusion, is a crucial factor, indicative of the very nature of art. It is neither chance nor caprice that has led aestheticians again and again to take account of it (and in a period dominated by a psychologistic outlook, to seek the explanation in a state of mind). In the element of "unreality," which has alternately troubled and delighted them, lies the clue to a very deep and essential problem: the problem of creativity.

What is "created" in a work of art? More than people generally realize when they speak of "being creative," or refer to the characters in a novel as the author's "creations." More than a delightful combination of sensory elements; far more than any reflection or "interpretation" of objects, people, events—the figments that artists *use* in their demiurgic work, and that have made some aestheticians refer to such work as "re-creation" rather than genuine creation. But an object that already exists—a vase of flowers, a living person—cannot be re-created. It would have to be destroyed to be re-created. Besides, a picture is neither a person nor a vase of flowers. It is an image, created for the first time out of things that are not imaginal, but quite realistic—canvas or paper, and paints or carbon or ink.

It is natural enough, perhaps, for naive reflection to center first of all round the relationship between an image and its object; and equally natural to treat a picture, statue, or a graphic description as an imitation of reality. The surprising thing is that long after art theory had passed the naive stage, and every serious thinker realized that imitation was neither the aim nor the measure of artistic creation, the traffic of the image with its model kept its central place among philosophical problems of art. It has figured as the question of form and content, of interpretation, of idealization, of belief and make-believe, and of impression and expression. Yet the idea of copying nature is not even applicable to all the arts. What does a building copy? On what given object does one model a melody?

A problem that will not die after philosophers have condemned it as irrelevant has still a gadfly mission in the intellectual world. Its significance merely is bigger, in fact, than any of its formulations. So here: the philosophical issue that is usually conceived in terms of image and object is really concerned with the nature of images as such and their essential difference from actualities. The difference is functional; consequently real objects, functioning in a way that is normal for images, may assume a purely imaginal status. That is why the character of an illusion may cling to works of art that do not represent anything. Imitation of other things is not the essential power of images, though it is a very important one by virtue of which the whole problem of fact and fiction originally came into the compass of our philosophical thought. But the true power of the image lies in the fact that it is an abstraction, a symbol, the bearer of an idea.

How can a work of art that does not represent anything—a building, a pot, a patterned textile—be called an image? It becomes an image when it presents itself purely to our vision, i.e. as a sheer visual form instead of a locally and practically related object. If we receive it as a completely visual thing, we abstract its appearance from its material existence. What we see in this way becomes simply a thing of vision— a form, an image. It detaches itself from its actual setting and acquires a different context.

An image in this sense, something that exists only for perception, abstracted from the physical and causal order, is the artist's creation. The image presented on a canvas is not a new "thing" among the things in the studio. The canvas was there, the paints were there; the painter has not added to them. Some excellent critics, and painters too, speak of his "arranging" forms and colors, and regard the resultant work primarily as an "arrangement." Whistler seems to have thought in these terms about his paintings. But even the forms are not phenomena in the order of actual things, as spots on a tablecloth are; the forms in a design —no matter how abstract—have a *life* that does not belong to mere spots. Something arises from the process of arranging colors on a surface, something that is created, not just gathered and set in a new order: that is the image. It emerges suddenly from the disposition of the pigments, and with its advent the very existence of the canvas and of the paint "arranged" on it seems to be abrogated; those actual objects become difficult to perceive in their own right. A new appearance has superseded their natural aspect.

An image is, indeed, a purely virtual "object." Its importance lies in the fact that we do not use it to guide us to something tangible and practical, but treat it as a complete entity with only visual attributes and relations. It has no others; its visible character is its entire being.

The most striking virtual objects in the natural world are optical— perfectly definite visible "things" that prove to be intangible, such as rainbows and mirages. Many people, therefore, regard an image or illusion as necessarily something visual. This conceptual limitation has even led some literary critics, who recognize the essentially imaginal character of poetry, to suppose that poets must be visual-minded people, and to judge that figures of speech which do not conjure up visual imagery are not truly poetic.[1] F. C. Prescott, with consistency that borders on the heroic, regards "The quality of mercy is not strained" as unpoetic because it suggests nothing visible.[2] But the poetic image is, in fact, not a painter's image at all. The exact difference, which is great and far-reaching, will be discussed in the following chapters; what concerns us right here is the broader meaning of "image" that accounts for the genuinely artistic character of non-visual arts without any reference to word painting, or other substitute for spreading pigments on a surface to make people see pictures.

The word "image" is almost inseparably wedded to the sense of sight because our stock example of it is the looking-glass world that gives us a visible copy of the things opposite the mirror without a tactual or other sensory replica of them. But some of the alternative words that have been used to denote the virtual character of so-called "aesthetic objects" escape this association. Carl Gustav Jung, for instance, speaks of it as "semblance." His exemplary case of illusion is not the reflected image, but the dream; and in a dream there are sounds, smells, feelings, happenings, intentions, dangers—all sorts of invisible elements—as well as sights, and all are equally unreal by the measures of public fact.

---

[1] See, for example, Remy de Gourmont, *Le problème du style*, especially p. 47, where the author declares that the only people who can "write" are visual-minded people.

[2] *The Poetic Mind*, p. 49.

Dreams do not consist entirely of images, but everything in them is imaginary. The music heard in a dream comes from a virtual piano under the hands of an apparent musician; the whole experience is a semblance of events. It may be as vivid as any reality, yet it is what Schiller called "Schein."

Schiller was the first thinker who saw what really makes "Schein," or semblance, important for art: the fact that it liberates perception—and with it, the power of conception—from all practical purposes, and lets the mind dwell on the sheer appearance of things. The function of artistic illusion is not "make-believe," as many philosophers and psychologists assume, but the very opposite, disengagement from belief—the contemplation of sensory qualities without their usual meanings of "Here's that chair," "That's my telephone," "These figures ought to add up to the bank's statement," etc. The knowledge that what is before us has no practical significance in the world is what enables us to give attention to its appearance as such.

Everything has an aspect of appearance as well as of causal importance. Even so non-sensuous a thing as a fact or a possibility *appears* this way to one person and that way to another. That is its "semblance," whereby it may "resemble" other things, and—where the semblance is used to mislead judgment about its causal properties—is said to "dissemble" its nature. Where we know that an "object" consists entirely in its semblance, that apart from its appearance it has no cohesion and unity—like a rainbow, or a shadow—we call it a merely virtual object, or an illusion. In this literal sense a picture is an illusion; we see a face, a flower, a vista of sea or land, etc., and know that if we stretched out our hand to it we would touch a surface smeared with paint.

The object seen is given only to the sense of sight. That is the chief purpose of "imitation," or "objective" painting. To present things to sight which are known to be illusion is a ready (though by no means necessary) way to *abstract* visible forms from their usual context.

Normally, of course, semblance is not misleading; a thing is what it seems. But even where there is no deception, it may happen that an object—a vase, for instance, or a building—arrests one sense so exclusively that it seems to be given to that sense alone, and all its other properties become irrelevant. It is quite honestly there, but is *important* only for (say) its visual character. Then we are prone to accept it as a vision; there is such a concentration on appearance that one has a sense of seeing sheer appearances—that is, a sense of illusion. [See Plate I.]

Herein lies the "unreality" of art that tinges even perfectly real objects like pots, textiles, and temples. Whether we deal with actual illusions or with such quasi-illusions made by artistic emphasis, what is presented is, in either case, just what Schiller called "Schein"; and a pure semblance, or "Schein," among the husky substantial realities of the natural world, is a strange guest. Strangeness, separateness, otherness —call it what you will—is its obvious lot.

The semblance of a thing, thus thrown into relief, is its direct aesthetic quality. According to several eminent critics, this is what the artist tries to reveal for its own sake. But the emphasis on quality, or essence, is really only a stage in artistic conception. It is the making of a rarified element that serves, in its turn, for the making of something else—the imaginal art work itself. And this form is the non-discursive but articulate symbol of feeling.

Here is, I believe, the clear statement of what Clive Bell dealt with rather confusedly in a passage that identified "significant form" (not, however, significant of anything) with "aesthetic quality." The setting forth of pure quality, or semblance, creates a new dimension, apart from the familiar world. That is its office. In this dimension, all artistic forms are conceived and presented. Since their substance is illusion or "Schein" they are, from the standpoint of practical reality, *mere* forms; they exist only for the sense or the imagination that perceives them—like the fata morgana, or the elaborate, improbable structure of events in our dreams. The function of "semblance" is to give forms a new embodiment in purely qualitative, unreal instances, setting them free from their normal embodiment in real things so that they may be recognized in their own right, and freely conceived and composed in the interest of the artist's ultimate aim—significance, or logical expression.

All forms in art, then, are abstracted forms; their content is only a semblance, a pure appearance, whose function is to make them, too, apparent—more freely and wholly apparent than they could be if they were exemplified in a context of real circumstance and anxious interest. It is in this elementary sense that all art is abstract. Its very substance, quality without practical significance, is an abstraction from material existence; and exemplification in this illusory or quasi-illusory medium makes the forms of things (not only shapes, but logical forms,[3] e.g. proportions among degrees of importance in events, or among different speeds in motions) present themselves *in abstracto*. This fundamental abstractness belongs just as forcibly to the most illustrative murals and most realistic plays, provided they are good after their kind, as to the deliberate abstractions that are remote representations or entirely non-representative designs.

But abstract form as such is not an artistic ideal. To carry abstraction as far as possible, and achieve pure form in only the barest conceptual medium, is a logician's business, not a painter's or poet's. In art forms are abstracted only to be made clearly apparent, and are freed from their common uses only to be put to new uses: to act as symbols, to become expressive of human feeling.

An artistic symbol is a much more intricate thing than what we usually think of as a form, because it involves *all* the relationships of its elements to one another, all similarities and differences of quality, not only geometric or other familiar relations. That is why qualities enter directly into the form itself, not as its contents, but as constitutive elements in it. Our scientific convention of abstracting mathematical forms, which do not involve quality, and fitting them to experience, always makes qualitative factors "content"; and as scientific conventions rule our academic thinking, it has usually been taken for granted that in understanding art, too, one should think of form as opposed to qualitative "content." But on this uncritical assumption the whole conception of form and content comes to grief, and analysis ends in the confused assertion that art is "formed content," form and content are one.[4] The solution of that paradox is, that a work of art is a structure whose interrelated elements are often qualities, or properties of qualities such as their degrees of in-

---

[3] Mr. I. A. Richards, in his *Principles of Literary Criticism*, declares that when people speak of "logical form," they do not know just what they mean. Perhaps he does not know, but I do; and if he really cares to know, he will find an elementary but systematic explanation in chapter 1 of my *Introduction to Symbolic Logic*.

[4] Morris Weitz, in his *Philosophy of the Arts*, offers an exhaustive analysis of the form-and-content problem, which shows up the conceptual muddles on which it rests. See Chap. 3, pp. 35–41.

tensity; that qualities enter into the form and in this way are as much one with it as the relations which they, and they only, have; and that to speak of them as "content," from which the form could be abstracted logically, is nonsense. The form is built up out of relations peculiar to them; they are formal elements in the structure, not contents.

Yet forms are either empty abstractions, or they do have a content; and artistic forms have a very special one, namely their *import*. They are logically expressive, or significant, forms. They are symbols for the articulation of feeling, and convey the elusive and yet familiar pattern of sentience. And as essentially symbolic forms they lie in a different dimension from physical objects as such. They belong to the same category as language, though their logical form is a different one, and as myth and dream, though their function is not the same.

Herein lies the "strangeness" or "otherness" that characterizes an artistic object. The form is immediately given to perception, and yet it reaches beyond itself; it is semblance, but seems to be charged with reality. Like speech, that is physically nothing but little buzzing sounds, it is filled with its meaning, and its meaning is a reality. In an articulate symbol the symbolic import permeates the whole structure, because every articulation of that structure is an articulation of the idea it conveys; the meaning (or, to speak accurately of a nondiscursive symbol, the vital import) is the content of the symbolic form, given with it, as it were, to perception.[5]

As though in evidence of the symbolic nature of art, its peculiar "strangeness" has sometimes been called "transparency." This transparency is what is obscured for us if our interest is distracted by the meanings of objects imitated; then the art work takes on literal significance and *evokes* feelings, which obscure the emotional content of the form, the feelings that are logically presented. That is, of course, the danger of representation, which is incurred whenever this device goes far beyond the needs of its primary office. It has secondary functions, too, in creating the artistic form (of which more will be said) wherefore many great artists have used their imitative powers lavishly; but in the work of a

---

[5]In the case of language this pregnance of the physically trivial form with a conceptual import verges on the miraculous. As Bernard Bosanquet said, "Language is so transparent that it disappears, so to speak, into its own meaning, and we are left with no characteristic medium at all." (*Three Lectures on Aesthetics*, p. 64.)

master hand the expressive form is so commanding, the transparency so clear that no one who has discovered the phenomenon of artistic import at all is likely to miss it there. The trouble is that many people have never felt it at all, because they have lived in a madhouse of too much art, wherein very great works are jumbled together with a multitude of ruinously bad ones, instead of standing out like peaks from the level of a modest, good tradition of design and workmanship. The very perception of form has been blunted by painful experience, instead of being exercised at the constant invitation of simple, gracious examples, as it is in less confused and less eclectic cultures. Tillyard remarked that the best preparation for reading great poetry is to read much good verse. Similarly, the surest training for the perception of great pictures is to live surrounded by good visual forms on the modest plane of textile designs and household utensils, and well-shaped decorated pitchers, jars, vases, nicely proportioned doors and windows, good carvings and embroideries—instead of "this eczemic eruption of pattern on all surfaces," whereof Roger Fry complained—and good illustrations in books, especially children's books. In a culture that has a seat and a tradition, certain basic forms are evolved that are true to simple feeling, and therefore comprehended by those who, lacking creative imagination, adopt current ideas, and apply what they have learned. But in a footloose society surfeited with influences, nothing is inviolate long enough to be governed by one clear feeling and to be really expressive of it. There are no simple significant forms to follow, and to compose suddenly, by an imaginative flash, into great creations, that are still continuous with the familiar principles they transcend. One filling station affects the style of the Taj Mahal, the next adapts itself to colonial surroundings, a third is a halfhearted pagoda, and next to it the gas pumps line up solemnly before a Swiss chalet. And we go about "liking" this and not that, and believing we *ought* to "like" the fifth sample, a functionally placed ark of glass and concrete, because it is American, modern, "our tradition," etc., etc.

Only an exceptional sensibility to form can survive this tangle of historical lines all ending in the snarl we call civilization. The average pictorial or musical instinct is confused to the point of complete frustration; and the natural defense is to abandon the language of plastic form, or music, or poetry, altogether and lean entirely on the standard-ized readings of sense experience that Coleridge called "primary imag-ination." Thus the representational power of art becomes a haven of refuge, a guarantee of meaning in the familiar mode of actuality; and the average man—as well as too many a critic—really believes that artists "re-create" fruits, flowers, women, and vacation spots, for him to possess in a pipe dream. As Ortega puts it, "The majority of people are unable to adjust their attention to the glass and the transparency which is the work of art; instead they penetrate through it to passion-ately wallow in the human reality which the work of art refers to. If they are invited to let loose their prey and fix their attention upon the work of art itself, they will say they see nothing in it, because, indeed, they see no human realities there, but only artistic transparencies, pure essences."[6]

We are not so much afflicted with bad taste, as with *no* taste. People tolerate the good and the bad, because they do not see the abstracted expressive form, the symbol of feeling, at all.

That is why the role of feeling in art has become an enigma. People who do rediscover the perceptual form, and realize that it is the truly essential factor, usually make it paramount by ruling out all its traffic with "meaning" of any sort. Thus they reject feeling, together with various associated "contents." What is left is an "exciting" mosaic of qualities, exciting us to nothing, a genuinely "aesthetic" object, an experiential dead end, pure essence. It is form and quality; form in quality; formed quality.

But people of artistic discernment (and only they could find per-ceptual form exciting) know that feeling does inhere somehow in every imaginal form. If, then, they cleave loyally to their pure realm of qual-ities, a quality it has to be. So here we have the curious phenomenological findings of Baensch, and the very similar conclusions of David Prall in his *Aesthetic Analysis*.

Prall's treatment is particularly interesting because it springs from the most serious and systematic analysis that has been made, so far as I know, of the sensuous element in the arts, which he calls the "aesthetic

---

[6]José Ortega y Gasset, *The Dehumanization of Art*, quoted in Rader's *A Modern Book of Aesthetics*.

surface." Each art, according to Prall, has a limited sensory realm de-fined by the selectiveness of a specialized sense, within which its whole existence lies. That is its "aesthetic surface," which can never be broken without breaking the work itself to which it relates, because it is the universe within which artistic form is articulated. The whole gamut of colors constitutes one such realm, and that of tones makes up another. In every case the "aesthetic surface" is something given by nature; so are the basic rules of structure, which spring from the nature of the material, as the diatonic scale, for instance, stems from the partial tones that lie in any fundamental of definite pitch. The several arts, therefore, are governed by the natural departments of sense, each giving the artist a particular order of elements out of which he may make combinations and designs to the limit of his inventive powers. Prall's philosophical approach to art is boldly technical, and guided by sound artistic sense in several departments. He treats every work of art as a structure, the purpose of which is to let us apprehend sensuous forms in a logical way. "The difference between perceiving clearly and understanding distinctly," he says, "is not the great difference we are sometimes led to think it."[7] And further: "Any conscious content is taken to be intelligible just so far as it is grasped as form or structure. This means, of course, as made up of elements in relations by virtue of which they actually come to-gether. . . . For elements not natively ordered by a relation of some sort will not make structures for us at all, nor will intrinsically related elements make structures for us unless we have become aware of the kinds of relation involved. You cannot make a spatial whole except with elements the very nature and being of which is spatial extension. You cannot make melodic structures except out of elements which are na-tively ordered by an intrinsic relation in pitch from which they cannot be removed. . . . The elements must lie in an order native to their very being, an order grasped by us as constituted by a relation. We call struc-tures intelligible . . . in so far as we find them capable of analysis into such elements so related."[8]

In other words, structures, or *forms* in the broad sense, must lie in some intellectual dimension in order to be perceived. Works of art are

[7] *Aesthetic Analysis,* p. 39.
[8] *Ibid.,* pp. 41–42.

made of sensuous elements, but not all sensuous materials will do; for only those data are *composable* which hold stations in an ideal continuum —e.g. colors in a scale of hues, where every interval between two given colors can be filled in with further elements given by implication, or tones in a continuous scale of pitches that has no "holes" for which a pitch is not determinable.

Prall's method seems to me impeccable: to study the work of art itself instead of our reactions and feelings toward it, and find some principle of its organization that explains its characteristic functions, its physical requirements, and its claims on our esteem. If, then, I start from a different premise, it is not because I disapprove Prall's statements —they are almost all acceptable—but because certain limitations of his theory seem to me to lie in the basic conception itself, and to disappear upon a somewhat different assumption. One of these limitations meets us in the analysis of poetry, where only one ingredient—the temporal pattern of sound, or "measure"—offers anything like a true "aesthetic surface" with commensurable elements to be deployed in formal relations, and this ingredient, though it is important, is not pre-eminent. In prose it is too free for scansion. Yet one feels that the true formal principle, whereby literature is constructed, must be just as evident and dominant in one gender as in another, and such characteristics as the pattern of poetic measure are merely specialized means for achieving it; and every distinct literary form must have some such means of its own, but not a new principle, to make it literature.

Another difficulty arises if we turn our attention to the art of dancing. Prall has not subjected this art to analysis, but indicated by cursory mention that he would treat it as a spatio-temporal form, and of course its constituent elements—motions—are mensurable and commensurable under both space and time. But such a conception of its basic forms brings it entirely and perfectly into the same category as mobile sculpture; even though one could adduce some characteristics that distinguished those two spatio-temporal arts, they would remain intimately related. Actually, however, they are very remotely related; mobile sculpture has no more connection with dance than stationary sculpture. It is *entirely sculpture,* and dance is entirely something else.

The art of acting becomes even more difficult to analyze than dancing, since the sensuous continuum of space and time, color and rhythm, is further complicated by sound elements, namely words. The fact is that Prall's theory is clearly applicable only to purely visual or purely auditory arts—painting and music—and its extension to other domains, even poetry, is a project rather than a natural consequence.

In short, the limitation inherent in Prall's theory is its bondage to those very "basic orders" to which it applies so excellently that practically everything he says about their artistic functions is true. The principle of the "aesthetic surface," consistently followed, actually leads to that purist criticism which has to condemn opera as a hybrid art, can tolerate drama only by assimilating it to literature, and tends to treat religious or historical themes in painting as embarrassing accidents to a pure design. It leads to no insight into the distinctions and connections of the arts, for the basic distinctions it makes between sensory orders are obvious. Consequently the connections it allows—e.g. between music and poetry, or music and dance, by virtue of their temporal ingredients —are obvious too; obvious, yet sometimes deceptive.

Limitation is not itself a reason for rejecting a theory. Prall knew the limitations of his inquiry and did not tackle the problems that lay beyond its reach. The only excuse for discarding a fundamental principle is that one has a more powerful notion, which will take the constructive work of the previous one in its stride, and then do something more. The weakness of Prall's aesthetics lies, I think, in a misconception of the dimensions underlying the various arts, and therefore of the fundamental principles of organization. The new idea of artistic structures, which seems to me more radical and yet more elastic than Prall's assumption of scales and spatio-temporal orders, causes a certain shift of focus in the philosophy of art; instead of seeking for elements of feeling among the sensuous contents, or qualia, literally contained in the art object, we are led straight to the problem of created form (which is not always sensuous) and its significance, the phenomenology of feeling. The problem of creativity, which Prall never had occasion to mention, is central here; for the elements themselves, and the wholes within which they have their distinct elementary existence, are created, not adopted.[9]

---

[9] Not the scales and geometries, for these are logical; but the exemplified continua of existence, the spaces and durations and fields of force.

A work of art differs from all other beautiful things in that it is "a glass and a transparency"—not, in any relevant way, a *thing* at all, but a symbol. Every good philosopher or critic of art realizes, of course, that *feeling* is somehow expressed in art; but as long as a work of art is viewed primarily as an "arrangement" of sensuous elements for the sake of some inexplicable aesthetic satisfaction, the problem of expressiveness is really an alien issue. Prall wrestles with it throughout a carefully reasoned psychological chapter, and although his psychology is clear and excellent, it leaves one with a sense of paradox; for the emotive element in art seems somehow more essential than the strictly "aesthetic" experience itself, and seems to be given in a different way, yet the work of art is aloof from real emotion, and can only suffer harm from any traffic with sentimental associations. In some sense, then, feeling must be *in* the work; just as a good work of art clarifies and exhibits the forms and colors which the painter has seen, distinguished, and appreciated better than his fellowmen could do without aid, so it clarifies and presents the feelings proper to those forms and colors. Feeling "expressed" in art is "feeling or emotion presented as the qualitative character of imaginal content."[10]

Here we have essentially the same treatment of feeling as in Baensch's essay, "Kunst und Gefühl," except that Baensch came to the conclusion that feeling could not even be found to lie entirely in the sensuous realm that one might regard as "content," but permeated the formal as well as the aesthetical elements of any art work. Both writers, however, seek salvation in the same tour de force of simply treating emotive elements as qualities of a concrete object, something which this inanimate object, and not its percipient, somehow "has"; and both know that the "expression" of real human feeling by a nonhuman object, which may be analyzed, without spatio-temporal relations, presents a paradox, and that their philosophic device is a counsel of despair.

"If it is asked how qualitative imaginal content can present feeling," says Prall, "how it can be actual feeling that art expresses, we arrive at the supposed miracle that art is so often said to be, the embodiment of spirit in matter. But thinking can have no intercourse with miracles. And since the simplest thinking finds that works of art do express feel-

---

[10]*Ibid.*, p. 145.

ing, we are forced by the obvious character of our data to look for feeling *within* the presented content, as an aspect of it, that is, integral to its actually present character, or as its unitary qualitative nature as a whole."[11]

The solution of the difficulty lies, I think, in the recognition that what art expresses is *not* actual feeling, but ideas of feeling; as language does not express actual things and events but ideas of them. Art is expressive through and through—every line, every sound, every gesture; and therefore it is a hundred per cent symbolic. It is not sensuously pleasing and *also* symbolic; the sensuous quality is in the service of its vital import. A work of art is far more symbolic than a word, which can be learned and even employed without any knowledge of its meaning; for a purely and wholly articulated symbol *presents* its import directly to any beholder who is sensitive at all to articulated forms in the given medium.[12]

An articulate form, however, must be clearly given and understood before it can convey any import, especially where there is no conventional reference whereby the import is assigned to it as its unequivocal meaning, but the congruence of the symbolic form and the form of some vital experience must be directly perceived by the force of *Gestalt* alone. Hence the paramount importance of *abstracting the form*, banning all irrelevancies that might obscure its logic, and especially divesting it of all its usual meanings so it may be open to new ones. The first thing is to estrange it from actuality, to give it "otherness," "self-sufficiency"; this is done by creating a realm of illusion, in which it functions as *Schein*, mere semblance, free from worldly offices. The second thing is to make it plastic, so it may be manipulated in the interests of expression in-

---

[11]*Loc. cit., infra.*

[12]Prall came so close to this realization that his avoidance of the term "symbol" for a work of art appears to be studied. Evidently he preferred the specious theory that assumes feelings to be contained in sensory qualities, to a semantic theory of art that would have laid him open to the charge of intellectualism or iconism. So he maintains that a feeling is *in* a picture, and that we "have" it when we look at the work. Compare, for instance the following passage with what has just been said about a perfected presentational symbol: "The point of the picture, its effective being, is just this embodied feeling that we have, if with open sensitive eyes we look at it and let its character become the content of our own affective conscious life at the moment." (*Ibid.*, p. 163.)

stead of practical signification. This is achieved by the same means—uncoupling it from practical life, abstracting it as a free conceptual figment. Only such forms can be plastic, subject to deliberate torsion, modification, and composition for the sake of expressiveness. And finally, it must become "transparent"—which it does when insight into the reality to be expressed, the *Gestalt* of living experience, guides its author in creating it.

Whenever craftsmanship is art, these principles—abstraction, plastic freedom, expressiveness—are wholly exemplified, even in its lowliest works. Some theorists assign different values to the various manifestations of art (e.g. pure design, illustration, easel painting), ranking them as "lower" and "higher" types, of which only the "higher" are expressive, the "lower" merely decorative, giving sensuous pleasure without any further import.[13] But such a distinction throws any theory of art into confusion. If "art" means anything, its application must rest on one essential criterion, not several unrelated ones—expressiveness, pleasantness, usefulness, sentimental value, and so forth. If art is "the creation of forms expressive of human feeling," then gratification of the senses must either serve that purpose or be irrelevant; and I agree wholeheartedly with Thomas Mann that there are no higher and lower, partial and supplementary arts, but, as he put it, "Art is entire and complete in each of its forms and manifestations; we do not need to add up the different species to make a whole."[14]

Pure design, therefore, is a test case, a touchstone of the concept of art developed in this book, and merits some closer examination here. For it is a basic phenomenon; all over the world one finds certain elements of graphic expression, patterns of color on naturally blank surfaces—walls, textiles, ceramics, wood or metal or stone slabs—addressed only to sight, and very delightful to that sense. Sometimes they serve as magic symbols, sometimes as proxies or reminders of natural objects; but, with or without such functions, they always fulfill one purpose to which they are pre-eminently adapted—decoration.

---

[13]Eugène Véron is the best known exponent of this view (see his *Aesthetics*, especially chap. vii). But compare also the much more recent judgment of Henry Varnum Poor, that "decoration pursued as decoration is apt to be so shallow and limited" that it requires some combination with "realistic painting" to stir the imagination. (*Magazine of Art*, August, 1940.)

[14]*Freud, Goethe, Wagner* (1937), p. 139.

What then, is "decoration"? The obvious synonyms are "ornamentation," "embellishment"; but, like most synonyms, they are not quite precise. "Decoration" refers not merely to beauty, like "embellishment," nor does it suggest the addition of an independent ornament. "Decoration" is cognate with the word "decorum"; it connotes fitness, formalization. But what is fitted and formalized?

A visible surface. The immediate effect of good decoration is to make the surface, somehow, *more visible;* a beautiful border on a textile not only emphasizes the edge but enhances the plain folds, and a regular allover pattern, if it is good, unifies rather than diversifies the surface. In any case, even the most elementary design serves to concentrate and hold one's vision to the expanse it adorns. [Cf. Plate II and III]

The similarity of forms in purely decorative painting and line drawing, such as one finds on pots and blankets, paddles and sails and tattooed bodies, in the most unrelated corners of the earth is so striking that André Malraux has suggested a prehistoric unity of culture to account for it.[15] The notion is not preposterous, even with regard to the most fundamental designs; but it does present such historical difficulty that one tends to look for a simpler one. It seems at least possible that those elementary forms—parallel lines and zigzags, triangles and circles and scrolls—have an instinctive basis in the principles of perception; that in them the impulse to some sort of organization of the visual field comes to expression so directly that it undergoes practically no distorting cultural influences, but brings forth a record of visual experience at its lowest terms. The late Albert Barnes treated sheer design in this way, when he wrote:

"The appeal of such decorative beauty is probably to be explained by its satisfaction of our general need of perceiving freely and agreeably. All our senses crave adequate stimulation, irrespective of what stimulates them. . . . This need of employing our faculties in a manner congenial to us, decoration meets and satisfies."[16]

This liberation of the senses is, indeed, an aspect of artistic perception;

---

[15]See his *The Psychology of Art,* Vol. II: *The Creative Act,* pp. 122–123. With respect to Altamira and Bushman art his hypothesis is, indeed, highly plausible, and has been advanced before by the anthropologist William J. Sollas in his *Ancient Hunters and Their Modern Representatives* (1924).

[16]*The Art in Painting,* p. 29.

there are certain forms that are "congenial" to vision—unbroken lines that lead the eye from one place to another without obstruction, and the simple shapes which the *Gestalt* psychologists have found to be the natural standards of perceptual judgment.[17] But comprehensibility, logical clearness, is not enough to create a virtual object and set it apart from actuality. Circles and triangles, taken by themselves, are not works of art, as decorative designs are. In an early part of *The Art in Painting*, Barnes make a distinction between decorative and expressive values,[18] which seems to me spurious; decoration is expressive,[19] not "adequate stimulation" but basic artistic form with an emotional import, like all created forms. Its office is not only to indulge perception, but to impregnate and transform it. It is the education of plastic imagination. Decorative design offers to the percipient—without any rule or explanation, purely by exemplification—a logic of vision. That fact has been noted before; but what has not been noted is the further, and crucial, fact that this logic is not the conceptual logic of space relations which leads to geometry (any and all geometries).[20] The principles of vision which become apparent in the structure of decorative forms are principles of *artistic vision,* whereby visual elements are carved out of the amorphous sensory chaos to conform not with names and predications, like the data of practical cognition, but with biological feeling and its emotional efflorescence, "life" on the human level. They are, *ab initio,* different from the elements that conform to discursive thought; but their function in the building up of human consciousness is probably just as important and deep. Art, like discourse, is everywhere the mark of man. As language, wherever it occurs, breaks up into words and acquires conventions for shuffling the patterns of those semi-independent words to express propositions, so the grammar of artistic vision develops plastic forms for the expression of basic vital rhythms. Perhaps that is why certain decorative devices are almost universal; perhaps it is convergence,

---

[17]See Wolfgang Köhler, *Gestalt Psychology* (1929), especially chap. v, "Sensory Organization."

[18]*Op. cit.,* pp. 30–31.

[19]In a later passage he admits this and, in fact, comes to much the same conclusion as I; but he never justifies or retracts his earlier statement.

[20]Failure to recognize this disinction is what made Birkhoff's ambitious work, *Aesthetic Measure*, the curious, inapplicable speculation on art that it is.

rather than divergence, that accounts for the astonishing parallels of design which may be found in such unrelated cultural products as Chinese embroideries, Mexican pots, Negro body decorations, and English printers' flowers.

Pure decorative design is a direct projection of vital feeling into visible shape and color. Decoration may be highly diversified, or it may be very simple; but it always has what geometric form, for instance a specimen illustration in Euclid, does not have—motion and rest, rhythmic unity, wholeness. Instead of mathematical form, the design has—or rather, it *is*—"living" form, though it need not represent anything living, not even vines or periwinkles. Decorative lines and areas express vitality in what they themselves seem to "do"; when they picture any creature that might really do something—a crocodile, a bird, a fish—that creature is just as likely (in some traditions even more likely) to be at rest as in motion. But the design itself expresses life. Lines that intersect in a central point "emanate" from that center, although they never actually change their relation to it. Similar or congruent elements "repeat" each other, colors "balance" each other, though they have no physical weight, etc. All these metaphorical terms denote relationships that belong to the virtual object, the created illusion, and they are just as applicable to the simplest design on a paddle or an apron, if the design is artistically good, as to an easel picture or a wall painting.

In a little textbook of decorative drawing, I found this naive, normative statement about ornamental borders: "Borders must move forward, and grow as they move."[20] What do the words "move" and "grow'" mean in this context? The border is fixed on the surface whereon it is painted, printed, embroidered or carved, and it would be hard to say, with respect to a tablecloth or a title page, which direction is "forward." The "movement" of the border is not really movement in the scientific sense, change of place; it is the semblance of rhythm, and "forward" is the direction in which the repeated elements of the design seem to be serried. Many borders move in either direction, as we choose to "read" them, but in some there is a strong feeling of one-way motion. Such effects spring directly from the design, and from nothing else; the motion of a design, forward, backward, outward, is inherent in its construction. Now, sec-

---

[20]Adolfo Best-Maugard, *A Method for Creative Design*, p. 10.

ondly, what is meant by "grow"? A border cannot grow bigger than the margin it adorns, nor would such a wonder be desirable. No, but the series of its repetitions seems to grow longer by a law of its own that makes it continue. That, again, is rhythm, the semblance of life (the definition of rhythm, which makes that term literally applicable to spatial as well as temporal forms, and, upon occasion, to other arrangements than series, cannot here be given, but is discussed in Chapter 7). *All motion in art is growth*—not growth of something pictured, like a tree, but of lines and spaces.

There is a tendency to this illusion in our "primary imagination," our practical use of vision. Movement and lines are intimately related in conception, as also lines and growth. A mouse running across the floor describes a path, an ideal line that grows with his progress. We say, the mouse *ran* under the sofa and along the wall; we may also say that his path *runs* that course. A person "writing in air" makes letters appear to our imagination, invisible lines that grow before us though our eyes see only his moving hand.

In an ornamental border there is no thing that moves at all, no mouse or hand that heads the advancing line. The border itself "runs" along the edge of the tablecloth or around the margins of a page. A spiral is an advancing line, but what really seems to grow is a space, the two-dimensional area it defines.

The classical explanation of such dynamic effects of what are, after all, perfectly static marks on a background, is that their powerful "persuasion of the eye" causes that organ truly and literally to move, and the sensation in the eye muscles makes us actually feel the motion.[21] But in ordinary life our eyes go from one thing to another in much greater muscular exertions, yet the things in a room do not seem to be running around. A little section of border such as we view here

is taken in at one glance, practically without ocular movement. Actually, nothing moves enough to give us a *sensation* of movement. The design, however, is a symbolic form which abstracts the continuity, directedness,

<hr />

[21]This hypothesis was advanced by Theodor Lipps in his *Aesthetic* and other writings, and defended by Violet Paget [Vernon Lee], especially in her well-known little book, *The Beautiful*.

and energy of motion, and conveys the idea of those abstracted characters exactly as any symbol conveys its meaning. In fact, it presents something more complex than the essence of motion, which it could not do if it merely *connoted* motion by stimulating diminutive movements in our eyes: namely, the idea of growth.

To understand how an advancing line begets the illusion of growth really involves one in the whole subject of created appearance; and the further question, why borders that "move" *should* "grow," raises the final issue of form and feeling in art. Let us see what light is shed on this problem, and what solution of it is offered by the theory of semblance and symbolic import.

In certain linear designs that, of course, physically lie perfectly still on a ground, there seems to be motion, though nothing is changing its place. On the other hand, where motion really takes place, it defines a lasting conceptual line even when it leaves no trace. The running mouse seems to cover a path lying on the floor, and the still, painted line seems to run. The reason is that both embody the abstract principle of *direction*, by virtue of which they are logically congruent enough to be symbols for one another; and in the ordinary, intelligent use of vision we let them stand proxy for each other all the time, though we do not know it. It is not a function that is first discursively conceived and then assigned to a possible symbol, but is non-discursively exhibited and perceived long before it is acknowledged in a scientific device (as it is in the language of physics, where vectors are conventionally indicated by arrows). Motion, therefore, is logically related to linear form, and where a line is unbroken, and supporting forms tend to give it direction, the mere perception of it is charged with the idea of motion, which shines through our impression of the actual sense datum and fuses with it in apperception. The result is a very elementary artistic illusion (not delusion, for, unlike delusion, it survives analysis), which we call "living form."

This term, again, is justified by a logical connection that exists between the half-illusory datum, and the concept of life, whereby the former is a natural symbol of the latter; for "living form" directly exhibits what is the essence of life—incessant change, or process, articulating a permanent form.

The path of a physical motion is an ideal line. In a line that "has movement," there is ideal motion. In the phenomenon we call "life," both continuous change and permanent form really exist; but the form is made and maintained by complicated disposition of mutual influences among the physical units (atoms, molecules, then cells, then organs), whereby changes tend always to occur in certain pre-eminent ways. Instead of a simple law of transformation such as one finds in inorganic change, living things exist by a cumulative process; they assimilate elements of their surroundings to themselves, and these elements fall under the law of change that is the organic form of "life." This assimilation of factors not originally belonging to the organism, whereby they enter into its life, is the principle of growth. A growing thing need not actually become bigger; since the metabolic action does not stop when a non-living substance has been assimilated and become alive, but is a continuous process of oxidation, separate elements also resign from the organic pattern; they break down again into inorganic structures, i.e. they die. When growth is more vigorous than decay the living form grows larger; when they are balanced it is self-perpetuating; when decay occurs faster than growth the organism is decadent. At a certain point the metabolic process stops all at once, and the life is finished.

Permanence of form, then, is the constant aim of living matter; not the final goal (for it is what finally fails), but the thing that is perpetually being achieved, and that *is* always, at every moment, an achievement, because it depends entirely on the activity of "living." But "living" itself is a process, a continuous change; if it stands still the form disintegrates—for *the permanence is a pattern of changes.*

Nothing, therefore, is as fundamental in the fabric of our feeling as the sense of permanence and change and their intimate unity. What we call "motion" in art is not necessarily change of place, but is *change made perceivable,* i.e. *imaginable,* in any way whatever. Anything that symbolizes change so we seem to behold it is what artists, with more intuition than convention, call a "dynamic" element. It may be a "dynamic accent" in music, physically nothing but loudness, or a word charged above others with emotion, or a color that is "exciting" where it stands, i.e. physically stimulating.

A form that *exemplifies* permanence, such as a fixed line or a delimited space (the most permanent anchors of vision), yet *symbolizes* motion, carries with it the concept of growth, because growth is the normal operation of those two principles conjoined in mutual dependence. Therefore the metaphorical statement: "Borders must move forward, and grow as they move," is perfectly rational if we consider that, and why, they *seem* to do these things. But why "must" they be drawn to seem like that? Because this illusion, this seeming, is the real symbol of feeling. The elementary pattern of feeling expressed in such world-accepted forms symbolizing "growth" is the *sense of life,* the most primitive "fulfillment"; and it is not mirrored in the physical lines, but in the created thing, the "motion" they have. The dynamic pattern, which is actually an illusion, is what copies the form of vital feeling. It is in order to be expressive that borders must move and grow.

Yet the "movement" of a design is always in a framework of felt stability; for unlike actual motion, it is not involved with change. The only person, so far as I know, who has clearly recognized this characteristic of plastic space is not a painter but a musician, Roger Sessions. In a remarkably discerning little essay, "The Composer and His Message"[22] (to which I shall probably return more than once), Mr. Sessions has written: "The visual arts govern a world of space, and it seems to me that perhaps the profoundest sensation which we derive from space is not so much that of extension as of permanence. On the most primitive level we feel space to be something permanent, fundamentally unchangeable; when movement is apprehended through the eye it takes place, so to speak, within the static framework, and the psychological impact of this framework is much more powerful than that of the vibrations which occur within its limits." This duality of motion-in-permanence is, indeed, what effects the abstraction of pure dynamism and creates the semblance of life, or activity maintaining its form.

"Expression" in the logical sense—presentation of an idea through an articulate symbol—is the ruling power and purpose of art. And the symbol is, from first to last, something created. The illusion, which constitutes the work of art, is not a mere arrangement of given materials in an aesthetically pleasing pattern; it is what results from the arrangement, and is literally something the artist makes, not something he finds. It comes with his work and passes away in its destruction.

[22]In *The Intent of the Artist,* edited by Augusto Centeno. See p. 106.

To produce and sustain the essential illusion, set it off clearly from the surrounding world of actuality, and articulate its form to the point where it coincides unmistakably with forms of feeling and living, is the artist's task. To such ends he uses whatever materials lend themselves to technical treatment—tones, colors, plastic substances, words, gestures, or any other physical means.[23] The making of the "semblance," and the articulation of vital form within its scaffold is, therefore, our guiding theme, from which all further problems of art—the ways of imagination, the nature of abstraction, the phenomena of talent and genius, etc.— will receive such light as the central idea can throw by implication, which is the philosophical strength and pragmatic value of concepts.

---

[23]The oft-asserted proposition that painting can incorporate nothing but color, music nothing but tone, etc., is, I think, not unconditionally true. This is one problem which the theory of created form is better fitted to solve than any theory based on the art medium (Alexander, Prall, Fry), because it admits the *principle of assimilation* discussed in Chap. 10.

Chapter five

VIRTUAL SPACE

The fundamental forms which occur in the decorative arts of all ages and races—for instance the circle, the triangle, the spiral, the parallel—are known as *motifs* of design. They are not art "works," not even ornaments, themselves, but they lend themselves to composition, and are therefore incentives to artistic creation. The word *motif* bespeaks this function: motifs are organizing devices that give the artist's imagination a start, and so "motivate" the work in a perfectly naive sense. They drive it forward, and guide its progress.

Some of these basic shapes suggest forms of familiar things. A circle with a marked center and a design emanating from the center suggests a flower, and that hint is apt to guide the artist's composition. All at once, a new effect springs into being, there is a new creation—a representation, the illusion of an object.

The floral rosette is one of the oldest and most widespread of these ornamental designs with obvious representational reference. We find it on Assyrian costumes, Chinese vases, implements of the Northwestern Indians, in Peruvian carvings, on Roman breastplates, peasant furniture and pottery all over Europe, and in the rose windows of Gothic cathedrals. The treatment is often very formal, botanically quite fantastic; the center may be a spiral, the petals simple radial lines, or circles surrounding a central ring, or enclosed in a large circle, or they may be ovals or triangles or even scalloped lines forming concentric rings. The interesting point is that in each of these inventions the form is so unmistakably a flower. [Cf. Plate IV] Suddenly the element of representation is not only present, but seems to be the ruling element. We do not usually think of such designs as geometric forms pictorially interpreted, but as conventionalized pictures of flowers. It is a common assumption that people first copied the appearance of real flowers and then, for no very evident reason, "abstracted" all these odd shapes from the faithful portrait. Actually, I think, a comparative study of decorative art and primitive representational art suggests forcibly that *form is first,* and the representational function accrues to it.[1] Gradually the decorative forms are modified more and more to picture all sorts of objects—leaves, vines, the intriguing shapes of marine life, flights of birds, animals, people, things. But the basic motifs remain: rings become eyes without undergoing any modification, triangles become beards, and spirals curls, ears, branches, breaking waves. [Cf. Plate V] The zigzag may decorate a snake as it decorates the edge of a pot, or it may represent the snake directly. Gradually the elementary forms are more and more synthesized into representational pictures, until they seem to disappear; but often a little attention reveals them even in advanced representational treatment, and wherever we find them their office is the primitive one of decorative design.

A similar shift occurs in the development of color. At first the primary colors are in sole possession, and seem to have only ornamental functions. In genuine folk art, black deer with blue eyes and blue deer with black eyes may alternate around a bowl, and warriors, as well as palm trees, come in all colors. Then convention fixes colors that have some relation to the actual hues of nature, but do not show any effort to copy specific effects. Thus in Egyptian paintings men are terra-cotta colored and women white or pale tan; in mediaeval psalters, angels often have literally golden hair, and in peasant art vermilion mustaches and canary pigtails are the order of the day. The use of color, like that of forms, is *first* ornamental and *afterwards* representative of natural attributes.

Decoration, based on quasi-geometric shapes that are "congenial" to our spatial intuition, and guided by interest in felt continuities, rhythms, and emotional dynamics, is a simple but pure and abstract order of expressive form. When designs include pictorial elements—dogs, whales, human faces—those images are simplified and distorted with perfect freedom to fit the rest of the pattern. Their graphic rendering is never a copy of direct visual impressions, but formulation, shaping, defining of the

---

[1] This is not a "law," supposed to be universally true, because there may be art forms that start directly from fetishes, signs, etc., i.e. from representations. But the most natural and potent source of *styles* is, I believe, decorative form, and even creations of more practical origin probably develop under its influence.

impressions themselves according to the principles of expressiveness, or vital form; it is symbolizing from the outset. But once the suggestion of objects has been followed, the representative interest makes art transcend its elementary motifs; a new method of organization arises—the adaptation of the old decorative devices to the systematic depiction of objects.[2]

The importance of this principle increases as the forms become more involved, asymmetrical, and subtle, created not only by obvious means like outlines and pure colors, but also by illusions of receding space and the orientation of units of design toward each other. The interpretation of such units as forms of objects is an inestimable aid in the creation of new spatial relationships, in distributing centers of interest and composing them into a visual unity. For centuries, in Europe and Asia, drawing and painting evolved mainly on representational guidelines; and, as in decorative design we speak of zigzags and circles as "motifs," so now we apply "motif" to what is pictured by the lines and shapes.

But no matter how many possibilities are opened to the artistic imagination by the power of representing things, imitation is never the main device in organization. The purpose of all plastic art is to articulate visual form, and to present that form—so immediately expressive of human feeling that it seems to be charged with feeling—as the sole, or at least paramount, object of perception. This means that for the beholder the work of art must be not only a shape in space, but a shaping *of* space—of all the space that he is given. When we investigate systematically all that is involved in this proposition, we are led ever to deeper and deeper questions, culminating in the problem of creation: What is created, and how is anything created, by the process of deploying colors on a ground?

Space as we know it in the practical world has no shape. Even in science it has none, though it has "logical form." There are spatial relations, but there is no concrete totality of space. Space itself is amorphous in our active lives and purely abstract in scientific thought. It is a substrate of all our experience, gradually discovered by the collaboration of

---

[2]Leonardo, in his *Treatise on Painting*, advises students to look at chance forms like cracks in plaster and knots in boards and try to make figures out of them, i.e. to read shapes of people and things into them. This, he says, is very good for the painter's imagination. It sounds silly; but was Leonardo silly? Or did he also feel that visual "reality" is made out of the forms that express man's inner life?

our several senses—now seen, now felt, now realized as a factor in our moving and doing—a limit to our hearing, a defiance to our reach. When the spatial experience of everyday life is refined by the precision and artifice of science, space becomes a coordinate in mathematical functions. It is never an entity. How, then, can it be "organized," "shaped," or "articulated"? We meet all these terms in the most serious literature of aesthetics.

The answer is, I think, that the space in which we live and act is not what is treated in art at all. The harmoniously organized space in a picture is not experiential space, known by sight and touch, by free motion and restraint, far and near sounds, voices lost or re-echoed. It is an entirely visual affair; for touch and hearing and muscular action it does not exist. For them there is a flat canvas, relatively small, or a cool blank wall, where for the eye there is deep space full of shapes. This purely visual space is an illusion, for our sensory experiences do not agree on it in their report. Pictorial space is not only organized by means of color (including black and white and the gamut of grays between them), it is created; without the organizing shapes it is simply not there. Like the space "behind" the surface of a mirror, it is what the physicists call "virtual space" —an intangible image.

This virtual space is the primary illusion of all plastic art. Every element of design, every use of color and semblance of shape, serves to produce and support and develop the picture space that exists for vision alone. Being only visual, this space has no continuity with the space in which we live; it is limited by the frame, or by surrounding blanks, or incongruous other things that cut it off. Yet its limits cannot even be said to *divide* it from practical space; for a boundary that divides things always connects them as well, and between the picture space and any other space there is no connection. The created virtual space is entirely self-contained and independent.

The first art theorist who recognized the purely visual and otherwise illusory nature of pictorial space, and understood its paramount importance for the aims and practices of painters, was Adolf Hildebrand. In a small but very serious book, *The Problem of Form in Painting and Sculpture,* he analyzed the process of pictorial representation from the standpoint of space creation, which he called the "architectonic" process.

The term is not altogether fortunate, since it suggests "architectural," which is not its meaning. He intended merely to connote that the artist's work is a *building up* of space for one sense alone, namely vision. He called that virtual image "perceptual space," meaning "visual"; and by the "architectonic method" he meant the systematic construction of forms that should present and articulate such space.

Everything that is relevant and artistically valid in a picture must be visual; and everything visual serves architectonic purposes. Where in practical life we employ other faculties than sight to complete our fragmentary visual experiences—for instance memory, recorded measurements, beliefs about the physical constitution of things, knowledge of their relations in space even when they are behind us or blocked by other things—in the virtual space of a picture there are no such supporting data. Everything that is given at all is given to vision; therefore we must have *visual substitutes* for the things that are normally known by touch, movement or inference. That is why a direct copy of what we see is not enough. The copy of things seen would need the same supplementation from non-visual sources that the original perception demanded. The visual substitutes for the non-visible ingredients in space experience make the great difference between photographic rendering and creative rendering; the latter is necessarily a departure from direct imitation, because it is a construction of spatial entities out of color alone (perhaps only varying shades of one color), by all sorts of devices in order to present at once, with complete authority, the primary illusion of a perfectly visible and perfectly intelligible total space.

"Material acquired through a direct study of nature," says Hildebrand, "is, by the architectonic process, transformed into an artistic unity. When we speak of the imitative aspect of art, we are referring to material which has not yet been developed in this manner. . . .

"Reviewing the artistic production of earlier times, we find that the architectonic structure of a work of art stands out everywhere as the paramount factor, whereas mere imitation is a thing which has only gradually developed."[3]

If we compare this observation with findings in the realm of folk art, the coincidence is striking. The architectonic process, as Hildebrand con-

[3]*The Problem of Form in Painting and Sculpture*, pp. 11–12.

ceives it, is *the construction and ordering of forms in space in such a way that they define and organize the space.* But a perceptually defined space is a shape: so the complete shaping of a given visual field is a work of pictorial art.

The central concept of Hildebrand's aesthetic is the concept of the visual field, or picture plane. His whole critique of art, in fact, is based on pictorial values—a curious idiosyncrasy in a sculptor! But within its limits, namely the graphic projection effected by painting, drawing, incising, or working in low relief, his analysis of the created space is so direct and illuminating that it merits some exposition.

The architectonic process, he says, always treats the elements of vision as spread out in a plane opposite the perceiving eye. The elementary forms out of which primitive painters made their representations lay exclusively in one such plane. But our eyes are actually able to focus at different depths, giving vision a power of penetrating into further distance. Nevertheless, with any change of distance, *sight is perfect only as it finds a new plane.* To organize vision again at a different depth requires the determination of a new ideal plane.

Experience in the composite and amorphous space of common perception has taught us to interpret certain lines as "foreshortened," i.e. as signals of things extending in the direction perpendicular to our field of vision. In graphic art, however, such lines serve only to mediate between the several planes, or layers of design, in complex visual space. As soon as we are preoccupied with construing what goes on in the direction away from us, we are no longer dealing with visual forms, but with things and their story. Artistically, things and goings on are only motifs on which forms are made, and whereby forms are related, in order to define the visual space and exhibit its character.

In relegating imitation and its natural models to their proper places, Hildebrand openly tackles the problem of reality and illusion. The character of things as we have seen, felt, or construed them by the concerted work of all our senses, he calls, with philosophical innocence, their "actual form." Apart from any naive ontological beliefs it may convey, "actual" is not a bad term, for it refers to the characteristics of things that are learned and valued in the sphere of our actions. This "actual form" is what an artist works *with;* what he works *for,* on the other hand, is to clarify their "perceptual form," or visible appearance. All that is important to him is what contributes to the perceptual form.

This form is a semblance of things, and the planes of vision, staggered one behind the other opposite the perceiving eye, are a semblance of space. They belong to that virtual space which is, I believe, the first creation in plastic art—the primary illusion in which all harmonious forms exist as secondary illusions, created symbols for the expression of feeling and emotion.

Virtual space, being entirely independent and not a local area in actual space, is a self-contained, total system. Whether it be two-dimensional or three, it is continuous in all its possible directions, and infinitely plastic. In any work of art, the dimensionality of its space and the continuous character of it are always implicitly assured. Perceptual forms are carved out of it and must appear to be still related to it despite their most definite boundaries. Hildebrand clinches this idea with a parable that is probably its best explication. "Let us imagine total space," he says, "as a body of water into which we may sink certain vessels, and thus be able to define individual volumes of the water without, however, destroying the idea of a continuous mass of water enveloping all." And in a later passage, he concludes: "Pictorial presentation has for its purpose the awakening of this idea of space, and that exclusively by the factors which the artist presents."[4]

If, therefore, the artist presents semblances of objects, people, landscapes, etc., it is for their visual values as portions of perceptual space. Unlike most writers on aesthetics, Hildebrand defines that important concept: "By the visual values of space we mean those values of an object which issue only in purely spatial perceptions tending toward the general conception of a segment of space. By purely spatial perceptions we mean perceptions independent of the organization or functioning of the object involved. Let us take a form which is given visual expression by contrasts of light and shade. Through their particular relations and respective positions, these different degrees of brightness and darkness affect the spectator as if they were actually modeling the object—a concerted effect is produced existing only for the eye, by factors which otherwise are not necessarily connected."[5]

---

[4] *Ibid.*, pp. 53–55.   [5] *Loc. cit.*

Representation, in other words, is for the sake of creating individual forms in visible relation to one another. It makes imagination help the eye to establish virtual proportions, connections, and focal points. The suggestion of familiar objects, used in this way, is essentially a device for constructing volumes, distances, planes of vision and the space between them; and as such it is a genuinely artistic factor. Again Hildebrand's concrete illustration is probably the best gloss to our text:

"To give the simplest example, think of a plane. It is evident that a plane is more clearly perceived when something is placed upon it, for instance, a tree—an upright. With something standing upon it, the horizontal portion of the surface expresses itself at once: one might say it becomes spatially active. The tree is affected in the same way. The upright tendency of its form is enhanced by the horizontal surface from which it springs. . . . A few streaks of cloud on the horizon draw our gaze, and we proceed from the vertical front plane into the background, thereby experiencing effectively by the simplest of means all the dimensions of space at once."[6]

Trees, clouds, horizons, buildings and ships, people in many postures, faces in various lights, all make sudden revelations of expressive form to a visually creative person. All may be represented in the virtual realm of purely apparent shapes and intervals. But it is not, as notably Croce and Bergson have said, the actual existence of the object to be depicted, that the artist understands better than other people. It is the semblance, the look of it, and the emotional import of its form, that he perceives while others only "read the label" of its actual nature, and dwell on the actuality.

The problem of "imitation," or reproducing the appearance of a model, has harassed philosophers ever since Plato censured art as "a copy of a copy." Almost every academic writer on aesthetics, faced with the antinomy of imitation and creation, today takes refuge in the doctrine that the artist selects certain sense impressions from the entire stock at his disposal, and that his creativity lies in the new effect gained by this judicious process; the result reveals his individual taste, i.e. his own personality, or else his emphases and deletions convey an insight into the "reality" of his object, which he sets forth as it really is—not as a kind

---

[6]*Op. cit.*, pp. 50–51.

of thing or such and such a creature, but a unique individual which he has "passionately seen." In either case, he suppresses what is unessential and heightens what is essential *to the subject,* to reveal its nature or his own feeling toward it.

But any such analysis leaves us with a fundamental confusion of nature and art, and binds artistic truth, ultimately, to the same post as propositional truth—that is, to the pictured thing. No wonder, then, if some aestheticians claim that our perception of things as the painter has seen them is not different in kind from our own perceptions in practical life, but differs from the latter only in context and use.[7] "Creation" becomes a somewhat pretentious word to apply to the modifications an artist may make in the appearance of things by selection and emphasis. Some modest souls, therefore, are content to call art a *"re*-creation" of experience, a "transcription" of the contemporary world. But there is no principle of free construction here; all deviations from the commonplace are signals of mental unbalance, "recreating" nightmare. The artist's freedom consists of little liberties, by-your-leave, editing the book of nature in the course of his transcription. When DeWitt Parker says that a painter recreates what he sees, but "to his critical eye there will be something . . . too much or too little, something to add or something to exclude, . . ."[8] there is no escape from the conclusion that the artist is adding touches to reality, prettifying the actual world.

Compare with this the bold statement of principle in Hildebrand's book: The factors which the artist presents are those which make us aware of related forms in the continuum of a total perceptual space. All accents and selections, as well as radical distortions or utter departures from any "actual form" of objects, have the purpose of *making space visible and its continuity sensible.* The space itself is a projected image, and everything pictured serves to define and organize it. Even representation of familiar objects, if it occurs, is a means to this end.

Virtual space, the essence of pictorial art, is a creation, not a re-creation. Yet most great artists, and especially those who made the boldest departures from the "actual form" of things, e.g. Leonardo and Cézanne, believed they were faithfully reproducing nature. Leonardo even advised

---

[7]Cf. Chapter 3, note 13.
[8]*The Analysis of Art* (1926), p. 51.

students to set up a glass through which objects could be seen, and trace their contours on it. (He himself, of course, did not need this aid, because he could draw freehand so well. Oddly enough, the method did not engender any further Leonardo.) But in Cézanne's reflections, that always center on the absolute authority of Nature, the relation of the artist to his model reveals itself unconsciously and simply: for the transformation of natural objects into pictorial elements took place *in his seeing,* in the act of looking, not the act of painting. Therefore, recording what he saw, he earnestly believed that he painted exactly what "was there." In his analysis of the object seen he expresses the principle of space construction to which his paintings bear witness.

"Nature reveals herself to me in very complex forms. . . . One must see one's model correctly and experience it in the right way. . . . To achieve progress nature alone counts, and the eye is trained through contact with her. It becomes concentric by looking and working. I mean to say that in an orange, an apple, a bowl, a head, there is a culminating point; and this point is always—in spite of the tremendous effect of light and shade and colorful sensations—the closest to our eye; the edges of the object recede to a center on our horizon."[9]

Here the great painter simply attributes to the object, *seen by him,* the properties Hildebrand found in virtual space. "The space of which we are clearly conscious when we attend to the distance plane [the "picture plane," the transformed surface] lies *behind* it. It commences with the plane. Space is conceived as a penetration into the distance. . . . All relations of solids and differences of solid form are read off from front to back . . ."[10] Cézanne was so supremely gifted with the painter's vision that to him attentive sight and spatial composition were the same thing. Virtual space was his mind's habitat. Perhaps Leonardo, too, could "copy nature" so naively because he actually saw only what, transferred to canvas or traced through glass, would create the primary illusion, the semblance of space. (In this way the painter's vision is indeed selective; but the line that "selects" a form was never found in actuality.) It takes a lesser artist, one who knows the light of common day, to note the process of interpretation whereby sense data, that are half-seen signals

---

[9]From two letters to Émile Bernard, 1904.
[10]Cf. Hildebrand, *op. cit.,* p. 60.

of physical conditions to the normal eye, are relieved of that function and, entirely seen, stand abstracted as new forms, in which the glow of feeling and the sense of vital process are visibly articulated. Hildebrand, who was no painter and at best a second-rate sculptor, often had the advantage as a theorist.

Creation of "virtual space" is common to all works of plastic art; but that is only the making of the universe in which the symbolic form exists. Expressiveness has endless degrees. Complete artistic success would be complete articulation of an idea, and the effect would be perfect livingness of the work. "Dead spots" are simply inexpressive parts. From beginning to end, every stroke is composition; where that is attained, there is truly "significant form." [See Plate VI]

Nothing demonstrates more clearly the symbolic import of virtual forms than the constant references one finds, in the speech and writings of artists, to the "life" of objects in a picture (chairs and tables quite as much as creatures), and to the picture plane itself as an "animated" surface. The life in art is a "life" of forms, or even of space itself.

In perusing a collection of theoretical utterances by a great many artists of the most varied schools and standpoints,[11] one can gather references to this fundamental effect on all levels of pictorial conception, from the simple desire to "imitate" human actions, to a mystical conception of dynamism to be conveyed by colors or geometric lines.

"The artistic form is living form," said Max Liebermann. "It is clear that this form is the basis of all pictorial art. But it is much more: it is also its end and its culmination."

Walter Sickert, speaking of Ingres' "Mme. Rivière," said: "The drawing has become a living thing, with a life, with a debit and credit of its own. What it has borrowed here it may, or may not, as it pleases, pay back there." And again: "Among Rembrandt's etchings the 'Boys Bathing' is pure drawing with no upholstery. There is not in it a line that is not alive."

Fernand Léger claims the same thing for colors that Sickert attributes to drawings and even to mere lines: ". . . color has a reality in itself,

---

[11]I have before me a most interesting anthology, *Artists on Art*, edited by Robert Goldwater and Marco Treves. All the following quotations are taken from this source unless otherwise noted.

a life of its own." Kandinsky carries the metaphor of "life" still further by assimilating it consciously to the literal meaning in his comparison of an abstract line and a fish:

"The isolated line and the isolated fish alike are living beings with forces peculiar to them, though latent. They are forces of expression for these beings and of impression on human beings, because each has an impressive 'look' which manifests itself by its expression.

"But the voice of these latent forces is faint and limited. It is the environment of the line and the fish that brings about a miracle: the latent forces awaken, the expression becomes radiant, the impression profound . . .

"The environment is the composition.

"The composition is the organized sum of the interior functions (expressions) of the work."

So we come to the more general idea of "life" in a picture, the "animation" of the canvas itself, the surface as a whole. This, too, is a natural conception to a painter; as Edward Wadsworth put it, "A picture is primarily the animation of an inert plane surface by a spatial rhythm of forms and colors." And Alfred Sisley: "The animation of the canvas is one of the hardest problems of painting. To give life to the work of art is certainly one of the most necessary tasks of the true artist. Everything must serve this end: form, color, surface."

What is it, then, this process of "animating" a surface that in actuality is "inert"? It is the process of transforming the actual spatial datum, the canvas or paper surface, into a virtual space, creating the primary illusion of artistic vision. This first reorientation is so important that some painters who have become keenly and consciously aware of it tend to be satisfied with the mere creation of space, regardless of anything further to be created in its virtual dimensions—like Malevich, enamored of the magic squares that, after all, yield space and only space. And those who have not figured out the distinction between the actual surface and the picture plane are none the less prone to feel it, as Redon did, undoubtedly, when he remarked on his "invincible peculiarity":

"I have a horror of a white sheet of paper. . . . A sheet of paper so shocks me that as soon as it is on the easel I am forced to scrawl on it with charcoal or pencil, or anything else, and this process gives it life."

It is now not a paper, but a *space*. To the great painters the illusion of space is usually so self-evident that even when they are talking about the actual material surface they cannot speak in terms of anything but the created element. Thus Matisse:

"If I take a sheet of paper of given dimensions I will jot down a drawing which will have necessary relation to its format. . . . And if I had to repeat it on a sheet of the same shape but ten times larger I would not limit myself to enlarging it: a drawing must have a power of expansion which can bring to life the space which surrounds it."

All this is, of course, metaphorical talk. But even as metaphor, what does it mean? In which sense can one possibly say that Van Gogh's yellow chair or a studio stove is alive? What does a surface do when it becomes, as Alfred Sisley said, "at times raised to the highest pitch of liveliness"?

Such questions, which are really perfectly fair, would seem philistine and even perverse to almost every artist. He would probably insist, quite seriously, that he was not using metaphor at all; that the chair really *is* alive, and an animated surface truly lives and breathes, and so on. This means simply that his use of "life" and "living" is a stronger symbolic mode than metaphor: it is myth.

The mark of a genuine myth is its power to impress its inventors as literal truth in the face of the strongest contrary evidence and in complete defiance of argument. It appears to be so sacred a truth that to ask in what sense it is true, or to call it a figure of speech, seems like frivolity. For it is a figure of *thought*, not merely of speech, and to destroy it is to destroy an idea in its pristine phase, just when it dawns on people. That is why mythic beliefs really are sacred. They are pregnant, and carry an unformulated idea.[12]

But the idea must mature some day, and taking logical form, emerge from the fantastic matrix. When this happens, it first begets factions of believers and scoffers, the latter simply at a loss to understand how anyone can hold to its absurdities. In the end no serious thinker questions the myth any more; it seems like an obvious figure of speech for a recog-

---

[12]This theory of the nature of myth, developed by Ernst Cassirer in his *Philosophie der symbolischen Formen*, I have already discussed in relation to philosophical doctrines, in *New Key*, chap. vii (Mentor ed., p. 159), and more fully in an earlier book, *The Practice of Philosophy*.

nized fact. The fact appears to have been found somewhere else, in rational discourse. Actually, discursive thinking has simply grown up to it and given the new idea literal expression, and facts may now be observed in its light.

"Living form" is the most indubitable product of all good art, be it painting, architecture, or pottery. Such form is "living" in the same way that a border or a spiral is intrinsically "growing": that is, it *expresses* life—feeling, growth, movement, emotion, and everything that characterizes vital existence. This expression, moreover, is not symbolization in the usual sense of conventional or assigned meaning, but a presentation of a highly articulated form wherein the beholder recognizes, without conscious comparison and judgment but rather by direct recognition, the forms of human feeling: emotions, moods, even sensations in their characteristic passage. The more intellectual artists (that is, those of keen mind, not those given to literal conception in art)—Delacroix, Matisse, Cézanne, and several younger men, not always as articulate—have understood this clearly; "living" form is the symbolism that conveys the idea of vital reality; and the emotive import belongs to the form itself, not to anything it represents or suggests. "All our interior world is reality," said Marc Chagall, "and that perhaps more so than our apparent world." It is this reality, certainly, that Mondrian extolled in his reflections: "'Art' is not the expression of the appearance of reality such as we see it, nor of the life which we live, but . . . it is the expression of true reality and true life . . . indefinable but realizable in plastics."

Art is a logical, not a psychological, expression, as Marsden Hartley observed: "Painters must paint for their own edification and pleasure, and what they have to say, not what they are impelled to feel, is what will interest those who are interested in them. The thought of the time is the emotion of the time."

One might vary the last sentence to read: the emotion in the work is the thought in the work. Just as the content of discourse is the discursive concept, so the content of a work of art is the non-discursive concept of feeling; and it is directly expressed by the form, the appearance before us. As Courbet said, "Once the beautiful is real and visible it contains its own artistic expression." Maurice Denis remarked the same thing:

"The emotion—bitter or sweet, or 'literary' as the painters say—springs from the canvas itself, a plane surface coated with colors.[13] There is no need to interpose the memory of any former sensation (such as of a subject derived from nature).

"A Byzantine Christ is a symbol; the Jesus of the modern painter, even in the most correctly drawn turban, is merely literary. In the one, the form is expressive; in the other, an imitation of nature wishes to be so."

But the most explicit statement is that of Henri Matisse: "Expression, to my way of thinking, does not consist of the passion mirrored upon a human face or betrayed by a violent gesture. The whole arrangement of my picture is expressive. The place occupied by the figures or objects, the empty spaces around them, the proportions—everything plays a part. . . . [See Plate IX]

"A work of art must carry in itself its complete significance and impose it upon the beholder even before he can identify the subject matter. When I see the Giotto frescoes at Padua I do not trouble to recognize which scene of the life of Christ I have before me, but I perceive instantly the sentiment which radiates from it and which is instinct in the composition in every line and color. The title will only serve to confirm my impression."

From the first line of decorative drawing to the works of Raphael, Leonardo, or Rubens, the same principle of pictorial art is wholly exemplified: the creation of virtual space and its organization by forms (be they lines, or volumes, or intersecting planes, or shadows and lights) that reflect the patterns of sentience and emotion. The picture space, whether conceived in two dimensions or in three, dissociates itself from the actual space in which the canvas or other physical bearer of it exists; its function as a symbol makes the objects in a picture as unlike normal physical objects as a spoken word is unlike the sounds of footsteps, rustlings, clatter and other noises that usually accompany and sometimes drown it. The faint little sound of a speaking voice arrests the ear in the midst of the medley of mechanical sounds and is something altogether different, because its significance is of a different order; similarly the space in a picture engages our vision completely because it is significant in itself and not as part of the surrounding room.

---

[13]In a sense, yes; but more properly, from the illusion created by means of the colors on canvas, the forms in virtual space. If these were not produced, the colors would convey nothing notable.

The primary illusion of virtual space comes at the first stroke of brush or pencil that concentrates the mind entirely on the picture plane and neutralizes the actual limits of vision. That explains why Redon felt driven, at the sight of a blank paper on his easel, to scrawl on it as quickly as possible with anything that would make a mark. Just establish one line in virtual space, and at once we are in the realm of symbolic forms. The mental shift is as definite as that which we make from hearing a sound of tapping, squeaking, or buzzing to hearing speech, when suddenly in midst of the little noises surrounding us we make out a single word. The whole character of our hearing is transformed. The medley of physical sound disappears, the ear receives language, perhaps indistinct by reason of interfering noises, but struggling through them like a living thing. Exactly the same sort of reorientation is effected for sight by the creation of any purely visual space. The image, be it a representation or a mere design, stands before us in its expressiveness: significant form.

That is why artists and trained art lovers have no need of cultivating the "aesthetic attitude." They are *not* selecting sense data from the actual world and contemplating them as pure qualitative experiences. The painter "selected" them, and he employed just those sensory qualities that he could use, in creating the illusory forms he wanted for the organization of his total virtual space. Our contemplation of his created forms, the whole organized semblance, should be made so easy for us that the return to actuality is a jolt. Sometimes, in the presence of great art, attention to the actual environment is hard to sustain.

The primary illusion of any art genre is the basic creation wherein all its elements exist; and they, in turn, produce and support it. It does not exist by itself; "primary" does not mean first-established, but *always* established where any elements are given at all. There are numberless ways of *making space visible,* i.e. virtually presenting it.

What are the "elements" of a work of art?

Elements are factors in the semblance; and as such they are virtual themselves, direct components of the total form. In this they differ from materials, which are actual. Paints are materials, and so are the colors they have in the tube or on the palette; but the colors in a picture are elements, determined by their environment. They are warm or cold, they advance or recede, enhance or soften or dominate other colors; they create tensions and distribute weight in a picture. Colors in a paintbox don't do such things. They are materials, and lie side by side in their actual, undialectical materialism.

Choice of materials may, to be sure, affect the range of available elements. One cannot always do the same things with diverse materials. The translucency of glass allows the making and use of special color elements that paint on a wooden ground could never create; therefore glass painting and wood painting set the artist different problems and suggest different ideas to be brought to expression. It is sometimes said that glass and wood have "different feelings." They permit, and even command, quite distinct forms, and of course equally distinct ranges of vital import.

All the discernible elements in a picture support the primary illusion, which is invariant, while the forms that articulate it may vary indefinitely. The primary illusion is a substrate of the realm of virtual forms; it is involved in their occurrence.[14]

But there are different modes even of the primary illusion, diverse major ways of constructing it, that lead to quite distinct realms of plastic art. To understand in what sense all plastic art is the same sort of thing is not enough, for it engenders hasty identifications and ruinous confusions. But in the light of the elementary function—the creation of the primary illusion as such—one may venture to pursue any and all distinctions that set various art forms apart, without danger of losing one's way in the pigeon-holes of purely academic description.

---

[14]There may also be "secondary illusions," certain non-visual created effects such as "a sense of time," what Malraux calls "holiness," dramatic feeling, "powers," etc., that support the plastic intent. The function of such secondary semblances will be considered later.

Chapter six

THE MODES OF VIRTUAL SPACE

So far we have been concerned solely with the "visual projection" in which space is perceived as a relation among things at the distance of some particular focus, and beyond it, behind the focal point. The picture plane counterfeits this pattern. But it does not simply substitute its surface for other impressions we might have. Physically, a picture is usually one of several things in our sight; it is surrounded by a wall, furniture, windows, etc. Very few pictures are so large as to fill our physical field of vision completely at normal distance, i.e. at a distance that lets us see the forms presented in them to best advantage. Yet a picture is a total visual field. Its first office is to create a single, self-contained, perceptual space, that seems to confront us as naturally as the scene before our eyes when we open them on the actual world. That is to say, the illusion created in pictorial art is a *virtual scene.* I do not mean a "scene" in the special sense of "scenery"—the picture may represent only one object or even consist of pure decorative forms without representative value—but it always creates *a space opposite the eye and related directly and essentially to the eye.* That is what I call "scene."

The notion of perceptual space as virtual scene derives from Hildebrand, and the idea of its creation through purely visual forms, even replacing all other normal means by visual ones, is his major contribution to the theory of art. Unhappily, however, he rides his hobby for a fall, by an injudicious leap. It is a great temptation to carry a theory over to further applications without examining how much of it is really general and how much is special, and consequently to distort new material to meet theoretical conditions that are not its own, instead of finding the exact version of the general principle which will meet the new case. But that Hildebrand, the sculptor, should succumb to it in the way he did is something of an oddity; for instead of reasoning from the realm he knew best, and perhaps misapplying some principles in other fields (which, however unfortunate, would be comprehensible enough), he carried over the concept of pictorial space to sculpture, lock, stock, and barrel; so he made his own art the stepchild, and analyzed it in essentially graphic terms.

Consequently, bas-relief is for him the matrix of sculptural form, and three-dimensionality either a minor characteristic or a device for combining many pictures (i.e. aspects of a figure) in one physical object by supreme technical skill. Just as the painter's problem of form is the creation of apparent volume by means of a two-dimensional surface, so, he holds, the sculptor's is the creation of a two-dimensional picture plane by means of actual volume.[1]

This assimilation of sculpture to painting, through the mediation of relief carving, certainly does violence to most people's sculptural sense; and the inward protest grows even more decided when architecture, too, is given cavalier treatment as just another form of picture-making, and buildings become collections of façades with no interior feeling. This is far too simple a way to pass from a special theory of pictorial space to the concept of perceptual space in general, which does underlie all the so-called "plastic arts," and which serves to make them one family. Each member has its own way of being; we need not be afraid to miss the basic relationship by recognizing such separate ways. The primary illusion is not the scene—that is only one articulation of it—but *virtual space*, however constructed. Painting, sculpture, and architecture are three great manifestations of spatial conception, equally original and equally destined to a complete development without confusion. Even where one subserves the other their several characters do not become identified. So we may look to sculpture for its own version of virtual space, and to architecture for its own, instead of treating pictorial art as the measure of all plastic expression. The differences among closely related arts are as interesting as the likenesses, and are really what gives this many-sided family its imposing richness and scope.

In the realm of sculpture the role of illusion seems less important

---

[1]Three-dimensional sculpture, for Hildebrand, serves the same purpose as Chinese scroll painting: it offers a continuous series of pictorial compositions. The only difference is that one unrolls the scroll and walks around the statue. See *The Problem of Form*, p. 95.

than in painting, where a flat surface "creates" a three-dimensional space that is obviously virtual. Sculpture is actually three-dimensional; in what sense does it "create" space for the eye? This is probably the question which led Hildebrand to say that the sculptor's task was to present a three-dimensional object in the two-dimensional picture plane of "perceptual space." But the answer, though it satisfies and, in fact, aptly completes his theory, lacks the confirmation of direct experience and artistic intuition. Sculptors themselves rarely think in terms of pictures, and of ideal planes of vision staggered one behind the other to define deep space (except in perfectly flat relief with rectangular cuts, or even mere graven lines, which is really pictorial art, substituting the graving tool for a pencil). Sculpture, even when it is wedded to a background as in true relief, is essentially *volume*, not *scene*.

The volume, however, is not a cubic measure, like the space in a box. It is more than the bulk of the figure; it is a space made visible, and is more than the area which the figure actually occupies. The tangible form has a complement of empty space that it absolutely commands, that is given with it and only with it, and is, in fact, part of the sculptural volume. The figure itself seems to have a sort of continuity with the emptiness around it, however much its solid masses may assert themselves as such. The void enfolds it, and the enfolding space has vital form as a continuation of the figure.

The source of this illusion (for empty space, unenclosed, has actually no visible parts or shape) is the fundamental principle of sculptural volume: the semblance of organism. In the literature of sculpture, more than anywhere else, one meets with reference to "inevitable form," "necessary form," and "inviolable form." But what do these expressions mean? What, in nature, makes forms "inevitable," "necessary," "inviolable"? Nothing but *vital function*. Living organisms maintain themselves, resist change, strive to restore their structure when it has been forcibly interfered with. All other patterns are kaleidoscopic and casual; but organisms, performing characteristic functions, *must* have certain general forms, or perish. For them there is a norm of organic structure according to which, inevitably, they build themselves up, deriving matter from their chance environment; and their parts are built to carry on this process as it becomes more complex, so the parts have shapes necessary to their respective functions; yet the most specialized activities are supported at every moment by the process which they serve, the life of the whole. It is the functional whole that is inviolable. Break this, and all the subordinate activities cease, the constituent parts disintegrate, and "living form" has disappeared.

No other kind of form is actually "necessary," for necessity presupposes a measure in teleological terms, and nothing but life exhibits any τήλος. Only life, once put in motion, achieves certain forms inevitably, as long as it goes on at all: the acorn becomes an oak, however stunted or varied, the sparrow's egg a sparrow, the maggot a fly. Other accretions of matter may have *usual* forms, but do not strive to achieve them, nor maintain themselves in them. A crystal broken in half yields simply two pieces of crystal. A creature broken in half either dies, i.e. disintegrates, or repairs one part, or both parts, to function again as a whole. It may even break just because the new wholes are preformed, the repair all but made, so the break is its dynamic pattern.

There is nothing actually organic about a work of sculpture. Even carved wood is dead matter. Only its form is the form of life, and the space it makes visible is vitalized as it would be by organic activity at its center. It is *virtual kinetic volume,* created by—and with—the semblance of living form.

Yet sculpture need not represent natural organisms. It may embody the appearance of life in non-representational shapes, like simple hewn monoliths, monumental pillars, pure inventions, or screens, urns, etc., representing no other objects than what they are, respectively, themselves. Or it may represent some inorganic thing, like Boccioni's bottles and Moore's baskets and birdcages, and yet be entirely living form; for it is expression of biological feeling, not suggestion of biological function, that constitutes "life" in sculpture. Where that feeling is really conveyed, we have the semblance of "inevitable," "necessary," "inviolable" form before our eyes, organizing the space it fills and also the space that seems to touch it and be necessary to its appearance.

Here we have the primary illusion, virtual space, created in a mode quite different from that of painting, which is *scene,* the field of direct vision. Sculpture creates an equally visual space, but not a space of direct vision; for volume is really given originally to touch, both haptic touch and contact limiting bodily movement, and the business of sculpture is to translate its data into entirely visual terms, i.e. *to make tactual space visible.*

The intimate relationship between touch and sight which is thus effected by the semblance of kinetic volume explains some of the complex sensory reactions which sculptors as well as laymen often have toward it. Many people feel a strong desire to handle every figure. In some persons the wish springs from obviously sentimental motives, anthropomorphizing the statue, imagining a human contact; this was the attitude Rodin expressed, and the knowledge that he would touch cold marble made him wistful, like Pygmalion.[2] But others—among artists, probably the majority—imagine the touch of stone or wood, metal or earth; they wish to feel the substance that is really there, and let their hands pass over its pure form. They know that the sensation will not always bear out the visual suggestion, perhaps will even contradict it. Yet they believe that their perception of the work will somehow be enhanced.

Sculptural form is a powerful abstraction from actual objects and the three-dimensional space which we construe by means of them, through touch and sight. It makes its own construction in three dimensions, namely the *semblance* of kinetic space. Just as one's field of direct vision is organized, in actuality, as a plane at the distance of a natural focus, so the kinetic realm of tangible volumes, or things, and free air spaces between them, is organized in each person's actual experience as his *environment,* i.e. a space whereof he is the center; his body and the range of its free motion, its breathing space and the reach of its limbs, are his own kinetic volume, the point of orientation from which he plots the world of tangible reality—objects, distances, motions, shape and size and mass.

Bruno Adriani, in his book *Problems of the Sculptor,* has written passage upon passage supporting the comparison of sculptural space with the subjective construction of the world as a realm centering in one's own kinetic volume. The convergence of our views—one a sculptor's, the other a theorist's—seems to me striking enough to warrant a literal quotation of his words. For example:

---

[2]Auguste Rodin, *Art,* p. 55.

"When we use the word 'space' in connection with artistic problems, neither the geometrical concept of three-dimensional space nor the physicist's theory of [the] four-dimensional unity space-time is applicable. They derive from abstract thinking and are not accessible to our senses.

"Space in art . . . can be perceived through our sensibility.

"It is the sensory scene of our human experiences, 'the sphere of our activity' and of our relations to our environment."[3]

"The sculpture intensifies the life of the sensory space, inducing its existence into our senses and into our consciousness. . . .

"While scientists distill abstract notions of 'space,' the artist endeavors to perceive a concrete space through intuition and to make it perceptible in a formal creation.

"The mathematician Henri Poincaré[4] . . . develops the idea that we take our own body as an instrument of measurement, in order to construct space—not the geometrical space, neither a space of pure representation, but a space belonging to an 'instinctive geometry'. . . .

"This system supplies the means necessary to fix our position in space.

"Poincaré concludes that every human being has to construct first this restricted space, . . . and then is capable of amplifying—by an act of imagination—the restricted space to the 'great space where he can lodge the universe'. . . .

"Extending the theory of Poincaré, we can establish an *analogy* between our instinctive procedure of constructing sensory space, and the mental activity of the sculptor determining through an organic system of axes the skeleton of his work. . . .

"Through the organism of his forms he creates a 'restricted space' as a symbol of the universe."[5]

A piece of sculpture is a center of three-dimensional space. It is a virtual kinetic volume, which dominates a surrounding space, and this environment derives all proportions and relations from it, as the actual environment does from one's self. The work is the semblance of a self, and creates the semblance of a tactual space—and, moreover, a visual semblance. It effects the objectification of self and environment for the

---

[3]*Problems of the Sculptor*, p. 16.
[4]In *Science et Méthode*.   [5]Adriani, *op. cit.*, p. 19.

sense of sight. Sculpture is literally the image of kinetic volume in sensory space.

That is why I say it is a powerful abstraction. And here I have to depart from Adriani; for he, still speaking of the sculptor, continues: "The space of his sculpture is his original world. . . . The 'ideal' beholder . . . transposes the system of coordinated axes, created by the sculptor, into his own organism." On the contrary, it seems to me that just because we do *not* identify the space which centers in a statue with our own environment, the created world remains objective, and can thus become an *image* of our own surrounding space. It is an environment, but not our own; neither is it that of some other person, having points in common with ours, so that the person and his surroundings become 'objects' to us, existing in our space. Though a statue is, actually, an object, we do not treat it as such; we see it as a center of a space all its own; but its kinetic volume and the environment it creates are illusory—they exist for our vision alone, a semblance of the self and its world.

This explains, perhaps, why the tactual encounter with stone or wood, contradicting as it does the organic appearance of sculpture, may nevertheless cause no disappointment, but may really enhance our appreciation of plastic form; it checks the anthropomorphic fancy, and heightens the abstractive power of the work. Yet handling a figure, no matter what it gives us, is always a mere interlude in our perception of the form. We have to step back, and see it unmolested by our hands, that break into the sphere of its spatial influence.

*　*　*

There is a third mode of creating virtual space, more subtle than the construction of illusory scene or even illusory organism, yet just as commandingly artistic, and in its scope the most ambitious of all; that is architecture. Its "illusion" is easily missed because of the obviousness and importance of its actual values: shelter, comfort, safekeeping. Its practical functions are so essential that architects themselves are often confused about its status. Some have regarded it as chiefly utilitarian, and only incidentally aesthetic, except in the case of monuments; others have treated it as "applied art," wherein practical considerations always force some sacrifice of the artist's "vision"; and some have tried to meet the prosaic demands of utility by making function paramount, believing that genuinely appropriate forms are always beautiful.[6] In architecture the problem of appearance and reality comes to a head as in no other art. This makes it a test case in aesthetic theory, for a true general theory has no exceptions, and when it seems to have them it is not properly stated. If architecture is utilitarian *except* in the case of monuments, then utility is not its essence; if it may be treated as sculpture *except* where practical needs interfere as in underground building, or necessities like bulkheads and chicken houses, then sculptural values are not essential to it. If functional interests can ever be adequately served without beauty, then form may follow function with all the happy effect in the world, but functionality is not the measure of beauty.

Architecture is so generally regarded as an art of space, meaning actual, practical space, and building is so certainly the making of something that defines and arranges spatial units, that everybody talks about architecture as "spatial creation" without asking what is created, or how space is involved. The concepts of *arrangement in space* and *creation of space* are constantly interchanged; and the primary illusion seems to have given way to a primary actuality. Nothing is more haphazard than the employment of the words: illusion, reality, creation, construction, arrangement, expression, form, and space, in the writings of modern architects.

But architecture is a plastic art, and its first achievement is always, unconsciously and inevitably, an illusion; something purely imaginary or conceptual translated into visual impressions. The influence of the

---

[6]Louis H. Sullivan was the first master to declare that, to be architecture, a building must be the image of its function; and his famous phrase: "Form follows function," has been quoted in and out of season. He obviously meant more than practical function, when he said: "If the work is to be organic the function of the part must have the same *quality* as the function of the whole; and the parts . . . must have the quality of the mass." (*Kindergarten Chats*, p. 47.)

Thirty-five years later László Moholy-Nagy observed: "In all fields of creation, workers are striving today to find purely functional solutions of a technical-biological kind: that is, to build up each piece of work solely from the elements which are required for its function." (*The New Vision*, p. 61.)

Cf. also Frank Lloyd Wright, *On Architecture*, p. 236: "'Form follows function' is but a statement of fact. When we say 'form and function are one,' only then do we take mere fact into the realm of creative thought."

underlying idea shows itself in such key phrases as "functional form,"[7] "life in space,"[8] "taking possession of space."[9] Functional form is a concept borrowed from biology or from mechanics; since, in cold fact, buildings are not active beings themselves, but only permit people to carry on activities in them, "functional form" is literally taken to mean convenient arrangement. "A machine to live in" is, then, the same thing, restricted to home architecture instead of applying to viaducts and tombs and radio towers as well. Prosaically speaking, all life is in space; and to "take possession" of space can mean nothing but to occupy it physically. Blankets put into a chest, filling it completely, take possession of the space in it. But certainly Moholy-Nagy did not mean physical filling-out when he wrote, in the triumphal last paragraph of *The New Vision:*

"A constant fluctuation, sideways and upward, radiant, all-sided, announces to man that he has taken possession, in so far as his human capacities and present conceptions allow, of imponderable, invisible, and yet omnipresent space."

This mystical conception of space is merely an ecstatically heightened form of a notion current and quite accepted among architects—the notion of space as an entity, with internal relations sometimes described as "dynamic," sometimes as "organic." One reads about "intersecting spaces" and "interval tensions of space."

Such expressions simply make no sense with reference to our practical or scientific concepts of space. Lines or light rays may intersect, but not spaces; there is only one space, conceived by common sense as the ideal receptacle that everything is in, and by scientific minds as the coordinate-system whereby everything is related. For the architect, however, this does not seem to be the case, else we would not have a whole literature about "living" and "activated" and "organic" and even "omnipresent" space—space to be lived with, experienced, intuited, and what not. The architect, in fine, deals with a *created space,* a virtual entity: the primary illusion of plastic art effected by a basic abstraction peculiar to architecture.

As *scene* is the basic abstraction of pictorial art, and *kinetic volume*

---

[7]Sullivan, *loc. cit.*

[8]Le Corbusier (C. E. Jeannert-Gris), *Toward a New Architecture*, p. 4.

[9]Moholy-Nagy, *op. cit.*, pp. 180 and 202.

of sculpture, that of architecture is *an ethnic domain*. Actually, of course, a domain is not a "thing" among other "things"; it is the sphere of influence of a function, or functions; it may have physical effects on some geographical locality or it may not. Nomadic cultures, or cultural phenomena like the seafaring life, do not inscribe themselves on any fixed place on earth. Yet a ship, constantly changing its location, is none the less a self-contained place, and so is a Gypsy camp, an Indian camp, or a circus camp, however often it shifts its geodetic bearings. Literally, we say the camp is *in* a place; culturally, it *is* a place. A Gypsy camp is a different place from an Indian camp, though it may be geographically where the Indian camp used to be.

A place, in this non-geographical sense, is a created thing, an ethnic domain made visible, tangible, sensible. As such it is, of course, an illusion. Like any other plastic symbol, it is primarily an illusion of self-contained, self-sufficient, perceptual space. But the principle of organization is its own: for it is organized as a functional realm made visible —the center of a virtual world, the "ethnic domain," and itself a geographical semblance.

Painting creates planes of vision, or "scene" confronting our eyes, on an actual, two-dimensional surface; sculpture makes virtual "kinetic volume" out of actual three-dimensional material, i.e. actual volume; architecture articulates the "ethnic domain," or virtual "place," by treatment of an actual place.

The architectural illusion may be established by a mere array of upright stones defining the magic circle that severs holiness from the profane, even by a single stone that marks a center, i.e. a monument.[10] The outside world, even though not physically shut out, is dominated by the sanctum and becomes its visible context; the horizon, its frame. The Temple of Poseidon at Sounion shows this organizing power of a composed form. On the other hand, a tomb carved out of solid rock may create a complete domain, a world of the dead. It has no outside; its proportions are internally derived—from the stone, from the burial—and define an architectural space that may be deep and high and wide, within but a few cubits of actual measure. The created "place" is essentially a semblance, and whatever effects that semblance is architecturally relevant.

---

[10]Cf. Sullivan, *op. cit.*, p. 121.

A lamp on the floor might make it a ghost den—an overhead light, bringing out the veins in the rock, the texture of ceiling and wall, transform it into a strangely dignified chamber. *All these possibilities are given with the architectural idea.* Le Corbusier said, "Architecture is the masterly, correct and magnificent play of masses brought together in light."[11] But light is a variable factor; therefore the elements of architecture—the constituents of the total semblance—must be protean to the extent of allowing, freely and safely, for the radical transformations that changes of light will make. In good buildings such changes are a source of richness and life; unusual lights bring out new forms, but all forms are beautiful, and every change yields a complete, perceptible mood.

A culture is made up, factually, of the activities of human being; it is a system of interlocking and intersecting actions, a continuous functional pattern. As such it is, of course, intangible and invisible. It has physical ingredients—artifacts; also physical symptoms—the ethnic effects that are stamped on the human face, known as its "expression," and the influence of social condition on the development, posture, and movement of the human body. But all such items are fragments that "mean" the total pattern of life only to those who are acquainted with it and may be reminded of it. They are ingredients in a culture, not its image.

The architect creates its image: a physically present human environment that expresses the characteristic rhythmic functional patterns which constitute a culture. Such patterns are the alternations of sleep and waking, venture and safety, emotion and calm, austerity and abandon; the tempo, and the smoothness or abruptness of life; the simple forms of childhood and the complexities of full moral stature, the sacramental and the capricious moods that mark a social order, and that are repeated, though with characteristic selection, by every personal life springing from that order. Once more I may resort to the words of Le Corbusier:

"Architecture . . . *should use those elements which are capable of affecting our senses, and of rewarding the desire of our eyes,* and should dispose them in such a way *that the sight of them affects us immediately* by their delicacy or their brutality, their riot or their serenity, their

---

[11]Le Corbusier, *op. cit.*, p. 29.

indifference or their interest; those elements are plastic elements, forms which our eyes can see and our minds can measure."[12]

"Architecture is the first manifestation of man creating his own universe, creating it in the image of nature. . . .

"The primordial physical laws are simple and few in number.

"The moral laws are simple and few in number."[13]

A universe created by man and for man, "in the image of nature"—not, indeed, by simulating natural objects, but by exemplifying "the laws of gravity, of statics and dynamics"—is the spatial *semblance* of a world, because it is made in actual space, yet is not systematically continuous with the rest of nature in a complete democracy of places. It has its own center and periphery, not dividing one place from all others, but limiting from within whatever there is to be. That is the image of an ethnic domain, the primary illusion in architecture.

The most familiar product of architecture is, of course, the *house*. Because of its ubiquity it is the most detailed, and yet the most variable general form. It may shelter one person or a hundred families; it may be made of stone or wood, clay, cement or metal, or many materials together—even paper, grass, or snow. People have made houses in the caves of barren mountains, and houses out of animal skins to take along on the march; they have used spreading trees for roofs, anchoring their houses to the live trunks. The imperative need of dwellings under all conditions, from the polar ice, almost as dead as the moon, to the prodigal Mediterranean lands, has caused every means of construction to be exploited; the house has been the builder's elementary school.

But the great architectural ideas have rarely, if ever, arisen from domestic needs. They grew as the temple, the tomb, the fortress, the hall, the theatre. The reason is simple enough: tribal culture is collective, and its domain therefore essentially public. When it is made visible, its image is a public realm. Most early architecture—Stonehenge, the Mounds, the Temple of the Sun—defines what might be called "religious space." This is a virtual realm; the temple, though oriented by the equinox points, merely symbolizes the "corners of the earth" to simple people who probably did not understand the astronomical scheme at all. The temple really

[12]*Ibid.*, p. 16
[13]*Ibid.*, p. 73.

made their greater world of space—nature, the abode of gods and ghosts. The heavenly bodies could be seen to rise and set in the frame it defined; and as it presented this space to popular thought it unified earth and heaven, men and gods. [See Plate VIII]

The same may be said of the more civilized edifices which serve to safeguard religious life against incursions of the profane. The Egyptian, Greek, and Roman temples, the church, the mosque, all present to outward view a wall, hiding the sanctum. The Children of the Zodiac are no longer invited to come and go, tracing their orbits between its columns. A cell encloses the altar. But the building dominates the community, and its outward appearance organizes the site of the town; religion, though no longer the whole of life, is the confluence of all ideas. Within the sanctuary the cultural domain is epitomized by the most economical and concentrated architectural means—a holy world, that one cannot live in, because it is too pure and moving, but that one enters for conscious communion with God and man.

The great tombs are the image of an Underworld; their windowless walls create a womb of Earth, though they be built above ground and in full sunlight. They are intended for silence and the reign of Death. Yet, artistically, nothing is more alive than the tense quietness of such chambers; nothing expresses a Presence and its domain as unequivocally as an Egyptian tomb. Even robbed of the corpse it enshrined, i.e. devoid of its actual function, it is the Realm of the Dead envisaged.

In a secular society, for instance the barbarian culture of the Goths, where swords had names and fealty was sworn to warlords instead of gods, the Hall was the natural symbol of a human world, where man found himself "Like the sparrow, flying in at one door, and immediately out at another . . . Into the dark winter from which he had emerged."

Architecture creates the semblance of that World which is the counterpart of a Self. It is a total environment made visible. Where the Self is collective, as in a tribe, its World is communal; for personal Selfhood, it is the home. And as the actual environment of a being is a system of functional relations, so a virtual "environment," the created space of architecture, is a symbol of functional existence. This does not mean, however, that *signs* of important activities—hooks for implements, convenient benches, well-planned doors—play any part in its significance. In that false assumption lies the error of "functionalism"—lies not very deep, but perhaps as deep as the theory itself goes. Symbolic expression is something miles removed from provident planning or good arrangement. It does not suggest things to do, but embodies the feeling, the rhythm, the passion or sobriety, frivolity or fear with which any things at all are done. That is the image of life which is created in buildings; it is the visible semblance of an "ethnic domain," the symbol of humanity to be found in the strength and interplay of forms.

Because we are organisms, all our actions develop in organic fashion, and our feelings as well as our physical acts have an essentially metabolic pattern. Systole, diastole; making, unmaking; crescendo, diminuendo. Sustaining, sometimes, but never for indefinite lengths; life, death.

Similarly, the human environment, which is the counterpart of any human life, holds the imprint of a functional pattern; it is the complementary organic form. Therefore any building that can create the illusion of an ethnic world, a "place" articulated by the imprint of human life, must seem organic, like a living form. "Organization" is the watchword of architecture. In reading the works of great architects with a philosophical bent—Louis Sullivan for instance, or his pupil Frank Lloyd Wright, or Le Corbusier—one is fairly haunted by the concepts of organic growth, organic structure, life, nature, vital function, vital feeling, and an indefinite number of other notions that are biological rather than mechanical. None of these terms applies to the actual materials or the geographic space required by a building. "Life" and "organism" and "growth" have no relevance to real estate or builders' supplies. They refer to virtual space, the created domain of human relations and activities. The place which a house occupies on the face of the earth—that is to say, its location in actual space—remains the same place if the house burns up or is wrecked and removed. But the place created by the architect is an illusion, begotten by the visible expression of a feeling, sometimes called an "atmosphere." This kind of place disappears if the house is destroyed, or changes radically if the building undergoes any violent alteration. The alteration need not even be very radical or extensive. Top-heavy added dormers, gingerbread porches, and other excrescences are very spectacular diseases; bad coloring and confused interior furnishing, though mild by comparison, may be enough to destroy the architectural illusion of an ethnic totality, or virtual "place."[14]

The proposition here advanced, that the primary illusion of plastic art, *virtual space,* appears in architecture as *envisagement of an ethnic domain,* has some interesting consequences. In the first place, it frees the conception of architecture from all bondage to special factors of construction, even the elementary ones of pier, lintel, and arch. The importance of such ancient devices is beyond dispute; yet even they may yield to new technical resources, and the creation that takes shape without their benefit may nonetheless be pure and unquestionable architecture. In the second place, it gives a new and forceful meaning to a principle insistently maintained by the great architects of our day—that architecture proceeds from the inside to the outside of a building, so that the façade is never a thing separately conceived, but like the skin or carapace of a living creature is the outer limit of a vital system, its protection against the world and at the same time its point of contact and interaction with the world.[15] A building may be entirely enclosed by a solid, masking wall, like a Renaissance palace or a Turkish harem, where life lies open only to the court within; or it may have practically no shell at all, being divided from its surroundings only by glass and movable shades, curtains, and screens. Its virtual domain may include terraces and gardens, or rows of sphinxes, or a great rectangular pool. Sea and sky may fill the intervals between its columns and be gathered to its space. In the third place, this conception offers a criterion of what things belong to architecture, as essentials, as variables (like roofs or rooms convertible for summer and winter), or as auxiliaries. Furnishings belong to architecture just in so far as they take part in creating the ethnic domain.[16] Pictures, treated by "interior decorators" as embellishments of

---

[14]A great deal could be said here about interior treatment, i.e. furnishing and decoration; but this topic bears rather interesting relations to the problem of *performance,* which arises in music, drama, and ballet, so I shall postpone it to a later chapter.

[15]Cf. László Moholy-Nagy, *op. cit.,* p. 198: "Since in architecture not sculptural patterns but spatial positions are the building elements, the inside of the building must be interconnected and connected with the outside by its spatial divisions."

[16]Nothing can appear more heretical to a musician than Wright's declaration that a piano in a room should be "built in," letting only the "necessary" parts—the keyboard, music rack and pedals—break a nice wall space. Quite apart from the effect on the tone, the affront to the instrument is outrageous; for the instrument is a living presence in the room, whose beauty should be respected instead of overridden by architectural plans.

a room may remain dissociated from it or even hostile. Yet a great picture *has a right to a room*, and a space frankly consecrated to it *is* an ethnic domain of a special sort, its function thus assigned. Many practical arrangements, on the other hand, have no architectural significance, though they be "built into" the house: steam or hot water heat, shutters in flues, etc. They affect the utility of the building, but not its semblance—not even its functional semblance. They are material factors, but not architectural elements.[17]

The most interesting result of the theory, however, is the light it throws on the relation of architecture to sculpture. The problem of interrelations among the arts, and indeed of their ultimate unity, really belongs to a much later part of my enquiry; but at this point the particular connection of these two arts (kindred as they are, anyway) becomes naturally apparent, so it would be pure pedantry to postpone the mention of it.

The earliest sculpture we know is entirely in the round, and independent: the primitive "Venuses" of prehistoric times. We have no architectural monuments of those days, unless the megalithic dolmen and certain mounds go back as far as the archaic fetishes. But almost as soon as buildings of hewn stone appear, sculpture becomes assimilated to architecture; and all over the world statuary merges into the altar, the temple wall, the column, the buttress. Relief and free figures are almost equally supported by the buildings with which they are associated, and which they are usually said to "adorn."

Yet great sculpture, no matter how intimately related to a building, is not an architectural element. The created place, instead of simply incorporating and thus overriding it, must give it room. For this reason only very strong, self-sufficient interiors can afford sculpture. The two art forms are, in fact, each other's exact complements: the one, an illusion of kinetic volume, symbolizing the Self, or center of life—the other, an illusion of ethnic domain, or the environment created by Selfhood. Each articulates one half of the life-symbol directly and the other by implication; whichever we start with, the other is its background. The temple

---

[17]They are, nevertheless, the architect's concern, and if he neglects them he does little honor to his own work—like a Leonardo who paints with experimental, perishable pigments.

housing the statue, or conversely the statue housed in the temple, is the absolute Idea; like all absolutes, intellectually motionless, a matrix of artistic expression rather than a directing principle.

Where the environment created by a building is far above the moral conceptions of its possessors, sculpture articulates its clear meaning, that would otherwise be lost. The great cathedrals give room to a wealth of statuary directly related to the architectural creation, yet *not creating architecture*.   [See Plate VII]   The cathedral is a place created for life-symbols rather than for actual life, which falls too far short of the architectural idea. In highly ideal creations sculpture and architecture often have to supplement each other; and in the most perfect cultures, where mental reaches were far beyond actual human grasps, they have always done so—to wit, in Egypt, Greece, mediaeval Europe, China, and Japan, the great religious periods in India, and in Polynesia at the height of its artistic life.

Modern sculpture returns to independent existence as the concept of social environment falls emotionally into confusion, becomes sociological and problematic, and "life" is really understood only from *within* the individual. Again the direct expression is of Self, and the ethnic domain created by implication, its emotive value but vaguely apprehended. And painting—the semblance of objective, visual *scene*—comes into its own as the paramount art of our day.

Painting has a different evolution, supported by other phenomena than architecture. I do not want to take up its history and connections at this point, except to remark that the attempts of some architects to assimilate "the art of the painter" to their own realm, when they discover the importance of color for architecture, is a mistake. Having a material in common does not link two arts in any important way. Color is one thing in a house and quite a different thing in a picture. Even the actual vista beyond a window is one sort of element and the plane of vision in virtual space is quite another. The connections here sought are in reality too difficult for such superficial solution, and belong to a different philosophical level.

Let us return to the primary illusion of the plastic arts, *virtual space* in its several modes. The fact that these modes are just so many ways of creating space relates them as definitely as it distinguishes them, and suggests good reasons why diverse minds find expression, respectively, through the diverse basic abstractions giving rise to the great forms, and yet have a far greater affinity for forms of plastic art other than their own than for arts which do not create virtual space at all; to speak in specific instances, why a painter is likely to be a competent judge of architecture, sculpture, textile design, jewelry, pottery, or any other visual space creation, but is no more likely than any layman (and, of course, no less likely either) to have a special understanding of music or literature. Indeed, he is apt to judge some other arts, such as ballet or theater, entirely from the standpoint of plastic form, which is not paramount in their realms at all.

The deep divisions among the arts are those that set apart their very worlds, namely the differences in what the various arts create, or differences of primary illusion. Many people—artists, critics, and philosophers—are averse to any serious study of these divisions, because they feel that somehow art is one, and the unity is more real than the multiplicity which, they insist, can be only specious, due to material differences, purely technical, at the most skin-deep. Yet such a hasty rejection of a problem usually bespeaks fear of it rather than a firm conviction of its unimportance. I also believe that art is essentially one, that the symbolic function is the same in every kind of artistic expression, all kinds are equally great, and their logic is all of a piece, the logic of non-discursive form (which governs literary as well as all other created form). But the way to establish these articles of faith as reasonable propositions is not just to say them emphatically and often and deprecate evidence to the contrary; it is, rather, to examine the differences, and trace the distinctions among the arts as far as they can be followed. They go deeper than, offhand, one would suppose. But there is a definite level at which no more distinctions can be made; everything one can say of any single art can be said of any other as well. *There lies the unity.* All the divisions end at that depth, which is the philosophical foundation of art theory.

Chapter seven

THE IMAGE OF TIME

From the plastic arts, which make space visible in the various modes in which we instinctively conceive and negotiate it, we turn to another great art genus, namely music. At once we are as in a different kingdom. The mirror of the world, the horizon of the human domain, and all tangible realities are gone. Objects become a blur, all sight irrelevant.

Yet the realm of experience, so radically changed, is entirely full. There are forms in it, great and small, forms in motion, sometimes converging to make an impression of complete accomplishment and rest out of their very motions; there is immense agitation, or vast solidity, and again everything is air; all this in a universe of pure *sound,* an audible world, a sonorous beauty taking over the whole of one's consciousness.

Ever since Pythagoras discovered the relation between the pitch of a sound and the vibration rate of the body producing that sound, the analysis of music has centered in physical, physiological and psychological studies of *tones:* their own physical structure and combinability, their somatic effects on men and animals, their reception in human consciousness. Acoustics became a valuable science that made possible not only better conditions of producing and hearing music, but, in the realm of music itself, the tempered scale, and the fixation of a standard pitch.

The objectivity of these gains inspired the hope that, however recalcitrant painting or poetry might be to scientific treatment, music at least could be comprehended and handled under relatively simple natural laws, which might then extend one's understanding, through analogy, to less abstract and less transparent arts. Again and again, therefore, attempts have been made to explain musical invention by the physical complexity of tones themselves, and find the laws and limits of composition on a basis of ratios or mathematical sequences to be exemplified. There is no use discussing the sheer nonsense or the academic oddities to which this hope has given rise, such as the Schillinger System of composition,[1] or the serious and elaborate effort of G. D. Birkhoff[2] to compute the exact degree of beauty in any art work (plastic, poetic and musical) by taking the "aesthetic measure" of its components and integrating these to obtain a quantitative value judgment.

The only artistically valid and valuable theory I know, based primarily on the composite nature of tone, is Heinrich Schenker's work. But the significance of Schenker will be much more apparent after my own fundamental thesis has been stated, so I shall postpone all comments on his analysis, except one: namely, that its value lies largely in the fact that it always remains analysis, and never pretends to any synthetic function. A work of art is a unit originally, not by synthesis of independent factors. Analysis reveals elements in it, and can go on indefinitely, yielding more and more understanding; but it will never yield a recipe. Because Schenker respects this relation between the theorist and his object, he never treats a masterpiece without reverence, even though his investigations extend to the smallest detail. There is no danger of being "overintellectual" where intellect is playing its proper part.[3]

But the philosophical question: What is music? is not answered even by Schenker; for it cannot be answered by researches into the ingredients out of which musical works are made. Almost all serious inquiry so far has been concerned with the materials of music and the possibilities of their combination. The fact that the tonal proportions were among the first physical laws to be mathematically expressed, tested, and systematized, has given music the name of a science, even of a scientific model

---

[1]See Joseph Schillinger, *The Schillinger System of Musical Composition*, and *The Mathematical Basis of the Arts*.

[2]G. D. Birkhoff, *Aesthetic Measure*. Another "academic oddity" (to speak politely) was my own youthful effort to apply symbolic logic to music; to which I confess, but will not refer by chapter and verse.

[3]Schenker speaks of "synthesis," but not in the sense of a veritable procedure. It is a mystical activity which he attributes to the Archetypal Line, the *Urlinie*, itself, not to the composer. "Diminution is to the Archetypal Line as a man's skeleton to his living flesh. . . . The Archetypal Line leads directly to the synthesis of the whole. It is the synthesis." (*Tonwille*, II, 5.)

for cosmology, from ancient times to our own day.[4] The material itself is interesting, and offers a definite, specialized field of inquiry. The order of pitches is continuous, and corresponds to an equally orderly series of vibration rates. Loudness, too, may be expressed in mathematical degrees of an unbroken scale, and reduced to a property of physical vibration. Even timbre—the most definitely qualitative characteristic of tones—is conditioned by the simplicity or complexity of the vibrations that produce the tone. Almost as soon as one proposes to think in strict terms about the phenomenon called "music," the physics of sound presents itself as the natural groundwork for any theory.

But sound, and even tone, as such is not music; music is something made out of sound, usually of definite intonation. Now there is just enough kinship between simple tone-relationships (8ve, 5th, 3rd) and agreeable sensation (consonance) to suggest a system of psychological "responses" corresponding exactly to the physical system of tonal "stimuli." So the science of acoustics acquired an alter ego, the psychology of music initiated by Carl Stumpf, which begins with the concept of separate auditory perceptions and seeks to build up the total musical experience as an emotional response to complex tonal stimuli, reinforced by sensations of contrast, surprise, familiarity, and above all, personal associations. There is, to date, a fairly large literature of psychological findings in this field. But far greater than the body of findings is the faith in the undertaking held mainly by persons who have not themselves gathered or interpreted such data. The program rather than its fulfillment has influenced both musical and unmusical people to think of the art of tone as a process of affective stimulation, and to suppose that musical experience will some day be describable in terms of "nervous vibrations" corresponding to the physical vibrations of sounding instruments.[5]

---

[4]See, e.g., Matila C. Ghyka, *Essai sur le rythme*, p. 78: "All this Vitruvian theory of proportions and eurythmics is nothing but a transposition, into the spatial dimension, of the Pythagorean theory of chords, or rather: musical intervals, as we find it reflected in the Timaeus (number as the soul of the world)."

[5]See, for instance, the chapter on music written by Paul Krummreich in L. W. Flaccus' *The Spirit and Substance of Art*, where the author, after asserting that music evokes instinctive reactions, says: "Instincts may be considered a phase of our unconscious life; and the unconscious we can discuss in terms of vibrations." But his discussion is *about* vibrations, never about something else *in terms of*

This ambitious hope rests, of course, on the widely held belief that the proper function of music is to cause a refined sort of sensuous pleasure that in turn evokes a well-timed, variegated succession of feelings. There is no need of reviewing this "stimulus theory" again after rejecting its credentials for art in general. Suffice it to point out that if music is art, and not an epicure's pleasure, then the study of vibration patterns on sound tracks and encephalographs may tell us astounding things about audition, but not about music, which is the illusion begotten by sounds.

The traditional preoccupation with the ingredients of music has had a somewhat unhappy effect on theoretical study, connoisseurship and criticism, and through criticism on the ideas and attitudes of the general public. It has led people to listen for the wrong things, and suppose that to understand music one must know not simply much music, but much *about* music. Concert-goers try earnestly to recognize chords, and judge key changes, and hear the separate instruments in an ensemble—all technical insights that come of themselves with long familiarity, like the recognition of glazes on pottery or of structural devices in a building —instead of distinguishing *musical elements,* which may be made out of harmonic or melodic material, shifts of range or of tone color, rhythms or dynamic accents or simply changes of volume, and yet be in themselves as audible to a child as to a veteran musician. For the elements of music are not tones of such and such pitch, duration and loudness, nor chords and measured beats; they are, like all artistic elements, something virtual, created only for perception. Eduard Hanslick[6] denoted them rightly: *"tönend bewegte Formen"*—"sounding forms in motion."

Such motion is the essence of music; a motion of forms that are not visible, but are given to the ear instead of the eye. Yet what are these forms? They are not objects in the actual world, like the forms normally revealed by light, because sound, though it is propagated in space, and is variously swallowed or reflected back, i.e. echoed, by the surfaces it encounters, is not sufficiently modified by them to give an impression

---

vibrations.

One of the most serious of these hopeful ventures is *La musique et la vie intérieure. Essai d'une histoire psychologique de l'art musical,* by L. Bourguès and A. Denéréaz.

See, further, F. E. Howard: "Is Music an Art or a Science?" *Connecticut Magazine,* VIII, no. 2 (1903), 255–288. There are dozens of other examples.

[6]*Vom Musikalisch-Schönen.*

of their shapes, as light does.[7] Things in a room may affect tone in general, but they do not influence tonal forms specifically, nor obstruct their motions, because forms and motions alike are only seemingly there; they are elements in a purely auditory illusion.

For in all the progressive movements we hear—fast movement or slow, stop, attack, rising melody, widening or closing harmony, crowding chords and flowing figures—there is actually nothing that moves. A word may be in order here to forestall a popular fallacy, namely the supposition that musical motion is actual because strings or pipes and the air around them move. Such motion, however, is not what we perceive. Vibration is minute, very fast, and if it comes to rest sound simply disappears. The movement of tonal forms, on the contrary, is large and directed toward a point of relative rest, which is no less audible than the progression leading to it. In a simple passage like the following:

the three eighth notes progress *upward* to C. Yet actually there is no locomotion. The C is their point of rest; but while it is sustained there is faster vibration than in any other part of the phrase. Musical motion, in short, is something entirely different from physical displacement. It is a semblance, and nothing more.

The last note of the example just given introduces another element that has no prototype in physical dynamics: the element of *sustained rest*. When a progression reaches its point of rest within a piece, the music does not therefore stand still, but moves on. It moves over static harmonies and persistent tones such as pedal points, and silences. Its forward drive may even carry it rhythmically beyond the last sound, as in some of Beethoven's works, e.g. in the finale of opus 9, no. 1, where

---

[7]This functional difference between light and sound was observed by Joseph Goddard some 50 years ago. "From a single central source light proceeds continually, which light the surfaces of objects reflect in ways corresponding to their character. . . . Although musical sound is more or less reflected and absorbed as it moves among objects, the result is to modify its general volume and character—as when music is performed in an empty or full room—not to give us impressions of those objects." (*On Beauty and Expression in Music*, pp. 25–27.)

the last measure is a silence:

The elements of music are moving forms of sound; but in their motion nothing is removed. The realm in which tonal entities move is a realm of pure *duration*. Like its elements, however, this duration is not an actual phenomenon. It is not a period—ten minutes or a half hour, some fraction of a day—but is something radically different from the time in which our public and practical life proceeds. It is completely incommensurable with the progress of common affairs. Musical duration is an image of what might be termed "lived" or "experienced" time— the passage of life that we feel as expectations become "now," and "now" turns into unalterable fact. Such passage is measurable only in terms of sensibilities, tensions, and emotions; and it has not merely a different measure, but an altogether different structure from practical or scientific time.

The semblance of this vital, experiential time is the primary illusion of music. All music creates an order of virtual time, in which its sonorous forms move in relation to each other—always and only to each other, for nothing else exists there. Virtual time is as separate from the sequence of actual happenings as virtual space from actual space. In the first place, it is entirely perceptible, through the agency of a single sense—hearing. There is no supplementing of one sort of experience by another. This alone makes it something quite different from our "common-sense" version of time, which is even more composite, heterogeneous, and fragmentary than our similar sense of space. Inward tensions and outward changes, heartbeats and clocks, daylight and routines and weariness furnish various incoherent temporal data, which we coordinate for practical purposes by letting the clock predominate. But music spreads out time for our direct and complete apprehension, by letting our hearing monopolize it —organize, fill, and shape it, all alone. It creates an image of time measured by the motion of forms that seem to give it substance, yet a substance that consists entirely of sound, so it is transitoriness itself. *Music makes time audible, and its form and continuity sensible.*

This theory of music is surprisingly corroborated by the observations of Basil de Selincourt in a short, little-known, but significant essay entitled "Music and Duration," which I have come across quite recently, and found remarkable on several counts, especially for the fact that the author distinguished, clearly and explicitly, between the actual and the virtual, with respect to both space and time. His words, written thirty years ago, may well be quoted here:

"Music is one of the forms of duration; it suspends ordinary time, and offers itself as an ideal substitute and equivalent. Nothing is more metaphorical or more forced in music than a suggestion that time is passing while we listen to it, that the development of the themes follows the action in time of some person or persons embodied in them, or that we ourselves change as we listen. . . . The space of which the painter makes use is a translated space, within which all objects are at rest, and though flies may walk about on his canvas, their steps do not measure the distance from one tone to another. . . . The Time of music is similarly an ideal time, and if we are less directly aware of it, the reason is that our life and consciousness are more closely conditioned by time than by space. . . . The ideal and the real spatial relations declare their different natures in the simplicity of the contrast which we perceive between them. Music, on the other hand, demands the absorption of the whole of our time-consciousness; our own continuity must be lost in that of the sound to which we listen. . . . Our very life is measured by rhythm: by our breathing, by our heartbeats. These are all irrelevant, their meaning is in abeyance, so long as time is music.

". . . If we are 'out of time' in listening to music, our state is best explained by the simple consideration that it is as difficult to be in two times at once as in two places. Music uses time as an element of expression; duration is its essence. The beginning and the end of a musical composition are only one if the music has possessed itself of the interval between them and wholly filled it."[8]

The second radical divergence of virtual time from actual lies in its very structure, its logical pattern, which is not the one-dimensional order we assume for practical purposes (including all historical and scientific purposes). The virtual time created in music is an image of time in a different mode, i.e. appearing to have different terms and relations.

The clock—metaphysically a very problematical instrument—makes a special abstraction from temporal experience, namely *time as pure sequence,* symbolized by a class of ideal events indifferent in themselves, but ranged in an infinite "dense" series by the sole relation of succession. Conceived under this scheme, time is a one-dimensional continuum, and segments of it may be taken from any extensionless "moment" to any succeeding one, and every actual event may be wholly located within just one segment of the series so as to occupy it completely.

Further descriptions of this ingenious time-concept are not relevant here; suffice it to point out that it is the only adequate scheme we know of for synchronizing practical affairs, dating past events, and constructing some perspective of future ones. It can, moreover, be elaborated to meet the demands of much more precise thought than "common sense." Modern scientific time, which is one coordinate of a many-dimensional structure, is a systematic refinement of "clock-time." But for all its logical virtues, this one-dimensional, infinite succession of moments is an abstraction from direct experiences of time, and it is not the only possible one. Its great intellectual and practical advantages are bought at the price of many interesting phases of our time perception that have to be completely ignored. Consequently we have a great deal of temporal experience—that is, intuitive knowledge of time—that is not recognized as "true" because it is not formalized and presented in any symbolic mode; we have only one way—the way of the clock—to think discursively about time at all.

---

[8] *Music and Letters,* I, no. 4 (1920), 286–293.

Compare also the following passage from "The Composer and His Message," by Roger Sessions (already mentioned in Chapter 4, note 22): "It seems to me that the essential medium of music, the basis of its expressive powers and the element which gives it its unique quality among the arts, is *time,* made living for us through its expressive essence, *movement.*"

The underlying principle of clock-time is *change,* which is measured by contrasting two states of an instrument, whether that instrument be the sun in various positions, or the hand on a dial at successive locations, or a parade of monotonous, similar events like ticks or flashes, "counted," i.e. differentiated, by being correlated with a series of distinct numbers. In any case it is the "states," "instants," or whatever we choose to call the terms of the series, that are symbolized, and therefore explicitly conceived, and "change" from one to the other is construed in terms of their differences. "Change" is not itself something represented; it is implicitly given through the contrast of different "states," themselves unchanging.[9]

The time-concept which emerges from such mensuration is something far removed from time as we know it in direct experience, which is essentially *passage,* or the sense of transience. Passage is just what we need not take account of in formulating a scientifically useful, i.e. measurable, order of time; and because we can ignore this psychologically prime aspect, clock-time is homogeneous and simple and may be treated as one-dimensional. But the experience of time is anything but simple. It involves more properties than "length," or interval between selected moments; for its passages have also what I can only call, metaphorically, *volume.* Subjectively, a unit of time may be great or small as well as long or short; the slang phrase "a big time" is psychologically more accurate than a "busy," "pleasant," or "exciting" time. It is this voluminousness of the direct experience of passage that makes it, as Bergson observed long ago, indivisible.[10] But even its volume is not simple; for it is filled with its own characteristic forms, as space is filled with material forms, otherwise it could not be observed and appreciated at all. The phenomena that fill time are *tensions*—physical, emotional, or intellectual. Time exists for us because we undergo tensions and their

---

[9] In 1926, Charles Koechlin published an article, "Le temps et la musique" (*La Revue Musicale,* VII, 3, p. 48), wherein I find this passage: "To certain minds, time appears as a resultant of our recollections of a great many states of mind, among which we 'assume' a continued duration that connects them as, given the limits of some measured distance, a path lies between those points. But actually those philosophers admit only the existence of the limits, and deny that of the path."

[10] In *Matière et Mémoire,* published originally in 1896, he wrote: "All movement, being indeed a passage from one point of rest to another, is absolutely indivisible." (46th ed., Paris, 1946, p. 209.)

resolutions. Their peculiar building-up, and their ways of breaking or diminishing or merging into longer and greater tensions, make for a vast variety of temporal forms. If we could experience only single, successive organic strains, perhaps subjective time would be one-dimensional like the time ticked off by clocks. But life is always a dense fabric of concurrent tensions, and as each of them is a measure of time, the measurements themselves do not coincide. This causes our temporal experience to fall apart into incommensurate elements which cannot be all perceived together as clear forms. When one is taken as parameter, others become "irrational," out of logical focus, ineffable. Some tensions, therefore, always sink into the background; some drive and some drag, but for perception they give *quality* rather than form to the passage of time, which unfolds in the pattern of the dominant and distinct strains whereby we are measuring it.[11]

The direct experience of passage, as it occurs in each individual life is, of course, something actual, just as actual as the progress of the clock or the speedometer; and like all actuality it is only in part perceived, and its fragmentary data are supplemented by practical knowledge and ideas from other realms of thought altogether. Yet it is the model for the virtual time created in music. There we have its image, completely articulated and pure; every kind of tension transformed into musical tension, every qualitative content into musical quality, every extraneous factor replaced by musical elements. The primary illusion of music is the sonorous image of passage, abstracted from actuality to become free and plastic and entirely perceptible.

Most readers have, undoubtedly, realized long ago that what is here called "subjective time" is the "real time," or "duration," which Henri Bergson attempted to capture and understand. Bergson's dream (one dares not say "concept" in connection with his thought) of *la durée réelle* brings his metaphysics very close to the musical realm—in fact, to the very brink of a philosophy of art. What prevented him from achieving

---

[11]Phenomenology attempts to describe in discursive terms this complex experience; and it tries to do so in terms of momentary impressions and actual feelings. The result is a tremendous complication of "states" in which the *sense of passage* is entirely lost in the parade of "moments" (*Augenblicke,* not *Momente*). See, for instance, the article by Philip Merlan, "Time Consciousness in Husserl and Heidegger," *Journal of Phenomenology,* VIII, 1 (September, 1947), 23–53.

a universal art theory was, essentially, a lack of logical daring; in his horror of a pernicious abstraction, he fled to a realm of no abstraction at all, and having wounded his spirit on the tools of physical science he threw away tools altogether.

Yet his nearness to the problems of art has made him pre-eminently the artists' philosopher. It is a curious fact that Croce and Santayana, who have both produced aesthetic theories, have never had the influence on artistic thought that Bergson still exercises; yet they have said many true things about the arts, whereas Bergson has said many sentimental and amateurish things.[12] But metaphysically he deals with matters that go to the core of all the arts, and especially of music.

His all-important insight is, briefly, that every conceptual form which is supposed to portray time oversimplifies it to the point of leaving out the most interesting aspects of it, namely the characteristic appearances of passage, so that we have a scientific equivalent rather than a conceptual symbol of duration. This criticism throws out a new challenge to the philosopher's powers of logical construction: find us a symbolism whereby we can conceive and express our firsthand knowledge of time!

But here the critic himself retires; the challenge was only an oratorical one; his own reply to it is a counsel of despair—namely, that such conception is impossible, its symbolic expression a metaphysical pitfall, because all symbolization is by its very nature a falsification. It is "spatialization," and every traffic with space is a betrayal of our real knowledge of time.[13] Philosophy must give up discursive thought, give up logical conception, and try to grasp intuitively the inward sense of duration.

But it is not the intervention of symbolism as such that balks our understanding of "lived" time; it is the unsuitable and consequently barren structure of the literal symbol. The demand Bergson makes upon philosophy—to set forth the dynamic forms of subjective experience— only art can fulfill. Perhaps this explains why he is the artists' phi-

---

[12]E.g. the passage in *La perception du changement:* "Without doubt, art causes us to discover in things more qualities and more shades of meaning than we would ordinarily perceive. It broadens our perception, but superficially rather than in depth. It enriches our present, but it does not lead us in any way to transcend the present."

[13]See *La pensée et le mouvant,* especially chap. 1; also, for a brief but fundamental presentation, his little *Metaphysics.*

losopher *par excellence.* Croce and Santayana make demands on art that are essentially philosophical; philosophers, therefore, find them interesting, but artists tend to ignore them. Bergson, on the other hand, sets up a task that is impossible to accomplish in the realm of discursive expression, i.e. is beyond the philosopher's pale (and cannot force entrance there by resort to instinct, either), but is exactly the artist's business. Nothing could seem more reasonable to a poet or a musician than Bergson's metaphyical aim; without asking whether it is feasible in philosophy, the artist accepts this aim and subscribes to a philosophy that lays claim to it.

As soon as the expressive symbol, the image of time, is recognized, one can philosophize about its revelations and correct certain Bergsonian errors actually in the light of better knowledge. There has been much astute refutation of Bergson's doctrine, but little constructive criticism, *except from musicians,* who recognized what he was driving at, and with the courage of innocence went straight to the solution, where his philosophical fears confused him. In particular, I have in mind two articles in *La Revue Musicale,* which attacked the chief obstacle to a philosophy of art in Bergson's rich and novel apprehension of time—its radical opposition to space, the repudiation of every property it might share with space. Art can build its illusion in space or in time; metaphysically, we can understand or misunderstand one realm as readily as the other; and it is hard to find the interesting characteristics of duration if there be too many things one is determined *not* to find.

The two articles, respectively, are Charles Koechlin's "Le temps et la musique," to which I have already referred,[14] and Gabriel Marcel's slightly earlier "Bergsonisme et musique."[15] Both authors are deeply in sympathy with Bergson's thesis, that the direct intuition of time must be our measure for its philosophical conception, and both realize what Bergson himself never clearly saw—that his "concrete duration," "lived time," is the prototype of "musical time," namely *passage* in its characteristic forms.[16] Furthermore, it is to their intellectual credit that they

---

[14]See footnote, p. 112.   [15]*Le Revue Musicale,* VII, 3.

[16]Marcel writes: "It is extremely difficult for the reader of M. Bergson not to suppose—contrary to reason—that a certain philosophy of music is wrapped up in the theory of concrete time. . . ." (*Op. cit.,* p. 221.) And Koechlin: "Heard time comes so close to pure duration that one might say it is the sensation of duration itself." (*Op. cit.,* p. 47.)

both distinguish between actual and musical duration, the living reality and the symbol.[17]

Bergson did, indeed, recognize a close relationship between musical time and *la durée pure*, but his ideal of thought without symbols would not let him exploit the power of the dynamic image. The desire to exclude all spatial structure led him to deny his "concrete duration" any structure whatever; when he himself uses the simile of musical time, he treats the latter as a completely formless flow, "the successive tones of a melody whereby we let ourselves be cradled." Consequently he misses the most important and novel revelation of music—the fact that time is not a pure succession, but has more than one dimension. His very horror of the scientific abstractions he finds typified in geometry makes him cling to the one-dimensional pure succession of "states," which looks suspiciously like the abstract structure of Newton's one-dimensional time-stream.

But musical time has form and organization, volume and distinguishable parts. In apprehending a melody we are not vaguely billowing along with it. As Marcel observed: "When we speak of the beauty of a melodic line, this aesthetic qualification does not refer to an inward progression, but to a certain object, to a certain non-spatial shape—for which the world of extension can merely furnish a symbolism that we know is inadequate. Gradually, as I pass from tone to tone, a certain *ensemble* emerges, a form is built up, which very surely cannot be reduced to an organized succession of states. . . . It is of the very essence of this form to reveal itself as duration, and yet to transcend, in its own way,

---

[17]Cf. Marcel, *op. cit.*, p. 222: "Concrete duration is not essentially musical. All the more can one say, though only with a turn of phrase . . . of which M. Bergson would heartily disapprove—melodic continuity furnishes an example, an illustration, of pure continuity, given for the philosopher to apprehend directly in a reality both universal and concrete."

Also Koechlin, listing the several concepts of time:

"1. Pure duration, attribute of our deepest consciousness, and seemingly independent of the external world: life unfolding.

2. Psychological time. This is the impression of time that we receive according to the events of life: minutes that seem like centuries, hours that pass too fast. . . .

3. Time measured by mathematical means. . . .

4. And finally, I would speak of musical time. . . . Auditory time is without doubt that which approaches most closely to pure duration. . . ." (*Op. cit.*, p. 46.)

the purely temporal order in which it is manifested." To regard musical form and relation as "spatial," as Bergson does, is precisely to miss the real being of music; true musical perception apperceives the form as something dynamic. "But this act of apperception . . . does not in any way resolve itself into that sympathy whereby I am wedded to the phrase and live it. I readily say, it is not an *abandon,* but on the contrary, a sort of mastery."[18]

The frequent references to "musical space" in the technical literature are not purely metaphorical; there are definitely spatial illusions created in music, quite apart from the phenomenon of volume, which is literally spatial, and the fact that movement logically involves space, which may be taking movement too literally. "Tonal space" is a different thing, a genuine semblance of distance and scope. It derives from harmony rather than from either movement or fullness of tone. The reason is, I believe, that harmonic structure gives our hearing an *orientation* in the tonal system, from which we perceive musical elements as holding *places* in an ideal range.[19] But the space of music is never made wholly perceptible, as the fabric of virtual time is; it is really an attribute of musical time, an appearance that serves to develop the temporal realm in more than one dimension. Space, in music, is a *secondary illusion.* But, primary or secondary, it is thoroughly "virtual," i.e. unrelated to the space of actual experience. Ernst Kurth, in his *Musikpsychologie,* likens it to "kinetic space,"[20] and in Werner Danckert's *Ursymbole melodischer Gestaltung* it figures as virtual "place."[21] J. Gehring, for his part, speaks of the staggered planes of musical depth.[22] Evidently, the spatial element which all these writers find in music is a plastic space, artistically transformed, yet in no specified visual mode. It is not an importation from actual

---

[18]Marcel, *op. cit.,* pp. 223–224.

[19]Cf. D. F. Tovey, *Essays in Musical Analysis,* V, 97: Speaking of Handel's modulations he says, "In the Chorus of Darkness . . . they traverse most of harmonic space."

[20]See p. 136: "In the light of all these phenomena one might, perhaps, best designate these subjective spatial impressions as 'kinetic space,' since they derive directly from the psychological vital energies. Only in its marginal manifestations does it [this space] resolve itself into perceptual factors. . . ."

[21]See p. 66: "Like all space in works of art, this [musical space] is nothing less than a cosmic symbol, a representation of Man's 'position,' 'location,' and 'range' in the greater nexus of the world."

[22]Gehring: *Grundprinzipien musikalischer Gestaltung.*

experience (though Kurth often flirts with sheer associationism), but neither is it the essential substance of the art. It simply arises from the way virtual time unfolds in this or that individual work—arises, and is eclipsed again.

The fact that the primary illusion of one art may appear, like an echo, as a secondary illusion in another, gives us a hint of the basic community of all the arts. As space may suddenly appear in music, time may be involved in visual works. A building, for instance, is the incarnation of a vital space; in symbolizing the feeling of the life that belongs to its precincts, it inevitably shows us time, and in some buildings this element becomes impressively strong. Yet architecture does not create a perceptible totality of time, as it does of space; time is a secondary illusion. The primary illusion always determines the "substance," the real character of an art work, but the possibility of secondary illusions endows it with the richness, elasticity, and wide freedom of creation that make real art so hard to hold in the meshes of theory.

As soon as we regard music as a thoroughgoing symbol, an image of subjective time, the appeal of Bergson's ideas to the artistic mind becomes quite comprehensible; for music presents reality no more directly than philosophical discourse, but it presents a sentient and emotional reality more adequately in a non-discursive image—*globalement,* as the French would say. With this tool it does exactly what he demanded of *la vraie métaphysique,* except one thing: to give a discursive account of itself in the end. That would be eating one's cake and having it too; and for this reason art is neither philosophy nor a substitute for philosophy, but is itself an epistemological datum about which we can philosophize.

The making of the symbol is the musician's entire problem, as it is, indeed, every artist's; and the special difficulties that confront us in dealing with music all spring from the nature of the musical illusion and the creative processes involved in forming and rendering it. Such subordinate issues are: the intervention of a performer between the composer and his audience; the wide range of "interpretations" of any given piece; the value and dangers of virtuosity, the bogey of "mere technique"; the process of "self-expression" attributed now to the composer, now to the performer, or in orchestral works to the conductor; the function of poetic texts; the principle of the *"petit roman,"* in default of a text, to inspire or to explain a composition; the opposite ideal of "pure music," upheld by the best musicologists and critics, and—paradoxically —the interest of most great composers in opera. All these problems have to be mooted in connection with our present subject. But they are far too complex, too great with implications affecting all the arts, to be passed with a mere bow of recognition. Their solution has to be prepared by a more detailed knowledge of the central theme—*what the musician is making, to what end, and by what means.*

Chapter eight

THE MUSICAL MATRIX

The musician, of course, is making a piece of music. Now music is something audible, as a picture is something visible, not merely in conception but in sensible existence. When a piece of music is completely made, it is there to be heard by the physical as well as the inward ear. For, Croce and many other serious aestheticians[1] to the contrary notwithstanding, the final process of figuring forth an idea in sensuous appearance is *not* a mechanical affair, but is part and parcel of the creative drive, controlled entirely, in every detail, by an artistic imagination.

Yet a great part of the making may take place without any overt expression. This physically non-sensuous structure has a permanent existence and identity of its own; it is what can be "repeated" in many transient appearances, which are its "performances," and in a sense it is all the composer can really call *his* piece. For, although he may carry it to absolute completion by performing it himself, and make a permanent gramophone record of his performance so this also may be repeated, the *composition* nevertheless exists, as something that could be committed to writing or to memory and that might be performed by another person.

The purpose of all musical labor, in thought or in physical activity, is to create and develop the illusion of flowing time in its passage, an audible passage filled with motion that is just as illusory as the time it is measuring. Music is an "art of time" in a more intimate and important

---

[1]Discussion of this contrary theory will be found below, in Chapter 20.

sense than the traditional one in which the phrase is commonly applied
not only to it but to literature, drama, and dance—the sense of *requiring
a definite time of perception.* In that sense the "arts of time" are opposed to the "arts of space." But music merits the title in two senses,
and *double-entendres* in philosophy are unfortunate. Therefore I shall
dispense with the expression, "arts of time," altogether, and distinguish
between the plastic and the *occurrent* arts (rather than "arts of performance," since literature for silent reading cannot be said to be "performed" except in a derivative and even Pickwickian sense).

Music is an occurrent art; a musical work grows from the first imagination of its general movement to its complete, physical presentation,
its *occurrence.* In this growth there are, however, certain distinguishable
stages—distinguishable, though not always separable.

The first stage is the process of conception, that takes place entirely
within the composer's mind (no matter what outside stimuli may start
or support it), and issues in a more or less sudden recognition of the
total form to be achieved. I say "more or less sudden," because the
point of this revelation probably varies widely in the typical experience
of different composers and even in the several experiences of any one of
them. A musician may sit at the keyboard, putting all sorts of themes
and figures together in a loose fantasy, until one idea takes over and
a structure emerges from the wandering sounds; or he may hear, all at
once, without the distinction of any physical tones, perhaps even without exact tone color as yet, the whole musical apparition. But however
the total *Gestalt* presents itself to him, he recognizes it as the fundamental form of the piece; and henceforth his mind is no longer free to
wander irresponsibly from theme to theme, key to key, and mood to
mood. This form is the "composition" which he feels called upon to
develop. (It is significant, at this point, that one speaks of "composition" in painting in an analogous sense; the basic form of the picture,
which is to be developed, and by which every line and every accent is
controlled.)

Once the essential musical form is found, a piece of music exists in
embryo; it is implicit there, although its final, completely articulate
character is not determined yet, because there are many possible ways
of developing the composition. Yet in the whole process of subsequent

invention and elaboration, the general *Gestalt* serves as a measure of right and wrong, too much and too little, strong and weak. One might call that original conception the *commanding form* of the work. It requires such things as ornamentation or intensification or greater simplicity; it may rule out some favorite device of its creator, and force him to find a new one; like a living organism it maintains its identity, and in the face of influences that should mold it into something functionally different, it seems to preserve its original purposes and become distorted from its true lines rather than simply replaced by something else.

It is, in fact, when the first semblance of organic form is achieved that a work of art exhibits its general symbolic possibilities, like a statement imperfectly made or even merely indicated, but understandable in its general intent. That central significance is, I think, what Flaubert called the "Idea," and its symbol is the commanding form that guides the artist's judgment even in moments of intense excitement and inspiration. In music the *fundamental movement* has this power of shaping the whole piece by a sort of implicit logic that all conscious artistry serves to make explicit. The relentless strain on the musician's faculties comes chiefly from the wealth of possibilities that lie in such a matrix and cannot all be realized, so that every choice is also a sacrifice. Every articulation precludes not only its own alternatives but all sorts of developments they would have made viable. Once the commanding form is recognized, the work is something like Leibniz's "best of possible worlds" —its creator's best choice among many possible elements, each of which, in an organic structure, requires so much clearance, preparation, and contextual aid from other factors that even the rendering of a small detail may commit him to a serious decision. If he is competent in his art, his mind is trained and predisposed to see every option in relation to others, and to the whole. He decides, and knows what his choice involves, and does not fumble. As Picasso said: "I have never made trials nor experiments. Whenever I had something to say I have said it in the manner in which I have felt it ought to be said."[2]

The matrix, in music the fundamental movement of melody or harmonic progression, which establishes the greatest rhythm of the piece

[2]See Goldwater and Treves, *Artists on Art*, p. 418.

and dictates its scope, is born of the composer's thought and feeling, but as soon as he recognizes it as an individual symbol and sets forth its outline it becomes the expression of an impersonal Idea, and opens, to him and others, a deep mine of musical resource. For the commanding form is not essentially restrictive, but fecund. A perfectly free imagination suffers from very lack of pressure; it is in the vague and groping state that precedes the conception of the total form. The great moment of creation is the recognition of the matrix, for in this lie all the *motives* for the specific work; not all the themes—a theme may be imported if it fits the place—but the tendencies of the piece, the need for dissonance and consonance, novelty and reiteration, length of phrase and timing of cadences. Because these general functions are demanded by the organic form itself, the composer's imagination has specific problems to solve, which he does not set himself capriciously, to try his powers of solution, but which spring from the objective form he has already created. That is why one may puzzle for a long time over the exact form of an expression, not seeing what is wrong with this or that, and then, when the right form presents itself, feel it going into place almost with a click. Since the emotional content of it is not clearly preconceivable without any expression, the adequacy of the new element cannot be measured by it with anything like the precision and certainty of that intuitive "click." It is the commanding form of the work that guarantees such a judgment.[3]

Under the influence of the total "Idea," the musician *composes* every part of his piece. The principles of articulating music are so various that each composer finds his own idiom, even within the tradition he happens to inherit. The Idea as it occurs to him already suggests his own way of composing; and in that process lies the individuation of the piece. Therefore the commanding form, greatest movement, or whatever one chooses to call it, is not what Schenker has termed the *Urlinie;* for, as Riezler pointed out, the *Urlinien* of very different pieces look peculiarly alike.[4] But the musical conceptions from which the respective works

---

[3]Cf. Roger Sessions, *op. cit.:* "[Sometimes] the inspiration takes the form, however, not of a sudden flash of music, but a clearly envisaged impulse toward a certain goal for which the composer was obliged to strive. When [in the case of Beethoven's 'Hammerklavier Sonata'] this perfect realization was attained, however, there could have been no hesitation—rather a flash of recognition that this was exactly what he wanted." (Pp. 126–27.)

[4]W. Riezler, "Die Urlinie," *Die Musik,* XXII[2], p. 502.

were developed must have been as distinct as the final products. That is because the initial "Idea" is the beginning of a creative process, and therefore activates a more definite plan of development than merely the breaking of a natural chord into successive tones, and of the resultant new overtone structures into new successions—the principle that Schenker calls *auskomponieren*. Some characteristic *way* of unfolding the tonal potentialities of the first harmonies is really the generative principle of a composition, and this may be implicit in a rhythmic figure, or in a consciousness of extreme vocal ranges (Schenker's *Intervalzug*, but without reference, at first, to the precise intervals involved) and of crowding changes or wide expanse, light, swift glow or arresting intensity. The *Urlinie*, on the other hand, is the end product of a structural analysis, and Schenker would probably be the last person to assume that the composer began with an explicit notion of his protomusical line, like a blueprint, and deliberately composed the piece within its frame. The idea of the piece contains the *Urlinie* as a statement contains its syntax; when we have a discursive thought to express, in a language we speak readily, we frame our statement without any thought of subject and predicate, yet our communication will flow in some traceable syntactical channel, to which the most involved constructions still maintain a relation of dependence.

The "language of music" as we know it has evolved its own forms, and these are traditional like the structural elements in speech. Yet it may be that even the *Urlinie* is not an unalterable law of all music, but only of our European development of music; that Schenker has discovered not so much the principle of the art itself, as of the "Great Tradition." His constant reliance on "masterpieces" and his resentment of all new idioms and departures make one think of the protagonists of so-called "representational" painting[5]; the laws of nature they claim to have discovered for all pictorial art are really the principles of the "Great Tradition" that inspired and supported its career in the history of our culture. If the *Urlinie* be the mark of our special kind of musical creation, then no wonder we can find it in all good compositions, and in many that are not good, too; and nothing could be more irrelevant than Riezler's charge against Schenker's analysis, that all *Urlinien* look alike,

---

[5]See, for example, Kenyon Cox, *The Classic Point of View*.

and one cannot tell by viewing them whether the works from which they have been abstracted be great or poor.[6]

What, then, is the essence of *all* music? The creation of virtual time, and its complete determination by the movement of audible forms. The devices for establishing this primary illusion of time are many; the recognition of related tones (fundamental and overtones, and by derivation our entire harmonic system) is the most powerful structural principle that has ever been employed, if artistic power be judged by the range and expressiveness of the structures to which the principle gives rise; but other musical traditions have used other devices. The drum has been used with wonderful effect to enthrall the ear, to push away, as it were, the world of practical time, and create a new time image in sound. In our own music the drum is a subsidiary element, but there are records of African music in which its constructive power is paramount.[7] The voice, in such performances, serves essentially to contrast with the steady tone of the drum—to wander and rise and fall where the purely rhythmic element goes on like Fate. The effect is neither melody nor harmony, yet it is music: it has motion and autonomous form, and anyone familiar with many works of that sort would probably feel their structure and mood almost from the opening beat.

Another ruling principle of music has been the intonation of speech. If chant, in its oldest sense, has a protomusical line, that line is not constructed harmonically, like Schenker's *Urlinie,* but rests on some other principle. Yet choric chant, no matter what its poetic content, is essentially music. It creates a dynamic form, purely sonorous movement, that metes out its own audible Time even to a person who cannot understand the words, though that person inevitably misses some of the richness of the musical texture. But this is a subject for future discussion. The point at issue here is merely that music is more universal than any one artistic tradition, and the difference between music and noise is not the absence

---

[6]W. Riezler, *op. cit.,* p. 509.

[7]For example, Victor P10–12 (89b), "Secret Society Drums, Bini Tribe" (5 drums). It is customary among Europeans to call all drum music "primitive"; but this drumming is not primitive at all—it is highly developed, the sophisticated product of a living tradition. If such African drumming be compared with the drummed dance accompaniments of European peasants (*L'anthologie sonore,* 16 [a, "Thirteenth Century Music"; b, "Fourteenth Century"]), the latter will sound truly "primitive," i.e. undeveloped, by contrast.

of this or that constructive principle, but of any commanding form whatever. Even noise may happen to furnish musical phenomena; hammers on anvils, rotary saws, dripping faucets are very apt to do so; but real music comes into being only when someone seizes on the motif and uses it, either as a form to be developed, or as an element to be assimilated to a greater form.

The essence of all composition—tonal or atonal, vocal or instrumental, even purely percussive, if you will—is the semblance of *organic* movement, the illusion of an indivisible whole. Vital organization is the frame of all feeling, because feeling exists only in living organisms; and the logic of all symbols that can express feeling is the logic of organic processes. The most characteristic principle of vital activity is rhythm. All life is rhythmic; under difficult circumstances, its rhythms may become very complex, but when they are really lost life cannot long endure. This rhythmic character of organism permeates music, because music is a symbolic presentation of the highest organic response, the emotional life of human beings. A succession of emotions that have no reference to each other do not constitute an "emotional life," any more than a discontinuous and independent functioning of organs collected under one skin would be a physical "life." The great office of music is to organize our conception of feeling into more than an occasional awareness of emotional storm, i.e. to give us an insight into what may truly be called the "life of feeling," or subjective unity of experience; and this it does by the same principle that organizes physical existence into a biological design—rhythm.

There have been countless studies of rhythm, based on the notion of periodicity, or regular recurrence of events. It is true that the elementary rhythmic functions of life have regularly recurrent phases: heartbeat, breath, and the simpler metabolisms. But the obviousness of these repetitions has caused people to regard them as the essence of rhythm, which they are not. The ticking of a clock is repetitious and regular, but not in itself rhythmic; the listening ear hears rhythms *in* the succession of equal ticks, the human mind organizes them into a temporal form.

The essence of rhythm is the preparation of a new event by the ending of a previous one. A person who moves rhythmically need not repeat a single motion exactly. His movements, however, must be complete gestures, so that one can sense a beginning, intent, and consummation, and see in the last stage of one the condition and indeed the rise of another. Rhythm is the setting-up of new tensions by the resolution of former ones. They need not be of equal duration at all; but the situation that begets the new crisis must be inherent in the denouement of its fore-runner.

Breathing is the most perfect exhibit of physiological rhythm: as we release the breath we have taken, we build up a bodily need of oxygen that is the motivation, and therefore the real beginning, of the new breath. If the release of one breath is not synchronous with the growth of the need for the next—for instance, if physical exertion exhausts our oxygen faster than we can exhale, so the new need grows imperative before the present breath is completed—breathing is not rhythmic, but gasping.

The heartbeat illustrates the same functional continuity: the diastole prepares the systole, and vice versa. The whole self-repair of living bodies rests on the fact that the exhaustion of a vital process always stimulates a corrective action, which in turn exhausts itself in creating conditions that demand new spending.

The principle of *rhythmic continuity* is the basis of that organic unity which gives permanence to living bodies—a permanence that, as I have remarked before (see p. 66), is really a pattern of changes. Now, the so-called "inner life"—our whole subjective reality, woven of thought and emotion, imagination and sense perception—is entirely a vital phe-nomenon, most developed where the organic unity of the precarious, individual form is most complete and intricate, i.e. in human beings. What we call mind, soul, consciousness, or (in current vocabulary) ex-perience, is an intensified vitality, a sort of distillate of all sensitive, teleological, organized functioning. The human brain, with all its rami-fications, is wide open to the world outside, and undergoes profound, more or less permanent changes by impressions that the "older," less variable organs record only by transient responses, the bodily symptoms of emotion. In animals, the intellect is almost as selective as the mouth in what it will receive; and what it does admit is apt to set the entire organism in motion. But the human brain is incomparably more tolerant of impressions, because it has a power of handling stimuli which must not be allowed to affect the total metabolic process deeply at all, on pain of death: that power is the *symbolic transformation* of perceptions.

Where the symbolic process is highly developed it practically takes over the domain of perception and memory, and puts its stamp on all mental functions. But even in its highest operations, the mind still follows the organic rhythm which is the source of vital unity: the building-up of a new dynamic *Gestalt* in the very process of a former one's passing away.

There are such genuine rhythms in inorganic nature, too; rhythm is the basis of life, but not limited to life. The swing of a pendulum is rhythmic, without our organizing interpretation (which is what makes a mere succession of sounds—all we perceive in listening to a watch, for instance—rhythmic for us). The kinetic force that drives the pendulum to the height of its swing builds up the potential that will bring it down again; the spending of kinetic energy prepares the turning point and the fall. The gradual decrease of the pendulum's arc due to friction is not usually visible in direct observation, so the motions seem exactly repetitious. A bouncing ball, on the other hand, shows rhythmic performance without equal measure. But the most impressive example of rhythm known to most people is the breaking of waves in a steady surf. Each new comber rolling in is shaped by the undertow flowing back, and in its turn actually hurries the recession of the previous wave by suction. There is no dividing line between the two events. Yet a breaking wave is as definite an event as one could wish to find—a true dynamic *Gestalt*.

Such phenomena in the inanimate world are powerful *symbols* of living form, just because they are not life processes themselves. The contrast between the apparently vital behavior and the obviously inorganic structure of ocean waves, for instance, emphasizes the pure semblance of life, and makes the first abstractions of its rhythm for our intellectual intuition. That is the prime function of symbols. Their second function is to allow us to manipulate the concepts we have achieved. This requires more than a recognition of what may be termed "natural symbols"; it demands the deliberate making of expressive forms that may be deployed in various ways to reveal new meanings. And such created *Gestalten,* that give us logical insight into feeling, vitality and emotional life, are works of art.

The commanding form of a piece of music contains its basic rhythm, which is at once the source of its organic unity and its total feeling. The concept of rhythm as a relation between tensions rather than as a matter of equal divisions of time (i.e. meter) makes it quite comprehensible that harmonic progressions, resolutions of dissonances, directions of "running" passages, and "tendency tones" in melody all serve as rhythmic agents. Everything that prepares a future creates rhythm; everything that begets or intensifies expectation, including the expectation of sheer continuity, prepares the future (regular "beats" are an obvious and important source of rhythmic organization); and everything that fulfills the promised future, in ways foreseen or unforeseen, articulates the symbol of feeling. Whatever the special mood of the piece, or its emotional import, the vital rhythm of subjective time (the "lived" time that Bergson adjures us to find in pure experience) permeates the complex, many-dimensional, musical symbol as its internal logic, which relates music intimately and self-evidently to life.

And what about repetition of forms, equal divisions, if recurrence is not the real basis of rhythm? What is the function of the countless regularities of accent, phrase, figure, and bar in the greatest masterpieces?

Repetition is another structural principle—deeply involved with rhythm, as all basic principles are with each other—that gives musical composition the appearance of vital growth. For what we receive, in the passage of sound, with a sense of recognition, i.e. as a recurrence, is oftentimes a fairly free variant of what came before, a mere analogy, and only logically a repetition; but it is just the sort of play on a basic pattern, especially the reflection of the over-all plan in the structure of each part, that is characteristic of organic forms. This is Schenker's principle of "diminution,"[8] Roger Sessions' "principle of association."[9] The fullest recognition of its "vitalizing" function that I know is in the article by Basil de Selincourt from which I have already had occasion to quote at length, and I cannot refrain from letting the author of that masterly little essay speak again:

---

[8]See especially *Das Meisterwerk in der Musik, passim.*
[9]*Op. cit.,* pp. 129 ff.

"Repetition begins with the bar, and continues in the melody and in every phrase or item into which we can resolve it. The growth of a musical composition may be compared to that of a flowering plant, . . . where not only the leaves repeat each other, but the leaves repeat the flowers, and the very stems and branches are like un-unfolded leaves. . . . To the pattern of the flower there corresponds a further pattern developed in the placing and grouping of flowers along the branches, and the branches themselves divide and stand out in balanced proportions, under the controlling vital impulse. . . . Musical expression follows the same law."[10]

As soon as a musical idea acquires organic character (no matter by what device this is achieved), it expresses the autonomous form of a *work,* the "commanding form" that controls its entire subsequent development. It is the comprehension of this organic unity and individuality that enables a composer to carry out a protracted piece of work on the strength of one initial "inspiration," and make the product more and more integral, instead of less and less so, by the constant importation of new ideas—sometimes even themes that occurred to him long ago, developments he has used elsewhere, traditional preparations—all to be assimilated and transfigured by the unique composition. As long as he can keep the musical organism alive in his imagination he needs no other rule or goal.

There are countless references in musicological literature and among the utterances of great musicians that bear witness to the central importance of living form, the semblance of spontaneous movement, in music; one could quote almost at random from Marpurg, Goddard, Tovey, Schweitzer, Schenker, Lussy, or from the notes and letters of Mozart, Chopin, Mendelssohn, Brahms—anyone, almost, who has written seriously and knowingly about music at all. One is forcibly reminded of the insistent note of vitalism, the universal agreement on the organic quality of all space composition, that runs through the comments of the masters of visual art, collected at the close of Chapter 5; and it would be hard, indeed, not to entertain at least the hypothesis that all art works, no matter in what special domain, are "organic" in the same sense. But let us be content with the hypothesis, until the proof takes care of itself; and without prematurely generalizing musical form, study it further.

---

[10]"Music and Duration," p. 288.

Perhaps the most striking thing about it is the *objective* character already mentioned. Once a matrix of musical thought, a "commanding form," has been grasped by one's artistic imagination, it assumes a peculiarly impersonal status, like an impression from outside, something "given." Great musicians have spoken of the musical "Idea" with an unmistakable feeling of moral obligation toward it, a sense of responsibility for its development and perfection. Thus Mendelssohn wrote to his friend Ferdinand Hiller, a gifted but superficial composer: "Nothing seems to me more reprehensible than to carp at a man's natural endowments . . . but if it be that, as here in your piece, all the themes, all that depends on talent or inspiration (call it what you will) is good and beautiful and moving, but the workmanship is not good, then, I think, one has no right to let it pass. . . . As I believe that a man of great capacities is duty-bound to become an excellent person, and is to be blamed if he does not develop to the full the powers he has been given, so, I maintain, it is with a piece of music. . . . I am quite aware that no musician can make his ideas and his talents other than what heaven has sent him; but just as surely do I know that if heaven has sent him great ideas he is bound to carry them out properly. Don't try to tell me . . . that your work is as good as your compositions are!"[11]

An even clearer statement, however, is Beethoven's, if we may trust Bettina Brentano's report to Goethe, which she assured him, on the strength of her extraordinary memory, was very nearly verbatim: "It takes spiritual [*geistigen*] rhythm to grasp music in its essence. . . . All genuine [musical] invention is moral progress. To submit to its inscrutable laws, and by virtue of these laws, to overcome and control one's own mind, so it shall set forth the revelation: that is the isolating principle of art. . . .

"Thus every true creation of art is independent, mightier than the artist himself. . . . Music gives the mind a relation to the [total] harmony. Any single, separate idea has in it the feeling of the harmony, which is Unity."[12]

I stress this objectivity and potency of the commanding form in a

---

[11]*Meisterbriefe*, II: "Felix Mendelssohn-Bartholdy," edited by Ernst Wolff. See pp. 128–129.

[12]Ludwig van Beethoven, *Briefe und Gespräche*, p. 146.

piece of music so heavily because I believe it is the key to almost all the moot problems of performance, understanding, adaptation, and even that dry old bone of contention, self-expression. From the matrix, the greatest movement, flows the life of the work, with all its contingencies, its powers and perils in the community of human minds.

Chapter nine

THE LIVING WORK

A great many considerations and puzzles that one meets sooner or later in all the arts find their clearest expression, and therefore their most tangible form, in connection with music. The philosophical problems of art are generally so interconnected that one might raise almost any one of them at any point; to avoid the aimlessness of a purely arbitrary order, therefore, I shall try to discuss such special topics not always at the first opportunity, but each one in the frame of that art which throws it into boldest relief. For instance, the question of literal meaning and artistic significance becomes most acute in the field of literature, that of "psychical distance" in drama. Once a more or less specialized artistic problem has been isolated and resolved one can usually find at least vestigial forms of it in all the great orders of art; but it is easiest to handle where it exhibits its classic instance.

In music, all sorts of interesting issues arise once a composition is given to the world, where it has a status and career as a living work of art. First of all, many different people are going to perform it, and on some occasions it will sound like a ghost of itself, if not (worse yet) a caricature. This contrast is so great that many musicians and psychologists have maintained there is no such thing as *the* piece, say Bach's first fugue in the *Well-Tempered Clavichord* (C-major), but as many pieces as there are performers of it, or even as many as its actual performances. What we call "the C-major fugue" is, they say, really a class of pieces, having only those properties in common which are symbolized by the notational devices of the score.

This is the sort of statement one meets with frequently in studio conversation; its protagonists are proud to designate it as "heretical," because what interests them is chiefly its divergence from common-sense opinion, which they call the "orthodox" view, as though there were a real body of doctrine behind what is casually accepted, and they were called upon to oppose its tenets. But the purpose of the heresy is not to evoke a far-reaching philosophical discussion; it is to justify, and even glorify, some unusual "liberty," say in this or that rendition of the Bach fugues, inattention to stylistic elements, questionable transcriptions, and so forth. Were the "heterodox" theory philosophically intended, the first part of it would not be a sweeping assertion, "there is no such thing as '*the* piece,' " but an answerable, though difficult question: "What do we mean by '*the* piece'?" And the second part—"There are as many pieces as performers, or even performances"—would be: "Where 'the piece' is taken to mean a complete, audible work, it is really a new phenomenon, somehow closely related to what we call 'the piece' in another sense, namely the composer's opus." Then the force of the disjunction—"performers *or* even performances" would present itself to open the next gambit, and so forth. For there is, of course, some truth in the "heresy," but it is not simple, and the only way to find it is to separate and study the several issues that are confusedly involved in the statement.

Let us begin with the first serious question: in speaking of a piece of music which almost everyone knows, e.g. the first fugue in the *Well-Tempered Clavichord,* what do we mean by "*the* piece," so called and known? We mean an organically developed illusion of time in audible passage. Here at once we stumble upon an ambiguity; for "audible" may refer to real or imaginary hearing. To a person who can read music as readily as most people read language, music becomes audible by the perusal of a score, as words do in ordinary reading. So one is naturally led to ask: Is silent reading of music the same sort of experience as silent reading of literature? If everyone were taught in early childhood to read music, as we are all taught to read words, would most people find musical satisfaction in silent reading, as they find literary satisfaction in perusing books?

Calvin Brown, in *Music and Literature: A Comparison of the Arts,* answers these questions with a simple "yes." Having remarked that silent reading of music is possible, he considers it proof enough that tonal structures and word structures are "presented to the ear" in the same essential way.[1] Yet there is a radical difference, which he overlooks, but which comes to light if one holds consistently to the central problem of *what is created* in a work of art: in music, the passage of time made audible by purely sonorous elements. These elements exist for the ear alone; all the musical helps to our actual perception of time are eliminated and replaced by tonal experiences in the musical image of duration. But the elements of literature are not sounds as such; even in poetry, words are not *merely* to be heard; instead of being pure sense objects that may become "natural" symbolic forms, like shapes and tones, they are symbols already, namely "assigned" symbols, and the artistic illusion created by means of them is not a fabric of *tönend bewegte Formen,* but a different illusion altogether. The phenomenon of silent reading, therefore, occurs in both arts, but has different values in the two respective contexts.

In music the relation of inward hearing and actual hearing underlies a whole phase of artistic production: the work of the performer. In this connection, then, it merits some exact study, which shows it to be more interesting than a vague general conception of it would let one suppose. The two kinds of hearing—physical and mental—differ from each other in ways that are not generally recognized, and their differences must be understood before one can find their exact relationships in musical experience.

Physical hearing, the actual sensory perception of sound, depends on the nature of an outside stimulus, and on what the sense organ transmits and the attentive mind registers, either as actual memory, or as "mental set" for further receptions. Even intelligent listening is to some degree passive, determined by the external cause. It is in large measure selective, filtering out what is irrelevant; yet a certain amount of irrelevancy always seeps through. Our perceptual apparatus is made for practical purposes, and only more or less successfully adapted to artistic ones. Those aspects of the physical tone which have practical importance tend,

---

[1]See p. 8: "No one mistakes the printed notes on a sheet of music for *music;* they are simply symbols which tell a performer what sounds he is to produce, and the sounds themselves are the music. Precisely the same thing holds true for literature and no illiterate would ever be guilty of this confusion. In fact, the only reason that we do not make the same error with respect to music is that we are largely musical illiterates."

therefore, to force themselves on our attention, and the more passively we listen the more prominently do they figure in what we hear. They are the most direct stimuli, the "sense data" given to the ear. Of course, human minds differ even in their sensitivity to such physical impressions; perception is so much influenced by conception that complete mental passivity would probably amount to insensibility. There are degrees of immediacy in our hearing, and perhaps the best way to determine these is to note what elements of musical experience we miss by careless listening, i.e. by giving only superficial attention, as a distracted or indifferent concertgoer does.

We do not miss the absolute pitch. This is not to say that we know *which* tone we hear, but each sound is heard to be just so and so high, according to the physical vibrations that cause it. Secondly, we hear its absolute duration. This is directly given; though we do not note what its value is, it lasts for a definite length of time. Thirdly, its timbre— the tone quality of brass or woodwind, viol or pianoforte or human voice. Where several instruments play together the orchestral timbre that prevails for the casual ear is indeed something nameless, yet the sheer impression of it is inescapably "given." In the fourth place, volume; loudness and softness are always directly heard, without special mental effort. So is a general quality of consonance or dissonance, though this varies widely, especially with the listener's habitual exposure to dissonant sounds (a person used to jazz becomes fairly indifferent to harmonic conflicts). Finally there is the element of stress. Dynamic accents are the most intrusive auditory effects. No matter how absent-mindedly we listen, we hear sharp attack, rhythmic beat or swing, gentle or stormy or speedy motion, and we hear it at some perfectly definite tempo.

What we miss by inattentive hearing is the logical connectedness of the tonal sequence. We have no clear awareness of what has passed, and therefore no impression of melodic or harmonic development, nor definite expectation of what is to come. Consequently, in what one might call purely physical listening, we can be startled by a sudden *sforzando*, without being puzzled at its unexpected incursion. We hear succession rather than progression, and miss all subordinate melody; where there is no obvious "tune" we may miss all melody whatever. Only the shifting actual tones, with specific pitch, endurance, timbre, volume, and over-all harshness or smoothness, pass at some definite tempo—hurrying, or easy, or interminably drawn out.

For mental hearing, as it is experienced in silent reading, exactly the opposite conditions hold: those tonal properties which are most definitely given to the physical ear, surviving even inattentive listening, are the very ones that may be quite vague or even completely lacking to the inward ear. To a person who cannot spontaneously identify an absolute pitch, the written note, say , means a more or less arbitrary sound, somewhere near the middle of the soprano register. He may or may not hear it as of a particular timbre, piano or voice or viol sound; certainly its tonal quality is not as definite as that of a physical sound, which is uniquely given, a good or a bad tone. Volume is only imagined where the composition obviously aims at the utmost power, or has prepared a special pianissimo. Moreover, the real length of tones is not always "heard," though it is somehow understood; in reading a slow movement one tends to read faster than the performance would pass in actual time.[2] One never misses structural elements, such as harmonic tensions and their resolutions, melody, even to the smallest figure, preparation and fulfillment, i.e. progression, theme and development, imitations, answers, and the essentially musical (rather than kinetic) rhythm that emerges from the deployment of harmonic changes and melodic accents. Inward hearing is a work of the mind, that begins with conceptions of form and ends with their complete presentation in imagined sense experience. It is supported by all sorts of symbolic devices: the guidance of printed scores, the specific, though minute muscular responses of breath and vocal cords that constitute subvocal singing, perhaps individual tonal memories and other references to experience. But the influence of exactly remembered sense impressions is very variable; inward hearing usually stops short of just that determinateness of quality and duration which characterizes actual sensation. This final imagination of tone itself, as something completely decided by the whole to which it belongs, requires a special symbolic support, a highly articulate bodily gesture; overtly, this gesture is the act of producing the tone, the per-

---

[2]I assert this on the authority of an eminent musician, Kurt Appelbaum, against whose wide experience I have checked my own observations.

former's expression of it; physiologically, it is the *feeling* for the tone in the muscles set to produce it, and is the symbol whereby the tone is imagined. Probably all aural imagination apart from such symbolic action is somewhat incomplete, unless it is based on a vivid memory of actually heard music.

Most composers carry the act of creative imagination from its inception as a "commanding form," or matrix idea (which Mendelssohn called "the composition"), to a point somewhere *before* the full realization of the musical work, which is the performed piece. The composer's piece is an incompleted work, but it is a perfectly definite piece carried to a perfectly definite stage. When we speak of "the first fugue in the *Well-Tempered Clavichord*," we mean something that is there for anybody's inward hearing, and may be completed by carrying out its tonal articulation to the limit, which is complete determinateness. A very competent musician may be able to do this in sheer imagination. As a rule, however, the performer's imagination is progressive, and is helped from moment to moment by the actuality of tone already realized in playing.

Performance is the completion of a musical work, a logical continuation of the composition, carrying the creation through from thought to physical expression. Obviously, then, the thought must be entirely grasped, if it is to be carried on. Composition and performance are not neatly separable at the stage marked by the finishing of the score; for both spring from the commanding form and are governed throughout by its demands and enticements. No general theory of phrasing, tempo, or study of periods and styles can enable the performer of a piece to begin his work at the printed page; all such general knowledge is a mere help in orientation, a knowledge of probabilities that may speed his understanding of the essential movement expressed in the score. The successive note-by-note reading that is a reaction pattern comparable to a typist's keyboard habit is not reading.[3] A well-trained typist would not claim to have read a book just because she has copied it; and many a sight reader at the piano has never read a piece of music, but only

---

[3]Robert Schumann, in his "Musikalische Haus-und Lebensregeln," wrote for the benefit of young students: "Only when the form is quite clear to you, will you understand its import." (*Gesammelte Schriften*, II, 170.)

reacted manually to the stimulus of note after note. Even the rendering of phrase after phrase, treating each one as a separate item, is not performing a piece; it is like a formal recitation:

"I, John"—"*I, John*"—
"Take thee, Mary"—"*Take thee, Mary*"—
"To be my wedded wife"—"*To be my wedded wife.*"

Or it might be compared to the reading of a Greek text by a person who knows perfectly well how to pronounce the words, and can speak continuously, raising his voice at the commas, dropping it at the periods, and pausing between the paragraphs, yet understands only occasional bits of what he prates.

Real performance is as creative an act as composition, just as the composer's own working out of the idea, after he has conceived the greatest movement and therewith the whole commanding form, is still creative work. The performer simply carries it on. He may be the composer himself; in that case, what he carries to completion may be a composition he has previously thought out, perhaps even written out (then he is said to "play his own piece"), or he may be inventing it then and there ("improvising"). If he is not the composer, then the commanding form is given to him; a variable but usually considerable amount of detail in the development of the form is given[4]; but the final decision of *what every tone sounds like* rests with him. For at a definite, critical point in the course of musical creation a new feeling sets in, that reinforces the tonal imagination, and at the same time is subject to it: the feeling of utterance.

A person in whom the feeling of utterance is strong and precise is a natural virtuoso. But such strength and precision are not the same thing as a mere desire for emotional expression. Artistic utterance always strives to create as complete and transparent a symbol as possible, whereas personal utterance, under the stress of actual emotion, usually contents itself with half-articulated symbols, just enough to explain the *symptoms* of inward pressure. Where music serves the primary purpose of direct emo-

---

[4]The mediaeval *numae*, because of their inexact meanings, required a great deal of judgment on the part of the performers. In modern notation the minimal prescription was the figured bass, which presupposed the performer's competence to carry out what today we consider definitely a part of the composer's work.

tive expression, the feeling of utterance is not altogether controlled by inward hearing, but is confused by unmusical gesture that is only imperfectly assimilated to the process of tone production. As a result, the dynamic stresses in every passage are exaggerated beyond the requirements of the melodic and harmonic tensions which, logically and artistically, they should simply illuminate; the effect is "romantic" in the bad sense.[5] In speech, a similar discrepancy between meaning and passional emphasis is called "oratorical." It is usually attributed to a lack of restraint, but that is not really its source. A performer whose utterance is inspired entirely by the commanding form of the work does not have to restrain anything, but gives all he has—all his feeling for every phrase, every resolving or unresolving harmonic strain in the work. Inward hearing, the muscular imagination of tone, the desire for outward hearing: these condition the final stage of making a musical work.

The possession of what I can only term "muscular imagination," the basis of vocal or instrumental technique, does not always accompany the power of inner hearing which is the foundation of all musical thinking. Many composers follow out their creative work only to a point short of complete tonal imagination; to them, the form is complete and self-evident before it reaches overt expression. In fact, their command of it sometimes fails in the last phase, so they actually perform their own work very imperfectly. Others are natural virtuosos; in many cases their thinking runs so infallibly the whole gamut from the first musical conception to and through the performed piece that their music sounds dedicated to the instrument. Chopin's pianistic art seems to have had a part in his very first thoughts. Chopin was truly and primarily a composer, so the influence of the piano was only one factor in his thinking, but when a person who is above all a performer turns his hand to composition, the power of the instrument becomes paramount; Kreisler's occasional compositions, for instance, sound as though they were suggested immediately by the vibrant strings, like cadenzas, impromptu variations, melodious *études;* the matrix is simple and small, the chief interest and enticement of the work is its easy, high development into physical tone.

Generally, however, the two kinds of musical imagination which may

---

[5]There is also "romantic music" in a good sense—music so composed that the genuinely tonal tensions motivate a great deal of dynamic coloring.

be called, respectively, conceptual and sonorous (to avoid the slippery word "interpretive"), occur separately; and the form of inward hearing that is necessary to a conceptual imagination, the composer's characteristic gift, is suggestive rather than fully sensuous. The significance of its sketchy quality is that such hearing is abstractive, concerned with the fundamental relationships whereby sound becomes music, a significant tonal form. The sonorous imagination, on the other hand, works toward the final goal of artistic conception—communication of the "Idea," articulate utterance.

This brings us to the problem of "self-expression" in a new and deepened form: not the subjective interpretation that makes art a vehicle for the performer's personal anxieties and moods, but the element of *ardor for the import conveyed*. This, of course, is actual feeling; it is not something symbolized by the music, but something that makes the symbol effective; it is the contagious excitement of the artist over the vital content of the work. Where it is missing, the symbol is "cold." But, being an actual and not virtual phenomenon, artistic "warmth" can never be planned and assured by any technical device. It shows itself in the final product, but always as an unconscious factor. In the plastic arts its mark is passionate presentation of the "Idea" from the first stroke to the last. In music it is the quality of impassioned utterance.

This quality belongs naturally to the human voice. But the voice is so much more an instrument of biological response than of art that all actual emotions, crude or fine, deep or casual, are reflected in its spontaneously variable tone. It is the prime avenue of self-expression, and in this demonstrative capacity not really a musical instrument at all. As Joseph Goddard remarked, "from intonation to melody is a jump. . . . So from timbre to harmony is a jump. . . . Intonation in language still fulfills that practical function of expression in virtue of which it was first developed. But melody and harmony have no practical function whatever; . . . they give rise to quite new orders of sensation."[6] Throughout its career as a bearer of musical ideas, the voice keeps its readiness for pathos, its association with actual feeling—what a German would call its *Lebensnähe*.

---

[6]Joseph Goddard: *The Deeper Sources of the Beauty and Expression in Music*, p. 23.

As long as direct pathos, springing from emotions of the moment, predominates in vocal utterance, the voice may be wailing or crooning or jubilating ever so freely, but it is not singing. Music begins only when some formal factor—rhythm or melody—is recognized as a framework within which accent and intonation are elements in their own right, not chance attributes of individual speech. Perhaps, in early religious life, the desire to make choric prayer reach further than the loudest speech, with less vocal effort and more articulation than in shouting, led people to discover the power of intonation to "carry" their words. We do not know. But as soon as syllables are fixed on a definite pitch, the breath has to be sustained, the vowels take precedence over the consonants, which merely serve to hold them apart, and the sound of the utterance, rather than the discourse, becomes the notable phenomenon; therefore, incantation would be a natural beginning of genuine song. On this level of speech organization the rich and variable ways of articulating sounds become apparent. Long or short vowels, open-mouthed and close-mouthed ones, sharp or soft consonants, syllabic accents, and such formal similarities as alliteration, rhyme, and rhythmic analogy, which are rarely noted in talking, tend to be conspicuous. All these factors serve to shift interest from the literal content of the words, the thing said, to the tonal form, the thing sung. Enunciation, originally intended to create words, now creates sonorities that are valued as ends rather than means; it punctuates and elaborates the full-throated tone that "carries" the words, and the product is an audible form, a piece of music.

Naturally the voice, even in chant, would be charged with so many emotional strains that its musical function would constantly be in jeopardy. The abstraction of such elements as pitch and measure (especially the complicated poetic measure of religious speech) is not easy in midst of a personal utterance. Formal concepts, before they are entirely familiar and clear, need reinforcement if they are not to slip away again. In primitive chant, the measure is often upheld by clapping or stamping. But such activity tends to interfere with music-hearing as much as to help it, because it is perceived more kinetically (as actual participation) than audibly (as sense impression). The drum, therefore, marks a great advance. With relatively little physical effort it furnishes a sharp, exact, and primarily audible accent, which can be manipulated far more easily and freely than gymnastic poundings. Its technique can be developed by individuals, which makes for virtuosity. Even monotone chanting to good drumming is unmistakably music, however schematic and bare it may sound to the tonally trained ear. But the crucial step in music is the conception of *melos,* the fixation and artistic use of pitch; and this probably owes its existence in large part to the discovery of inanimate, physical sources from which sounds of definite pitch may be obtained by plucking, striking, rubbing, or blowing. By means of pitched instruments, intonation is at once objectified; instruments furnish a standard to which vocal pitch may be held.

In Europe, where music has certainly had its fullest development, melody instruments were used for centuries primarily to accompany song. An important exception is the flute, which achieved an early independence for two reasons: first, that it is a variant of the shepherd's pipe, which was invented by solitary men who could either blow on a reed or sing, but not both, so the existence of wordless, instrumental music was revealed to them by the very limitation of their means; and secondly, that among early instruments the woodwinds come nearest to having a vocal quality.

The essential contributions of voice and instruments, respectively, come from opposite poles in the realm of music. The structural elements are evolved most easily by the aid of vibrant strings and pipes, whose fully developed range far exceeds that of any voice, or even the combined ranges of high and low voices. Vocal music can only approximate to the flexibility, the distinctness, the tonal and rhythmic accuracy of instruments. Jumps of intonation, figures, trills, and runs that are easy on the violin or the piano are a singer's dream of technical control. The voice as an instrument, free from all interference by the physiological duties of the lungs, emotional constrictions of the throat, or the non-musical habits of the tongue, is the ideal that governs his tonal imagination and work. By listening and by practice he purifies the element that is the dangerous, but chief and irreplaceable asset of vocal music —the element of *utterance.*

The player's problem is the opposite. The conceptual framework of melody and harmony is expressed by the very construction of musical instruments, but the semblance of song is something achieved only in the course of their gradual perfection, and above all in their use under the stimulation of "kinetic hearing." Instrumental music strives for the expressiveness of song, the sound of direct utterance, "voice."

This, I believe, is the basis of the qualitative difference, which has often been noted, between singing and all other kinds of music.[7] It is not, as Goddard thought, the power of our emotional association with the voice that makes it pre-eminently "human," but the fact that utterance, which is an intellectual function of the human organism, has always a fundamentally vital form. When it is abstracted from any actual context, as in music-conscious song, it becomes art, but it keeps its *Lebensnähe*. The fact that song grows in musical power by constant formalization, approaching the sound of instruments, whereas all other sources of tone are somewhat schematic and lifeless until they attain "voice," the semblance of singing, marks a peculiar dialectic in the total phenomenon of music, which accounts, perhaps, for the existence of two distinct talents —the inventive, at home in musical abstraction, and the interpretive, centering on the kinetic tonal imagination that leads to the making of perfectly intended and controlled sounds. The latter kind is derived from the natural connection between mind and voice. On this basis, the development of song is not too hard to understand; but what is truly puzzling is the emergence, with the evolution of sonorous instruments, of something that can only be called "utterance" in playing. There is a transference of the ideo-motor response from the vocal organs to the hand. A musician's hands, supplemented by his familiar instrument, become as intuitively responsive to imagined tone as the throat. No one could possibly figure out, or learn by rote, the exact proper distance on the fingerboard for every possible interval; but conceive the interval

---

[7]For example, Joseph Goddard: "When music is produced by the human voice it ceases to be naked in associations, being then enrobed in the manifold associations of humanity. . . . It is this vast change from abstract sound to sound rich in human associations—from tones strange to tones familiar—which we feel as so striking and grateful when human voices break in on instrumental music. In vocal music the mystic features of musical sound have a human aspect. Thus it is that high musical emanation in vocal form has something of the character of inspired utterance." (*Op. cit.*, pp. 87–88.)

The same contrast in feeling was noted by Guido M. Gatti, "Composer and Listener," *Musical Quarterly*, XXXIII, 1 (January, 1947), 52–63; Schumann, *op. cit.*, II; Günther Stern, "Zur Phänomenologie des Zuhörens," *Zeitschrift für Musikwissenschaft*, IX (1926–27), 610–619; and by Francis Tovey, *op. cit.*, V, 1.

clearly and the finger will find it precisely, and even adjust, after a single exploration, to an instrument that frets a tiny bit differently from the accustomed standard. As for the varying qualities and nuances of tone, produced chiefly by the bow, they depend patently on "kinetic hearing." The mind hears, the hand follows, as faithfully as the voice itself obeys the "inward ear."[8] That is probably why the natural and the artificial instrument, direct and indirect utterance, can finally merge as completely as they do in the masterpieces of opera, cantata, and lyric song, which are very close to perfect form completely uttered.

It also means that the instrumentalist as well as the singer has a psychologically sensitive medium at his disposal; so the values and dangers of personal feeling are the same for the one as for the other. *As long as personal feeling is concentrated on the musical content, i.e. the significance of the piece, it is the very nerve and "drive" of the artist's work.* It is the dynamism which makes him create the audible symbol in the way that seems to him clearest, most fully perceivable, most impressive. This is intense conception, which makes for the utmost power of musical expression. Every tension and movement in the frame of created time seems like a personal emotion, but one that lives apart from the concerns of the actual day.

If, on the other hand, the player lets his own need for some emotional catharsis make the music simply his outlet, he is likely to play passionately, with exciting dynamics, but the work will lack intensity because its expressive forms are inarticulate and blurred. The performance is a symptom of emotion, and like all such symptoms—laughter, tears, trembling—it is contagious for the moment; but no one carries anything away from such a personal exhibition, because passage after passage of the

---

[8]Cf. Philippe Fauré-Fremiet, *Pensée et ré-création:* "I recite, in my mind, each note with its right time-value and my entire nervous system is so spontaneously keyed to it that my fingers are practically at the point of execution. Again, I think a particular melodic theme, a development, and I think this also note by note like a concrete reality and with its proper time-values . . . If it is given to woodwinds or cellos, for instance, it does not evoke in me any apparent impulse to give manual expression to it, but I almost hum it, as if my throat and lips had been in turn alerted, as if I were going to sing, or more exactly to reproduce it, transposing. . . . I almost live the piece with my whole being, the entire gamut of my physical resources, and in a time and pace with which I cannot permit myself any liberties whatever, because the expression I am seeking depends on it." (Pp. 32–33.)

composition, deriving logically from a central movement, has been cut short of its natural completion and adapted to convey a new and extraneous feeling.

Yet every performer has what one might call a "proper repertoire," consisting of the pieces he is temperamentally able to play: music that is within his emotional ken. For, although he need not have actually experienced every feeling he conveys, he must be able to *imagine* it, and every idea, whether of physical or psychical things, can be formed only within the context of experience. That is to say, a form of sentience, thought, or emotion that he can imagine must be *possible for him*. Within the range of his own emotional possibilities, however, he can even learn, purely through music, some way of feeling that he never knew before.[9] In the rich fabric of our own subjective existence we make discoveries, as we make them in the outer world, by the agency of adequate symbols. Through art we learn the character and range of subjective experience, as through discourse we learn in great detail the ways of the objective world.

Oddly enough, the player who projects irrelevant feelings into music, emotional fragments of his own life, is the one who is in danger of exhibiting "mere technique," because he is not thinking the music entirely. Since he does play what is written, all the details of his playing that are mentally unrealized are sheer physical responses, and give the impression that his fingers are "prating" except for the expression of musically unmotivated and unintended passions. The intricacies of the composition receive no meaning from the commanding form itself, and especially if they pass swiftly he cannot adapt them to his own emotions, which have no such distinct and elaborate form; so he rattles off whole passages simply because they are written, and all he conveys is the fact that he can make the mechanical responses to so many notes. But if a virtuoso is free of confusing emotions to think in musical forms and feel only

---

[9]The following account was given me by one of the great pianoforte artists, in conversation: "When I first read a composition, I conceive it according to the range of my experience. But as I study it, there comes a point—sometimes after a long time, but always quite definitely and rather suddenly—when I feel that my personality has changed under the influence of the piece. I have learned to feel a new way, or to understand a new feeling. Then I have grasped the musical idea, and practice differently—practice entirely to articulate."

their import, the highest physical achievement is absorbed by the thing rendered, the organized virtual duration, the image of sentient life. He cannot suffer from too much technique: it is his mental articulateness and his power of utterance.

So far our whole concern has been with the making of music; but there is another, equally important function, namely listening, which exhibits almost as great a range between utmost effectiveness and total obtuseness as we find in performance. Musical hearing is itself a talent, a special intelligence of the ear, and like all talents it develops through exercise. A person used to listening takes in with ease the most extended or involved compositions, whereas even a naturally musical individual without a background of much music, perhaps casually heard, but often heard, finds it hard to listen for more than a few minutes. That is probably why provincial concerts, lay orchestras, and even fairly serious amateurs' clubs usually present programs consisting of short pieces and snatches of longer works: one movement of a sonata, one movement of a trio, the Serenade from Haydn's Quartet, Op. 3 No. 5, and so forth. The audience cannot listen to a whole Haydn quartet or a whole Beethoven sonata.

The first principle in musical hearing is not, as many people assume, the ability to distinguish the separate elements in a composition and recognize its devices, but to experience the primary illusion, to feel the consistent movement and recognize at once the commanding form which makes this piece an inviolable whole. Even young children do this when they listen delightedly to a tune. If their elders make more ambitious music in the home, and the children are taught as a matter of courtesy to keep reasonably quiet during a performance, their listening power will grow by incidental use, as their power of reading grows whenever they read signs, headlines, and captions here or there. Lying in bed and hearing good singing or playing before going to sleep is a natural education. The radio, of course, offers all the means of learning to listen, but it also harbors a danger—the danger of learning *not* to listen; and this is greater, perhaps, than its advantage. People learn to read and study with music —sometimes beautiful and powerful music—going on in the background. As they cultivate inattention or divided attention, music as such becomes more and more a mere psychological stimulant or sedative (as the case may be, both functions are possible), which they enjoy even during conversation. In this way they cultivate *passive hearing,* which is the very contradiction of *listening.*

The real basis of music appreciation is the same as of music making: the recognition of forms in virtual time, charged with the vital import of all art, the ways of human feeling. It is the perception of feeling through a purely apparent flow of life existing only in time. Anything the listener does or thinks of to make this experience more telling is musically good. This is not to say, however, that anything people like to do during music is good, since they often confuse "enjoying music" with enjoying themselves unmusically during music. But anything that helps concentration and sustains the illusion—be it inward singing, following a half-comprehended score, or dreaming in dramatic images—may be one's personal way to understanding. For *listening* is the primary musical activity. The musician listens to his own idea before he plays, before he writes. The basis of all musical advance is more comprehensive hearing. And the one support that every artist must have if he is to go on creating music is a world that listens.

Chapter ten

THE PRINCIPLE OF ASSIMILATION

In the previous chapter the special character of vocal music was considered at some length because it brought the problem of personal utterance into clearest focus. This, however, is not the only philosophical issue that arises peculiarly in the realm of song. A second and equally fundamental one is the much-debated principle of "purity" of the artistic medium. For song is normally wedded to words. It probably began with the intonation of words, to make them more potent in prayer or magic. In earlier times, song and poetry are supposed to have been one, for all recitation was intoned. Throughout the history of music the importance of words has been asserted by one school and denied by another. The Italian *Camarati* regarded the conveyance of the words as the prime office of music; the popes have protested against elaborate anthems and cantatas which obscured the sacred texts, pulled them apart or overlapped the lines so no sentence could be heard plainly. Gluck, in the famous dedication of *Alceste* to the Archduke Leopold of Tuscany, is supposed to have asserted the primacy of words over music in opera, though I do not think his statement should be taken to mean that the work is, in effect, poetry or even drama rather than music. Gluck is universally regarded as a composer, not a dramatist, nor an arranger of Calzabigi's poetry for the stage; and no one, to my knowledge, has ever spoken of the piece as Calzabigi's play with music by Gluck. This indicates that however superficially people may paraphrase the words of his preface, their artistic perception belies the theory they have read into them. The true meaning of Gluck's deference to the text will be evident a little later, so we may postpone the issue here.

The historical fact is that no matter what doctrines about the relationship between words and music have held sway, composers have made as free as they liked with their texts. Bach has sometimes followed the verbal pattern faithfully in recitative fashion, sometimes built his music on the already composed poetic line, as in the chorales, and sometimes torn the sentences asunder, repeating phrases or separate words, and weaving these fragments of language into the most intricate vocal *fugati*, for instance in the motets. Palestrina had done all those things before him, Mozart did them after him, Prokofiev does them today. Yet no one could have more understanding or respect for words than Bach had for the sacred texts. What all good composers do with language is neither to ignore its character, nor to obey poetic laws, but to transform the entire verbal material—sound, meaning, and all—into musical elements.

When words enter into music they are no longer prose or poetry, they are elements of the music. Their office is to help create and develop the primary illusion of music, virtual time, and not that of literature, which is something else; so they give up their literary status and take on purely musical functions. But that does not mean that now they have only sound-value. Here the theory of David Prall, that the "aesthetic surface" of music is pure sound in orders of pitch, loudness, and timbre, and that in hearing music we perceive designs in the compass of this "aesthetic surface," requires a little emendation if it is not to lose its significance in the face of some of the greatest musical endeavors—song, cantata, oratorio and opera. *For what we perceive is not the aesthetic surface.* What we hear is motion, tension, growth, living form—the illusion of a many-dimensional time in passage. The "aesthetic surface" is something that underlies this illusion. If we assume an "aesthetic attitude" and try to perceive only the abstracted tonal elements, we really discount the forcible semblance in order to understand its sensory vehicle. Such an interest commits us to the principle of treating words as pure phonemes, and leads into artificialities that increase in proportion to the freedom and power of vocal and dramatic music; for in the composer's imagination words simply do not figure as vowels held apart by consonants, despite the fact that intonation stresses their phonetic attributes, and gives these, too, possible independent functions in the audible structure.

The work is, as Prall says, composed of sounds; but everything that gives the sounds a different appearance of motion, conflict, repose, emphasis, etc., is a musical element. Anything that binds figures together, contrasts or softens them, in short: *affects the illusion,* is a musical element.

Words may enter directly into musical structure even without being literally understood; the *semblance of speech* may be enough. The most striking illustration of this principle is found in plain-song. In such mediaeval chant the tonal material is reduced to the barest minimum: a single melodic line, small in compass, without polyphonic support, without accompaniment, without regular recurrent accent or "beat." Play such a line on the piano or on any melody instrument, it sounds poor and trivial, and seems to have no particular motion. But as soon as the words are articulated it moves, its wandering rhythmic figures cease to wander as they incorporate intoned speech rhythms, and the great Latin words fill the melodic form exactly as chords and counterpoints would fill it. The fact that the syllables supporting the tones are concatenated by their non-musical, original character into words and sentences, causes the tones to follow each other in a more organic sequence than the mere succession which they exhibit in an instrumental paraphrase. It is not the sentiment expressed in the words that makes them all-important to Gregorian chant; it is the cohesion of the Latin line, the simplicity of statement, the greatness of certain words, which causes the composer to dwell on these and subordinate what is contextual to them. Even a person who has no inkling of Greek—perhaps does not recognize the incursion of Greek words into the Latin mass—feels the sacred import of the text:

> *Kyrie Eleison,*
> *Christe Eleison,*

because the exploitation of those four words is a full musical event.[1]

Furthermore, the paucity of musical means requires the vividness and warmth that belong to the human voice. But where words and voice are pitted against such very slight formal elements as homophonic melody without bar lines, without any tonic-and-dominant anchorage, without the mechanically fixed pitch that strings or pipes assure, there is an ob-

---

[1]This function of the text persists in later music. Francis Tovey says of the "Magnificat" of Bach's *B-minor Mass:* "It is a concerto in which the chorus-voices play the part of the solo-instrument." (*Essays in Musical Analysis,* V, 52.) The one word is "Magnificat."

vious danger of losing the artistic illusion altogether under the impact of personal utterance. Here the work demands something to assure its impersonality and objectivity; and in fact, it keeps these virtues mainly by the formalities of its performance. Choric song is a strong antidote to sentimentalism, because the expressions of actual feeling that threaten the musical illusion cancel each other out in group singing. A chorus, therefore, is always an impersonal influence. Where this safeguard does not operate—that is, where a single cantor intones the service—it is the spirit of his vicariate, his own depersonalized status, that preserves the artistic integrity of the chant, which is conceived as something objective and efficacious and not as an opportunity for self-expression. The self with all its actual desires is in abeyance as the priest celebrates his office.

The point of this whole discussion of plain-song is to show by a classic example how music may absorb and utilize phenomena that do not belong to its normal material, the "aesthetic surface" of tones in their several relational orders, at all. But whatever importations it admits to its precincts it transforms, lock, stock, and barrel, into *musical elements*. What helps and what hinders musical expression depends on what the primary illusion can completely swallow up. The sense of words, the fervor of utterance, devotional duties, choric responses—these are all foreign materials, but in so far as they affect the image of time, either by assuring its dissociation from actual experience, or stressing its vital import, or furnishing genuine structural factors, they are virtual elements in a realm of purely musical imagination. Anything that can enter into the vital symbolism of music belongs to music, and whatever cannot do this has no traffic with music at all.

When words and music come together in song, music swallows words; not only mere words and literal sentences, but even literary word-structures, poetry. Song is not a compromise between poetry and music, though the text taken by itself be a great poem; song is music. It need not even have, in the strict European sense, melody; a monotone chant punctuated with changing chords,[2] an African drummed piece on which the long, wailing declamation breaks in, rising and falling within a stationless tonal continuum, is song, not speech. The principles of music

---

[2]An example of this is given—in European music, at that—by Karl Orff's *Antigone*.

govern its form no matter what materials it uses, from rattling gourds to holy names.

When a composer puts a poem to music, he annihilates the poem and makes a song. That is why trivial or sentimental lyrics may be good texts as well as great poems. The words must convey a *composable* idea, suggest centers of feeling and lines of connection, to excite a musician's imagination. Some composers, for instance Beethoven, are thus excited by great literature[3]; others find a musical core in quite insignificant verses as often as in real poetry. Schubert has composed the undeniably second-rate poems of Müller into a song cycle just as beautiful and important as his settings of Heine's and Shakespeare's poetic treasures. Müller's works are much poorer literature, but just as good texts; and in the musical works to which they have given rise their inferiority is redeemed, because as poetry they have disappeared.

Eminent aestheticians have repeatedly declared that the highest form of song composition is a fusion of perfect poetry with perfect music.[4] But actually a very powerful poem is apt to militate against all music. Robert Schumann made this discovery when he turned from his original literary and critical interests to musical composition. In his youth he wrote an essay "On the Intimate Relationship between Poetry and Music," in which he said, after a long, romantic passage in praise of each separate art: "Still greater is the effect of their union: greater and fairer, when the simple tone is enhanced by the winged syllable, or the hovering word is lifted on the melodious billows of sound, when the light rhythm of verse is gently combined with the orderly measure of the bars in gracious alternation. . . ."[5] This is typical literary music criticism,

---

[3]Bettina Brentano, in a letter to Goethe, tells him of Beethoven's comments on his poetry, quoting the composer's words from her excellent memory: "Goethe's poems have great power over me, not only because of their content, but by their rhythm. I get excited, and put into the mood for composing by this language that seems to build itself up like a work of higher spiritual beings, and to contain already the secret of its harmonies. It forces me to pour out the melody in all directions, from the burning-point of my enthusiasm. I pursue it, passionately overtake it again. . . . I cannot part from it, and with eager joy I have to repeat it in all possible modulations, and in the end, at last, I am triumphant over musical ideas." (Beethoven, *Briefe und Gespräche*, p. 145.)

[4]The most famous is, of course, Wagner, who dreamed of a work that should unite *all* arts on an equal footing, a *Gesamtkunstwerk*.

[5]*Gesammelte Schriften über Musik u. Musiker*, Vol. II, p. 173.

that treats music as a soft romantic accompaniment duplicating the sound-effects of poetry. But as a mature musician he wrote in a different vein. He had produced many songs and knew that the composition of a text was no gentle compromise, no gracious alternation of poetic and musical values. In reviewing Joseph Klein's renderings of the lyrics from Goethe's *Wilhelm Meister*, he said: "To speak frankly, it seems to me that the composer has too much respect for his poem, as though he were afraid to hurt it by seizing it too ardently; so at every turn we find rests, hesitations, embarrassments. But the poem should lie like a bride in the minstrel's arm, free, happy, and entire; then it sounds like something from heaven afar." And further, with special reference to Mignon's song "Kennst du das Land": "Indeed I know no musical setting of this song, except Beethoven's, that can approach the impression it makes all by itself, without music."[6]

Here is the key to a radical difficulty in song writing. A poem that has perfect form, in which everything is said and nothing merely adumbrated, a work completely developed and closed, does not readily lend itself to composition. It will not give up its literary form. This is true of most of Goethe's poems. The poetic creations are so entirely autonomous and self-contained that many abler composers than Klein have shrunk from violating them to transform them into a mere plastic substance for another work, and use them anew as musical elements without independent form. A second-rate poem may serve this purpose better because it is easier for the music to assimilate its words and images and rhythms. On the other hand, some very fine lyrics make excellent texts, for instance Shakespeare's incidental songs, the robust, simple verses of Burns, most of Verlaine's poetry, and notably Heine's. The reason is that all these poets imply as much as they speak; the form is frail, no matter how artful (as it certainly is with Verlaine and Heine), the ideas it conveys are not fully exploited, the feelings not dramatically built up as they are in Goethe's poems. All their potentialities are still there and are emphasized by the ironically casual form. Consequently the poetic work can dissolve again at the touch of an alien imaginative force, and the beautiful, overcharged words—"My love is like a red, red rose"—or: "Les

[6]*Ibid.*, Vol. I, p. 272.

sanglots longues des violons"—can motivate entirely new expressive forms, musical instead of poetic.

This, above all, is what the text must do in all music that is based on words. There is a musical form anciently known as the "air," which begins with a text, but takes from it chiefly the pattern of metric accents to frame a simple, self-contained melody, which may be played without words or sung to any verses that follow its meter. The folk song and the hymn tune are examples of such abstractable vocal music. The air is characteristically neither sad nor happy; but the way it can take such specific coloring from the various words on which it may be carried shows how closely sadness and happiness, exaltation and rage, contentment and melancholy really resemble each other in essence. The same tune may be a drinking song or a national anthem, a ballad or a ditty.[7] But even where words may be freely varied, they are assimilated by the tune as elements that make the music lighter or deeper, drive it forward or hold it back, soften it or slow it. A folk song played without words may be lovely, but it always sounds a little bit simple-minded. It is, in fact, empty, incomplete. Consider the difference between hearing four stanzas of such a song, e.g. "Marleborough s'en va-t-en guerre," in a foreign language, i.e. without being able to understand the words, and hearing the tune played four times in succession on an instrument! The articulation of the words, the element of utterance they contribute, is part of the music, without any literary appeal. Francis Tovey, though I think he never really distinguished the musically important function of the text from its one-time literary functions, none the less recognized its active responsibilities in song, when he wrote: "I have not yet had an opportunity of producing any vocal music without words, such as Medtner's Vocal Sonata or Debussy's *Sirenes,* and so I have not gone into the interesting questions that arise when the human voice thrusts all instruments aside, as it inevitably does, only to disappoint the expectation of human speech."[8]

In so-called "art song," there may be a conscious irony achieved when

---

[7]"The Star-Spangled Banner" appears first as an English drinking song. Thomas Moore's "Believe me, if all those endearing young charms" was written to an Irish air, which was already serving, at the time, as "Fair Harvard."

[8]*Op. cit.,* Vol. V, "Vocal Music," p. 1.

the same words are put to different musical phrases, e.g. in Schubert's "In grün will ich mich kleiden" ("With green will I bedeck me"), where the words "Mein Schatz hat's Grün so gern" ("My love's so fond of green") appear in a bright, high phrase, to be immediately repeated in a low and level one that follows like a somber undertone:

Mein Schatz hat's Grün so gern,   mein Schatz hat's Grün— so gern.

Here the text is the unchanging factor that throws the contrast of the two musically given moods into relief, and unites them in one reference. But, whatever the particular function of the words, they normally enter into the very matrix of the song.[9]

The fundamental principle of art which makes the transformation of a poetic line into musical thought possible is briefly but clearly stated in a little article by Mario Castelnuovo-Tedesco, wherein he says: "The poem must have an 'expressive core'; it should express a 'state of soul.' . . . It should express the 'core' in a perfect, simple and clear, and harmonious form, but without too many words. A certain 'margin' should be left for the music; from this point of view, an intimate and restrained poem is preferable to a too sonorous and decorative one.

". . . When I find a poem that particularly interests me and arouses my emotion, I commit it to memory. . . . After some time . . . I sing it quite naturally; the music is born. . . . So much for the vocal part. But in a song there is also the instrumental part. . . . To produce it properly is a matter of finding the right atmosphere, the 'background,' the

---

[9]There is a letter from Beethoven to his publishers, Breitkopf & Härtel in Leipzig, which bears testimony to this fact: "In the Chorus of the Oratorio 'We have beheld Him,' you have persisted, in spite of my note to adhere to the old text, in adhering to the unfortunate alterations. Good heavens, do they believe in Saxony that the word makes the music? If an unsuitable word can ruin this music, which is certainly so, then one should be happy if one finds that words and music are inseparable, and not try to improve them just because the words in themselves are unpoetic." Beethoven, *op. cit.*, p. 82.

environment that surrounds and develops the vocal line. . . . This something exists in the poetry too. I have already said that every poem-for-music must have, above all, an 'expressive core'—which may be formed of one or several fundamental elements—a core that provides the key to the poem itself. It is this key, it is these elements, that one must discover and to which one must give utterance through almost 'symbolic' musical means."[10]

The principle of assimilation, whereby one art "swallows" the products of another, not only establishes the relation of music to poetry, but resolves the entire controversy about pure and impure music, the virtues and vices of program music, the condemnation of opera as "hybrid," versus the ideal of the *Gesamtkunstwerk*.

There is no such thing as an "inferior" or "impure" *kind* of music. There is only good or bad music. Of course there are different kinds—vocal and instrumental, lyric and dramatic, secular and religious, naive and cultivated—but no kind is "higher" or "purer" than any other. I cannot agree at all with W. J. Henderson (whose book, *What is Good Music?* seems to me a sort of musical etiquette book setting up a social standard of good taste) when he says categorically: "Music unaccompanied by text is called absolute music, and this is surely the highest form of the art."[11] Neither can I subscribe to the opinion of Paul Bertrand, that there are two opposed aims in music making, the one to create form, the other to express feeling, and that the first is the ideal of "pure," the second of "dramatic" music.

"It is universally recognized," says M. Bertrand, "that music, pre-eminently the language of feeling, may be expressed in two very different ways that are essentially distinct.

"Pure music aims above all else at the esthetic grouping of sounds; having no direct recourse to poetry it expresses feeling only in a way that is vague and general, undetermined by precision of language. Here music holds sovereign sway. Having to suffice unto itself, it is compelled to maintain, of itself alone, a balance of form calculated to satisfy the

---

[10]"Music and Poetry: Problems of a Song Writer," *Musical Quarterly*, XXX, no. 1 (January, 1944), 102–111. The phrase, "almost 'symbolic' musical means," indicates he knows the utterance *is* symbolic, but no definition of "symbol" fits the character of a musical work, so he treats his expression as metaphorical.

[11]W. J. Henderson, *What is Good Music?*, p. 87.

intellect at all times and consequently to sacrifice part of its intensity of expression.

"Dramatic music, on the other hand, subordinates music to words, gestures, actions, largely absolving it of all concern as regards balance of form, seeing that poetry, the language of intellect, intervenes in direct fashion, and music simply strengthens it by contributing all the power of expression it can supply.

"These two terms therefore, pure music and dramatic music, do not represent an arbitrary classification of musical productions, but two different—and to some extent opposite—conceptions of the role of music. . . . One of these two conceptions has always grown and developed at the expense of the other."[12]

This passage not only illustrates the popular confusion between musical expression, which is formulation of feeling, and self-expression, the catharsis of more or less inarticulate feeling, but also reveals the inconsistency that vitiates a theory of music based on that confusion. For if music be *"preeminently* the language of feeling," as M. Bertrand says, then why is not pure music purely such a language? Why should the pre-eminent instrument, used alone, be able to express feeling "only in a way that is vague and general"? And if its true function be to act as a sensuous stimulus enhancing the emotionality of drama or poetry, then why should it ever be composed into a mere "esthetic grouping of sounds" to satisfy the intellect?

A theory that makes music appear as an art divided against itself, doing by turns two essentially incommensurable, if not incompatible, things, certainly does not go deep into its problems. The truth is, I think, that the range of musical forms is enormous, as the diversity of vital experiences is enormous, taking in flamboyant passions that can be presented only on a grand scale, and also the profound unspectacular emotive life that demands subtle, intricate, self-contained symbols, intensive and anything but vague, for its articulation. When music is strong and free it can "swallow" and assimilate not only words, but even drama. Dramatic actions, like the "poetic core," become motivating centers of

---

[12]"Pure Music and Dramatic Music," *Musical Quarterly*, IX (1923), 545. (Originally published in French in *Le Ménestrel*, June, 1921, and translated by Fred Rothwell.)

feeling, musical ideas. Mendelssohn, composing Goethe's *Walpurgisnacht,* wrote to the author: "When the Druid makes his sacrifice, and the whole thing becomes so solemn and immeasurably great, one really doesn't need to make up any music for it, the music is so apparent in it already, it is all full of the sound, and I have sung the verses to myself without thinking [about composing them]. . . . I only hope that one will be able to hear in my music how deeply the beauty of the words has moved me."[18]

The simple belief that all arts do the same thing in the same way, only with different sensuous materials, has led most people to a serious misconception concerning the relationship of music to poetry and drama. The text, written in advance, certainly has literary form. If the procedures of the several arts were really analogous, a composer could only translate that form into its musical equivalent. Then it would make sense to say, as Henderson does, that operatic music "is governed absolutely by the text."[14] But a shadow-like following of verse forms and literary concepts does not produce a musical organism. Music must grow from its own "commanding form." Let Mendelssohn speak once more: "I can conceive music [for a poem] only if I can conceive a mood that produces it; mere artfully arranged sounds that aptly follow the accent of the words, *forte* on strong words and *piano* on mild ones, but without really expressing anything, I have never been able to understand. Yet for this poem I can't imagine any other kind of music than this—not intensive, integral, poetic, but accompanying, parallel, musical music; but I don't like that sort."

The expression "musical music" is puzzling at first glance; it becomes clear enough, however, by comparison with the previous term "poetic." The feeling of the poem must enter into the matrix itself. Music in which the very gist of a poem has been incorporated is, I think, what Mendelssohn meant by "poetic" music; specifically, music which does *not* parallel the literary structure. A song conceived "poetically" sounds not as the poem sounds, but as the poem *feels;* in the process of composition, individual words, images, and actions merely present opportunities for the development of the composer's ideas. Details of story or imagery that do not give such openings simply disappear in the new

---

[18]Felix Mendelssohn-Batholdy, *Meisterbriefe,* edited by Ernst Wolff, pp. 37–38.
[14]*Op cit.*, p. 86.

creation; they may be present, but they are not discerned. What he called "musical music," on the other hand, is something independent of the poem, externally similar in structure, but manufactured out of entirely independent material to "match" the verses, which remain essentially unchanged by it.

The measure of a good text, a good libretto, even a good subject for music, is simply its transformability into music; and that depends on the composer's imagination. Thus Mozart, working on *The Abduction from the Serail,* wrote to his father, who had found all sorts of fault with the libretto: "As for Stephanie's work, you are quite right, of course. . . . I know well enough that his versification is not of the best; but it falls in so well with my musical ideas (which are disporting themselves in my head all in advance), that I can't help liking it, and I am ready to bet that in the performance of the work you won't notice any shortcomings."[15]

Because the text must be, first of all, an ingredient in the commanding form, the musical conception as a whole, a conscious collaboration between poet and composer is not really as valuable as people are prone to believe. Not that is it worthless; Mozart certainly availed himself of Stephanie's services in the course of his work,[16] and Beethoven, a much less facile worker than Mozart, wrote an oratorio in a fortnight with the ready aid of his librettist; yet he felt that the union of those entirely subservient words with his music was a *mariage de convenance.* "For my part," he wrote at that time, "I had rather compose even Homer, Klopstock, Schiller. Though they present great difficulties to be overcome, those immortal poets at least are worthy of one's effort."[17]

In view of the practice and comments of these great composers, Wagner's criticism, that the great fault of opera had always been the subordination of the dramatic elements to the whims, inclinations and tastes

[15]Albert Leitzmann, ed., *Mozarts Briefe.* Letter dated at Vienna, October 15, 1781.

[16]In another letter, again to his father, he wrote: "At the beginning of the third act is a charming quintet or rather finale, but I would rather have this at the close of the second act. In order to manage this, a great change has to be wrought, an entirely new departure, and Stephanie is up to his ears in work." *Ibid.,* letter dated Vienna, September 26, 1781.

[17]*Op. cit.,* letter to the *Wiener Gesellschaft der Musikfreunde,* dated January 25, 1824.

of the composer, whereas the drama should really predominate and the music be mere emotional expression accompanying it,[18] sounds oddly pointless and unjustified. Odder yet is the practical effect of his resolution to make music a mere means to enhance the action and lend it emotional intensity. Mozart cut his scores ruthlessly wherever he felt that arias or ensembles impeded the action, or, as he said, "made the scene grow pale and cold, and very embarrassing for the other actors, who had to stand around"; but in Wagner's operas, however exciting the music, the action drags interminably, and the actors stand around most of the time. Above all, no opera is more unmistakably music and not drama. One may hear Wagner's overtures, or *Liebestod,* or *Feuerzauber,* in many a symphony concert; but has any theater company ever offered even his best libretto, the *Meistersinger,* as a play without music? Would anyone think of enacting *Tristan* as spoken tragedy? What holds for his playwrighting holds also for his other non-musical efforts. The spectacle may be ever so grand, the staging ever so ambitious (as in his day the revolving stage for *Parsifal* certainly was), Wagner's theatrical inspiration is not expert stagecraft; the libretto is never great poetry; the scenery he demanded is no more great painting than any other, for scenery is not pictorial art at all; in short, his music drama is not the *Gesammtkunstwerk,* the work-of-all-arts, which he had projected in theory, but a work of music, like all the "reprehensible" operas that went before it.

This brings us back to the first great composer of opera who had proposed to subordinate his music to the dramatic action: Gluck. He, too, produced works essentially musical, though unlike Wagner he took finished plays for his librettos. But the play as such disappears in the great, single, and truly dramatic movement of the music. Not only the emotions of the *personae dramatis,* but the very sense of the action, the scope of the subject, *the feeling of the play as a whole,* are elements in the first musical conception. The music is "subordinated" only in the sense of being *motivated* by the text.

There is a discerning little article by an author who calls himself "an

---

[18]Cf. Richard Wagner, *Gesammelte Schriften und Dichtungen,* Vol. III, "Oper u. Drama," p. 231: "If, then, I declare that the error in the art-form of opera lay in the fact that a means of expression (music) was treated as an end, and the purpose of the expression (drama) as a means, I do so . . . to combat the miserable half-measures that infest our art and criticism."

amateur, who has long pursued musical interests via his instrument, and sometimes in the realm of theory," on the subject of Gluck's dramatic art. Emil Staiger, this modest amateur, conceives the significance of Gluck's project and its musical result in a way that makes his essay a direct testimony to the principle of "assimilation" here discussed.[19]

"Wagner employs music to elucidate the text psychologically and philosophically," says Staiger. "With this intent he develops his *Leitmotiv* device, which permits him to follow every turn of the poetic phrase, to allude to mythical or psychical circumstances and mention things whereof his heroes are perhaps still unaware, or on which they keep discreet silence. But the more Wagner's music traffics with such details of the text, the more is he in danger of losing the larger line. Indeed, the 'Ring' cycle, and even separate parts or acts of it, cannot really be apprehended as a unit except by intellectual reflection on the ideational structure. The great single span is missing in this musical epic. From the depths of the soul his tones and figures arise, endowed with tremendous magic—who could seriously deny that? But they fall back again without support, and only rarely does the work exhibit any great forms.

"Not so Gluck! He too was possessed with a human interest, as much as Wagner. . . . [But] his music seeks to represent his characters not by a *Leitmotiv*—rather, one might say, through tonal relations—chiefly, however, by means of something that really eludes description, a peculiar tracing of musical lines, a sort of melodic profile, which remains unaltered through all external changes. Thus Orpheus, in all his singing, is [the embodiment of] great and noble sorrow, so controlled that even his most moving lament occurs in a major key; and Eurydice is pure chastity, as transparent almost as glass. And if, in comparison with Wagner's intricate psychology, this might be called primitive, we can only say that in just this matter Gluck was guided by a truer dramatic insight, which was lost to Wagner's epoch as it is to ours, but which demands the subordination of psychological interest. . . .

"Hölderlin draws the comparison, somewhere, between the progress of an ancient tragedy and the progress of a poetic verse. A verse has a beginning, and sooner or later reaches a point of highest intonation. Then it sinks back again and dies away. The Attic drama runs a similar

---

[19]See "Glucks Bühnentechnik," in his *Musik und Dichtung*.

course. . . . The poet begins with an agonized situation that cries for its resolution. He intensifies the unbearable. He introduces scenes of relative calm and starts a further increase of feeling, till a crisis occurs and the tension is swiftly or gradually resolved. The spectator is delighted far more than he himself knows by the rhythmic sequence of scenes, the wise meting-out of emotions, the great arc of passion that spans the piece from beginning to end."

This "great arc of passion," rising from a troubled beginning to sublime heights, and subsiding at last to a serene, final cadence, Staiger finds in the very structure, the "commanding form," of Gluck's operas. Gluck himself was so aware of its source in the Greek story, that he credited Calzabigi with the lion's share of his own works. But the librettos are, after all, far from Greek tragedy in literary and dramatic power and form. The "happy ending" of the *Orpheus* violates the myth so that as a play it would be unbearable. Gluck, however, felt the spirit of the myth even in the softened form. Just because he read it from the first as that which his music was to make of it, to him it had form and beauty. In reality, however, Staiger says quite truly: "To the composer it was given to distribute the stresses, here to restrain the burst of passion, there to strike with full force, and then, muting his tone, to descend from the terrible height back to the level again. It was the composer who created the new operatic art."

And finally he states the secret of Gluck's relation to the unfolding plot:

". . . He wished, as he said in the introduction to *Alceste,* that the music should enhance the interest of the dramatic situation without interrupting the action. Now we know what this means. It is not a matter of satisfying the curiosity of the audience without interpolating musical obstacles; the point is, not to lose the single span of feeling, the vast rhythmic unity of the whole. . . .

"If we review [Gluck's work] from this standpoint, his much-debated dictum, that music should subserve the text, suddenly appears in a new light. Although Gluck was determined to let his music play handmaiden to the poetic work, he was not obliged for one moment to betray his music, because from the very first moment he conceived drama itself, the tragic art of the ancient Greeks, in the spirit of music, i.e. as an art that uses passions and mutually attuned characters and events *to create music*."[20]

Now this is simply the principle of assimilation, whereby the words of a poem, the biblical allusions in a cantata, the characters and events in comedy or tragedy become musical elements when they are musically used. If the composition is music at all, it is pure music, and not a hybrid of two or more arts. The *Gesamtkunstwerk* is an impossibility, because a work can exist in only one primary illusion, which every element must serve to create, support, and develop. That is what happened to Wagner's operas in spite of himself: they are music, and what is left of his non-musical importations that did not undergo a complete change into music, is dross.

There remains one major question, perhaps to many minds the most important: the purity or impurity, merit or demerit, of "program music." So much has been written for and against it that we shall do best, perhaps, to cut across the familiar arguments, and apply the same measure to the concept of the "program" as to all previous problematical concepts. That measure lies in the fundamental question: "How does the 'program' affect the making, the perception, or the comprehension of the musical piece as an expressive form?" The answer to this query reveals, I think, the uses and misuses of the *petit roman* in their proper contrast.

Ever since music became an independent art, separate from intoned speech and danced rhythms (and perhaps even before), there has been melody obviously suggested by natural sounds or movements, that might be called, in a general way, "program music." The imitation of the cuckoo's cry in "Sumer is i-cumen in" is usually quoted as the oldest instance we can recover. Then came the time of "musical hermeneutic" when upward and downward movements of melodic phrases were interpreted as symbols of rising spirit and sinking spirit, respectively, i.e. of joy and sorrow, life and death. Then semiquavers trembled, chromatics mourned, arpeggios praised the Lord. In the age of Bach and Handel such interpretations had become conventional enough to furnish a large store of suggestions to the composer setting a text to music. And herein lay the value of this decorous "tone painting": it suggested *musical devices* to be used in the most varied total forms and original contexts,

---

[20]*Op. cit.*, pp. 29–37.

much as the Bible offers its language for the most spontaneous and special prayers. The devices were recognized melodic figures and rhythmic patterns, and their general acceptance actually relieved the composer of any obligation to imitate natural intonations and gestures. And furthermore, while direct imitations are bound to the ideas they are supposed to convey, the traditional renderings are free musical elements; they may be used for purely creative purposes in the making of expressive forms not motivated by any poetic text. Schweitzer's contention, that Bach used certain musical figures regularly in conjunction with emotionally tinged words like "death," "joy," "suffering," "heaven," and that those figures recurring in his purely instrumental music still carried the same poetic connotations, so that his fugues and suites should be viewed as "poems" translated into music,[21] seems to me entirely unjustified. As Tovey said of the fabric of musical gestures, obviously inspired by the words in vocal music, "Bach took it for granted, and did not attach to it anything like the importance it is apt to assume in the minds of readers who learn of its rediscovery today. Good music was to him a thing that could be used to any good new purpose, regardless of what its details may have symbolized in their first setting."[22]

Actually, the same figures that in religious cantatas accompany mortal fear or self-abasement may be humorously used to connote sinuous worms in Haydn's *Creation,* and may occur in Mozart's minuets where certainly nobody is groveling at all. The words of the cantatas may have suggested tonal renderings by their emotive values, but what it all comes to is that those words, with all their religious or human significance, have been assimilated by a purely musical form, the matrix of the cantata, from which the rhythmic and melodic figures that are their characteristic settings emerge with the same logic as the evolution of functional details in an organism.

Such composition is not "program music," but simply music. To a genuine tonal imagination everything that sounds harbors the possibility of tonal forms and may become a motif, and many silent things, too, offer their rhythms as musical ideas. Anything is good out of which one can make a theme, a passage, a movement: the cuckoo's call that pro-

---

[21]Schweitzer, *J. S. Bach, Le musicien-poet.*
[22]*Op. cit.,* Vol. V, "Vocal Music," p. 51.

vides a canon, the bells that ring the bass of Musorgsky's Easter music, the heartbeat skillfully given to the violins (for much greater transformation than tympani could make) in Mozart's *Abduction from the Serail,* or ideas of dramatic action and passion. All such ideas motivate the course of the music which develops by their suggestion. But it does not imitate as closely as possible, approximating natural noises and undramatized self-expression; for, as Mozart said, "Music must always remain music."[23]

Music must remain music, and everything else that enters in must *become* music. That is, I think, the whole secret of "purity," and the only rule that determines what is or is not relevant. Music may be "representational" in the sense of taking themes from bird songs and marketplace calls, hoofbeats or heartbeats, echo-effects, dripping waters, or the motions of ships and machines. It may also "represent" the emotional connotations of words by the devices familiar to Bach and Buxtehude, or with less convention, the rise and fall of passions enacted on the stage. But where music is really music, though ideas of things or situations may underlie its forms, such ideas are never necessary to account for what one hears, to give it unity, or—worst of all—to give it emotive value.

"Program music" in the strict sense is a modern vagary, the musical counterpart of naturalism in the plastic arts. The source of its wide popularity is that the unmusical can enjoy it, and in a mass-civilization, where audiences number thousands instead of scores of listeners, the majority are, of course, not really musical. Music affects most people, but not necessarily as art; just as pictures activate almost everyone's imagination, but only clear and intuitive minds really understand the

---

[23]"The rage of Osmin is turned into comedy by the use of Turkish music. . . . The aria, 'So, by the beard of the prophet' is in the same tempo, it is true but with rapid notes, and since his anger is constantly heightened and it would seem as if the aria were already ending, the *Allegro assai* must be most effective in a totally different time and a different tonality, for a person who is in a violent rage oversteps all bounds of order, moderation and sound purpose, he is beside himself, and so the music too must know itself no more. But as passions, whether violent or not, must never be expressed to the point of disgust and the music, even in the most terrific situation, . . . must always remain music, therefore I haven't chosen a key totally unrelated to F [the key of the aria] but A minor, a related key. Now the aria of Belmonte [is] in A major: 'Oh how fearful, Oh how passionate,' you know how it is expressed, and the agitated beating of the heart is indicated too, the violins in octaves." (Leitzmann, *op. cit.*, letter to Leopold Mozart, dated Vienna, September 26, 1781.)

vital import, while the average person reacts to the things depicted, and turns away if he can find nothing to promote his discursive thoughts or stimulate his actual emotions. A program reporting imaginary pranks, listing the subjects of pictures in a gallery, or announcing that now so-and-so does this, now he does that, like the radio broadcast of a game or a fight, is a voice from the realm of actuality, even if its statements are fanciful. If the "interpretation" correctly reviews the composer's own raw material, it brings it back as such, i.e. as material, untransformed, unassimilated, to disturb the illusion of a flowing Time in which all feeling takes audible form. Sometimes, however, the commentator does not even furnish such workshop data, but retails merely what he himself dreams about when he listens to the music, and invites the audience officially to share a banal literary synopsis under the hypnotic influence of sound.

All the arts exercise a certain hypnotism, but none so promptly and patently as music. Something like it emanates from architectural works like the great cathedrals, Greek temples, and some especially impressive public places, such as museum halls that seem to enclose their treasures in a completely harmonious world. Everything said or done in such places seems to be augmented by the vastness of the living space and dramatized by its atmosphere. The influence extends over things not belonging to art at all. Architecture, however, can hypnotize the average person only through its greatest effects, whereas music exerts this power at almost all times. When one is half listening and thinking of something else, and one's emotions are engaged by the subject matter, they are enhanced by the mere sensuous background of music. Where thought and feeling are really determined by a problem under contemplation, the tonal forms convey no ideas at all. The whole function of the music then is something that is always involved in artistic presentations of any sort—the power of *isolation*. This is what makes mere "background music" facilitate some people's unmusical thinking and heighten its emotional tone. Because our ears are open to the whole world, and hearing, unlike seeing, requires no exclusive focus, aural impressions reach us without demanding our conscious attention. Perhaps that is why we can experience the hypnotic influence of music and stop there—stop short of any significant perception—in a way what we cannot do as readily with any other art.

Between real listening, which is actively thinking music, and not listening at all, like the student who solves an algebraic problem while the radio broadcasts a symphony, there is a twilight zone of musical enjoyment where tonal perception is woven into daydreaming. This is probably the most popular way of receiving music, for it is easy and highly pleasurable, and aestheticians who regard any sort of pleasure as the purpose of art, and any enjoyment therefore as tantamount to appreciation, encourage the practice. Yet its effect on the musical mind is questionable. To the entirely uninitiated hearer it may be an aid in finding expressive forms at all, to extemporize an accompanying romance and let the music express feelings accounted for by its scenes. But to the competent it is a pitfall, because it obscures the full vital import of the music noting only what comes handy for a purpose, and noting only what expresses attitudes and emotions the listener was familiar with before. It bars everything new or really interesting in a work, since what does not fit the *petit roman* is passed over, and what does fit is the dreamer's own. Above all, it leads attention not to the music, but away from it – via the music to something else that is essentially an indulgence. One may spend a whole evening in this sort of dream, and carry nothing away from it at all but the "tired businessman's" relaxation—no musical insight, no new feeling, and actually *nothing heard.*

The reason nothing really musical remains is that in the process of daydreaming the music is assimilated to the dream, just as in song a poem is "swallowed" by music, and in opera the drama meets this fate. A dream is not a work of art, but it follows the same law; it is not art because it is improvised for purely self-expressive ends, or for romantic satisfaction, and has to meet no standards of coherence, organic form, or more than personal interest. The result of listening to music in this way is the free creativity that belongs to adolescence, when sentiment is anchorless and demands prodigious amounts of fictive adventure. Perhaps it is natural and proper to that age to use music, too, primarily as a road to romance. But the whole process really takes one away from art in the direction of sheer subjectivity.

Yet music truly heard and imaginatively grasped may be artistically "used," assimilated to works in other orders of illusion—"swallowed" just as it may itself "swallow" poetry or drama. That is a different story, which will engage us especially in the next chapter.

Chapter eleven

VIRTUAL POWERS

No art suffers more misunderstanding, sentimental judgment, and mystical interpretation than the art of dancing. Its critical literature, or worse yet its uncritical literature, pseudo-ethnological and pseudo-aesthetic, makes weary reading. Yet this very confusion as to what dancing is—what it expresses, what it creates, and how it is related to the other arts, to the artist, and to the actual world—has a philosophical significance of its own. It stems from two fundamental sources: the primary illusion, and the basic abstraction whereby the illusion is created and shaped. The intuitive appreciation of dance is just as direct and natural as the enjoyment of any other art, but to analyze the nature of its artistic effects is peculiarly difficult, for reasons that will soon be apparent; consequently there are numberless misleading theories about what dancers do and what the doing signifies, which turn the beholder away from simple intuitive understanding, and either make him attentive to mechanics and acrobatics, or to personal charms and erotic desires, or else make him look for pictures, stories, or music—anything to which his thinking can attach with confidence.

The most widely accepted view is that the essence of dance is musical: the dancer expresses in gesture what he feels as the emotional content of the music which is the efficient and supporting cause of his dance. He reacts as we all would if we were not inhibited; his dance is self-expression, and is beautiful because the stimulus is beautiful. He may really be said to be "dancing the music."

This view of dance as a gestural rendering of musical forms is not merely a popular one, but is held by a great many dancers, and a few —though, indeed, very few—musicians. The music critic who calls himself

Jean D'Udine[1] has written, in his very provocative (not to say maddening) little book, *L'art et le geste:* "The expressive gesticulation of an orchestra conductor is simply a dance. . . . All music is dance—all melody just a series of attitudes, poses."[2] Jacques Dalcroze, too, who was a musician and not a dancer by training, believed that dance could express in bodily movement the same motion-patterns that music creates for the ear.[3] But as a rule it is the dancer, choreographer, or dance critic rather than the musician who regards dance as a musical art.[4] On the assumption that all music could be thus "translated," Fokine undertook to dance Beethoven symphonies; Massine has done the same—both, apparently, with indifferent success.

Alexander Sakharoff, in his *Reflexions sur la musique et sur la danse,* carried the "musical" creed to its full length: "We—Clotilde Sakharoff and I—do not dance *to* music, or with musical accompaniment, we dance *the music*." He reiterates the point several times. The person who taught him to dance not *with* music, but to dance the music itself, he says, was Isadora Duncan.[5] There can be no doubt that she regarded dance as the visible incarnation of music—that for her there was no "dance music," but only pure music rendered as dance. Sakharoff remarked that many critics maintained Isadora did not really understand the music she danced, that she misinterpreted and violated it; he, on the contrary, found that she understood it so perfectly that she could dare to make free interpretations of it.[6] Now, paradoxically, I believe both Sakharoff and the critics were right. Isadora did not understand the music *musically*, but for her

---

[1]Albert Cozanet.

[2]*L'art et le geste,* p. xiv.

[3]The best known exponent of this view is, of course, Jacques Dalcroze; but it has received far more systematic statement by L. Bourguès and A. Denéréaz, in *La musique et la vie intérieure,* where we find: "Every musical piece establishes in the organism of the listener a dynamogenic global rhythm, every instant of which is a totality of all its dynamogenic factors, intensity, scope, duration, manner of production, timbres, combined into simultaneous effects and reacting upon the listener according to their succession." (P. 17.)

"If 'cenesthetics' is the soul of feeling, then kinesthetics is after all but the 'soul of gesture.' " (P. 20.)

[4]See, for example, George Borodin, *This Thing Called Ballet;* Rudolf Sonner, *Musik und Tanz: vom Kulttanz zum Jazz.*

[5]*Reflexions sur la musique et sur la danse,* p. 46.

[6]*Ibid.,* p. 52.

purposes she understood it perfectly; she knew what was balletic,[7] and that was all she knew about it. In fact, it was so absolutely all she knew that she thought it was all there was to know, and that what she danced was really "the music." Her musical taste as such was undeveloped—not simply poor, but utterly unaccountable. She ranked Ethelbert Nevin's "Narcissus" with Beethoven's C♯ Minor Sonata, and Mendelssohn's "Spring Song" with some very good Chopin *Études* her mother played.

Isadora's lack of musical judgment is interesting in view of the alleged basic identity of music and dance (Sakharoff considers them "as closely related as poetry and prose"—that is, two major forms of one art). Most artists—as we had occasion to note before, in connection with the plastic arts—are competent judges of works in any form and even any mode of their own art: a painter usually has a true feeling for buildings and statues, a pianist for vocal music from plain-song to opera, etc. But dancers are not particularly discerning critics of music, and musicians are very rarely even sympathetic to the dance. There are those, of course, who write for ballet and undoubtedly understand it; but among the hosts of musicians—composers and performers alike—the ones who have a natural proclivity for the dance are so few that it is hard to believe in the twinship of the two arts.

The existence of an intimate relation—identity or near-identity—has indeed been repudiated, vehemently denied, by some dancers and dance enthusiasts who maintain—quite properly—that theirs is an independent art; and those few defenders of the faith have even gone so far as to claim that the world-old union of music and dance is a pure accident or a matter of fashion. Frank Thiess, who has written a book of many remarkable insights and judgments, lets his conviction that dance is not a mode of musical art confuse him utterly about the balletic function of music, which he deprecates as a mere "acoustically ornamented rhythm" running parallel to the independent dance.[8]

There is another interpretation of dance, inspired by the classical

---

[7]"Balletic" is used here in its general sense of *concerning dance,* and not with particular reference to the type of dance known as "ballet." There is no accepted English adjective from a word meaning "dance" that avoids false connotations; in Merle Armitage's admirable collection of essays, *Modern Dance,* the German word "tänzerisch" is translated by "dancistic" (p. 9), but the word sounds unnatural.

[8]Frank Thiess, *Der Tanz als Kunstwerk,* pp. 42–43.

ballet, and therefore more generally accepted in the past than in our day: that dance is one of the plastic arts, a spectacle of shifting pictures, or animated design, or even statues in motion. Such was the opinion of the great choreographer Noverre who, of course, had never seen actual moving pictures or mobile sculpture.[9] Since these media have come into existence, the difference between their products and dance is patent. Calder's balanced shapes, moved by the wind, define a truly sculptural volume which they fill with a free and fascinating motion (I am thinking, in particular, of his "Lobster Pot and Fishtail" in the stair well of the Museum of Modern Art in New York), but they certainly are not dancing. The moving picture has been seriously likened to the dance on the ground that both are "arts of movement";[10] yet the hypnotic influence of motion is really all they have in common (unless the film happens to be of a dance performance), and a peculiar psychological effect is not the measure of an art form. A screenplay, a newsreel, a documentary film, has no artistic similarity to any sort of dance.

Neither musical rhythm nor physical movement is enough to engender a dance. We speak of gnats "dancing" in the air, or balls "dancing" on a fountain that tosses them; but in reality all such patterned motions are *dance motifs*, not dances.

The same thing may be said of a third medium that has sometimes

---

[9]See his *Lettres sur les arts imitateurs*, reflections on the dance-plots appended to Letter XXIV: "That which produces a picture in painting also produces a picture in the dance: the effect of these two arts is similar; they both have the same role to play, they must speak to the heart through the eyes . . . everything that is used in dance is capable of forming pictures, and anything that can produce a pictorial effect in painting may serve as a model for the dance, as also everything that is rejected by the painter, must be likewise rejected by the ballet master." Compare also his *Lettres sur la danse, et sur les ballets*, Letter XIV: Pantomime is a bolt which the great passions discharge; it is a multitude of lightning strokes which succeed each other with rapidity; the scenes which result are their play, they last but a moment and immediately give place to others."

[10]Cf. Borodin, *op. cit.*, p 56: "The basic materials of both the ballet and the film are similar. Both depend upon the presentation of a picture in motion. . . . Like the ballet, the film is pattern in movement, a sequence of pictures constantly changing but presented according to an artistic plan—at least in its higher forms. So, too, the ballet. It is, in fact, only that the idiom, the turn of phrase, is different. The difference between ballet and film is very similar to that between two languages having a common origin—as, for example, Italian and Spanish, or Dutch and English. The foundations are almost the same in both cases but the development has in each proceeded along different lines."

been regarded as the basic element in dance: pantomime. According to the protagonists of this view, dancing is a dramatic art. And of course they have a widely accepted theory, namely that Greek drama arose from choric dance, to justify their approach. But if one looks candidly at the most elaborate pantomimic dance, it does not appear at all like the action of true drama;[11] one is far more tempted to doubt the venerable origins of acting than to believe in the dramatic ideal of dance motions. For dance that begins in pantomime, as many religious dances do, tends in the course of its subsequent history to become more balletic, not more dramatic.[12] Pantomime, like pure motion patterns, plastic images, and musical forms, is dance material, something that may become a balletic element, but the dance itself is something else.

The true relationship is well stated by Thiess, who regards pantomime itself as "a bastard of two different arts," namely dance and comedy,[13] but observes: "To conclude from this fact that it [pantomime] is therefore condemned to eternal sterility, is to misapprehend the nature of some highly important formative processes in art. . . . A true dance pantomime may indeed be evolved, purely within the proper confines of the dance . . . a pantomime that is based entirely, from the first measure

---

[11]Noverre, accused by certain critics of having violated the dramatic unities of Greek themes in his dances, replied: "But suffice it to say that ballet is not drama, that a production of this kind cannot be subjected to strict Aristotelian rules. . . . These are the rules of my art; those of the drama are full of shackles; far from conforming to them, I should avoid knowing anything about them, and place myself above these laws that were never made for the dance." (*Lettres sur les arts imitateurs,* Reflection XXIV on the dance-plots, pp. 334–336.)

[12]Evidence for this contention may be found in Sachs' *World History of the Dance,* despite the fact that the author himself believes drama to have arisen from dance that was built on a mythical or historical theme (see pp. 226, 227). In discussing the evolution of animal dances, he says: "From these examples we may see that it has been the fate of the animal dance to grow continually away from nature. The urge to compose the movements into a stylized dance, therefore to make them less real, has taken more and more of the natural from the steps and gestures." (P. 84.)

[13]Compare Isadora Duncan's comment: "Pantomime to me has never seemed an art. Movement is lyrical and emotional expression, which can have nothing to do with words and in pantomime, people substitute gestures for words, so that it is neither the art of the dancer nor that of the actor, but falls between the two in hopeless sterility." (*My Life,* p. 33.)

I also consider pantomime not a kind of art at all—but, rather, like myth and fairy tale, a proto-artistic phenomenon that may serve as motif in many different arts—painting, sculpture, drama, dance, film, etc.

to the last, on the intrinsic law of the dance: the law of rhythmic motion." As the first master of such truly balletic miming he names Rudolf von Laban. "In his work," he says, "as in pure music, the content of an event disappears entirely behind its choreographic form. . . . Everything becomes expression, gesture, thrall and liberation of bodies. And by the skillful use of space and color, the balletic pantomime has been evolved, which may underlie the ensemble dance of the future."[14]

What, then, is dance? If it be an independent art, as indeed it seems to be, it must have its own "primary illusion." Rhythmic motion? That is its actual process, not an illusion. The "primary illusion" of an art is something created, and created at the first touch—in this case, with the first motion, performed or even implied. The motion itself, as a physical reality and therefore "material" in the art, must suffer transformation. Into what?—Thiess, in the passage just quoted, has given the answer: "Everything becomes expression, *gesture*. . . . "

All dance motion is gesture, or an element in the exhibition of gesture—perhaps its mechanical contrast and foil, but always motivated by the semblance of an expressive movement. Mary Wigman has said, somewhere: "A meaningless gesture is abhorrent to me." Now a "meaningless gesture" is really a contradiction in terms; but to the great dancer all movement in dance was gesture—that was the only word; a mistake was a "meaningless gesture." The interesting point is that the statement itself might just as well have been made by Isadora Duncan, by Laban, or by Noverre. For, oddly enough, artists who hold the most fantastically diverse theories as to what dancing is—a visible music, a succession of pictures, an unspoken play—all recognize its gestic character. *Gesture* is the basic abstraction whereby the dance illusion is made and organized.

Gesture is vital movement; to the one who performs it, it is known very precisely as a kinetic experience, i.e. as action, and somewhat more vaguely by sight, as an effect. To others it appears as a visible motion, but not a motion of things, sliding or waving or rolling around—it is *seen and understood* as vital movement. So it is always at once subjective and objective, personal and public, willed (or evoked) and perceived.

In actual life gestures function as signals or symptoms of our desires, intentions, expectations, demands, and feelings. Because they can be consciously controlled, they may also be elaborated, just like vocal sounds,

---

[14]Thiess, *op. cit.*, pp. 44–47.

into a system of assigned and combinable *symbols,* a genuine discursive language. People who do not understand each other's speech always resort to this simpler form of discourse to express propositions, questions, judgments. But whether a gesture has linguistic meaning or not, it is always spontaneously expressive, too, by virtue of its form: it is free and big, or nervous and tight, quick or leisurely, etc., according to the psychological condition of the person who makes it. This self-expressive aspect is akin to the tone of voice in speech.

Gesticulation, as part of our actual behavior, is not art. It is simply vital movement. A squirrel, startled, sitting up with its paw against its heart, makes a gesture, and a very expressive one at that. But there is no art in its behavior. It is not dancing. Only when the movement that was a genuine gesture in the squirrel is *imagined,* so it may be performed apart from the squirrel's momentary situation and mentality, it becomes an artistic element, a possible dance-gesture. Then it becomes a free symbolic form, which may be used to convey *ideas* of emotion, of awareness and premonition, or may be combined with or incorporated in other virtual gestures, to express other physical and mental tensions.

Every being that makes natural gestures is a center of vital force, and its expressive movements are seen by others as signals of its will. But virtual gestures are not signals, they are symbols of will. The spontaneously gestic character of dance motions is illusory, and the vital force they express is illusory; the "powers" (i.e. centers of vital force) in dance are created beings—created by the semblance gesture.

The primary illusion of dance is a virtual realm of Power—not actual, physically exerted power, but appearances of influence and agency created by virtual gesture.

In watching a collective dance—say, an artistically successful ballet —one does not see *people running around;* one sees the dance driving this way, drawn that way, gathering here, spreading there—fleeing, resting, rising, and so forth; and all the motion seems to spring from powers beyond the performers.[15] In a *pas de deux* the two dancers appear to

---

[15]Compare Cyril W. Beaumont's account of a rehearsal of the Alhambra Ballet: "The pianist renders the theme of the movement . . . while the dancers perform evolution after evolution which Nijinska controls and directs with dramatic gestures of her arms. The dancers swirl into long, sinuous lines, melt into one throbbing mass, divide, form circles, revolve and then dash from sight." (Published in *Fanfare,* 1921, and quoted in the same author's *A Miscellany for Dancers,* p. 167.)

magnetize each other; the relation between them is more than a spatial one, it is a relation of forces; but the forces they exercise, that seem to be as physical as those which orient the compass needle toward its pole, really do not exist physically at all. They are dance forces, virtual powers.

The prototype of these purely apparent energies is not the "field of forces" known to physics, but the subjective experience of volition and free agency, and of reluctance to alien, compelling wills. The consciousness of life, the sense of vital power, even of the power to receive impressions, apprehend the environment, and meet changes, is our most immediate self-consciousness. This is the feeling of power; and the play of such "felt" energies is as different from any system of physical forces as psychological time is from clock-time, and psychological space from the space of geometry.

The widely popular doctrine that every work of art takes rise from an emotion which agitates the artist, and which is directly "expressed" in the work, may be found in the literature of every art. That is why scholars delve into each famous artist's life history, to learn by discursive study what emotions he must have had while making this or that piece, so that they may "understand" the message of the work.[16] But there are usually a few philosophical critics—sometimes artists themselves —who realize that the feeling in a work of art is something the artist *conceived* as he created the symbolic form to present it, rather than something he was undergoing and involuntarily venting in an artistic process. There is a Wordsworth who finds that poetry is not a symptom of emotional stress, but an image of it—"emotion recollected in tranquillity"; there is a Riemann who recognizes that music *resembles* feeling, and is its objective symbol rather than its physiological effect;[17] a Mozart who knows from experience that emotional disturbance merely interferes with artistic conception.[18] Only in the literature of the dance,

---

[16]Margaret H'Doubler says explicitly: "The only true way of appreciating works of art is by becoming familiar with the conditions and causes which produce them." (*Dance: A Creative Art Experience*, p. 54.)

[17]A statement of Riemann's attitude may be found quoted in *New Key*, p. 245 *n.;* (Mentor ed., p. 199 *n.*).

[18]In a letter to his father (dated at Vienna, June 9, 1781), Mozart wrote: "I, who must always be composing, need a clear mind and a quiet heart." And on an-

the claim to direct self-expression is very nearly unanimous. Not only the sentimental Isadora, but such eminent theorists as Merle Armitage and Rudolf von Laban, and scholars like Curt Sachs, besides countless dancers judging introspectively, accept the naturalistic doctrine that dance is a free discharge either of surplus energy or of emotional excitement.

Confronted with such evidence, one naturally is led to reconsider the whole theory of art as symbolic form. Is dance an exception? Good theories may have special cases, but not exceptions. Does the whole philosophy break down? Does it simply not "work" in the case of dance, and thereby reveal a fundamental weakness that was merely obscurable in other contexts? Surely no one would have the temerity to claim that *all* the experts on a subject are wrong!

Now there is one curious circumstance, which points the way out of this quandary: namely, that the really great experts—choreographers, dancers, aestheticians, and historians—although explicitly they assert the emotive-symptom thesis, implicitly contradict it when they talk about any particular dance or any specified process. No one, to my knowledge, has ever maintained that Pavlova's rendering of slowly ebbing life in "The Dying Swan" was most successful when she actually felt faint and sick, or proposed to put Mary Wigman into the próper mood for her tragic "Evening Dances" by giving her a piece of terrible news a few minutes before she entered on the stage. A good ballet master, wanting a ballerina to register dismay, might say: "Imagine that your boy-friend has just eloped with your most trusted chum!" But he would not say, with apparent seriousness, "Your boy-friend told me to tell you goodby from him, he's not coming to see you any more." Or he might suggest to a sylph rehearsing a "dance of joy" that she should fancy herself on a vacation in California, amid palms and orange groves, but he probably would not remind her of an exciting engagement after the rehearsal, because that would distract her from the dance, perhaps even to the point of inducing false motions.

It is *imagined feeling* that governs the dance, not real emotional conditions. If one passes over the spontaneous emotion theory with which almost every modern book on the dance begins, one quickly comes to the

other occasion (July 27, 1782): "My heart is restless, my mind confused, how can one think and work intelligently in such a state?"

evidence for this contention. Dance gesture is not real gesture, but virtual. The bodily movement, of course, is real enough; but *what makes it emotive gesture*, i.e. its spontaneous origin in what Laban calls a "feeling-thought-motion,"[19] is illusory, so the movement is "gesture" only within the dance. It is *actual movement*, but *virtual self-expression*.

Herein, I think, lies the source of that peculiar contradiction which haunts the theory of balletic art—the ideal of a behavior at once spontaneous and planned, an activity springing from personal passion but somehow taking the form of a consummate artistic work, spontaneous, emotional, but capable of repetition upon request. Merle Armitage, for instance, says: ". . . Modern dance is a point of view, not a system. . . . The principle underlying this point of view is that emotional experience can express itself directly through movement. And as emotional experience varies in each individual, so will the outer expression vary. *But form, complete and adequate, must be the starting point if the modern dance as an art-form is to live.*"[20] How form can be the starting point of a direct emotional reaction remains his secret. George Borodin defines ballet as "the spontaneous expression of emotion through movement, refined and lifted to the highest plane."[21] But he does not explain what lifts it, and why.

The antinomy is most striking in the excellent work of Curt Sachs, *A World History of the Dance*, because the author understands, as few theorists have done, the nature of the dance illusion—the illusion of Powers, human, daemonic or impersonally magical, in a non-physical but symbolically convincing "world"; indeed, he calls dancing "the vivid representation of a world seen and imagined" (p. 3). Yet when he considers the origins of the dance, he admits without hesitation that the erotic displays of birds and the "spinning games" and vaguely rhythmic group antics of apes (reported by Wolfgang Köhler with great reserve

---

[19]Rudolf von Laban, who constantly insists that gesture springs from *actual* feeling (Cf. *Welt des Tänzers: Fünf Gedankenreigen*, especially p. 14), understands nonetheless that dance begins in a *conception* of feeling, an apprehension of joy or sorrow and its expressive forms: "At a stroke, like lightning, understanding becomes plastic. Suddenly, from some single point, the germ of sorrow or joy unfolds in a person. Conception is everything. All things evolve from the power of gesture, and find their resolution in it."

[20]*Op. cit.*, p. vi.

[21]*Op. cit.*, p. xvi.

as to their interpretation) are genuine dances; and having been led so easily to this premise, he passes to an equally ready conclusion: "The dance of the animals, especially that of the anthropoid apes, proves that the dance of men is in its beginnings a pleasurable motor reaction, a game forcing excess energy into a rhythmic pattern" (p. 55).

The "proof" is, of course, no proof at all, but a mere suggestion; it is at best a corroboration of the general principle discussed in *Philosophy in a New Key*, that the first ingredients of art are usually accidental forms found in the cultural environment, which appeal to the imagination as usable artistic elements.[22] The sportive movements that are purely casual among apes, the instinctive, but highly articulated and characteristic display-gestures of birds, are obvious *models* for the dancer's art. So are the developed and recognized "correct" postures and gestures of many practical skills—shooting, spear-throwing, wrestling, paddling, lassooing—and of games and gymnastics. Professor Sachs is aware of a connection between such phenomena and genuine art forms, but does not seem to realize—or at least, does not express—the momentousness of the step from one to the other. Like John Dewey, he attributes the serious performance of these play-gestures as dance, to the wish for a serious purpose, a conscientious excuse for expending energy and skill.[23] I have countered Professor Dewey's explanation elsewhere, and will not repeat the argument here;[24] suffice it to say that as soon as a characteristic gesture is strikingly exhibited to someone who is not completely absorbed in its practical purpose,—e.g. the gestures of play and free exercise, that have none—it becomes a gestic *form*, and like all articulate forms it tends to assume symbolic functions. But a symbol-seeking mind (rather than a purposive, practical one) must seize upon it.

The reason why the belief in the genuinely self-expressive nature of dance gestures is so widely, if not universally, held is twofold: in the first place, any movement the dancer performs is "gesture" in two different senses, which are systematically confused, and secondly, *feeling* is variously involved in the several sorts of gesture, and its distinct functions are not kept apart. The relationships among actual gestures and

---

[22] Cf. *New Key*, chap. ix, especially p. 248 (Mentor ed., p. 201).

[23] *Op. cit.*, p. 55.

[24] Cf. *New Key*, pp. 156–158 (Mentor ed., pp. 127–128).

virtual ones are really very complex, but perhaps a little patient analysis will make them clear.

"Gesture" is defined in the dictionary as "expressive movement." But "expressive" has two alternative meanings (not to mention minor specializations): it means either "self-expressive," i.e. symptomatic of existing subjective conditions, or "logically expressive," i.e. symbolic of a concept, that may or may not refer to factually given conditions. A sign often functions in both capacities, as symptom and symbol; spoken *words* are quite normally "expressive" in both ways. They convey something the speaker is thinking about, and also betray *that* he is (or sometimes, that he is not!) entertaining the ideas in question, and to some extent his further psycho-physical state.

The same is true of gesture: it may be either self-expressive, or logically expressive, or both. It may indicate demands and intentions, as when people signal to each other, or it may be conventionally symbolic, like the deaf-mute language, but at the same time the *manner* in which a gesture is performed usually indicates the performer's state of mind; it is nervous or calm, violent or gentle, etc. Or it may be purely self-expressive, as speech may be pure exclamation.

Language is primarily symbolic and incidentally symptomatic; exclamation is relatively rare. Gesture, on the contrary, is far more important as an avenue of self-expression than as "word." An expressive word is one that formulates an idea clearly and aptly, but a highly expressive gesture is usually taken to be one that reveals feeling or emotion. It is *spontaneous* movement.

In the dance, the actual and virtual aspects of gesture are mingled in complex ways. The movements, of course, are actual; they spring from an intention, and are in this sense actual gestures; but they are not the gestures they seem to be, because they seem to spring from feeling, as indeed they do not. The dancer's actual gestures are used to create a semblance of self-expression, and are thereby transformed into virtual spontaneous movement, or virtual gesture. The emotion in which such gesture begins is virtual, a dance element, that turns the whole movement into dance-gesture.

But what controls the performance of the actual movement? An actual body-feeling, akin to that which controls the production of tones in musical performance—the final articulation of *imagined* feeling in its appropriate physical form. The conception of a feeling disposes the dancer's body to symbolize it.

Virtual gesture may create the semblance of self-expression without anchoring it in the actual personality, which, as the source only of the actual (non-spontaneous) gestures, disappears as they do in the dance. In its place is the created personality, a dance element which figures simply as a psychical, human or superhuman Being. It is this that is expressing itself.

In the so-called "Modern Dance" the dancer seems to present his own emotions, i.e. the dance is a self-portrait of the artist. The created personality is given his name. But self-portraiture is a motif, and though it is the most popular motif of solo dancers today, and has become the foundation of a whole school, it is no more indispensable to "creative dancing" than any other motif. Quite as great dance may be achieved by other devices, for instance by simulating necessary connection of movements, i.e. mechanical unity of functions, as in *Petroushka,* or by creating the semblance of alien control, the "marionette" motif in all its varieties and derivatives. This latter device has had at least as great a career as the semblance of personal feeling which is the guiding principle of so-called "Modern Dance." For the appearance of movement as gesture requires only its (apparent) emanation from a center of living force; strangely enough, a mechanism "come to life" intensifies this impression, perhaps by the internal contrast it presents. Similarly, the mystic force that works by remote control, establishing its own subsidiary centers in the bodies of the dancers, is even more effectively *visible power* than the naturalistic appearance of self-expression on the stage.

To keep virtual elements and actual materials separate is not easy for anyone without philosophical training, and is hardest, perhaps, for artists, to whom the created world is more immediately real and important than the factual world. It takes precision of thought not to confuse an imagined feeling, or a precisely conceived emotion that is formulated in a perceptible symbol, with a feeling or emotion actually experienced in response to real events. Indeed, the very notion of feelings and emotions not really felt, but only imagined, is strange to most people. Yet there are such imaginary affects—in fact, there are several kinds:

those which we imagine as our own; those which we impute to actual people on the stage in drama or dance; those which are imputed to fictitious characters in literature, or seem to characterize the beings portrayed in a picture or in sculpture, and are therefore part and parcel of an illusory scene or an illusory self. And all these emotive contents are different from the feelings, moods, or emotions, which are expressed in the work of art as such, and constitute its "vital import"; for the import of a symbol is not something illusory, but something actual that is revealed, articulated, made manifest by the symbol. Everything illusory, and every imagined factor (such as a feeling we imagine ourselves to have) which supports the illusion, belongs to the symbolic form; the feeling of the whole work is the "meaning" of the symbol, the reality which the artist has found in the world and of which he wants to give his fellow men a clear conception.

Imagined feelings, illusory emotive symptoms, and portrayals of sentient subjects have long been recognized as ingredients in art. Konrad Lange, some fifty years ago, called such feeling-elements *Scheingefühle*.[25] But under this rubric he lumped all the different sorts of feeling—imagined, simulated, portrayed—that *go into* a work of art, and interpreted the reaction of the percipient as a process of "make-believe," i.e. playfully treating the work as an actuality and pretending to experience the feelings represented or suggested in it. The idea of presenting feeling to our intellect through an artistic symbol was, of course, not conceivable in the frame of Lange's genetic and utilitarian premises; the only "message" a work could have was, from his standpoint, its thematic content, i.e. what it *r*epresented, and as the only epistemological issue was the settlement of *beliefs* in terms of common-sense conception, the sole relation between art and reality was that of sense datum and scientific fact. Since a picture of a horse is obviously not a horse one can ride on,

---

[25]See *Das Wesen der Kunst*, which appeared in 1901. There is an essay by J. Sittard, "Die Musik im Lichte der Illusions-Aesthetik" (*Die Musik*, II[2], p. 243) which is a serious contemporary review of that book; Sittard passes over the illusion of objects and events, and dwells on the notion of *Scheingefühle*. "An illusory feeling," he says, "is the real core of the aesthetic illusion." (P. 244.) After making clear the difference between real and imagined feelings, he remarks: "The basis of real greatness in an artist is, after all, the power of identifying himself with every emotion, even one which is alien to him and in which he does not fulfill his own being."

and a still life of apples not something one can eat, belief could not account for one's interest in paintings and fictions; the only explanation, then, was a psychology of "make-believe," or play, in which the knowledge that the "belief" was a pretense would make it possible to enjoy even sad scenes and intrinsically undesired objects, as art lovers evidently do.

The advance of epistemological thinking in the twentieth century is strikingly attested by the difference between Lange's naive treatment of feeling-contents in art and the analysis made by Baensch in the article "Kunst und Gefühl," quoted at some length in Chapter 3.[26] Oddly enough, while Lange missed the distinctions among feelings experienced and feelings perceived, and classed them all as "experienced" with different degrees of seriousness, Baensch missed the distinction between a feeling itself, which is an actual biological event, and the concept of it, which is an intellectual object, or meaning of a symbol; therefore he found himself faced with the paradox of actually present feelings that nobody was undergoing. The resulting philosophical quixotisms, and their disappearance when art forms are taken as symbols instead of actualities, have already been discussed, and merit no repetition. The salient point is that in dance the basic abstraction itself involves a *Scheingefühl.* Real gesture springs from feeling (physical or psycho-physical); the semblance of gesture, therefore, if it is made by means of actual movement, must be a movement that *seems* to spring from feeling. But the feeling that is implied in such an apparently spontaneous "gesture" is itself a created dance element—a *Scheingefühl*—and may even be attributed not to the dancer, but to some natural or supernatural power expressing itself through him. The conscious will that seems to motivate or animate him may be imagined to lie beyond his person, which figures as a mere receptacle or even momentary concentration of it (Laban's *"Ballung von Tanzenergien"*).

The almost universal confusion of self-expression with dance expression, personal emotion with balletic emotion, is easy enough to understand if one considers the involved relations that dance really has to feeling and its bodily symptoms. It is, furthermore, not only induced by the popular conception of art as emotional catharsis, but is aggravated

[26]See pp. 19 ff.

by another, equally serious and respected doctrine (which is, I think, untenable on many counts, though it is the theory held by Croce and Bergson) namely that an artist gives us insight into actualities, that he penetrates to the nature of individual things, and shows us the unique character of such completely individual objects or persons. In so-called "Modern Dance" the usual motif is a person expressing her or his feelings. The absolutely individual essence to be revealed would, then, be a human soul. The traditional doctrine of the soul as a true substance, entirely unique, or individual, meets this theory of art more than half-way; and if the person whose joys and pains the dance represents is none other than the dancer, the confusions between feeling *shown* and feeling *represented*, symptom and symbol, motif and created image, are just about inescapable.

The recognition of a true artistic illusion, a realm of "Powers," wherein purely imaginary beings from whom the vital force emanates shape a whole world of dynamic forms by their magnet-like, psycho-physical actions, lifts the concept of Dance out of all its theoretical entanglements with music, painting, comedy and carnival or serious drama, and lets one ask *what belongs to dancing,* and what does not. It determines, furthermore, exactly how other arts are related to the ancient balletic art, and explains why it is so ancient, why it has periods of degeneration, why it is so closely linked with amusement, dressing-up, frivolity, on the one hand and with religion, terror, mysticism and madness on the other. Above all, it upholds the insight that dance, no matter how diverse its phases and how multifarious, perhaps even undignified its uses, is un-mistakably and essentially art, and performs the functions of art in worship as in play.

If one approaches the literature of dancing in the light of this theory, one finds the theory corroborated everywhere, even where an entirely different conception of dance is explicitly professed. Implicitly there is always the recognition of created dance forces, impersonal agencies, and especially of controlled, rhythmicized, formally conceived gesture beget-ting the illusion of emotions and wills in conflict. Writers who fill their introductions or opening paragraphs with statements committing them to a daily round of emotions enough to kill any normal person, and to spontaneous exhibits of them on schedule, do not talk about any specific emotions and feelings when they enter into discussion of specific dance problems, but almost invariably speak of setting up tensions, exhibiting forces, creating gestures that *connote* feelings or even thoughts. The actual thoughts, memories, and sentiments that lie behind them are purely personal symbols that may help the artistic conception, but do not appear. As Mary Wigman has put it: "How the dance experience manifests itself to the individual may remain his own secret. The artistic achievement alone is the only valid testimony."[27]

It was this achievement which Arthur Michel, fully aware though he was of the passionate personality behind it, described purely in terms of dance forces, virtual tensions, virtual centers or "poles" of energy: "To realize the human being as tension in space; that is, the dissolution of the dancer into swaying movement discharging tension, was the idea, the task, the aim of Mary Wigman. No one but a being so superbly and demoniacally possessed, so stretched between heaven and hell as was Mary Wigman could ever have succeeded, in the dancistic sense, in embodying human existence as tension within herself. Only such a person, perhaps, could have conceived the idea of creative dancing as the oscillation of a human being between two external poles of tension, thus transplanting the dancing body from the sensually existing sphere of materialism and real space into the symbolic supersphere of tension space."[28]

"When she is dancing, her torso and limbs seem to be governed by a power of nature acting after secret laws."[29]

"Mary Wigman's dance creativeness more and more insistently demanded that the polarity of space tension be made visible by a second dancer, or by a group, in addition to its manifestation by a single dancer."[30]

"The dancing group is a personality, an aching, suffering creature assailed by dance tension which drives it to struggle with a visible (or invisible) partner. The chorus, on the contrary, is a dancistic mass. Its movements are not the expression of what it is feeling individually. It moves according to impersonal laws. It might be compared to some work of architecture come to life, moving, transforming itself from one shape

---

[27]"The New German Dance," in *Modern Dance*, p. 22.
[28]"The Modern Dance in Germany," *Ibid*, p. 5.
[29]*Ibid.*, p. 6.   [30]*Ibid.*, p. 7.

to another . . . it is a space-shaping creation and recreation of this form of body tension . . . architecture which, in its incessant change, produces a spiritual atmosphere."[31]

Now obviously the group personality is not an actual creature suffering attacks of anything; neither are the dancers of the chorus actually a subhuman organic mass. All these entities are *dance elements* that emerge from the interplay of virtual forces of "space tensions" and "body tensions" and even less specific "dance tensions" created by music, lights, décor, poetic suggestion, and what not.

The writings of the most thoughtful dancers are often hard to read because they play so freely across the line between physical fact and artistic significance. The complete identification of fact, symbol, and import, which underlies all literal belief in myth,[32] also besets the discursive thinking of artists, to such an extent that their philosophical reflections are apt to be as confused as they are rich. To a careful reader with ordinary common sense they sound nonsensical; to a person philosophically trained they seem, by turns, affected or mystical, until he discovers that they are *mythical*. Rudolf von Laban offers a perfect instance: he has very clear ideas of what is created in dance, but the relation of the created "tensions" to the physics of the actual world involves him in a mystic metaphysics that is at best fanciful, and at worst rapturously sentimental.[33]

The chief source of such abortive speculations is the failure to distinguish between what is actual and what is virtual in the making of the symbol, and furthermore, between the "virtual" symbol itself and its import, which refers us back to actuality. But this telescoping of symbols and meanings, word and world, into one metaphysical entity is the very hallmark of what Cassirer has termed "the mythical consciousness"; and that is *structurally* the same as the artistic consciousness. It is metaphorical almost from first to last. But as one remembers that the statements Laban makes about emotions refer to *body feelings,* physical feelings that spring from the *idea* of an emotion and initiate symbolic gestures which articulate this idea, and that his "emotional forces" are semblances of physical or magical forces, one can turn his specious

---

[31]*Ibid.,* p. 9.   [33]Cf. *op. cit., passim.*
[32]Cf. *New Key*, Chap. vi.

physical account of the world and its energies into a description of the illusory realm of "powers," and then his analyses all make sense.[34] Especially his treatment of objects as complexes of intersecting forces in balletic space[35] is a piece of bold logical construction, for it lets one conceive the entire world of dance as a field of virtual powers—there are no actualities left in it at all, no untransformed materials, but only elements, living Beings, centers of force, and their interplay.

The most important result, however, of recognizing the primary illusion of dance and the basic abstraction—virtual spontaneous gesture—that creates and fills and organizes it, is the new light this recognition sheds on the status, the uses, and the history of dancing. All sorts of puzzling dance forms and practices, origins, connections with other arts, and relations to religion and magic, become clear as soon as one conceives the dance to be neither plastic art nor music, nor a presentation of story, but a play of Powers made visible. From this standpoint one can understand the ecstatic dance and the animal dance, the sentimental waltz and the classical ballet, the mask and the mime and the orgiastic carnival, as well as the solemn funeral round or the tragic dance of a Greek chorus. Nothing can corroborate the theory of artistic illusion and expression here advanced, so forcibly as an authoritative history of dancing, re-read in the light of that theory; the following chapter, therefore, will present at least a few significant facts, historical or current, to substantiate the conception of dance as a complete and autonomous art, the creation and organization of a realm of virtual Powers.

---

[34]Cf. *op. cit.*, *Zweiter Reigen*, where a pseudo-scientific discussion of physical nature ends with the paragraph: "The tensions which we experience, suddenly, everywhere, in motionlessness, in the sudden sensation of falling, of swinging, are the sparks, the organic parts of a great, invisible, and for us perhaps terrifying world, of which we are little aware."

[35]Tension (*Spannung*) he describes as "a harmonious, simultaneous self-awareness, self-perception, self-exploration, self-experiencing of the infinite transformations and potentialities of transformation in the world with relation to each other." After this heroic effort at cosmic definition, he continues: "From this universal process arises something physically perceivable, a form of being which in this work I call nucleation (*Ballung*). This nucleation arises, endures, expires and begets by this play of tensions the impressions of Time, Space, Power, and the like.

". . . A nucleation derived from the special modes of sympathetic vibrations of the homogeneous infinite will be sensibly and coarsely received by the eye. 'Sensibly,' that is to say, as 'making sense.' Our experience interprets that phenomenon as a space-filling nucleation, a Thing." (P. 6.)

Chapter twelve

THE MAGIC CIRCLE

All forces that cannot be scientifically established and measured must be regarded, from the philosophical standpoint, as illusory; if, therefore, such forces appear to be part of our direct experience, they are "virtual," i.e. non-actual semblances. This applies to chthonic powers, divine powers, fates and spells and all mystic agencies, the potency of prayer, of will, of love and hate, and also the oft-assumed hypnotic power of one's mind over another (hereby, I do not mean to call in question the *phenomenon* of hypnotizing a subject, but only the concept of a psychical "force" emanating from the "master mind").

The assumption of mysterious "powers," or concentrations of forces not theoretically calculable in mathematical terms, dominates all pre-scientific imagination. The world picture of naive men naturally stems from the pattern of subjective action and passion. Just as the envisagement of spatial relations begins with what Poincaré called our "natural geometry,"[1] so the comprehension of dynamic relations starts from our experience of effort and obstacle, conflict and victory or defeat. The conception of "powers" in nature operating like impulses, and of force inhering in things as strength is felt to be in the body, is an obvious one. Yet it is a myth, built on the most primitive symbol—the body (just as most of our descriptive language is based on the symbolism of head and foot, leg and arm, mouth, neck, back, etc.: the "foothills" of a range, the mountain's "shoulder," the "leg" of a triangle, the "bottleneck," the "headland," etc.). This envisagement of the world as a realm of individual living forces, each a being with desires and purposes that bring it into conflict with other teleologically directed powers, is really the key idea of all mythical interpretations: the idea of the Spirit World.

Ernst Cassirer, in his voluminous writings on the evolution of sym-

---

[1]Compare *supra* Chap. 6, p. 91.

bolic forms,[2] has traced this principle of "spiritualizing" (which is not really "anthropomorphizing," since it affects the image of man himself in strange ways) through the entire fabric of language, and has shown how human minds thinking with words have built up their whole world out of "powers," which are modeled on subjective feelings of potency. Religion, history, politics, and even the traditional abstractions of philosophy reflect this fundamental *Weltanschauung* which is incorporated in language. The formulation engendered by the subjective model is really a great metaphor, in which our "natural" conception of the world is expressed; but where the human mind has only one symbol to represent an idea, the symbol and its meaning are not separable, because there is no other form in which the meaning could be thought and distinguished from the symbol. Consequently the great metaphor is identified with its meaning; the feelings of power that serve as symbols are attributed to the reality symbolized, and the world appears as a realm of potent Beings.

This conception of nature characterizes what Cassirer calls the "mythic consciousness." But, as mythic thinking determines the form of language and then is supported and furthered by language, so the progressive articulation and sharpening of that supreme instrument ultimately breaks the mythic mold; the gradual perfection of *discursive form*, which is inherent in the syntax of language as metaphor is inherent in its vocabulary, slowly begets a new mode of thought, the "scientific consciousness," which supersedes the mythic, to greater or lesser extent, in the "common sense" of different persons and groups of persons. The shift is probably never complete, but to the degree that it is effected, metaphor is replaced by literal statement, and mythology gives way to science.[3]

The primitive phases of social development are entirely dominated by the "mythic consciousness." From earliest times, through the late tribal stages, men live in a world of "Powers"—divine or semidivine Beings, whose wills determine the courses of cosmic and human events. Painting, sculpture, and literature, however archaic, show us these Powers already fixed in visible or describable form, anthropomorphic or zoomorphic—a sacred bison, a sacred cow, a scarab, a Tiki, a Hermes or

---

[2] See especially Vols. I and II of *Die Philosophie der symbolischen Formen;* also *Sprache und Mythos* (*Language and Myth*), and *An Essay on Man*, Part I, *passim*, especially chap. 2, "A Clue to the Nature of Man: the Symbol."

[3] Cf. his *Substance and Function.*

Korê, finally an Apollo, Athena, Osiris, Christ—the God who has a personal appearance even to the cut of his beard, a personal history of birth, death, and glorification, a symbolic cult, a poetic and musical liturgy. But in the first stages of imagination, no such definite forms embody the terrible and fecund Powers that surround humanity. The first recognition of them is through the feeling of personal power and will in the human body and their first representation is through a bodily activity which abstracts the sense of power from the practical experiences in which that sense is usually an obscure factor. This activity is known as "dancing." The dance creates an image of nameless and even bodiless Powers filling a complete, autonomous realm, a "world." It is the first presentation of the world as a realm of mystic forces.

This explains the early development of dance as a complete and even sophisticated art form. Curt Sachs, in his compendious *World History of the Dance,* remarks with some surprise: "Strange as it may sound—since the Stone Age, the dance has taken on as little in the way of new forms as of new content. The history of the creative dance takes place in prehistory."[4] Dance is, in fact, the most serious intellectual business of savage life: it is the envisagement of a world beyond the spot and the moment of one's animal existence, the first conception of life as a whole—continuous, superpersonal life, punctuated by birth and death, surrounded and fed by the rest of nature. From this point of view, the prehistoric evolution of dancing does not appear strange at all. It is the very process of religious thinking, which begets the conception of "Powers" as it symbolizes them. To the "mythic consciousness" these creations are realities, not symbols; they are not felt to be created by the dance at all, but to be invoked, adjured, challenged, or placated, as the case may be. The symbol of the world, the balletic realm of forces, *is* the world, and dancing is the human spirit's participation in it.

Yet the dancer's world is a world transfigured, wakened to a special kind of life. Sachs observes that the oldest dance form seems to be the *Reigen,* or circle dance, which he takes to be a heritage from animal ancestors.[5] He regards it as a spontaneous expression of gaiety, non-

---

[4]*World History of the Dance,* p. 62.

[5]"The origins of human dancing . . . are not revealed to us either in ethnology or prehistory. We must rather infer them from the dance of the apes: the gay,

representative and therefore "introvert," according to his (rather unfortunate) adaptation of categories borrowed from Jung's dynamic psychology. But the circle dance really symbolizes a most important reality in the life of primitive men—the sacred realm, the magic circle. The *Reigen* as a dance form has nothing to do with spontaneous prancing; it fulfills a holy office, perhaps the *first* holy office of the dance—it divides the sphere of holiness from that of profane existence. In this way it creates the stage of the dance, which centers naturally in the altar or its equivalent—the totem, the priest, the fire—or perhaps the slain bear, or the dead chieftain to be consecrated.

In the magic circle all daemonic powers are loosed. The mundane realm is excluded, and with it, very often, the restrictions and proprieties that belong to it. Dr. Sachs has said quite truly that all dance is ecstatic —the holy group dance, the vertiginous individual whirl dance, the erotic couple dance. "In the ecstasy of the dance man bridges the chasm between this and the other world, to the realm of demons, spirits, and God."[6] Sometimes the fight against powers of darkness is enacted in a weapon dance with an invisible partner; sometimes military prowess is represented as a clash of visible contestants. The virtue of weapons themselves may be celebrated by flinging, catching, twirling and flourishing them. All vital and crucial activities have been sanctified by dance, as in birth, puberty, marriage, death—planting and harvest, hunting, battle, victory—seasons, gatherings, housewarmings. The occasions of such sacred dances naturally led to pantomime illustrating the objects of desire or fear; pantomime furnished new dance forms, often capable of great elaboration; the elaborations required properties—costumes, implements,

---

lively circle dance about some tall, firmly fixed object must have come down to man from his animal ancestors. We may therefore assume that the circle dance was already a permanent possession of the Paleolithic culture, the first perceptible stage of human civilization." (*Ibid.*, p. 208.)

Dr. Sachs certainly oversimplifies the problem of art and overestimates the evidence (from Köhler) for the solution he accepts. We do not know that the apes experience only lively fun as they trot around a post; perhaps some fickle forerunner of mystical excitement awakens in them at that moment. Perhaps their antics are merely playful. Perhaps the tendency to rhythmic tramping was set off by Prof. Köhler's example, and would never have developed in the jungle unless they watched human dancers somewhere. We know too little to infer anything from "the dance of the apes."

[6]*Ibid.*, p. 4.

masks—and these in turn created *dance characters,* spirits and animals, ghosts and gods, according to the conceptual stock in trade of the dancers. The "Country Devil" of the Congo is a giant dance mask whose dread habitat is a tree in the jungle, where it hangs between dances, at a safe distance from the compound.[7] The "May Queen" of European tradition is a dance personage, probably taking the place of a fertility goddess to whom the dance was originally addressed. The secondary character of the "King of the May," sometimes crowned and exalted beside the queen, suggests that the center of the whole ceremony may have been an erotic couple dance, invoking the procreative forces in fields and vineyards and flocks, or urging them along by "sympathetic magic."

No matter what the dance is supposed to achieve, what dramatic or ritualistic elements it embraces, its first move is always the creation of a realm of virtual Power. "Ecstasy" is nothing else than the feeling of entering such a realm. There are dance forms that serve mainly to sever the bonds of actuality and establish the "otherworldly" atmosphere in which illusory forces operate. Whirling and circling, gliding and skipping and balancing are such basic gestures that seem to spring from the deepest sources of feeling, the rhythms of physical life as such. Because they present no ideas of things outside the organism, but only objectify vitality itself, Dr. Sachs has designated these elements as "imageless," and regards them as the special stock in trade of "introvert" peoples. The distinction between "introvert" and "extravert" dancers, measured by the uses of "imageless dances" and "image dances" (miming) respectively, goes through the whole book. But it never rests on any psychological findings that prove the purely ecstatic dancers—dervishes, devil dancers, contortionists—to be more introvert than (say) the maenads who enact the death and resurrection of Dionysus, or to distinguish the mentality of persons who dance on the village green in a simple ring from that of the dancers who wind a "chain-dance," borrowing their motif from the process of weaving, or who wave outstretched hands to simulate birds in flight. As he traces the history of "imageless dances," they appear to merge with dramatic pantomime; and conversely his account of imitative gestures shows their choric development to be generally away from

---

[7]According to a lecture by Pearl Primus, upon her return from Africa (winter of 1949–50)

mimicry, toward pure rhythmic and expressive gesture. In summary of his findings he notes this himself. "From these examples," he says, "we may see that it has been the fate of the animal dance to grow continually away from nature. The urge to compose the movements into a stylized dance, therefore to make them less real, has taken more and more of the natural form from the steps and gestures. All too quickly the duck walk becomes a simple squatting step. . . .

"On the other hand, perhaps motions of a purely individual motor origin have been considered mimetic and animal-like and given a new interpretation."[8]

Reflecting on these facts, he makes a general observation that shows the whole imitative business of art in what I consider its proper light —as a guiding concept, or *motif*. "There are therefore in the animal dance exactly the same relationships," he says, "which are familiar in the history of decoration: have we to deal with the abstraction and geometrization of an animal theme or with the zoomorphic naturalization of an abstract and geometric theme?" (Compare this remark with the reflections on design-motifs in Chapter 4: at once a fundamental relation between two very different arts becomes apparent, namely their strictly similar use of *natural forms*.)

The distinction between extravert and introvert, representative and non-representative dance, which becomes more and more tenuous throughout the work, is really much less useful than the consideration of *what is created* in the various kinds of dance, and what purposes, therefore, the various rhythmic, mimetic, musical, acrobatic, or other elements serve. What is created is the image of a world of vital forces, embodied or disembodied; in the early stages of human thought when symbol and import are apprehended as one reality, this image is the realm of holiness; in later stages it is recognized as the work of art, the expressive form which it really is. But in either case, the several dance elements have essentially constructive functions. They have to establish, maintain, and articulate the play of "Powers." Masquerading and miming alone cannot do this, any more than naturalistic representation of objects can of itself create or shape pictorial space. But histrionic motifs assure the illusion, the "dance ecstasy." "It aims simply at ecstasy," says Dr. Sachs,

[8]*Op. cit.*, pp. 84–85.

"or it takes over the form of the mystic circling, in which power jumps across from those on the outside to the one on the inside or vice versa . . . the people encircle the head of an enemy, the sacrificial buffalo, the altar, the golden calf, the holy wafer, in order that the power of these objects may flow across to them in some mysterious way."[9]

Whatever motifs from actual life may enter into a dance, they are rhythmicized and formalized by that very ingression. Within the Magic Circle every action grows into balletic motion and accent: the lifting of a child or of a grail, the imitations of beasts and birds, the kiss, the war whoop. Free dance movement produces, above all (for the performer as well as the spectator) the illusion of a conquest of gravity, i.e. freedom from the actual forces that are normally known and felt to control the dancer's body. Frank Thiess remarked this fact in his excellent book, already quoted in the previous chapter. After some pertinent comments on the excessive use of stretching, leaping, and balloon-bouncing techniques in otherwise quite empty performances, "in which the ballerinas seek to demonstrate that the earth's gravitation has practically no hold upon them," he adds: "None the less, this demand for conquest of gravity was based on a correct conception of the nature of dance; for its main tendency is always to surmount the bonds of massive weight, and lightness of movement is, perhaps, the cardinal demand one has to make on a dancer. . . . It is, after all, nothing but the conquest of material resistance as such, and therefore is not a special phenomenon at all in the realm of art. Consider the triumph of sculpture over the stone, of painting over the flat surface, of poetry over language, etc. It is, then, precisely the material with which any particular art has to work that is to be overcome, and to a certain degree is to be rendered no longer apparent."[10] Somewhat later, still in this connection, he designates the toe dance as "the frozen symbol of this ideal," especially intended to show that the body has lost nearly all its weight, so that it can be supported by the tips of its toes. And here he adds a comment significant for the theory of semblance: "In actuality," he says, "the toes are securely boxed, the support of the body is the instep. But that is neither here nor there; the body is supposed to *appear* weightless, and thus, from the artistic standpoint, to *be* so."[11]

---

[9]*Ibid.*, p. 57.   [10]*Der Tanz als Kunstwerk*, p. 63.   [11]*Ibid.*, p. 67.

Even the toe dance, so much despised by Isadora Duncan and by the schools she inspired, is essentially creative, not athletic. The art of dancing is a wider category than any particular conception that may govern a tradition, a style, a sacred or secular use; wider than the cult dance, the folk dance, the ballroom dance, the ballet, the modern "expressive dance." Isadora, convinced that the exhibition of personal feeling was the only legitimate theme for terpsichorean art, could not understand her own reactions to the dancing of Kschinsky and Pavlova, which captivated her despite her beliefs and ideals.

"I am an enemy of the Ballet," she wrote, "which I consider a false and preposterous art, in fact, outside the pale of all art. But it was impossible not to applaud the fairylike figure of Kschinsky as she flitted across the stage more like a lovely bird or butterfly than a human being. . . . Some days later I received a visit from the lovely Pavlova; and again I was presented with a box to see her in the ravishing Ballet of Gisèle. Although the movement of these dances was against every artistic and human feeling, again I could not resist warmly applauding the exquisite apparition of Pavlova as she floated over the stage that evening."[12]

How a ballet could be "ravishing," in which every movement was contrary to art and human feeling, was a problem that she evidently did not pursue in her theoretical musings. Had she thought more deeply about her own words, she might have found the answer, the key to the loveliness of Kschinsky and Pavlova and their entire "false and preposterous art," and the very thing her own dance seems to have lacked most grievously: the dancer as an apparition.

The play of virtual powers manifests itself in the motions of illusory personages, whose passionate gestures fill the world they create—a remote, rationally indescribable world in which forces seem to become visible. But what makes them visible is not itself always visual; hearing and kinesthesia support the rhythmic, moving image, to such an extent that the dance illusion exists for the dancer as well as for the spectators. In tribal society some dances include all persons present, leaving no spectators at all. Now, a person dancing has visual impressions, but never the actual impression of the performance as a whole.

---

[12]*My Life*, p. 164.

A solitary dancer does not even see other members of some group in which he takes a part. Yet dance is essentially addressed to sight. I know of no cult that practices dancing in total darkness, nor of any accomplished dancer who is blind. Near darkness is often courted, but *precisely for its visual effects,* the blurring and melting of forms, the mystery of black spaces. Moonlight and firelight are used by primitive dancers as artfully as footlights and colored spotlights by modern choreographers, except that the dance is brought to the light source, so to speak, so that a given illumination is exploited, instead of bringing prescribed light effects to bear on a performance for which they are deliberately invented.[13]

The solution to this difficulty lies in the realization that the basic abstraction is virtual gesture, and that gesture is both a visible and a muscular phenomenon, i.e. may be seen or felt. Conscious gesture is essentially communication, like language. In total darkness it loses its communicative character. If we commune with ourselves, we imagine its visible character, and this, of course, we can do also in the dark; but to a blind person conscious gesture is as artificial as speech to the deaf. Our most direct knowledge of gestic expression is muscular feeling, but its purpose is to be seen. Consequently the illusion of gesture may be made in terms of visual or kinesthetic appearance; but where only one sense is actually appealed to, the other must be satisfied by implication. Because dance-gesture is symbolic, objectified, every dance which is to have balletic significance primarily for the people engaged in it is necessarily ecstatic. It must take the dancer "out of himself," and it may do this by an astounding variety of means: by the merest suggestion of motion, when physical preparations have been made in advance through drink, drugs, or fasting; by music at once monotonous and exciting, such, for instance, as the dervishes listen to for a long period before they arise; by strong musical and physical rhythms that enthrall the dancer almost instantly in a romantic unrealism (this is the usual technique of the secular "ballroom" dance); or—most primitive and natural of all—by weaving the "magic circle" round the altar or the deity, whereby every dancer is exalted at once to the status of a mystic. His every motion becomes dance-gesture because he has become a spirit,

---

[13] This observation, too, was made by Pearl Primus after her visit to "the bush."

a dance-personage, which may be more or less than a man—more, if the appeal of the tribe is concentrated in his particular performance; less, if he simply merges his moving limbs with the greater movement of the *Reigen,* and his mind with the vague and awful Presence that fills the circle.

Every dancer *sees* the dance sufficiently to let his imagination grasp it as a whole; and with his own body-feeling he understands the gestic forms that are its interwoven, basic elements. He cannot see his own form as such, but he *knows* his appearance—the lines described by his body are implied in the shifts of his vision, even if he is dancing alone, and are guaranteed by the rhythmic play of his muscles, the freedom with which his impulses spend themselves in complete and intended movements. He sees *the world in which his body dances,* and that is the primary illusion of his work; in this closed realm he develops his ideas.

The dance in its pristine strength is completely creative. Powers become apparent in a framework of space and time; but these dimensions, like everything else in the balletic realm, are not actual. Just as spatial phenomena in music are more like plastic space than like the spaces of geometry or of geography,[14] so in dance both space and time, as they enter into the primary illusion, and occasionally appear in their own right as secondary illusions, are always created elements, i.e. virtual forms. Primitive dance makes its own realm, and assures its own duration, chiefly by the unbroken tension of its circling and shifting, its acrobatic balances and rhythmic completion of movements.

The "body set" of the dancers, maintained by the ecstatic concentration for great feats of leaping, whirling, stamping piston-like beats, holds the time structure together, and the activity itself gives rise to the tonal accompaniment that is at once a musical by-product and a strong binding device. The Indian's "how-how-how" is an integral part of the war dance, as the fakir's hum is of his mystic actions. Sachs points out that animal dances are quite naturally accompanied by sounds reminiscent of the represented animal, and remarks: "The genuine animal dance has need of no other music." The tonal element is a dance activity, a means of filling and vitalizing the time frame of the performance.

---

[14]Compare *supra* Chap. 7, p. 117.

Musical and pictorial effects, which have been widely and variously regarded as the essence, the aim, or the controlling models of the dancer's art, seem rather to have been developed quite independently of plastic arts or of harmony, as dance elements with structural, purely balletic functions. Because of the complex nature of its primary illusion—the appearance of Power—and of its basic abstraction—virtual gesture, primitive dance holds a complete hegemony over all artistic materials and devices, though without exploiting them beyond its own needs. There are several dancers, and also aestheticians of the dance, whose writings bear witness to the importance of terpsichorean space and time, and to their essentially artistic, illusory nature. Hanns Hasting, in a study entitled "Music for the Dance," makes this telling observation: "When a dancer speaks of space, he does not only, nor even principally mean actual space, but space which signifies something immaterialistic, unreal, imaginary, which goes beyond the visible outlines of one or more gestures."[15]

The real profundity, however, of the relationship among the arts by virtue of their characteristic symbolic creations is attested by a passage in Rudolf Sonner's *Musik und Tanz*, where he says: "On lower cultural levels, dance is a typical symbol of space, and begets an intense space-experience. For there is, as yet, no place of worship save possibly a plotted field (sacred grove), a holy ground. But from the moment when, by the building of temples, a new, deep space-experience is created in terms of another symbolism, dance as a [spatial] cult ceremony seems to be superseded by the forces of architecture. . . ."[16]

The relation between dance and music is more obvious, and has been studied far more exhaustively. Whether a dance is accompanied by music or not, it always moves in *musical time;* the recognition of this natural relation between the two arts underlies their universal affinity. In highly ecstatic performances the temporal autonomy of the dance does

---

[15]In *Modern Dance*, p. 39. The passage goes on: "Out of this feeling springs a need for musical forms which create the same musical space." Although such emphasis on spatial values may sometimes be advantageous, I cannot agree with the writer on the general principle of parallelism which he develops from this point on. There is no reason why *generally* the space effect achieved in dance should be duplicated by a similar secondary illusion in music.

[16]*Musik und Tanz: vom Kulttanz zum Jazz.* See p. 76.

not require a very well-made musical fabric to emphasize and assure it; fragments of song and the atonal beats of sticks or drums, mere punctuations of sound, suffice. The bodily sensations of the dancers, merging with sights and sounds, with the whole kaleidoscope of figures (frequently masked) and mystic gestures, hold the great rhythm together. The individual dancer dances not so much with his fellows—they are all transformed into dance-beings, or even into mere parts of a daemonic organism —as he dances with the world; he dances with the music, with his own voice, with his spear that balances in his hand as though by its own power, with light, and rain, and earth.

But a new demand is made on the dance when it is to enthrall not only its own performers, but a passive audience (rustic audiences that furnish the music by singing and clapping are really participants; they are not included here). The dance as a spectacle is generally regarded as a product of degeneration, a secularized form of what is really a religious art.[17] But it is really a natural development even within the confines of the "mythic consciousness," for dance magic may be projected to a spectator, to cure, purify, or initiate him. Tylor describes a savage initiation ceremony in which the boys solemnly witnessed a dog dance performed by the older men. Shamans, medicine men, witch doctors and magicians commonly perform dances for their magical effects not on the dancer, but on the awed spectators.

From the artistic standpoint this use of the dance is a great advance over the purely ecstatic, because addressed to an audience the dance becomes essentially and not only incidentally a spectacle, and thus finds its true creative aim—to make the world of Powers visible. This aim dictates all sorts of new techniques, because bodily experiences, muscular tensions, momentum, the feelings of precarious balance or the impulsions of unbalance, can no longer be counted on to give form and continuity to the dance. Every such kinesthetic element must be replaced by visual,

---

[17]Cf. Rudolf Sonner, *op. cit.*, p. 9: "In the last analysis dance always goes back to a religious-ceremonial practical motive. Only in a late stage do dances descend to a sphere of purely aesthetic hedonism, in which they lose all serious meaning."

Also Curt Sachs, *op. cit.*, p. 6: "As early as the Stone Age, dances became works of art. As early as the Metal Ages, legend seizes the dance and raises it into drama. But when in higher cultures it becomes art in the narrower sense, when it becomes a spectacle, when it seeks to influence men rather than spirits, then its universal power is broken."

audible, or histrionic elements to create a comparable ecstatic illusion for the audience. At this stage, the problems of the tribal or cult dance are practically those of the modern ballet: to break the beholder's sense of actuality and set up the virtual image of a different world; to create a play of forces that *confronts* the percipient, instead of engulfing him, as it does when he is dancing, and his own activity is a major factor in making the dance illusion.

The presence of an audience gives dance its artistic discipline; and where this audience commands great respect, for instance where the dancers perform to royal spectators, choreographic art soon becomes a highly conscious, formalized, and expert presentation. It may, however, still be religious; in the Orient it has never entirely lost its cult significance, although its long tradition has brought it, by this time, to a state of technical perfection and cultural sophistication that our own balletic efforts cannot match, and indeed, our balletic thinking probably cannot fathom. "In southeastern Asia," says Dr. Sachs, "where the wrench dance has moved into a more restricted province, the limbs are methodically wrenched out of joint. . . .

"In Cambodia, as also in Burma, the arms and legs are bent at an angle, the shoulder blades are pushed together, the abdomen is contracted, and the body as a whole is in 'bit and brace position'. . . .

"There is a very conscious relationship to the puppet dance—where according to absolute standards the dance as a high art has reached one of its peaks—in the dances of the Sultan families of Java, and, somewhat degenerated, in those of the Javanese professional dancers, who use the former dances as a model. For the dance of living men and women on the stage of Java and the presentation in pantomime on a white screen of old hero stories by means of dolls cut out of leather, have stood for centuries side by side stylistically and otherwise. . . . The Javanese dance is almost in two dimensions, and since every limb of the body must reveal itself complete and unforeshortened, it is incomparably expressive."[18]

Such dancing is designed entirely to present a unified and complete appearance to an audience. Yet the most theatrical dance may still have religious connotations. "According to the strict Hindu view, dance with-

---

[18]*Op. cit.*, pp. 45–46.

out prayer is considered vulgar; he who witnesses it will be childless and will be reincarnated in the body of an animal."[19]

The most important effect of the passive audience on the history of dancing is, I think, the separation of the dance as spectacle from the dance as activity, and the consequent separate histories of these two distinct phases. From one we have derived the ballet, which is entirely a professional affair, and from the other the social dance, which is almost as completely an amateur pursuit. The tap dance and clog dance hold an intermediate position; like the square dance, they are really folk art, not wholly divorced from the village dance in which the audience participates by singing, and sometimes clapping, stamping, or jigging. As such they have really not developed under the influence of the passive audience, but belong to a more primitive order. Perhaps this has something to do with their revival and popularity in our society, which bears many marks of primitivism—fairly crude face painting, artificially altered eyebrows, dyed finger- and toe-nails, etc.; a love of louder and louder noises, music learned from savage peoples; a strong tendency to myth and cult activity in political life, and a return to all-out, tribal soldiery instead of the more specialized reliance on professional armies that had allowed seventeenth- and eighteenth-century Europe to develop an essentially civil culture.

Be that as it may, the separation of stage dancing from the purely ecstatic took place long ago—probably much longer ago in some parts of Asia than in Europe—and ever since this schism, the two kinds of dance have followed different lines of development, and each has been affected in its own way by the great trauma that Western civilization has of necessity inflicted on all the arts—secularization.

Why, without motives of worship or magic-making, did people go on dancing at all? Because the image of Powers is still, in some sense, a world image to them. To the "mythic consciousness" it presents reality, nature; to a secular mind it shows a romantic world; to the knowing psychologist this is the infantile "world" of spontaneous, irresponsible reactions, wish-potency, freedom—the dream world. The eternal popularity of dance lies in its ecstatic function, today as in earliest times; but instead of transporting the dancers from a profane to a sacred state,

[19] *Ibid.*, p. 223.

it now transports them from what they acknowledge as "reality" to a realm of romance. There are quite genuine "virtual powers" created even in social dance; artistically they may be trivial—merely the magnetic forces that unite a group, most simply a couple, of dancers, and the powers of rhythm, that "carry" the body through space with seemingly less than its usual requirement of effort—but they are convincing. For this reason even social dancing is intrinsically art, though it does not achieve more than elementary forms before it is put to non-artistic uses —delusion, self-deception, escape. The dream world is essentially a fabric of erotic forces. Often the dance technique serves merely to set up its primary illusion of free, non-physical powers, so that a daydream may be "started" by the dancer's ecstatic removal from actuality, and after that the dance becomes confused and makes way for self-expression pure and simple. Dancing which ends in making actual indecent passes at the girl, like the Bavarian *Schuhplattler,* in hugging and kissing, as the early waltz usually did, or even quite innocently in a game of genuine competition—trying to catch a ring, trying to escape from a circle, etc.—such dancing is merely instrumental. Its creativity is the lowest possible, and as soon as it has served a practical purpose the dance itself collapses.

But this is an extreme picture of the degeneration of dance due to secularization. Its normal fate is simply the shift from religious to romantic uses. Undoubtedly the artistic virtues of some religiously ecstatic dances, practiced year in, year out by dancing sects, are no greater than those of the saraband, the minuet, the waltz, or the tango. In fact, the divine Powers contacted in traditional mystic dancing are often but vaguely distinguishable from the erotic forces, the bonds of love and the communing selves, or the freedom from gravity, which enthusiastic ballroom dancers experience.

The most important, from the balletic standpoint, is the last—the sense of freedom from gravity. This ingredient in the dance illusion is untouched by the shift from cult values to entertainment values. It is a direct and forceful effect of rhythmicized gesture, enhanced by the stretched posture that not only reduces the friction surfaces of the foot, but also restricts all natural bodily motions—the free use of arms and shoulders, the unconscious turnings of the trunk, and especially the automatic responses of the leg muscles in locomotion—and thereby produces a new body-feeling, in which every muscular tension registers itself as something kinesthetically new, peculiar to the dance. In a body so disposed, no movement is automatic; if any action goes forward spontaneously, it is induced by the *rhythm* set up in imagination, and prefigured in the first, intentional acts, and not by practical habit. In a person with a penchant for the dance, this body-feeling is intense and complete, involving every voluntary muscle, to the fingertips, the throat, the eyelids. It is the sense of virtuosity, akin to the sense of articulation that marks the talented performer of music. The dancer's body is *ready for rhythm*.

The rhythm that is to turn every movement into gesture, and the dancer himself into a creature liberated from the usual bonds of gravitation and muscular inertia, is most readily established by music. In the highly serious, invocative, religious dance, the music often had to establish a complete trance before the dancers moved; but in the secular pleasure-dance the illusion to be created is so elementary, the gesture pattern so simple, that a mere metric rhythm is usually enough to activate the performers. Two bars, four bars, the feet begin to tap, the partners to conjoin their motions, and the ecstasy builds up in repetition, variation, and elaboration, supported by a pulse beat of sound more felt than heard.

Popular dancing so motivated, carried on in a spirit of romance, escape, relief from the burden of actuality, without any spiritually strenuous achievement—that is to say, the erotic and entertaining pleasure-dance—has begotten a corresponding genre of musical composition, originally intended merely as part of the dance: the whole literature of "dance music." This in turn has produced musical forms which are independent, today, of that original connection: the suite, sonata, and symphony. Even the waltz, the tango, the rumba, have suggested works of music that are not really intended to be danced.[20] But such developments are musical events, not balletic. The dance, in relation to the concert suite that begins with an *intrata* and ends with a *gigue,* serves as a musical motif, which is fairly well dropped by the time Haydn takes the sonata in hand. Real "dance music" is a different thing, and every age has its harvest of it —music expressly fashioned to be "swallowed" by the simple, entranc-

---

[20]A study of this influence of dance on the history of music may be found in Evelyn Porter's *Music Through the Dance.*

ing, but ephemeral, amateur dance of the ballroom. Usually it is artistically as negligible as the romantic creations it serves. But here—as in all the labyrinthine byways of art—a piece of music so conceived may be a work of true art. And then it does something to the dance, as soon as it comes to the ears of a gifted dancer; for the social dance, too, has all the possibilities of serious art. There is no theoretical limit to the expressiveness of the Exhibition Dance. Its one requirement for objective significance and beauty is—balletic genius.

To make the dance a work of art requires that translation of kinesthetic experience into visual and audible elements, which I mentioned above as the artistic discipline imposed by the presence of passive spectators. The dancer, or dancers, must transform the stage for the audience as well as for themselves into an autonomous, complete, virtual realm, and all motions into a play of visible forces in unbroken, virtual time, without effecting either a work of plastic art or of "melos." Both space and time, as perceptible factors, disappear almost entirely in the dance illusion, serving to beget the appearance of interacting powers rather than to be themselves apparent. That is to say, music must be swallowed by movement, while color, pictorial composition, costume, décor —all the really plastic elements—become the frame and foil of gesture. The sudden effects of pure time or perfect space that sometimes occur are almost immediately merged again into the life of the dance.

The primary illusion of dance is a peculiarly rich experience, just as immediate as that of music or of the plastic arts, but more complex. Both space and time are implicitly created with it. Story runs through it like a thread, without linking it at all to literature; impersonation and miming are often systematically involved in its basic abstraction, virtual gesture, but dance pantomime is not drama; the mummery of masks and costumes, to which its thematic gestures belong, is depersonalizing rather than humanly interesting. Dance, the art of the Stone Age, the art of primitive life par excellence, holds a hegemony over all art materials.

Yet like all art it can harbor no raw material, no things or facts, in its illusory world. The virtual form must be organic and autonomous and divorced from actuality. Whatever enters into it does so in radical artistic transformation: its space is plastic, its time is musical, its themes are fantasy, its actions symbolic. This accounts, I think, for the many different notions which dancers and aestheticians have held as to what is the essence of dance. Every one of its secondary illusions has been hailed as the true key to its nature, assimilating the whole phenomenon of dance to the realm wherein the given illusion is primary; dance has been called an art of space, an art of time, a kind of poetry, a kind of drama.[21] But it is none of those things, nor is it the mother of any other arts—not even drama, as I think a study of dramatic creation will presently show.[22]

As a rule, the dancers who take dance motion to be essentially musical are those who think mainly in terms of the solo dance, and are not quite weaned away from the subjective, kinesthetic experience of dance forms as the full apprehension of them. Musical rhythm enters somewhat more directly and insistently into the kinesthetic perception of one's own gestures than into the objective perception of gestures performed by others, no matter how well the music is used in the latter case. On the other hand, those who regard dance as an art of space are usually the true stage dancers and masters of ballet. Yet both parties are misled by their awareness of secondary illusions, which are really devices that support the total creation or enhance its expressiveness.

In the possibility of such passing artistic effects, which really suggest, for the moment, an excursion into some different realm of art, lies the clue to one of the deepest relations among the great art genders—the kinship of their primary illusions. This relation, however, is always kinship and not identity, so that two radically distinct orders never merge; a work never belongs to more than one realm, and it always establishes that one completely and immediately, as its very substance. But the distinct appearance of a simpler illusion, e.g. pure space or pure time, in the context of the more complex illusion of dance or of literature,[23] often effects a sudden revelation of emotive import by stressing a formal aspect and abstracting it, which makes its feeling-content apparent. The same emphasis is sometimes achieved by passing momentarily to another mode of the primary illusion; Sullivan remarked that sculptural decoration in architecture serves for the intensification of feeling,[24] and D. G. James,

---

[21]Cf. Chap. 11, especially pp. 169–172.

[22]See below, Chap. 17.

[23]The reader is referred to the next chapter for an account of the literary illusion.

[24]*Kindergarten Chats*, p. 188.

in *Skepticism and Poetry,* claims that each one of Shakespeare's central characters achieves a "depersonalization of feeling" in a lyrical passage, which is really the apotheosis of the play.[25]

In the dance, the rich fabric of its primary illusion confuses the theorist, but to the creative artist everything is part of his dance that can serve to make the semblance of psychic and mystic Powers an image of the "powers" directly felt in all organic life, physical or mental, active or passive. "Strong and convincing art," said Mary Wigman, "has never arisen from theories. It has always grown organically. Its carriers and supporters have been those few creative natures for whom a path of work has been determined by destiny."[26]

Today, in our secular culture, those artists are the dancers of the stage, of the Russian ballet and its derivatives, of the various schools of "Modern Dance," and occasionally of the revue, when some number in its potpourri of good and bad entertainment rises to unscheduled heights, through the inadvertent engagement of a genius. The work of dance composition is as clear and constructive, as imaginative and as contrived as any plastic or musical composition; it springs from an idea of feeling, a matrix of symbolic form, and grows organically like every other work of art. It is curious to compare the further words of Mary Wigman, in the essay from which I have just quoted, with the testimonies of musicians[27] on the creative process:

"All dance construction arises from the dance experience which the performer is destined to incarnate and which gives his creation its true stamp. The experience shapes the kernel, the basic accord of his dance existence around which all else crystallizes. Each creative person carries with him his own characteristic theme. It is waiting to be aroused through experience and completes itself during one whole creative cycle in manifold radiations, variations and transformations."[28]

The substance of such dance creation is the same Power that enchanted ancient caves and forests, but today we invoke it with full knowledge of its illusory status, and therefore with wholly artistic in-

---

[25]*Skepticism and Poetry,* p. 118.
[26]"The New German Dance," in *Modern Dance,* p. 20.
[27]See Chap. 8.
[28]*Op. cit.,* p. 21.

tent. The realm of magic around the altar was broken, inevitably and properly, by the growth of the human mind from mythic conception to philosophical and scientific thought. The dance, that most sacred instrument of sorcery, worship, and prayer, bereft of its high office, suffered the degeneration of all cast-off rituals into irrational custom or social play. But it has left us the legacy of its great illusions, and with them the challenge to an artistic imagination no longer dependent on delusions for its motive powers. Once more human beings dance with high seriousness and fervor; the temple dance and the rain dance were never more reverent than the work of our devout artists.

Serious dance is very ancient, but as art it is relatively new, except possibly in some old Asiatic cultures. And as art it creates the image of that pulsating organic life which formerly it was expected to give and sustain. "The image which has assumed form gives evidence of the primary vision conceived through the inner experience. That creation will ever be the most pure and forceful in its effect, in which the most minute detail speaks of the vibrating, animated unity which called forth the idea. The shape of the individual's inner experience . . . will also have the unique, magnetic power of transmission which makes it possible to draw other persons, the participating spectators, into the magic circle of creation."[29]

---

[29]*Ibid.*, p. 23.

Chapter thirteen

POESIS

Literature is one of the great arts, and is more widely taught and studied than any other, yet its artistic character is more often avowed than really discerned and respected. The reason why literature is a standard academic pursuit lies in the very fact that one can treat it as something else than art. Since its normal material is language, and language is, after all, the medium of discourse, it is always possible to look at a literary work as an assertion of facts and opinions, that is, as a piece of discursive symbolism functioning in the usual communicative way. This deceptive aspect of verbal art has made "literature" one of our principal examination subjects, whereas the study of other arts is generally deemed to require special inclination or talent and is therefore left to the student's choice.

Whole libraries of books have been written on the principles of literary art, because the intellectual approach which is natural to scholars makes those principles at once very intriguing and very confounding. The significance of any piece of literature must lie, supposedly, in what the author says; yet every critic who is worth his salt has enough literary intuition to know that *the way of saying things* is somehow all-important. This is especially obvious in poetry. How, then, is the reader to divide his interest between the value of the assertion and the special way it is made? Isn't the wording everything? And yet, must not the wording itself be judged by its adequacy to state the author's ideas?

The essential task of criticism seems to be to determine what the special mode of expression is, and how serviceable it is for saying what the author wants to say. There are numberless introductions to poetry that urge one to determine "what the poet is trying to say," and to judge of "how well he says it." But if the reader can make clear what the poet

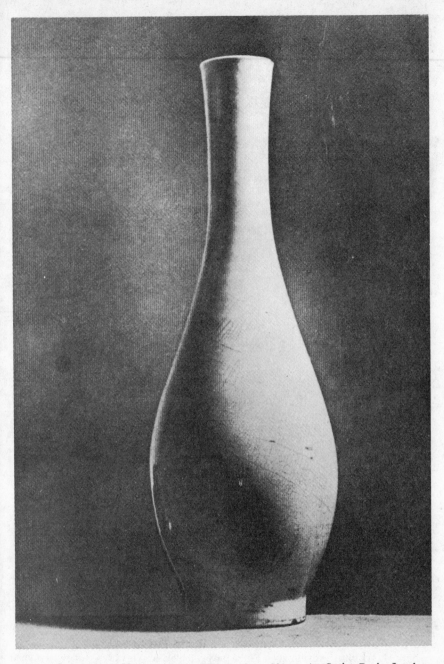

Plate I STONEWARE VASE   MING DYNASTY; from *Chinese Art*, Spring Books, London.

"There is such a concentration on appearance that one has a sense of seeing sheer appearances."

Plate II WOVEN BEDSPREAD   Photo by Phillip A. Viscutti, Courtesy of Lyman Allyn Museum, New London, Conn.

"Even the most elementary design serves to concentrate and hold one's vision to the expanse it adorns."

Plate III MAORI MAN

"The immediate effect of good decoration is to make the surface, somehow, more *visible*."

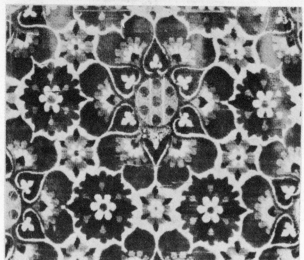

VENETIAN
Courtesy of the
Metropolitan Museum of Art,
Fletcher Fund, 1946

MEXICAN
Courtesy of the
American Museum
of Natural History

CHINESE   Courtesy of the State of Washington Campus Studios

ASSYRIAN   Courtesy of the Metropolitan Museum of Art

Plate IV

"The interesting point is that in
each of these inventions the form
is so unmistakably a flower."

INDONESIAN   Courtesy of the
                 Smithsonian Institution

Plate V

"Rings become eyes . . . and spirals tails, curls, ears, branches, breaking waves."

MEXICAN
Courtesy of the
American Museum
of Natural History

CHINESE
From a Booklet by
H. T. Morgan, Los Angeles

CHINESE   Courtesy of the State of Washington Campus Studios

Plate VI G<small>IOTTO</small> *The Salutation*   Alinari

"From beginning to end, every stroke is composition."

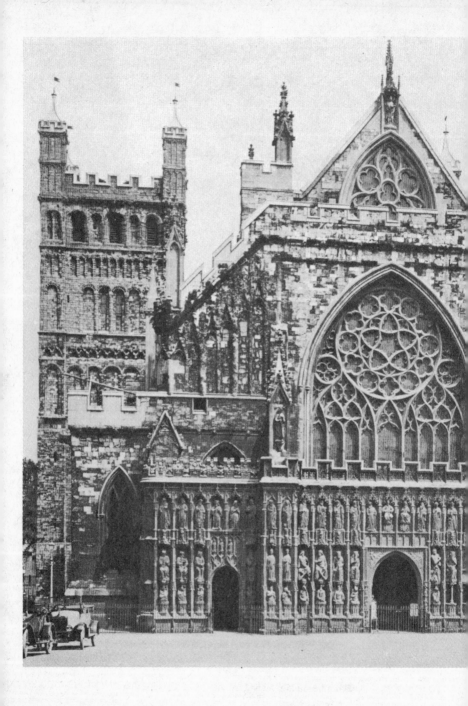

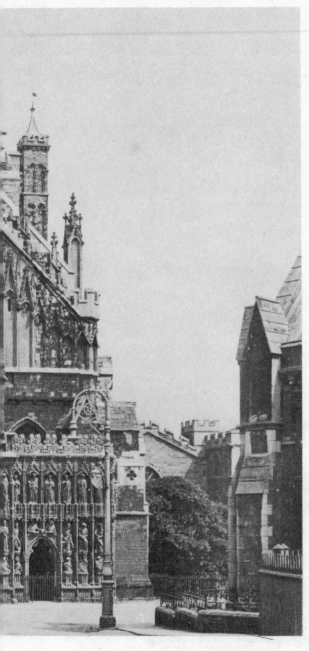

"The great cathedrals give room to a wealth of statuary directly related to the architectural creation, yet *not creating architecture.*"

Plate VII
EXETER CATHEDRAL,
WEST FRONT

Courtesy of National
Buildings Record, London
Photograph copyright
by Mrs. F. H. Crossley

Plate VIII Stonehenge   Courtesy of British Information Service

"The temple really made their greater world of space . . . The Heavenly bodies could be seen to rise and set in the frame it defined."

Plate IX MATISSE *Interior at Nice*　Courtesy of The Art Institute of Chicago;
gift of Mrs. Gilbert W. Chapman
© SPADEM 1964 by French Reproduction Rights, Inc

" 'The whole arrangement of my picture is expressive'."

is trying to say, why cannot the poet say it clearly in the first place? We often have to construe for ourselves what a foreigner speaking our language is trying to say; but is the poet thus incapable of handling his words? If it is we who are unfamiliar with *his* language, then we have not to determine what he is trying to say, but what he does say; and how well he says it is not ours to judge, since we are tyros.

The oddest thing about this apparent linguistic difficulty is that it besets people who are not novices in the realms of poetry at all. Professor Richards, who has made a serious study of "the widespread inability to construe meaning," remarks with some surprise that "it is not only those with little experience of poetry who fail in this. Some who appear to have read widely seem to make little or no endeavor to understand, or, at least, to remain strangely unsuccessful. Indeed, the more we study this matter the more we shall find 'a love for poetry' accompanied by an incapacity to understand or construe it. This construing, we must suppose, is not nearly so easy and 'natural' a performance as we tend to assume."[1] Yet he is convinced that it is a necessary step to appreciation, and that it can and should be taught, since the only alternative to "understanding" the poetry one reads must be some sort of "sentimental" pleasure in the words. For "it is not doubtful that certain 'sentimental' addictions to poetry are of little value, or that this poor capacity to interpret complex and unfamiliar meanings is a source of endless loss. . . ."[2]

It is a truism for modern pragmatists that there are only two essential functions of language (however much they talk about its many, many uses), namely to convey information, and to stimulate feelings and attitudes in the hearer. The leading questions of poetry criticism, therefore, must be: What is the poet trying to say? and: What is the poet trying to make us feel? That the feelings he wishes to invoke are appropriate responses to the propositions he has stated, is another truism. But between the peculiar difficulty of understanding what the poem says, and the distractions that may interfere with the "appropriate" emotional response, the appreciation of poetry seems to be a highly refined mental and neural exercise. I think Professor Richards would agree that it is,

---

[1] I. A. Richards, *Practical Criticism*, p. 312.
[2] *Ibid.*, p. 313.

for he says of the literal understanding alone: "It is a craft, in the sense that mathematics, cooking, and shoemaking are crafts. It can be taught. . . ."[3] And then come all the hazards of the response! " 'Making up our minds about a poem' is the most delicate of all possible undertakings. We have to gather millions of fleeting semi-independent impulses into a momentary structure of fabulous complexity, whose core or germ only is given us in the words. What we 'make up,' that momentary trembling order in our minds, is exposed to countless irrelevant influences. Health, wakefulness, distractions, hunger and other instinctive tensions, the very quality of the air we breathe, the humidity, the light, all affect us. No one at all sensitive to rhythm, for example, will doubt that the new pervasive, almost ceaseless, mutter or roar of modern transport . . . is capable of interfering in many ways with our reading of verse."[4]

Now, this is the exact counterpart in poetics of Prall's "young musical fanatic," whose experience cannot be completely musical so long as he is aware of his body and its surroundings (compare Chapter 3, p. 37). It is another instance of the preciousness which results from the stimulus-response theory of art—from treating art as a special way of "experiencing" things that are not different, in themselves, from the things we meet in real life. I shall not repeat here the objections which I have already brought against that psychological approach,[5] but only present, here as there, what seems to me a more promising conception of the work of art.

It is the fashion among teachers of poetry, today, to begin by telling us that the word "poet" means "maker." But what has the writer of a poem really *made?* An arrangement of words is no more a creation than the arrangement of plates on a table. Some people who realize this choose to keep the term nonetheless, and consequently call every deliberate ordering of elements—plates on the table, linen on the shelf, words in an inventory or words in a poetry book—a "creation." This practice goes more than halfway to meet the pragmatist theory that poetry differs only "in degree" from anything else in life. In degree of what? "Certain responses," "certain integrations," "certain values." Science has not progressed far enough to analyze these certainties any further.[6]

---

[3]*Ibid.*, pp. 312–313.   [4]*Ibid.*, pp. 317–318.   [5]See Chap. 3, p. 37.
[6]Cf. I. A. Richards, *Principles of Literary Criticism*, especially pp. 226–227.

If, however, we ask the same questions about poetry that I have raised about the other arts, the answers prove to be exactly parallel to those concerning painting or music or dance. The poet uses discourse to create an illusion, a pure appearance, which is a non-discursive symbolic form. The feeling expressed by this form is neither his, nor his hero's, nor ours. It is the meaning of the symbol. It may take us some time to perceive it, but the symbol expresses it at all times, and in this sense the poem "exists" objectively whenever it is presented to us, instead of coming into being only when somebody makes "certain integrated responses" to what a poet is saying. We may glance at a page and say to ourselves almost immediately "Here's a good poem!" Even though the light of one bare bulb makes the room horrid, the neighbors are boiling cabbage, and our shoes are wet.[7] For the poem is essentially something to be perceived, and perceptions are strong experiences that can normally cut across the "momentary trembling order in our minds" resulting from assorted stimuli—whether comfort and sweet air, or cold and dreariness and cabbage.

The initial questions, then, are not: "What is the poet trying to say, and what does he intend to make us feel about it?" But: "What has the poet made, and how did he make it?" He has made an illusion, as complete and immediate as the illusion of space created by a few strokes on paper, the time dimension in a melody, the play of powers set up by a dancer's first gesture. He has made an illusion by means of words— words having sound and sense, pronunciations and spellings, dialect forms, related words ("cognates"); words having derivations and derivatives, i.e. histories and influences; words with archaic and modern meanings, slang meanings, metaphorical meanings. But what he creates is not an arrangement of words, for words are only his materials, *out of which* he makes his poetic elements. The elements are what he deploys and balances, spreads out or intensifies or builds up, to make a poem.

The readiest way, perhaps, to understand what sort of thing the poet creates, is to consider a rather trivial experience that probably everyone has had at one time or another: namely, being told, in response to a perfectly candid and true statement, "It sounds so dreadful when you

---

[7]Compare Clive Bell's observation on recognizing a picture as good at a glance, quoted in Chap. 3, p. 33.

put it like that!'" Now the fact referred to is actually not more dreadful for being conveyed by one verbal symbol rather than another; the fact simply is what it is. But it *seems* most horrible when stated in some particular way. And the listener does not protest, "It *is* so dreadful when you put it like that," but "It *sounds* so dreadful. . . ." Or we may sum up the content of a speech with complete faithfulness, merely stating each point briefly, and be met with the comment: "Of course, if you put it like that, it just seems silly!" Again, the content of our summary, if it be accurate, is no sillier than that of the speech; but there, the propositions asserted seemed wonderful, and in the dry short version they seem ridiculous.

What is altered in the telling is not the fact or belief expressed, but the appearance of it. The same event may appear quite differently to two people who experience it. The differences are undoubtedly due to associations, attitudes, insights, and other psychological factors that determine integrated total responses. But such causes cannot be controlled by a poet, since he is not an inspired psychologist knowing the state of mind of the reader and working on it with the skill of an advertising expert. The appearances of events in our actual lives are fragmentary, transient and often indefinite, like most of our experiences—like the space we move in, the time we feel passing, the human and inhuman forces that challenge us. The poet's business is to create the appearance of "experiences," the semblance of events lived and felt, and to organize them so they constitute a purely and completely experienced reality, a piece of *virtual life*.

The piece may be great or small—as great as the Odyssey, or so small that it comprises only one little event, like the thinking of a thought or the perception of a landscape. But its distinguishing mark, which makes it quite different from any actual segment of life, is that the events in it are simplified, and at the same time much more fully perceived and evaluated than the jumble of happenings in any person's actual history. Not that there may not be a jumble in virtual life too; nothing could be more jumbled than, for instance, the ideas and scenes in *The Waste Land*. But there is artistic purpose in such confusion, it is not merely copied from things which happened that way in fact. The virtual experience created out of those very adroitly jumbled impressions is a full and clear vision of social tyrannies, with all of the undertones of personal dread, reluctance, half-delusion, and emotional background to hold the assorted items together in a single illusion of life, as a color scheme unifies all the figures of a variegated picture in the realm of its virtual space.

That *illusion of life* is the primary illusion of all poetic art. It is at least tentatively established by the very first sentence, which has to switch the reader's or hearer's attitude from conversational interest to literary interest, i.e. from actuality to fiction. We make this shift with great ease, and much more often than we realize, even in the midst of conversation; one has only to say "You know about the two Scotchmen, who . . ." to make everybody in earshot suspend the actual conversation and attend to "the" two Scots and "their" absurdities. Jokes are a special literary form to which people will attend on the spur of the moment. Children listen with the same readiness to stories and verses, just as they are always prepared to look at pictures.

In this chapter I shall deal only with poetry, especially lyric, for several reasons: in the first place, most people can feel, even if they cannot explain, the difference between literal import and artistic import in lyric poetry, far more strongly than in other kinds of literature; secondly, the purely verbal materials—metrical stresses, vowel values, rhyme, alliteration, etc.—are more fully exploited in poetry than in prose, so the technique of writing is more strikingly apparent in verse and more easily studied in that restricted field; and thirdly, all forms of literary art, including so-called "non-fiction" that has artistic value, may be understood by the specialization and extension of poetic devices. All writing illustrates the same creative principles, and the difference between the major literary forms, such as verse and prose, is a difference of devices used in literary creation. So, just as I developed the concept of "virtual space" first with reference to pictorial art alone,[8] I shall discuss the illusion of experience, or "virtual life," in this chapter only with regard to poetry in the strict sense. The transition to prose literature is very easily made once the principle of poetic creation is understood.

The word "life" is used in two distinct general senses, ignoring the many esoteric or special senses it may have besides: the biological sense,

---

[8]Cf. Chaps. 4 and 5.

in which "life" is the characteristic functioning of organisms, and is opposed to "death"; and the social sense, in which "life" is *what happens*, what the organism (or, if you will, the soul) encounters and has to contend with. In the first sense, all art has the character of life, because every work must have organic character,[9] and it usually makes sense to speak of its "fundamental rhythm." But "life" in the second sense belongs peculiarly to poetic art, namely, as its primary illusion. The semblance of experienced events, the illusion of life, is established with the opening line; the reader is confronted at once with a virtual order of experiences, which have immediately apparent values, without any demonstrable reasons for the good or evil, importance or triviality, even the natural or supernatural characters they seem to have. For illusory events have no core of actuality that allows them to appear under many aspects. They have only such aspects as they are given in the telling; they are as terrible, as wonderful, as homely, or as moving as they "sound."

> Tyger, tyger, burning bright
> In the forests of the night—

At once the "tyger" exists as a supernatural animal, not a beast for British sportsmen to hunt and have skinned. A common tiger would prowl in a dark jungle, not burn in "forests of the night." The turn of phrase: "forests of the night" makes the place as unrealistic and symbolic as the creature himself, because the grammatical construction (nothing more!) assimilates the forests to the night, instead of making darkness an attribute of the forests, as common sense would do, by the usual adjectival construction, "dark (or gloomy) forests." Blake's "tyger" has no natural birth, no daily habits; he is *the* "tyger" made by God, with a heart of satanic emotions and a master brain. The mystery of Nature is in him: "Did He who made the Lamb make thee?"

The vision of such a tiger is a virtual experience, built up from the first line of the poem to the last. But nothing can be built up unless the very first words of the poem effect the break with the reader's actual environment. This break is what makes any physical condition that is not intensely distracting irrelevant to the poetic experience. Whatever

---

[9]Cf. Chap. 8, *passim*.

our integrated organic response may be, it is a response not to cumulative little verbal stimuli—a precariously sustained progress of memories, associations, unconscious wishes, emotions—but a response to a strongly articulated *virtual experience,* one dominant stimulus. We have no way of noting and following our psychological integrations (which makes me doubt whether "science" will ever give an interesting account of artistic values), but we can trace in considerable detail the making of the virtual presentation, to which different persons have different reactions, but which enough people perceive in *essentially* the same way to make its symbolic function effective.

In a poem like "The Tyger" the enthralling unreality is so evident that the break with actual existence may seem like something special, something peculiar to mystical poems, which cannot fairly be set up as a principle of poetry as such. What about poems that are close to common experience, like the fine, concentrated verses written by ancient Chinese poets, mentioning real places, and often addressed to real people? Consider the simple, precise statements of this little poem:[10]

A FAREWELL IN THE EVENING RAIN

To Li Ts'ao

Is it raining on the river all the way to Ch'u?—
The evening bell comes to us from Nan-king.
Your wet sail drags and is loath to be going
And shadowy birds are flying slow.
We cannot see the deep ocean-gate—
Only the boughs of Pu-kou, newly dripping.
Likewise, because of our great love,
There are threads of water on our faces.

Even in translation, without the original verse conventions of Chinese literature (whatever they be), this is poetry, not a report of Li Ts'ao's departure. A complete subjective situation is created by the things mentioned; but everything of common-sense importance—where the friend is going, how far, why, or with whom—is radically omitted. The rain on the river, in the sails, on the obstructing boughs, finally becomes a flow of tears. It is brought in throughout the poem, in approximately every other line, so that the further items—the bell, the shadowy birds, the

---

[10]By Wêi Ying-wu, translated by Witter Bynner. *The Jade Mountain*, p. 207.

invisible ocean-gate—merge with it, and are consequently gathered up with it into the great love for which the whole poem is weeping. Further-more, those apparently casual local events interspersed between the rain-lines are all symbols of the bond that makes parting painful. Nan-king is calling; the sail is heavy, sailing is hard; the birds, which are going away, are slow, and they are shadowy—The Shadow; the "deep ocean-gate," the greater place that is Li Ts'ao's next destination, is not to be seen for the near precious place, "the boughs of Pu-kou," obstructing all interest in the venture. And so the apparently simple description builds up to the confession of human feeling which is treated, by a master stroke of indirectness, as a mere simile to the external events that really serve only to prepare it:

> *Likewise,* because of our great love,
> There are threads of water on our faces.

"We," and the rain, the river, the parting, the motions and sounds and the time of day, are the *poetic elements* created by words alone, by being mentioned. The place and the incident take their character as much from what is left out as from what is named. Everything in the poem has a double character: each item is at once a detail of a perfectly con-vincing virtual event, and an emotional factor. There is nothing in the whole structure that has not its emotional value, and nothing that does not contribute to the illusion of a definite and (in this case) familiar human situation. That illusion would not be helped at all by additional knowledge—by actual familiarity with the place referred to, further in-formation about the career or personality of Li Ts'ao, or footnotes on the authorship of the poem and on the circumstances of its composition. Such further additions would only clutter the poetic image of life with irrelevant items—irrelevant because they do not spring from the organ-izing principle whereby the illusion is wrought: that every element in the action is also an expression of the feeling involved in the action, so that the poet creates events in a psychological mode rather than as a piece of objective history.

This experiential character of virtual events makes the "world" of a poetic work more intensively significant than the actual world, in which secondhand facts, unrelated to personal existence, always make the scaffolding, so that orientation *in* the world is a major problem. In a literary framework, the *dramatis personae* may be disoriented, but the reader is not; even T. S. Eliot's world of sham and futility, that disconcerts J. Alfred Prufrock, has a perfectly definite character—distressing perhaps, but not confusing—for the reader. If the reader cannot grasp the presented "world," something is wrong with the poem or with his literary comprehension.

The virtual world in which poetic events develop is always peculiar to the work; it is the particular illusion of life those events create, as the virtual space of a picture is the particular space of the forms in it. To be imaginatively coherent, the "world" of a poem must be made out of events that are in the imaginative mode—the mode of naive experience, in which action and feeling, sensory value and moral value, causal connection and symbolic connection, are still undivorced. For the primary illusion of literature, the semblance of life, is abstracted from immediate, personal life, as the primary illusions of the other arts—virtual space, time, and power—are images of perceived space, vital time, felt power.

Virtual events are the basic abstraction of literature, by means of which the illusion of life is made and sustained and given specific, articulate forms. One small event may fill a whole poem, unfolding its details in the simplified, isolating framework of a purely poetic reality. That is the principle on which some Elizabethan lyrics are made from thematic materials which are really trivial. Consider the smallness and even banality of the actual assertion contained in Herrick's "Delight in Disorder." He prefers a casual air in female attire to neatness and care. Is that a statement worth preserving for more than three hundred years? As a factual statement—like the bits of information inserted to fill small spaces in newspapers—certainly not. But what did Herrick make of it? A psychological event: the occurrence and passage of a thought. At once the theme comes to life. The thought begins with contemplation of the general effect and its source:

> A sweet disorder in the dress
> Kindles in clothes a wantonness:

The very first words, "sweet disorder," make the break with actuality, because they express an extraordinary valuation as nonchalantly as though everyone could be expected to share it. And in the same breath the sweetness is explained: such disorder is tantalizing. The word "kindles" tells the whole story. The wantonness is said to be "kindled" in *clothes;* this keeps the whole amorous fancy, the passion kindled in the gentleman by the wantonness of the lady, on a superficial plane of *galanterie;* in speculation he proceeds to muster her from top to toe:

> A lawn about the shoulders thrown
> Into a fine distraction:
> An erring lace, which here and there
> Enthralls the crimson stomacher:
> A cuff neglectful, and thereby
> Ribbands to flow confusedly:
> A winning wave (deserving note)
> In the tempestuous petticoat:
> A careless shoestring, in whose tie
> I see a wild civility:
> Do more bewitch me, than when art
> Is too precise in every part.

The last two lines express his considered judgment, and the thought is finished. From its whimsical inception to the candid conclusion, it is a flirtatious reverie; the completely regular couplets, regular even to the sameness of punctuation, supply a background of decorum to the erring and enthralling, the confusion, winningness, tempestuousness, and carelessness of the clothes, that gives the obvious play of double intent an air of sophisticated naughtiness. The form of the poem expresses the tacitly accepted frame of the gentleman's musings, which is a very conventional one—a tight, regular pattern of social safeguards, in which one can afford to be intrigued.[11]

---

[11]Professor F. W. Bateson, in *English Poetry and the English Language,* asserts that this poem, "instead of being the mere *jeu d'esprit* that it would seem to be, is essentially a plea for paganism." I am sorry that I cannot agree with this moral interpretation. I can find no anti-Puritanism, nor anti-anything; the preciseness to which the gentleman objects is not the demure neatness of Puritan maidens, but is "art," intended to bewitch, and his charge is that it fails to do so. The use of "art" is not what he objects to; the true naturalness of Wordsworth's "Lucy" would not thrill him at all. It is understood that the lady tries to charm him, and he gallantly remarks on "A winning wave (deserving note). . . ." Only an intentional accident *deserves* to be noted.

A poem that is *essentially* a plea for something should certainly express its

Now, all this analysis is not intended as an exercise in the New Criticism, but merely to show that all poetry is a creation of illusory events, even when it looks like a statement of opinions, philosophical or political or aesthetic. The occurrence of a thought is an event in a thinker's personal history, and has as distinct a qualitative character as an adventure, a sight, or a human contact; it is not a proposition, but the entertainment of one, which necessarily involves vital tensions, feelings, the imminence of other thoughts, and the echoes of past thinking. Poetic reflections, therefore, are not essentially trains of logical reasoning, though they may incorporate fragments, at least, of discursive argument. Essentially they create the *semblance* of reasoning; of the seriousness, strain and progress, the sense of growing knowledge, growing clearness, conviction and acceptance—the whole experience of philosophical thinking.

Of course a poet usually builds a philosophical poem around an idea that strikes him, at the time, as true and important; but not for the sake of debating it. He accepts it and exhibits its emotional value and imaginative possibilities. Consider the Platonic doctrine of transcendental remembrance in Wordsworth's "Ode: Intimations of Immortality": there are no statements pro and con, no doubts and proofs, but essentially the experience of having so great an idea—the excitement of it, the awe, the tinge of holiness it bestows on childhood, the explanation of the growing commonplaceness of later life, the resigned acceptance of an insight. But to cite Wordsworth as the proponent of a bona fide philosophical theory is a mistake; for he could not and would not have elaborated and defended his position. The Platonic doctrine to which the poem commits him is actually rejected by the Church whose teachings he professed. As he presents it in the Ode, however, it has nothing to do with any further theology; it does not go beyond the poem. Few people who admire the poem feel actually persuaded to a belief in pre-

---

pathos somewhere, however subtly. But there is no social protest in this poem, not even a rebellious rhythm; a reader who did not know that the poet wrote in Puritan times would never guess from the poem that there must have been some such oppressive circumstance. But meanings and motives which only historical scholarship can supply add nothing to the poetic events or their poetic significance. The speaker in the poem does not plead for liberties, he takes them, howbeit in the safe form of musing; and the poem itself is not a moral plea, but "a fine distraction."

vious existence, and there really is no prophecy in it of a life hereafter, save by implication in scattered lines:

> Thou, over whom thy Immortality
> Broods like the Day. . . .

or:

> Our Souls have sight of that immortal sea
> Which brought us hither. . . .

The logical structure of the thought is really very loose; yet the whole composition sounds like a piece of metaphysical reasoning, and the semblance of fresh ideas occurring in very unacademic surroundings gives it a peculiar depth, which is really depth of experience rather than depth of intellect.

Thinking is part of our instinctive activity—the most human, emotional, and individual part. But this highly personal talent is also our most unmistakably social response, for it is so intimately bound up with language that meditation is inseparable from ways of speaking; and no matter how original we may be in our use of language, the practice itself is a purely social heritage.[12] But discursive thought, so deeply rooted in language and thereby in society and its history, is in turn the mold of our individual experience. We observe and hold in mind essentially what is "speakable." The ineffable may intrude on our consciousness, but it is always something of a fearful guest, and we admit or deny it, according to our temperament, with a sense of mystery. The formulation of thought by language, which makes every person a member of a particular society, involves him more deeply with his own people than any "social attitude" or "community of interests" could do; for this original mental bond holds the hermit, the solitary outlaw, the excommunicate as surely as the most perfectly adjusted citizen. Whatever brute fact may be, our experience of it bears the stamp of language.

In poetic events, the element of brute fact is illusory; the stamp of language makes the whole thing, it creates the "fact." That is why peculiarities of language—liturgical phraseology, archaisms, infantilisms[13]— are poetical devices, and why dialect poetry is a distinct literary form. Dialect bespeaks a mode of thinking that enters into the very events

---

[12]A more detailed consideration of language may be found in *New Key*, chap. v.
[13]E.g. the expression *"ein Ueberall"* in Rainer Maria Rilke's "Der Idiot."

encountered or contemplated in the poem. Burns probably could not have addressed or even noted the field mouse in the king's English, without making his reflections slightly ridiculous or sentimental. The farmer's language holds the incident in the homely frame of clod and corn and hoeing and gathering, a life so close to the soil that the man is doing with his tools and team what the mouse does by her nibbling and carrying. The mouse's plight is a common rural disaster, and no one could appreciate it better than the farmer: "tha maun live." The reality of the parallel with his own dependence on that same corn is stressed by the dialect, which casts the whole experience in the mold of a mind familiar with winter problems.

Dialect is a valuable literary tool, which may be employed in subtler ways than straightforward writing in its vocabulary; for it shades imperceptibly into colloquial *use* of words, turns of phrase that reflect quaint thoughts rather than fixed speech habits. Walter de la Mare, for instance, uses all shades of formal and vernacular English in the little fairy piece called "Berries":

> There was an old woman
> Went blackberry picking
> Along the hedges
> From Weep to Wicking.
> Half a pottle—
> No more she had got,
> When out steps a Fairy
> From her green grot;
> And says, 'Well, Jill,
> Would 'ee pick 'ee mo?'
> And Jill, she curtseys,
> And looks just so.
> 'Be off,' says the Fairy,
> 'As quick as you can,
> Over the meadows
> To the little green lane,
> That dips to the hayfields
> Of Farmer Grimes:
> I've berried those hedges
> A score of times;
> Bushel on bushel
> I'll promise 'ee, Jill,
> This side of supper

> If 'ee pick with a will.'
> She glints very bright,
> And speaks her fair;
> Then lo, and behold!
> She had faded in air.

(Jill hurries to the lane and finds the hedges, that shine "like William and Mary's bower," and picks as much as she can carry.)

> When she comes in the dusk
> To her cottage door,
> There's Towser wagging
> As never before,
> To see his Missus
> So glad to be
> Come from her fruit-picking
> Back to he.
> As soon as next morning
> Dawn was grey,
> The pot on the hob
> Was simmering away;
> And all in a stew
> And a hugger-mugger
> Towser and Jill
> A-boiling of sugar,
> And the dark clear fruit
> That from Faërie came,
> For syrup and jelly
> And blackberry jam.
> Twelve jolly gallipots
> Jill put by;
> And one little teeny one,
> One inch high;
> And that she's hidden
> A good thumb deep,
> Half way over
> From Wicking to Weep.

The diction in this poem is held to a fair level of literate speech as long as the events are realistic, and falls into dialect whenever they are essentially products of the old Goodie's mind. The Fairy, in the first moment of surprise, speaks in the vernacular, and her disappearance, though impersonally described by the poet, is still in Jill's language:

> She glints very bright,
> And speaks her fair—

That makes the whimsical yet quite unextravagant character of the poem. The real touch of genius, however, is the objective reporting of the dog's thought with a popular grammatical distortion:

> To see his Missus
> So glad to be
> Come from her fruit-picking
> Back to he.

What the dog "thinks" is, after all, *her* interpretation of his wagging: "Yes, Jill's back, Jill's back! Yes, yes, she's glad to be back to he!" And the poet lifts this thought, condensed but undisturbed, to the level of objective fact simply by his narrative construction.

Here we come to the principle of poetic creation: virtual events are qualitative in their very constitution—the "facts" have no existence apart from values; their emotional import is part of their appearance; they cannot, therefore, be stated and then "reacted to." They occur only as they seem—they are *poetic facts,* not neutral facts toward which we are invited to take a poetic attitude.

There is a book by E. M. W. Tillyard, entitled *Poetry, Direct and Oblique,* which sets up the thesis that there are two distinct kinds of poetry: the direct, or "statement poetry" which simply states the ideas the poet wishes to convey, and the indirect "poetry of obliquity" that does not state his most important ideas at all, but implies or suggests them by subtle relations among the apparently trivial statements he does make, and by the rhythm, images, references, metaphors, and other elements that occur in them. The book is full of interesting reflections on rhetoric, myth, character, thematic materials, and literary procedure; in short, it is a very good book. Yet I think its main thesis is, if not false, certainly out of kilter. The distinction between "statement poetry" and "oblique poetry" is fair enough, but rests on a difference of technical means rather than of poetic excellence, and consequently is not as deep as Professor Tillyard supposes; and his account of "oblique" meanings all but cancels the insight into poetic meanings as such, which probably prompted his whole analysis.

"Oblique" meanings are what DeWitt Parker called "depth meanings," to be read "between the lines."[14] Tillyard illustrates this concept by

---

[14]*The Principles of Aesthetics,* especially p. 32.

comparing two poems on essentially the same topic, Goldsmith's "The Deserted Village," and Blake's "The Echoing Green." Goldsmith's poem is a long one, of which he quotes only that portion which describes the village; I shall have more to say about his interpretation of it a little later, and therefore omit the matter here. But Blake's poem may be quoted in its entirety:

THE ECHOING GREEN

The sun does arise,
And make happy the skies;
The merry bells ring
To welcome the Spring;
The skylark and thrush,
The birds of the bush,
Sing louder around
To the bells' cheerful sound,
While our sports shall be seen
On the Echoing Green.

Old John, with white hair,
Does laugh away care,
Sitting under the oak,
Among the old folk.
They laugh at our play,
And soon they all say:
"Such, such were the joys
When we all, girls and boys,
In our youth time were seen
On the Echoing Green."

Till the little ones, weary,
No more can be merry;
The sun does descend,
And our sports have an end.
Round the laps of their mothers
Many sisters and brothers,
Like birds in their nest,
Are ready for rest,
And sport no more seen
On the darkening Green.

Goldsmith, Professor Tillyard claims, "wants the reader to think primarily of villages when he talks of Auburn. . . . We believe this because the formal parts of the poetry reinforce the statement, rather than suggest thoughts alien to it. The couplets evolve in a simple explicatory sequence; they unfold the scene with no hint of ulterior meaning; their freshness and unobstructedness are those of the clear sunny day they describe."[15] Of "The Echoing Green," on the other hand, he says: "I believe that Blake in this poem is expressing an idea, an idea that has nothing in itself to do with birds, old and young folk, or village greens, and one most common in Blake's poetical works. It is the idea that there is virtue in desire satisfied. Though desire is not mentioned, yet the keynote of the poem is fruition. . . . The poem gives the sense of the perfectly grown apple that comes off at a touch of the hand. It expresses the profound peace of utterly gratified desire. . . .

"Thus explained, 'The Echoing Green' is as nearly perfect an example of poetical obliquity as can be found. . . . The abstract idea, far from being stated, has been translated into completely concrete form; it has disappeared into apparently alien facts. Through its major obliquity 'The Echoing Green' is in a different category from Goldsmith's lines and must be judged by different standards."[16]

"Granted the interpretation that there is virtue in gratified desire, the poem can be said to express a great human commonplace, and one which in Blake's day more than in our own especially called for expression."[17]

What Professor Tillyard is obviously (and rightly) seeking is the poetic import of the piece; but what does he find, for us? A moral, which he is able to state in six words; a proposition, to be accepted by humanists and rejected by the followers of more ascetic cults. There is nothing about such a "great commonplace" that eludes in principle the grasp of discursive language; it may be, as he suggests, that "no direct statement of it is likely to carry weight," that "we require the speaker to talk about most things before saying what he most has to say," and that "we may even prefer the ultimate obliquity of his omitting what he has to say altogether and implying it through an elaborate pattern of seeming irrelevancies."[18] But the fact remains that the "great commonplace" is a moral, a truth which could be stated. Blake himself has made direct statement of it:

---

[15]*Poetry, Direct and Oblique*, p. 8.
[16]*Ibid.*, pp. 11–12.   [17]*Ibid.*, p. 25.   [18]*Ibid.*, p. 28.

> Abstinence sows sand all over
> The ruddy limbs and flaming hair,
> But Desire Gratified
> Plants fruits of life and beauty there.

Yet in analyzing "The Echoing Green" Professor Tillyard found the "emotional core" of the poem, which he had probably recognized intuitively at the first reading; for he said the poem both repelled and fascinated him—repelled, because he thought it was a mere description of a village green, and fascinated, he knew not why until he discovered its "obliquity."[19] And in pointing out the supposed moral, he mentions what I think is the real meaning, the feeling developed and revealed in the little work: "The keynote of the poem is fruition." Fruition is the life process itself, and the direct experience of it is the profoundest harmony we can feel. This experience is what the poem creates in three short stanzas, by the devices to which he has called attention, and some that he has passed over. Gratified desire is only the end of this experience; the desire itself, the whole joy of beginning, freedom, strength, then mere endurance, and finally weariness and the dark, held in one intensive view of humanity at play, are all equally important in creating the symbol of *life completely lived*. The completeness is felt; and the peculiar *élan* and progress of this feeling is the abstraction that the poetic form makes. But this same emotional pattern shines through many experiences and on many levels of life, as emotional patterns generally do; that is why a true artistic symbol always seems to point to other concrete phenomena, actual or virtual, and to be impoverished by the assignment of any one import—that is to say, by the logical consummation of the meaning-relation.

In reading a "great commonplace" into the poem, Professor Tillyard has to pass over some of its strongest elements, for instance the title, which is an integral part of the piece. A village green is usually flat and open, the houses standing too far back to produce noticeable echoes. But Blake's use of "echoing" is not descriptive, it is the opposite; it counteracts the flatness and openness of the ordinary green, and holds his image of life together as in an invisible frame. The "echo" is really that of the repeating life story—the old laughing at the young and recalling their

---

[19]*Ibid.*, pp. 10-11.

own youth, the young returning to a previous generation—"Round the laps of their mothers, many sisters and brothers . . ." and there is another level of "echoing" life—one form of life being typified in another: the children "like birds in their nest," and the aged people gathered under the oak. Here, I think, Professor Tillyard missed a trick, when he said: "Why in the second [stanza] does old John sit under the oak? To keep off the noonday sun." True, it is noon in the second stanza, but this is implied more by the fact that the children's play is at its height than by any function of the tree. The oak is the latest-leafing of the shade trees, and when "The merry bells ring to welcome the Spring," it would actually still be bare. But the oak is a traditional and "natural" symbol of enduring life—the old folks' tree. Even the line "Old John with white hair" achieves the interweaving of age and youth, for "John" means "The Young," and Blake was sufficiently steeped in the New Testament to attach the idea of the Youngest Disciple to the name. Its prevalence as a name in English village life gave him his opening for a subtle choice here.

One can go on almost from word to word in this poem, tracing the construction of an artistic form that is completely organic, and therefore able to articulate the great vital rhythms and their emotional overtones and undertones. What such a symbolic form presents cannot be expressed in literal terms, because the logic of language forbids us to conceive the pervasive ambivalence which is characteristic of human feeling. Professor Tillyard speaks of "the primal Joy-Melancholy";[20] and to indicate such feeling by a paradoxical name is about as much as philosophy can do with it.

Were poetry essentially a means of stating discursive ideas, whether directly or by implication, it would be more nearly related to metaphysics, logic, and mathematics than to any of the arts. But propositions—the basic structures of discourse, which formulate and convey true or false beliefs "discursively"—are only materials of poetry. What Professor Tillyard calls "statement poetry" is poetry that does not use any merely implied propositions; but of course it uses other devices to create the illusion of life. When he lists pure sensibility among the meanings conveyed by "oblique statement,"[21] "obliquity" seems to mean simply the

---

[20] *Ibid.*, pp. 44 ff.   [21]*Ibid.*, pp. 18 ff.

possession of vital import of some sort. But any collection of lines that is not "oblique" in this sense is not poetry. Tillyard realizes this ultimate weakness of his distinction between "oblique" and "direct" poetry, but pleads for its pragmatic value as a principle of criticism.[22] What he does not realize is that the entire difficulty arises from treating poetry as a set of statements instead of a created appearance, a fabric of virtual events.

If, however, we ask how the primary illusion is established and sustained, what poetic elements are created, and how they are deployed, we shall not have to resort to any artificial contrasts or classifications in order to understand the difference between Blake and Goldsmith, Wordsworth and Pope, and judge their respective poems by one and the same standard, yet do justice to their differences of intent.

Poetry creates a virtual "life," or, as it is sometimes said, "a world of its own." That phrase is not altogether happy because it suggests the familiar notion of "escape from reality"; but a world created as an artistic image is given us to look at, not to live in, and in this respect it is radically unlike the neurotic's "private world." Because of the unhealthy association, however, I prefer to speak of "virtual life," although I may sometimes use the phrase "the world of the poem" to refer to the primary illusion as it occurs in a particular work.

After all that has been written to the effect that the literal content of a poem is not its real import, the resort to a theory of even "relatively direct" poetry, and of a special standard to judge it by, seems a strange one for a truly literary mind to take; if direct statements occur in a good poem, their directness is a means of creating a virtual experience, a non-discursive form expressing a special sort of emotion or sensibility; that is to say, their *use* is poetic, even if they are bald assertions of fact. To take the bull fairly by the horns, I shall illustrate my point by the very poem Professor Tillyard adduces as an example of "direct poetry,"

---

[22]"Finally, I had better own up to a deliberate piece of fraud. The terms 'direct' and 'oblique' poetry are a false contrast. All poetry is more or less oblique: there is no direct poetry. But . . . the only way to be emphatic or even generally intelligible is by fraud and exaggeration to force a hypothetical and convenient contrast." (*Op. cit.*, p. 5.) Unfortunately, inexactness does not make a statement "hypothetical."

which has supposedly no (or next to no) mission but to convey the ideas that its sentences state. His example is the old hymn:

> Stabat mater dolorosa
> iuxta crucem lacrimosa
> dum pendebat filius;
> cuius animam gementem
> contristatem et dolentem
> pertransivit gladius.
>
> O quam tristis et afflicta
> fuit illa benedicta
> mater unigeniti,
> quae moerebat et dolebat
> et tremebat, cum videbat
> nati poenas inclyti!

"However impressive," he declares, "this hymn is direct; it does not go beyond describing and emphasizing the scene it describes." But actually it is describing this scene in a very special way—in short lines, which do not really *describe* what is happening at all, but merely allude to the familiar events, and use as many scriptural elements and liturgical phrases as possible—the sword piercing the soul, the Blessed Mother, the Only Begotten Son, the Virgin-Born Son. There is an extraordinary amount of stock material even in these first two stanzas. In stanza 3 is added the Mother of Christ, in 4 His dying for the sins of His children, an allusion by a single word to His flagellation, then the laconic mention: "dum emisit spiritum." The interspersed references to emotion are entirely common currency: groaning and weeping, sorrowing, suffering, mourning.

If there were no ulterior motive in all this borrowing and stringing together of traditional material and obvious words, the first four stanzas would be purely manufactured verse, and I do not know how Professor Tillyard could find them impressive. But the poem *is* impressive; in the fifth stanza, which begins:

> Pia mater, fons amoris!

The words "fac, ut" are introduced, and after that "fac" occurs nine times, always in strong positions—all but once, in fact, at the beginning of a line. The poem has changed from statement to prayer; there are no more chains of monotonous words ("quae moerebat et dolebat et tremebat cum videbat" or in 4: ". . . suum dulcem natum, morientem, desolatum" (between "subditum" and "spiritum"), but a flowing movement to the incredibly musical and solemn close:

> Quando corpus morietur,
> fac ut animae donetur
> Paradisi gloria.

In the poem as a whole, the four declarative stanzas form an introduction that is strikingly static. The first words—"Stabat mater"—prepare this impression by their sense, and the extraordinary hardness of the second line, *"iuxta crucem lacrimosa,"* supports "stabat," by its sound. Then comes the monotony, and the undeveloped allusions. The effect is one of *rehearsed ideas,* all familiar (even the mentioned emotions), all held in one small compass by catchwords, and immovable as rock. The direct statements are not really "describing and emphasizing the scene," at all; they are creating a feeling that is not in the least appropriate to that melodramatic scene—a feeling that belongs to faith, the acceptance of doctrine, a sense of certainty and dogmatic rightness: the blessing of the Creed. From this *felt faith* the much less confident and more passionate prayer takes off: and the tempo and tone of the poem rise from contemplation of the Crucifixion (in 6 and 7) to "Virgo virginum praeclara," the Judgment, and the glory of Paradise in a crescendo of sound and sense. To quote only the first two stanzas is deceptive; they change their character entirely in the whole; their statements are "direct," but the poetic purpose of this directness is an obliquity that Blake could not surpass.

To treat *anything* that deserves the name of poetry as factual statement which is simply "versified," seems to me to frustrate artistic appreciation from the outset. A poem always creates the symbol of a feeling, not by recalling objects which would elicit the feeling itself, but by weaving a pattern of words—words charged with meaning, and colored by literary associations—akin to the dynamic pattern of the feeling (the word "feeling" here covers more than a "state"; for feeling is a process, and may have not only successive phases, but several simultaneous developments; it is complex and its articulations are elusive). Look at the poem, or rather the fragment, which Professor Tillyard quotes in contrast to "The Echoing Green"—Goldsmith's description of Auburn and its holiday pleasures, at the beginning of "The Deserted Village":

> How often have I loitered o'er thy green,
> Where humble happiness endeared each scene!
> How often have I paused on every charm,
> The sheltered cot, the cultivated farm,
> The never-failing brook, the busy mill,
> The decent church that topt the neighboring hill,
> The hawthorn bush, with seats beneath the shade,
> For talking age and whispering lovers made!
> How often have I blessed the coming day,
> When toil remitting lent its turn to play,
> And all the village train from labour free
> Led up their sports beneath the spreading tree,
> While many a pastime circled in the shade,
> The young contending as the old surveyed;
> And many a gambol frolicked o'er the ground,
> And sleights of art and feats of strength went round;
> And still as each repeated pleasure tired,
> Succeeding sports the youthful band inspired.

"This," he says, "is a fair example of what I call the poetry of direct statement: it is to some degree concerned with what the words state as well as with what they imply." In spite of slight obliquities, such as the absence of a direct moral comment, the poet "wants the reader to think primarily of villages when he talks of Auburn. . . . We believe this because the formal parts of the poetry reinforce the statement rather than suggest thoughts alien to it."

If we regard the non-literal import of a poem as a *thought* alien to the subject matter, a moral or a judgment of value, then Goldsmith's reminiscence of the village green has, indeed, no "obliquity," for it has no such content. But if we view it as a *created virtual history*, the couplets which "evolve in a simple explicatory sequence" do so for quite another purpose than to make the reader "think primarily of villages": their purpose is to construct that history in an exact and significant form. The "formal parts" do not reinforce the statement; they are reinforced by it. The items referred to are "chosen" (which means, they occurred to the poet) because they serve the formal whole.

The keynote of the poetic form is intricacy, not simplicity; and *it is the intricacy of a group dance*. Line after line, there is either a reference to smooth motion, continuous, circling, processional, or to changing places. This last form especially occurs again and again, even where no motion is involved. There is an artistic reason for this. But first the generally active nature of the village is established: "The never-failing brook, the busy mill." Note that, as a piece of direct word painting, these are out of place; we began with the green. The brook and the mill are probably not in the center of the village; neither are the sheltered cot and the cultivated farm. But the green is the dancing place, and everything else in the village is, for Goldsmith's purpose, related to it: shelter, "cultivated" surroundings, then the symbol of natural activity, the brook, and human activity, the mill. And why

> The *decent* church that topt the neighboring hill?

The church is the social sanction of this symbolic dance: divine chaperonage, aloof and apart, but present. The whole action takes place as under a canopy: "with seats beneath the shade," or "in the shade," "beneath the spreading tree." That draws the Magic Circle. Then the procession: "the village train" that "led up their sports." In Blake's poem there is no such phrase, because he was not creating a dance image. All through Goldsmith's lines there goes a pattern of turning, circling, alternating, repeating, succeeding.

> When toil remitting *lent its turn* to play,
>
> While many a pástime *circled* in the shade,
>
> And many a gambol *frolick'd o'er the ground,*
> And sleights of art and feats of strength *went round;*
> And still, as each *repeated* pleasure tired,
> *Succeeding* sports the youthful band inspired.

Finally, there are two lines which let one feel who the partners in this folk dance really are:

> For talking age and whispering lovers made,

and

> The young contending as the old surveyed.

The alternating partners are youth and age, the dance is the Dance of Life, and Goldsmith's village is the human scene. As such, the fragment Professor Tillyard chose to treat as "statement poetry" is only one half of the contrast which is the guideline of the whole poem: element for element the dance is opposed to the later scene, wherein the green is overgrown, the brook choked and marshy, the church unvisited, the farms abandoned. Had Goldsmith limited the description of Auburn revisited to this antithesis, and given the reason—the encroachment of an irresponsible aristocracy on the sober, balanced, rural economy—in a few striking words, he would have written a strong poem. The moral would have been an artistic element, the shadow of unfeeling and brute force dispelling the natural rhythm of human life. But the poem is longer than his poetic idea; that is why it ends up "moralizing," and gets lost in weak literal appeal.

There is nothing the matter with an ardent moral idea in poetry, provided the moral idea is used for poetic purposes. Shelley, the avowed enemy of moral verse, used the hackneyed old theme of the vanity of earthly power for one of his best poems, "Ozymandias." The sonnet form is particularly suited to moral motifs. Consider the themes of some famous sonnets:

> The world is too much with us; late and soon,
> Getting and spending, we lay waste our powers. . . .

> Let me not to the marriage of true minds
> Admit impediment. Love is not love
> Which alters when it alteration finds,
> Or bends with the remover to remove. . . .

> Leave me, O Love! which reachest but to dust;
> And thou, my mind, aspire to higher things. . . .

> O how much more doth beauty beauteous seem
> By that sweet ornament which truth doth give!

If we regard them as "moral verse," their messages are familiar to the point of banality. But just because there is no interesting literal content to invite argument, we can take the moral as a *theme,* motivating the poetic creation, which is a virtual experience of serious reflection coming to a conclusion. This experience involves much more than reasoning; even the first lines indicate that each sonnet begins its reflection with a different initial feeling. Wordsworth's opens with a finished recognition; the first one of Shakespeare's, with an insistent argumentative tone that expresses desire to believe rather than objective insight; Sidney's

starts in the midst of a mental struggle; and the second of Shakespeare's
with an exclamation, a sudden idea.

Blake's "The Echoing Green" is a better poem than Goldsmith's "The
Deserted Village," but this does not mean that the latter, being of a
different sort, requires a different standard of judgment; Blake's poem
is better because it is entirely expressive, whereas Goldsmith did not
sustain his poetic idea throughout his composition. The fact that their
chief devices are different is immaterial; atmosphere, suggestiveness, sober
exposition, morals and maxims, all serve but one purpose in the hands
of the poet: to create a virtual event, to develop and shape the illusion
of directly experienced life.

Since every poem that is successful enough to merit the name of
"poetry"—regardless of style or category—is a non-discursive symbolic
form, it stands to reason that the laws which govern the making of poetry
are not those of discursive logic. They are "laws of thought" as truly
as the principles of reasoning are; but *they never apply to scientific or
pseudo-scientific (practical) reasoning.* They are, in fact, the laws of
imagination. As such they extend over all the arts, but literature is the
field where their differences from discursive logic become most sharply
apparent, because the artist who uses them is using linguistic forms, and
thereby the laws of discourse, at the same time, on another semantic
level. This has led critics to treat poetry indiscriminately as both art and
discourse. The fact that something seems to be asserted leads them astray
into a curious study of "what the poet says," or, if only a fragment of
assertion is used or the semblance of propositional thought is not even
quite complete, into speculations on "what the poet is *trying* to say."
The fact is, I think, that they do not recognize the real process of poetic
creation because the laws of imagination, little known anyway, are obscured for them by the laws of discourse. Verbal statement is obvious,
and hides the characteristic forms of verbal figment. So, while they speak
of poetry as "creation," they treat it, by turns, as report, exclamation,
and purely phonetic arabesque.

The natural result of the confusion between discourse and creation is
a parallel confusion between actual and virtual experiences. The problem
of "Art and Life," which is only of secondary importance for the other
arts, becomes a central issue in literary criticism. It troubled Plato, and

it troubles Thomas Mann; and at the hands of less profound theorists, it promises well to throw the whole philosophy of art into a welter of morals and politics, religion and modern psychiatry. So, before passing from poetry to even more deceptively "factual" literature, we had better consider the functions of language, and try to understand the relation of fact and fiction, and therewith the connections between literature and life, explicitly and clearly first.

Chapter fourteen

LIFE AND ITS IMAGE

Philosophers have been slow to recognize the fact that there are any general laws governing imagination, except insofar as its processes interfere with those of discursive reason. Hobbes, Bacon, Locke, and Hume noted the systematic tendencies of the mind to error: the tendencies to associate ideas by mere contiguity in experience, hypostatize concepts once abstracted and treat them as new concrete entities, attribute power to inert objects or to mere words, and several other vagaries that lead away from science to a state of childish error. But until recently, no one asked *why* such fantastic errors should occur with monotonous persistence.

As it often happens in the history of thought, the problem presented itself suddenly to a number of people in different fields of scholarship. The outstanding answer to it was given by Ernst Cassirer, in his great work, *Die Philosophie der symbolischen Formen*. The first of Cassirer's three volumes concerns language, and uncovers, in that paradigm of symbolic forms, the sources both of logic and of its chief antagonist, the creative imagination. For in language we find two intellectual functions which it performs at all times, by virtue of its very nature: to fix the pre-eminent factors of experience as entities, by giving them *names*, and to abstract concepts of relationship, by talking *about* the named entities. The first process is essentially hypostatic; the second, abstractive. As soon as a name has directed us to a center of interest, there is a thing or a being (in primitive thinking these alternatives are not distinguished) *about* which the rest of the "specious present" arranges itself. But this arranging is itself reflected in language; for the second process, assertion, which formulates the *Gestalt* of the complex dominated by a named being, is essentially syntactical; and the form which language thus impresses on experience is discursive.

The beings in the world of primitive man were, therefore, creations of his symbolizing mind and of the great instrument, speech, as much as of nature external to him; things, animals, persons, all had this peculiarly ideal character, because abstraction was mingled with fabrication. The naming process, started and guided by emotional excitement, created entities not only for sense perception but for memory, speculation, and dream. This is the source of mythic conception, in which symbolic power is still undistinguished from physical power, and the symbol is fused with what it symbolizes.

The characteristic form, or "logic," of mythic thinking is the theme of Cassirer's second volume. It is a logic of multiple meanings instead of general concepts, representative figures instead of classes, reinforcement of ideas (by repetition, variation, and other means) instead of proof. The book is so extensive that to collect here even the most relevant quotations would require too much space; I can only refer the reader to the source.

At the very time when the German philosopher was writing his second volume, an English professor of literature was pondering precisely the same problem of non-discursive symbolism, to which he had been led not by interest in science and the vagaries of unscientific thought, but by the study of poetry. This literary scholar, Owen Barfield, published in 1924 a small but highly significant book entitled *Poetic Diction, A Study in Meanings*. It does not seem to have made any profound impression on his generation of literary critics. Perhaps its transcendence of the accepted epistemological concepts was too radical to recommend itself without much more deliberate and thorough reorientation than the author gave his readers; perhaps, on the exact contrary, none of these readers realized how radical or how important its implications were. The fact is that this purely literary study reveals the same relationships between language and conception, conception and imagination, imagination and myth, myth and poetry, that Cassirer discovered as a result of his reflection on the logic of science.[1]

---

[1]Cassirer's philosophy of symbolic forms developed out of his earlier work, *Substance and Function*.

The parallel is so striking that it is hard to believe in its pure coincidence, yet such it seems to be. Barfield, like Cassirer, rejects Max Müller's theory that myth is a "disease of language," but praises his distinction between "poetic" and "radical" metaphor; then goes on to criticize the basic assumption contained even in the theory of "radical metaphor," that the carrying over of a word from one sphere of sense to another, or from sensory meanings to non-sensory ones, is really "metaphor" at all.

"The full meanings of words," he says, "are flashing, iridescent shapes like flames—ever-flickering vestiges of the slowly-evolving consciousness beneath them. To the Locke-Müller-France way of thinking,[2] on the contrary, they appear as solid chunks with definite boundaries and limits, to which other chunks may be added as occasion arises."

He goes on to question the supposed occurrence of a "metaphorical period" in human history, when words of entirely physical meaning were put to metaphorical uses; for, he says, "these poetic, and *apparently* metaphorical values were latent in meaning from the beginning. In other words, you may imply, if you choose, with Dr. Blair,[3] that the earliest words in use were 'the names of sensible material objects' *and nothing more*—only, in that case, you must suppose the 'sensible objects' themselves to have been something more; you must suppose that they were not, as they appear at present, isolated, or detached, from thinking and feeling. Afterwards, in the development of language and thought, these single meanings split up into contrasted pairs—the abstract and the concrete, particular and general, objective and subjective. And the poesy felt by us to reside in ancient language consists just in this, that, out of our later, analytic, 'subjective' consciousness, a consciousness which has been brought about along with, and partly because of, this splitting up of meaning, we are led back to experience the original unity."[4]

---

[2]The reference is to the works of John Locke, Max Müller, and Anatole France, respectively. *Poetic Diction, A Study in Meanings*, p. 57.

[3]Hugh Blair, *Lectures on Rhetoric and Belles Lettres* (1783).

[4]Barfield, *op. cit.*, p. 70. Concerning the subject-object dichotomy, compare Cassirer, *Philosophie der symbolischen Formen*, II, p. 32 on the primeval function of symbolism: "Just because, at this stage, the ego is not yet conscious and free, flourishing in its own productions, but is only on the threshold of those mental processes which shall presently dichotomize 'Self' and 'World,' the new world of signs must appear to the mind as something absolutely, 'objectively' real."

"In the whole development of consciousness . . . we can trace the operation of two opposing principles, or forces. Firstly [*sic*], there is the force by which . . . single meanings tend to split up into a number of separate and often isolated concepts. . . . The second principle is one which we find given us, to start with, as the nature of language itself at its birth. It is the principle of living unity."[5]

". . . Not an empty 'root meaning to shine,' but the same definite spiritual reality which was beheld on the one hand in what has since then become pure human thinking; and on the other hand, in what has since become physical light; . . . not a metaphor, but a living figure."[6]

These passages could almost pass for a paraphrase of Cassirer's *Language and Myth,* or fragments from the *Philosophie der symbolischen Formen.* The most striking parallel, however, is the discussion of mythic imagination, which begins:

"Perhaps nothing could be more damning to the 'root' conception of language than the ubiquitous phenomenon of myth." Barfield then states briefly the theory of multiple meanings and fusion of symbol and sense, and concludes: "Mythology is the ghost of concrete meaning. Connexions between discriminate phenomena, connexions which are now apprehended as metaphor, were once perceived as immediate realities. As such the poet strives, by his own efforts, to see them, and to make others see them, again."[7]

Meanwhile, in a totally different department of learning, namely the newborn science of psychiatry, another man had come upon the existence of an "irrational" mode of thought—a mode having its own symbolism and "logic"—and had made practical applications of the idea, with spectacular success. This man was Sigmund Freud. At first—when he began to publish his theory of neuroses and analytic studies of dreams, around the turn of the century—the relevance of his discovery to aesthetics was not apparent, and its danger for traditional ethics fully engaged the attention of his critics. But even in the preface to the third edition of his *Traumdeutung,* the edition of 1913, he himself observed that in the future it should be revised "to include selections from the rich material of poetry, myth, usage of language [idiom], and folklore. . . ."

[5]*Ibid.,* p. 73.
[6]*Ibid.,* p. 75.   [7]*Ibid.,* pp. 78–79.

Why did not Cassirer and Barfield take cognizance of Freud's work? Because by the time they undertook their respective studies, its influence on art theory, especially poetics, as well as on comparative religion and mythology, was widespread and profound, but had already shown its peculiar weakness, namely that it tended to put good and bad art on a par, making all art a natural self-expressive function like dream and "make-believe" instead of a hard won intellectual advance. Similarly it equated myth and fairy tale. Anyone who recognized artistic standards, like Barfield, or knew the intricate problems of epistemology as Cassirer did, could not but feel that this excursion must somehow end in a blind alley.

The literature of aesthetics based on Freud's psychoanalysis belongs chiefly to the nineteen-twenties.[8] During those years, C. G. Jung published his much-softened and somewhat mystical version of "dynamic psychology," and expressed his far more reasonable views about its bearing on art criticism. But to admit the "limitations" of a procedure still does not dispose of one's difficulties if the procedure happens to be fundamentally mistaken. Freud's studies of non-discursive symbolism, and Jung's consequent speculations about "archetypes," were all made in the interest of tracing dream symbols to their sources, which are ideas expressible in literal terms—the "dream thoughts" which the "manifest dream content" represents. The same thing can, indeed, be done with every product of imagination, and interesting psychological facts will come to light through the analysis. Every poem, novel or play contains a wealth of dream material which stands proxy for unspoken thoughts. But psychoanalysis is not artistic judgment, and the many books and articles that have been written on the symbolic functions of painting, music, and literature actually contribute nothing to our understanding of "significant form." The Freudian conception of art is a theory of "significant motif."[9]

Non-discursive form in art has a different office, namely to articulate

---

[8]For example, F. C. Prescott's *The Poetic Mind,* 1922; *Poetry and Myth,* 1927; J. M. Thorburn's *Art and the Unconscious,* 1925; DeWitt Parker, *The Principles of Aesthetics,* 1920; *The Analysis of Art,* 1924; Sigmund Freud, *Psychoanalytische Studien an Werken der Dichtung und Kunst,* 1924. These are only a few.

[9]Motif may play a role in artistic expression, as I shall try to show a little later. But its artistic function is neither the revelation of "dream thoughts" nor the catharsis of emotions.

knowledge that cannot be rendered discursively because it concerns experiences that are not *formally* amenable to the discursive projection. Such experiences are the rhythms of life, organic, emotional and mental (the rhythm of attention is an interesting link among them all), which are not simply periodic, but endlessly complex, and sensitive to every sort of influence. All together they compose the dynamic pattern of feeling. It is this pattern that only non-discursive symbolic forms can present, and that is the point and purpose of artistic construction.

The laws of combination, or "logic," of purely aesthetic forms—be they forms of visible space, audible time, living forces, or experience itself—are the fundamental laws of imagination. They were recognized long ago by poets, who praised them as the wisdom of the heart (much superior to that of the head), and by mystics who believed them to be the laws of "reality." But, like the laws of literal language, they are really just canons of symbolization; and the systematic study of them was first undertaken by Freud.

Since his interest in such epistemological research was only incidental to his project of finding the disguised motif of a fantasy, his own statements of these canons are scattered through many hundred pages of dream analysis. But summed up briefly, they turn out to be the very same "laws" that Cassirer postulated for "mythic consciousness," that Émile Durkheim found operative in the evolution of totemism,[10] and that Barfield noted in "poetic meaning," or "true metaphor."

The cardinal principle of imaginative projection is what Freud calls *Darstellbarkeit*, which Brill translates as "presentability." Since Freud's alleged "true" meanings are so often not "presentable" in the usual sense, this translation is unfortunate; for *darstellbar* means "capable of presentation," and does not refer to propriety. I shall therefore translate it as "exhibitable." Every product of imagination—be it the intelligently organized work of an artist, or the spontaneous fabrication of a dreamer —comes to the percipient as an experience, a qualitative direct datum. And any emotional import conveyed by it is perceived just as directly; that is why poetic presentation is often said to have an "emotional quality."[11]

---

[10]In *Les formes élémentaires de la vie religieuse.*

[11]Cf. the passage quoted from Baensch's "Kunst und Gefühl" in Chap 2, pp. 20–21.

Associated meanings are not, as many aestheticians assume, a part of the import of poetry; they serve to *expand the symbol,* and this is a technical aid on the level of symbol making, not of artistic insight. Where associations are not evoked the symbol is not enhanced, and where its poetic use depends on such tacit extension, it may simply fail. (T. S. Eliot sometimes counts on associations that normally fail to occur, so that his richest fabric of oblique historical references produces no imaginative enrichment for the reader. This criticism of Eliot is analogous to one I heard a musician make of the Pro Arte Quartet, whose pianissimo was so perfect that it was inaudible beyond the stage: "What is the use of a beautiful pianissimo if one can't hear it?" The members of the quartet might have answered, in the spirit of Mr. Eliot, that the audience should be following the score.)

The first logically disturbing feature of non-discursive expressive forms is what Freud calls "over-determination." The same form may have more than one import; and, whereas the assignment of meaning to an acknowledged symbol (e.g. of literal or accepted hyperbolic meaning to a word) precludes other possibilities in its given context, the significance of a pure perceptible form is limited by nothing but the formal structure itself. Consequently references that could be rationally taken only as alternatives are simply co-present as "the import" in art. This makes it possible to fuse even two contradictory affects in one expression. The "primal Joy-Melancholy" of which Tillyard speaks is exactly such a content, which cannot be carried through in any symbolism bound to the logic of discourse, but is a familiar content to the poetic mind. Freud calls this the *principle of ambivalence.* I believe the power of artistic forms to be emotionally ambivalent springs from the fact that emotional opposites—joy and grief, desire and fear, and so forth—are often very similar in their dynamic structure, and reminiscent of each other. Small shifts of expression can bring them together, and show their intimate relations to each other, whereas literal description can only emphasize their separateness.

Where there is no exclusion of opposites, there is also, strictly speaking, no negative. In non-verbal arts this is obvious; omissions may be significant, but never as negatives. In literature, the words, "no," "not," "never," etc., occur freely; but what they deny is thereby created. In poetry there is no negation, but only contrast. Consider, for instance, the last stanza of Swinburne's "The Garden of Proserpine," in which almost every line is a denial:

> Then star nor sun shall waken,
> Nor any change of light:
> Nor sound of waters shaken,
> Nor any sound or sight:
> Nor wintry leaves nor vernal;
> Nor days nor things diurnal;
> Only the sleep eternal
> In an eternal night.

Sun and star, light, sounding waters, leaves, and days all appear even as they are denied; out of them is woven the background that sets off the final assurance:

> Only the sleep eternal
> In an eternal night.

The long process of denial, meantime, has furnished the monotonous "nor—nor—nor" that makes the whole stanza sink to sleep almost without the closing lines; the negative word thus exercising a creative function. The literal sense, furthermore, being a constant rejection of the emerging ideas, keeps them pale and formal—faded, "gone"—in contrast with the one positively stated reality, Sleep.

I mentioned heretofore that in poetry there is no genuine logical argument; this again is paralleled by the speciousness of reasoning in dreams.[12] The "fixation of belief" is not the poet's purpose; his purpose is the creation of a virtual experience of belief or of its attainment. His "argumentation" is the semblance of thought process, and the strain, hesitatation, frustration, or the swift subtlety of mental windings, or a sense of sudden revelation, are more important elements in it than the conclusion. Sometimes a conviction is perfectly established by mere reiteration ("If I say it three times it's true," as Lewis Carroll's Bellman said).

One of the most powerful principles governing the use of "natural symbols" is the *principle of condensation*. This, too, was discovered by Freud in the course of his dream analysis.[13] It is, of course, related to

---

[12]See Freud, *Interpretation of Dreams*, chap. vi: "The Dream Work," pp. 227 ff.
[13]*Ibid.*, pp. 284 ff.

over-determination; indeed, all the principles of non-discursive projection are probably interrelated, just as those of discursive logic—identity, complementarity, excluded middle, etc.—are all of a piece. But condensation of symbols is not the same thing as over-determination; it is essentially a fusion of forms themselves by intersection, contraction, elision, suppression, and many other devices. The effect is usually to intensify the created image, heighten the "emotional quality"; often to make one aware of complexities of feeling (this, I think, is James Joyce's purpose in carrying condensation to such lengths that his language becomes a distorted dream language). The real master of condensation is Shakespeare:

> And Pity, like a naked newborn babe,
> Striding the blast, or Heaven's Cherubin, hors'd
> Upon the sightless couriers of the air,
> Shall blow the horrid deed in every eye
> That tears shall drown the wind.

A student trained by Professor Richards could probably paraphrase the last line to the effect that "the sound of weeping shall be louder than the wind"; but the paraphrase sounds improbable, and the line itself, tremendous; and besides, what Shakespeare said was: "Tears shall drown the wind," so he probably did not intend anything else. Furthermore, what paraphrase can make sense out of a newborn babe and a mounted guard of cherubin that *blow* a *deed* in people's eyes? The literal sense of these prophecies is negligible, though that of the words is not; the poetic sense of the whole condensed and exciting figure is perfectly clear. Shakespeare's poetry rings with such diction.

There are other characteristics of imaginative expression, but the ones I have just adduced must serve here to mark the basic distinction between discursive and non-discursive thinking and presentation. These principles seem to govern equally the formation of dreams, mythical conceits, and the virtual constructions of art. What, then, really sets poetry apart from dream and neurosis?

Above all, its purpose, which is to convey something the poet knows and wishes to set forth by the only symbolic form that will express it. A poem is not, like dream, a proxy for literal ideas, intended to hide wishes and feelings from oneself and others; it is meant to be always emotionally transparent. Like all deliberate expression, it meets a public standard of excellence.[14] One does not say of a sleeper that he dreams clumsily, nor of a neurotic that his symptoms are carelessly strung together; but a poet may certainly be charged with ineptitude or carelessness. The process of poetic organization is not a spontaneous association of images, words, situations, and emotions, all amazingly interwoven, without effort, through the unconscious activity Freud called "the dream work." Literary composition, however "inspired," requires invention, judgment, often trial and rejection, and long contemplation. An air of unstudied spontaneous utterance is apt to be as painstakingly achieved as any other quality in the poetic fiction.

Every successful work of literature is wholly a creation, no matter what actualities have served as its models, or what stipulations set up its scaffold. It is an *illusion of experience*. It always creates the semblance of mental process—that is, of living thought, awareness of events and actions, memory, reflection, etc. Yet there need not be any person in the virtual "world" who sees and reports. The semblance of life is simply the *mode* in which virtual events are made. The most impersonal account of "facts" can give them the qualitative imprint which makes them "experiences," able to enter into all sorts of contexts, and taking on significance accordingly. That is to say, literature need not be "subjective," in the sense of reporting the impressions or feelings of a given subject, yet everything that occurs in the frame of its illusion has the semblance of a *lived* event. This means that a virtual event exists only in so far as it is formed and characterized, and its relations are only such as are apparent in the virtual world of the work.

To create the poetic primary illusion, hold the reader to it, and develop the image of reality so it has emotional significance above the suggested emotions which are elements in it, is the purpose of every word a poet writes. He may use his own life's adventures or the contents of his dreams, just as a painter may picture his bedroom chair, his studio stove, the chimney pots outside his skylight, or the apocalyptic images before his mind's eye. A poet may take doctrines and moral convictions for his theme, and preach them in heroic couplets or in iambic pentameter

---

[14]The problem of applying this standard is another story; here I would remark that, although it is not always possible to say how a poet has met the standard, it is always possible to point out the causes if he failed.

or in wisps of free verse. He may intersperse references to public events, and use names of real personages, just as painters have often painted faithful portraits, or given the features of their patrons to the worshipers depicted in sacred pictures. Such materials, turned to artistic purposes, need not disturb the work at all, which consequently is no less "pure art" than it would otherwise be. The only condition is that materials from any source whatever must be put to completely artistic use, entirely transformed, so that they do not lead away from the work, but give it, instead, the air of being "reality."

There are countless devices for creating the world of a poem and articulating the elements of its virtual life, and almost every critic discovers some of these means and stands in wondering admiration of their "magic." It may happen that a poet himself falls in love with a poetic resource, as Swinburne did with alliterative words and Browning with the sound of conversation, and uses it so freely and obviously that one hears the technique itself instead of perceiving only the virtual events it serves to create. The poet has become a theorist, like the awe-struck critic (a critic who cannot be awe-struck is not equal to his material), and is tempted to set up a recipe for poetic work. If other writers are impressed with his recipe they form a "school," and perhaps issue a manifesto, asseverating the essential nature of poetry, and as a corollary the basic importance of their technique, which achieves the essence. The poetry of the past, and especially the recent past,[15] is then censured as "impure" in so far as most of it does not strive for this essence (not to attain it is unsuccessful rather than impure; but to *aim* at anything else is considered as importing non-poetic factors, adulterating the poem).

The question of "pure poetry" has exercised literary critics (some of whom are poets) in England and especially in France, and to a lesser extent in other countries, for at least three decades now. L'Abbé Bremond gave it a succinct statement and entirely bootless answer in his famous lecture *La poésie pure*,[16] which ends with a description of poetic essence whereby one can only interpret "essence" as "magic." Now, any avid reader of poetry will probably agree that there is something about

---

[15]F. A. Pottle, in *The Idiom of Poetry*, p. 28, remarks on this reaction to the immediately preceding age, and subsequently explains it.

[16]This appeared as a little book in 1920.

poetry that may be called "poetic magic"; but that this quality does not depend on sound or imagery, meaning or emotion, but is something else that inheres in the poem, separate and mystical, is not an enlightening assumption. Like all mystical beliefs, it is irrefutable, but has no theoretical value whatever.

The value of the lecture was that it provoked a controversy in the course of which some serious thinkers found it necessary to account for the "magical" quality, define their own notions of poetic essence, and set up a criterion of "pure poetry" which should not measure poems by the standard of a poetry beyond all language, above words, a "poetry of silence." Yet many critics followed l'Abbé Bremond in principle, i.e. in thinking of "pure poetry" as *purified,* freed upon non-poetic ingredients or non-poetic functions; and in this they and he were carrying on the thought of Poe, Shelley, Coleridge, Swinburne, all of whom had sought for the "poetic essence" as *one of the elements* in poetic discourse, and pleaded for an increase of this element, whatever it was, and for the elimination of other elements *as far as possible.* Shelley would leave out all didactic statements; that was not too difficult, and most literary aestheticians seconded him. Even lovers of didactic poetry usually agreed that what they loved was not "pure poetry." Poe went further, regarding all "explicit" statement as unpoetic. He did not make quite clear whether the opposite of "explicit" was "implicit," "figurative," or "vague"; in one case at least he lets one infer that he means "vague," for he praises music as the *vaguest* of all communications. But figurative expression satisfied him, too. Like most philosophically untrained writers (for, although most of the poet-critics read philosophy, they were not disciplined thinkers), he let the opprobrious term "explicit" mean by turns "explicit," "precise," "literal," "objective," "naturalistic," and other objectionable characters. What he was trying to do was to exclude "untransformed" ideas, single words, or statements that would cause the reader to think of things in the actual world instead of holding him to the virtual world of the poem. His mistake was the common one of trying to exclude supposedly offending *materials* rather than demanding consistent artistic *practices.*

His modern successors are subtler. Mr. Eliot is not philosophically undisciplined. He also tries to purify poetry by leaving out as much explicit statement as possible; and for him the opposite of "explicit" is, quite properly, "implicit." The moot point of his theory arises in its application: can the purely implicit in a statement always be made effective? How can remote implications be given to the reader's intuition? His answer is that the reader must be educated to read pure poetry: he must have such wide associations with words that even assonance with a line of famous literature, English or foreign, causes in him a reverberation of that line, and a veiled reference to some obscure mediaeval monk at once suggests this worthy's history or legend. Eliot's famous footnotes may be a poetic device to create a sense of abstruseness, rather than genuine glosses to allay it; but this does not alter the fact that his avowed cultural presupposition is fantastic, and bespeaks a desperate nostalgia for a vanished culture, smaller and surer and systematically compact. Great poets often hold odd theories, and write good poetry nonetheless; Eliot's is a case in point. But there is always a danger that poetry so preciously conceived may be read not as poetry, but as an esoteric game between poet and reader, which gives those who can play it an intellectual rather than a poetic thrill.

The interesting parallel between Bremond's and Eliot's theories is that both tend to reduce the discursive material of the poem, or *the poem on paper*, in order to enhance the true "poetic" element, which is an experience created by the verbal stimulus; the tacit premise being that this experience is most intense where the stimulus is most reduced. As Bremond's ideal limit is a "poetry of silence," Eliot's should properly be that of the single all-implying word. All that saves him from embracing this ideal is, I think, poetic common sense (l'Abbé Bremond, being a mystic, has no such simple safeguard, and does not need it). The poet is better than his poetics.

The ideal of pure poetry is, of course, closely bound up with the problem of what constitutes poetry of any sort—that is, with the definition of poetry. If we know what we mean by "poetry" we can judge of its pure instances, and should be able to find the causes of impurity in poems that suffer from it. The great majority of writers who raise the question: "What is poetry?" do not answer it at all, but discuss what is poetic, or define "poetic experience." Some of them do, indeed, call the poetic experience the poem itself, and the "poem on paper" only a symbol of it. Prescott, for instance, stated this view explicitly in *Poetry and Myth:*

"Poetry in the true sense is obviously not something that can be fixed on a printed page and bound up in volumes; it is rather made up of the series of thoughts and feelings, induced by the printed symbols, succeeding each other in the reader's mind." But, most surprisingly, this poetry may not be poetic! For he went on directly to say: "The response to these symbols may not be poetical at all; it may be some quite rational construction in place of the series of images, spontaneously accompanied by appropriate thoughts and feelings, which the poet intended, and for which the symbols have at best served him as a very imperfect means of communication."[17]

Here we have *two* poems, the writer's and the reader's, related to each other through a very imperfect medium, words. Yet one of these two poems may not be poetic. It may be "a quite rational construction." Surely enough, a few pages later we find: "The essential element in poetry is non-reasonable. This element it is that generates the true poetic beauty, which is dream-like; which cannot be steadily or attentively contemplated, but may be seen only in glimpses; of which we can say only that it has the charm or magic that is the mark of its presence; which therefore is inexplicable."[18]

Here we have everything: the irrationality postulated by Poe, the "presence" of a *Something* beyond words or thoughts, the magic, the all-but-dispensable mediating words, the "poetic experience," the "poetic intent." And of course, we must have creativity: "The distinguishing mark of poetry, whatever its external form, is in its creation. This fictional creation . . . is expressive of and motivated by the poet's wish, or aspiration."[19] It may seem strange that a series of thoughts and feelings in the reader's mind should have as its distinguishing mark somebody else's symptoms of dynamic pressure; but, pointing out that the poet's vision (imperfectly conveyed by words) is an illusion, "a making over of outward impressions into a mere phantasm of the mind," he explains that the reader may borrow it and elaborate it to suit his

---

[17]*Poetry and Myth*, p. 1.　　[18]*Ibid.*, p. 7.　　[19]*Ibid.*, p. 4.

own needs. "Even the merest sketch, if it once starts the imagination, will be amply filled out;—and all this filling out, the largest part of every work of art, is mere dream and illusion."[20]

The real purpose of communicating the poet's daydream is to set the reader daydreaming; and whatever dream results is (by the first statement, quoted above) *the poem* (though it may not be poetic).

I have given so much space to an obviously muddled theory of poetry because it exhibits almost *all* the muddles from which current theory suffers, and soon falls into the helpless condition to which they give rise —that none of its "principles" really works, freely and without exception, in all instances. Poetry is essentially the same as myth; but, says Prescott, "Before trying to bring out the mythical element in poetry I should say that it is of course not to be found everywhere in our actual poetry." That is because, although poetry is the language of imagination, "In much verse, and even much that we quite properly call poetry, the imagination is not directly or constantly at work." Poetry (presumably, here, the "poem on paper") starts a vision and imposes rhythm (form, meter, music); "Poetry therefore may be called a matter of *seeing* and *singing*. It is not, however, always actually both." And so on; ideally, poems should be mythic creations, imaginative, visionary, musical; but no poem in anyone's mind or book actually meets the standard.

So we come back to the problem of pure poetry. There are two ways of making poetry "pure"; either by leaving out what is repudiated as non-poetic—as Shelley, Poe, Valéry and Moore advocated—leaving poetry as pure as possible; or else by using an avowed principle such as report of emotions, or sheer sound, or metaphor to generate the whole poem, making it simon-pure, and consequently small and rarified, a gem. This is the way of the imagists, the impressionists, the symbolists.

In the face of all these efforts, Professor F. A. Pottle has raised the naive but pertinent question: Should poetry be entirely pure, or even as pure as possible? And his well-considered answer is, *"Poetry should be no purer than the purpose demands."*[21] What the poet's purpose is, he discussed earlier, and arrived at this general principle:

"Poetic language is language that expresses the qualities of experi-

---

[20] *Ibid.*, p. 40.
[21] *Op. cit.*, p. 99.

ence, as distinguished from language that indicates its uses. Since all language is to some extent expressive in this sense, all human speech is, strictly speaking, poetry in various degrees of concentration. *In the ordinary or popular sense of the term, poetry is language in which expression of the qualities of experience is felt to predominate greatly over statement concerning its uses."*[22]

"Poetry" and "poetic language" are here made synonymous. Poetry, then, is a kind of language, and moreover, a kind that shades off by degrees into another kind, which at furthest remove is its opposite. The purpose of using poetic language is to make the reader aware of the qualities of experience.[23] What sort of "experience" is here referred to we are not told, but presumably actual human experience in general. This conception of the mission of poetry is the counterpart, in poetics, to Roger Fry's belief that the function of pictorial art is to make us aware of "what things really look like."[24]

Poetry "in the ordinary or popular sense of the term" is, I take it, language selected for its qualitative rather than practical reference, and brought together in discourses about the writer's experience, known as "poems." A poem is a statement, in the same sense as any practical statement, but in terms that achieve a high concentration of "qualitative expressiveness." But Professor Pottle holds that there is no need of sustaining a very quintessence of expressiveness throughout such a discourse; a poem may contain a good deal of "prose," or informative language, which serves as a foil for too much intensity of perception, and tends to set off the high moments of "experience" to better advantage when they come.[25]

There is good artistic judgment in Professor Pottle's treatment of the demand for "purity." But philosophically it is a makeshift, which does not solve the problems of poetic versus unpoetic language, "expression of quality" versus "expression of fact," because it does not touch the confusing assumption from which those problems stem. The hapless assumption is his own basic tenet, that to be poetic is a function of language,

---

[22]*Ibid.*, p. 70.
[23]*Op. cit.*, p. 66: "What do I mean by language that is 'expressive'? It is language that makes us more sharply conscious of experience as experience. . . ."
[24]*Vision and Design*, p. 25.
[25]*Op. cit.*, *chap.* v, pp. 93 ff.

so that "all human speech is, strictly speaking, poetry in various degrees of concentration." This makes poetry a species of discourse, pointing out characteristics of experience as all discourse does, but concerned with qualitative instead of practical aspects. Since experience has, of course, both aspects, the distinction between poetry and literal discourse is thus conceived to be not radical, but gradual.

Now I maintain that the difference is radical, that poetry is not genuine discourse at all, but is the creating of an illusory "experience," or a piece of virtual history, by means of discursive language; and that "poetic language" is language which is particularly useful for this purpose. What words will seem poetic depends on the central idea of the poem in question. Legal language, for instance, is not ordinarily deemed poetical; there is nothing "qualitative" about words like "charter," "deed," "patent," "lease," "bonds," "estimate," "grant"; but consider how Shakespeare used them:

> Farewell! Thou art too dear for my possessing,
> And like enough thou know'st thy estimate.
> The charter of thy worth gives thee releasing;
> My bonds in thee are all determinate.
> For how do I hold thee but by thy granting,
> And for that riches where is my deserving?
> The cause of this fair gift in me is wanting,
> And so my patent back again is swerving.
> Thyself thou gav'st, thy own worth then not knowing,
> Or me, to whom thou gav'st it, else mistaking:
> So thy great gift, upon misprision growing,
> Comes home again, on better judgment making.
>   Thus have I had thee as a dream doth flatter—
>   In sleep a king, but waking no such matter.

The hard, technical terms have a purpose here, to which, by the way, Shakespeare often used them: they create the semblance of ineluctable fact. The impersonal and sovereign nature of law is infused into an intensely personal situation, and the result is a sense of absolute finality. This sense is achieved by the daring metaphor of a legal discourse; the barrister's jargon here is true "poetic diction."

There is no successful poetry that is not pure poetry. The whole problem of "purity" is a pseudo-problem arising from a misconception as to *what is poetry*, and from mistaking certain powerful and *almost* ubiquitous devices for the basic principle of poetry, and calling "pure poetry" only what is effected by those means. Dwelling on the sensuous, the qualitative, is such a major device for creating the image of experience; the use of irony is another, for the very structure of human feeling is ironical; ambiguity, metaphor, personification, "hypnotic" rhythms and words—all these are major factors in the making of poetry. But the creation of a virtual history is the principle which goes through all literature: the principle of *poesis*.

If poetry is never a statement about actuality, has it, then, nothing to do with life, beyond the ultimate reference of its composed forms to vitality itself, i.e. through their artistic function of expressing the morphology of real human feeling? Has nothing of the artist's own biography gone into the illusion, except by accident, as dross rather than gold?

Every good work of art has, I think, something that may be said to come from the world, and that bespeaks the artist's own feeling about life. This accords with the intellectual and, indeed, the biological importance of art: we are driven to the symbolization and articulation of feeling when we *must* understand it to keep ourselves oriented in society and nature. So the first emotional phenomena a person wants to formulate are his own disconcerted passions. It is natural to look for expressive materials among the events or objects that begot those passions, that is, to use images associated with them, and under the stress of real emotion, events and objects perceived are prone to appear in a *Gestalt* congruent with the emotion they elicited. So reality quite normally furnishes the images; but they are no longer anything in reality, they are forms to be used by an excited imagination. (They may, indeed, be metaphorical in the "Freudian" fashion, too, symptomatic fantasies on which feeling is concentrated.) And now begins the work of composition, the struggle for complete expressiveness, for that understanding of the form which finally makes sense out of the emotional chaos.

The motif, often springing from deeper sources of imagination than art itself, and the feeling the artist has toward it, give the first elements of form to the work; its dimensions and intensity, its scope and mood. Sometimes the technique is subdued where the subject is violent, as in Thomas Wolfe's "Death in the City," so that the whole treatment has an air of understatement that is part of the fundamental artistic conception. The motif itself, far from being indifferent or alien, then becomes a structural element, the polar opposite of the rendering. But if the

artist chooses for his motif an image or event that is exciting only to
him, i.e. as a private symbol, such a use of it would set up no tension
in the work, but only in his mind, and the intended device would fail.
To achieve the sense of understatement he could not use the subject
matter as such, but would have to create an element of exciting quality
to pull against the restraint of his handling. Art that contains purely
personal symbols as structural elements is impure, and such impurity
is fatal.

It is usually with the advance of conceptual competence that an artist
becomes able to find material outside his own situation, because he becomes more and more apt to see all things, possibilities as well as actualities, half-wrought already into expressive forms in terms of his own
art. A poet thinks poetry a good part of the time, and can view experience—not only his own—emotionally, because he understands emotion.
Some poets, for instance Wordsworth, usually take a start from personal
experience as some painters always paint from models, or "on location";
but the experiences they use are not subjective crises, they are objectively interesting events. Other writers, like Coleridge, compound their
poetic visions of suggestions found in books, old memories, dreams, hearsay, and an occasional striking experience. Where a theme comes from
makes no difference; what matters is the excitement it begets, the importance it has for the poet. The imagination must be fed from the world
—by new sights and sounds, actions and events—and the artist's interest
in ways of human feeling must be kept up by actual living and feeling;
that is, the artist must love his material and believe in his mission and
his talent, otherwise art becomes frivolous, and degenerates into luxury
and fashion.

As surely as some experience of real life must inspire art, it must be
entirely transformed in the work itself. Even the personality called "I"
in an autobiography must be a creature of the story and not the model
himself. "My" story is what happens in the book, not a string of occasions in the world. Failure to make this distinction has led, I think, to
George Moore's rejection of all "subjective" poetry as impure.[26] The

---

[26]See *An Anthology of Pure Poetry*, p. 19: ". . . art for art's sake means pure
art, that is to say, a vision almost detached from the personality of the poet."
And on page 34 he speaks of "pure poetry" as "something that the poet creates
outside his own personality."

subjective passages in a good poem are just as removed from actuality as the descriptions of nature or the Pre-Raphaelite tales of mediaeval ladies which he accepts as poetically pure. There is, of course, a great deal of poetry in our literary heritage that is ruined by unimaginative report of emotion. But it is neither the moral idea nor the mention of feelings that makes such passages bad; it is the lapse from creativity, from creating the illusion of a moral illumination or a passional experience, into mere discourse about such matters; that is, the fallacy of using the poem simply to state something the poet wishes to tell the reader.[27] Mr. Moore, however, does not discriminate good from bad poetry by a standard of creativity; he throws out all passages that make use of the materials he has placed under taboo. Attitudes toward anything, beliefs, principles, and all general comments are impurities. Sometimes, indeed, the poem itself may not even sound didactic, but if the critic knows from the poet's other works, or even from biographical data, that a moral interest motivated the composition, it can no longer give him pleasure. Moore relates such a discovery, and the change of heart it produced in him:

"My father used to admire the sonnet on Westminster Bridge, [28] and I admired it until I could no longer escape from the suspicion that it was not the beautiful image of a city overhanging a river at dawn that detained the poet, but the hope that he might once more discern a soul in nature. . . . And after reading the sonnet again and considering the general tone of it, I discovered a carefully concealed morality in it. . . . He would Christianise the soul in nature if he got it, I said; wherefore the poem comes under the heading of proselytism in poetry."[29]

The measure of "pure poetry" which Moore sets up as the standard of *good* poetry relegates most of the world's great lyrical heritage to an inferior rank.[30] This leaves him with a slender store of masterpieces, as

[27]The worst example I can think of, offhand (apart from amateur poetry in provincial newspapers) is Longfellow's "A Psalm of Life."

[28]Wordsworth's sonnet, beginning: "Earth has not anything to show more fair."

[29]Moore, *op. cit.*, pp. 19–20.

[30]On page 34 of his Introduction he lets De la Mare remark: "Many of the most beautiful poems in the language would have to be barred." Yet he himself says of his [projected] collection: "The value of the anthology (if we compile it) would be that it creates a new standard."

he predicted that it would; and although most of the poems he brought together in his anthology as examples of the highest art are lovely, none of them is great and vigorous. Their loveliness, in fact, becomes a little cloying; the tripping rhymes and gliding rhythms carry too much whimsey and delight, and the occasional laments and wistful fairy tragedies are not forceful enough to break the monotony.

To forbid poets any traffic with serious thought is to cut out a whole realm of poetic creation, namely the presentation of deep and tragic feeling. Any pain harsher than the gentle melancholy of singing "Willow, willow, willow," requires a framework of subject matter stronger than Moore would admit.[31] A remark in the introduction (which is written in the form of a conversation between him and his friends, John Freeman and Walter de la Mare), that a book of "Pure Poetry" could include most of Blake's *Songs of Innocence* but none of the *Songs of Experience*,[32] shows up the confining and cramping influence of his aesthetic standard; even so inspired a poet as Blake must watch himself not to mention the wrong things. "The Tyger," presumably, is not a pure poem because it contemplates the contrasts in creation ("Did He who made the Lamb make thee?"), and because it mentions "God" (Blake's own God) instead of obsolete "gods." "The Sick Rose" is not pure, because of the obvious meaning, that in all joy there is incipient sorrow, in all life incipient death, or whatever "Great Commonplace" one chooses to make the implicit theme. But "The Echoing Green" is included in the anthology; and did not Professor Tillyard find a "Great Commonplace" in that, too—like the "Soul in Nature" that spoiled "Westminster Bridge"?

Ideas and emotions are *dangerous* subjects for poetry, the former because a weak poet may be led into discourse on his topic, the latter because he may be tempted to direct utterance, exclamation, and catharsis of his own feelings. But a good poet can and certainly may handle even the most treacherous material; the only law that binds him—and, indeed, binds all other artists—is that every bit of the subject matter must be used for artistic effect. Everything must be virtual experience. There

---

[31]Cf. C. Day Lewis, *The Poetic Image*, p. 133: "A poetry which excludes the searchings of reason and the promptings of the moral sense is by so much the less impassioned, the less various and human, the less a product of the whole man at his full imaginative height."

[32]*Op. cit.*, p. 36.

is no trafficking with actualities in poetry, no matter how much the creator of the semblance has drawn on his own feelings, his deepest convictions, his memories and secret wishes. Poetry on moral themes may be undidactic, for the same reason that Goethe found poetry on immoral themes to be uncorrupting:[33] it does not express any proposition, and therefore does not advocate or confess anything. Similarly, subjective poetry is not a genuine display of subjectivity, because it is fiction. The very intensity of personal consciousness in it is something created by means of wording, cadence, completeness or incompleteness of statement, and every other ruse known in literature. The most perfect example of *virtual subjectivity* that comes to my mind happens to be in prose form, not verse, but it is a case in point, for it is a complete poetic transformation: James Joyce's *Portrait of the Artist as a Young Man*. The telling makes the scene, the life, the personage—there is not a line of "purely informative language," it is all fiction, though it is portraiture. Literary events are *made,* not reported, just as portraits are painted, not born and raised.

It is a common custom among poets and critics to oppose poetry to prose not as one art form to another, but as art and non-art—that is, to identify prose with the discursive language of practical thinking. Coleridge, Poe, and in our own day Professor Pottle among many others, mean by "prose" the *un*poetic. In reality, however, prose is a literary use of language, and therefore, in a broad but perfectly legitimate sense (considering the meaning of "poesis"), a *poetic form*.[34] It is derived from poetry in the stricter sense, not from conversation; its function is creative. This holds not only for prose fiction (the very term, "fiction," bespeaks its artistic nature), but even for the essay and for genuine historical writing. But that is a further subject.

---

[33]"Art is intrinsically noble; for this reason the artist is not afraid of commonness. For by his very use of it he ennobles it; and so we see the greatest artists exercising with utmost boldness their royal prerogative." (*Maximen und Reflexionen über Kunst.*)

[34]The belief that prose is the same thing as conversational language is so generally held that everyone is innocently ready to laugh at the gentleman who was amazed to find that all his life he had been talking prose. In my opinion, M. Jourdain had reason to be *étonné;* his literary instinct told him that conversation was something different from prose, and only lack of philosophy forced him to accept the popular error.

Chapter fifteen

VIRTUAL MEMORY

Everything actual must be transformed by imagination into something purely experiential; that is the principle of poesis. The normal means of making the poetic transformation is language; the way an event is reported gives it the appearance of being something casual or something momentous, trivial or great, good or bad, even familiar or new. A statement is always a formulation of an idea, and every known fact or hypothesis or fancy takes its emotional value largely from the way it is presented and entertained.

This power of words is really astounding. Their very sound can influence one's feeling about what they are known to mean. The relation between the length of rhythmic phrases and the length of chains of thought makes thinking easy or difficult, and may make the ideas involved seem more or less profound. The vocal stresses that rhythmicize some languages, the length of vowels in others, or the tonal pitch at which words are spoken in Chinese and some less known tongues, may make one way of wording a proposition seem gayer or sadder than another. This rhythm of language is a mysterious trait that probably bespeaks biological unities of thought and feeling which are entirely unexplored as yet.

The fullest exploitation of language sound and rhythm, assonance and sensuous associations, is made in lyric poetry. That is why I have considered this kind of literary composition first; not, as some people may suppose, because it is somehow superior to other kinds, the oldest or the purest or the most perfect sort of poetry. I do not think it has any higher artistic value than narrative poetry or prose. But it is the literary form that depends most directly on pure verbal resources—the sound and evocative power of words, meter, alliteration, rhyme, and other rhythmic devices, associated images, repetitions, archaisms, and grammatical twists. It is the most obviously linguistic creation, and therefore the readiest instance of poesis.

The reason why lyric poetry draws so heavily on the sound and the emotional character of language is that it has very scant materials to work with. The motif (the so-called "content") of a lyric is usually nothing more than a thought, a vision, a mood, or a poignant emotion, which does not offer a very robust framework for the creation of a piece of virtual history. Just as the composers of plain-song had to exploit the rhythms and accents of their Latin texts and the registers of human voices (the cultivation of the eunuch choir stems from this musical need), because they had none of the resources of meter, polyphony, keynote and modulation, nor instrumental support to work with, so the lyric poet uses every quality of language because he has neither plot nor fictitious characters nor, usually, any intellectual argument to give his poem continuity. The lure of verbal preparation and fulfillment has to do almost everything.

The virtual history that a lyric poem creates is the occurrence of a living thought, the sweep of an emotion, the intense experience of a mood. This is a genuine piece of subjective history, though usually it is a single episode. Its differences from other literary products are not radical, and there is no device characteristic of lyric composition that may not also be met in other forms. It is the frequency and importance of certain practices, rather than their exclusive use, that make lyric poetry a special type. Speech in the first person, for instance, may be found in ballads, novels, and essays; but there it is a deviation from the usual pattern, and in the lyric it is normal. Direct address to the reader may be found in romances, ballads, novels—but in the lyric such lines as:

> Hast thou named all the birds without a gun?

or:

> Never seek to tell thy love
> Love that never can be told

or:

> Tell me, where is fancy bred

hardly seem like personal apostrophe; the address is formal rather than exhortatory. In reflecting on lyric expression in the light of other literary work we shall find, presently, that neither the person speaking nor the person spoken to is an actual human being, the writer or the reader; the rhetorical form is a means of creating an *impersonal subjectivity,* which is the peculiar experiential illusion of a genre that creates no characters and no public events.

What a poet sets out to create, rather than what he feels or wants to tell us, determines all his practices, and leads to the establishment of literary forms like the lyric, the romance, the short story, the novel. Critics who do not recognize this universal aim of every art, and every work of art, are easily misled by usages that have meanings in art quite different from their meanings in real discourse; such critics assume that a poet who says "you," without putting the words into the mouth of a character addressing another, is speaking to the reader; and that the most notable characteristic of lyric poetry—the use of the present tense —means that the poet is uttering his own momentary feelings and thoughts.

The study of tense and its literary uses is, in fact, a revealing approach to the problem of poetic creation; and English is a particularly interesting language for such a study, because it has certain subtleties of verb formation that most other languages lack, notably the "progressive" forms "I am doing," "I was doing," "I have been doing," etc., as distinct from the formal conjugates: "I do," "I did," and the past participle tenses.[1] In the use of verb forms one finds devices that disclose the real nature of the literary dimension in which the image of life is created; the present tense proves to be a far more subtle instrument than either grammarians or rhetoricians generally realize, and to have quite other uses than the characterization of present acts and facts.

As soon as we pass from the intensive, small form of the lyric to works of greater compass, we encounter a new dominant element—narrative. This element is not unknown in lyric verse, but it is incidental there;

---

[1]On the other hand, it lacks independent forms corresponding to the French "imperfect" and "definite" past tenses. Our "present perfect" corresponds to the French "past indefinite," but the distinction between "j'étais" and "je fus" we cannot make without circumlocution.

or :

> She dwelt among the untrodden ways,

> A sunny shaft did I behold,
> From sky to earth it slanted,

are narrative lines, but they only serve to introduce a situation, an image, or an object for reflection and emotion. When, however, narrative is treated as the central motif of a composition, a new factor is introduced, which is *story interest*. This changes the entire form of thought which governs the work. A course of impersonal happenings is a strong framework for the making of a poetic illusion; it tends to become the ground plan, or "plot," of the entire piece, affecting and dominating every other means of literary creation. Personal address, for instance, which is usually a rhetorical device in lyric writing, becomes an action in the story, as one fictitious person addresses himself to another. Imagery, which is often the chief substance of a lyric poem, and may appear to be generated by free association, each vision evoking another,[2] is no longer paramount in narrative poetry, and no longer free; it has to serve the needs of the action. If it fails to do so, the work loses the organic character that makes poetry seem like a piece of nature though everything in it be physically impossible.

Narrative is a major organizing device. It is as important to literature as representation to painting and sculpture; that is to say, it is not the essence of literature, for (like representation in plastic art) it is not indispensable, but it is the structural basis on which most works are designed. It underlies the "Great Tradition" of poetic art in our culture, much as representation underlies the "Great Tradition" in sculptural and pictorial art.

The profound influence of narrative on any literary work into which it enters is most pervasively shown in the change of tense from the present, which is normal for lyric expression, to the perfect, the characteristic tense of story. Since most literature is narration, the perfect tense is by far the most common verb form in fiction. It is so accepted that it does not seem to require explanation, until we reflect on the fact that daydream—often regarded as the source of all literary invention—is usually

---

[2]Shelley built the first three sections of his "Ode to the West Wind" by means of such dreamlike concatenation of images.

formulated in the present tense. Daydream is a process of pretending, i.e. of "make-believe," akin to the imaginative play of children; the story is "lived" in the telling, both by its author and by the listeners. If the purpose of literary art were, as Tolstoi maintained,[3] to make the reader live in the story, feel with the characters, and vicariously experience their adventures, why is not the present its natural tense, as it is in free imagination?

Because literature, however fantastic, emotional, or dreamlike, is never present fantasy, served by bare ideas of action and emotional situations, voluntarily as in play or involuntarily as in dream. Virtual life, as literature presents it, is always a self-contained form, a unit of experience, in which every element is organically related to every other, no matter how capricious or fragmentary the items are made to appear. That very caprice or fragmentation is a *total effect,* which requires a perception of the whole history as a fabric of contributive events.[4]

Actual experience has no such closed form. It is usually ragged, unaccentuated, so that irritations cut the same figure as sacrifices, amusements rank with high fulfillments, and casual human contacts seem more important than the beings behind them. But there is a normal and familiar condition which shapes experience into a distinct mode, under which it can be apprehended and valued: that is memory. Past experience, as we remember it, takes on form and character, shows us persons instead of vague presences and their utterances, and modifies our impressions

---

[3]Leo Tolstoi, *What is Art?*

[4]F. W. Bateson, in *English Poetry and the English Language*, p. 77, quotes an interesting passage from Geoffrey Scott's *The Architecture of Humanism* in this connection: "The detail of the baroque style is rough. . . . It is rapid and inexact. But the purpose was exact, though it required 'inexact' architecture for its fulfilment. They [the baroque architects] wished to communicate, through architecture, a sense of exultant vigour and overflowing strength . . . a huge gigantic organism through which currents of continuous vigour might be conceived to run. A lack of individual distinctness in the parts . . . was thus not a negative neglect, but a positive demand. Their 'inexactness' was a necessary invention." And Bateson goes on: "The baroque style is rapid and inexact: it is rapid *because* it is inexact. And so with poetic diction. The style of such poets as Thomson, Young, Gray, and Collins is a rapid style; but their diction is conventional. And the diction is conventional because the style is rapid. A more precise and concrete diction would have destroyed the impression of rapidity that the style conveys. It is only because the individual words attract so little attention to themselves that the poetry is able to attain its unrivalled and almost headlong sense of movement."

by knowledge of things that came after, things that change one's spontaneous evaluation. Memory is the great organizer of consciousness. It simplifies and composes our perceptions into units of personal knowledge. It is the real maker of history—not recorded history, but the *sense of history* itself, the recognition of *the past* as a completely established (though not completely known) fabric of events, continuous in space and time, and causally connected throughout.[5] Whitehead has remarked on the peculiar aloofness of the past from all our wishes and strivings, as something formed and fixed, whereas the present is still amorphous, unused, unfashioned.[6]

To remember an event is to experience it again, but not in the same way as the first time. Memory is a special kind of experience, because it is composed of selected impressions, whereas actual experience is a welter of sights, sounds, feelings, physical strains, expectations, and minute, undeveloped reactions. Memory sifts all this material and represents it in the form of distinguishable events. Sometimes the events are logically connected, so that sheer remembering can date them with respect to each other; that is, in a vivid recollection of (say) coming down a hill, the sense of being high up and of treading dry gravel has merged into that of accelerated motion, of the horizon's lifting all around, of places near the bottom of the path; and the whole series of changes may be remembered. Any special adventure along the way then finds its temporal frame in the memory itself. But most events are recalled as separated incidents, and can be dated only by being thought of in a causal order in which they are not "possible" except at certain times. The other items in this causal order are one's various other memories, but the order itself is an intellectual system. Young children have no historical sense. The past is simply "before"; "where we were yesterday" and "where we were three days ago" are not meaningful expressions unless the two places have been otherwise identified and connected with

---

[5]Cf. Georg Mehlis, "Das aesthetische Problem der Ferne" (*Logos*, VI, 1916–17, 173–184): "The enigmatic depths of memory have never been plumbed and exhaustively searched by any man. . . . Each life-span organizes itself into a particular nexus of events which we can recall and in which we may dwell. . . . These worlds of experience and memory are our permanent possessions. . . . They have the virtue of finished products . . . a completeness which the present does not have."

[6]See *Symbolism: Its Meaning and Effect*, especially pp. 58–59.

those relative dates. Before we know any names for the days of the week, for the months, for the times of day, even very recent memories have no order. Children's experiences either still belong to the specious present —like the bump that still hurts—or they have become recollections, and belong to an essentially timeless past.

Even our personal history as we conceive it is, then, a construction out of our own memories, reports of other people's memories, and assumptions of causal relations among the items thus furnished. It is by no means all recollection. We are not really aware of our existence as continuous. Sometimes the memories of different places and activities in which we have found ourselves are so incongruous that we have to recall and arrange a series of intervening events before we really feel convinced that two such diverse situations belong to the same life. Especially when memory is very vivid it has no continuity. The deeply impressed incident seems to rise out of the past all alone, sometimes with such extraordinary detail that it suggests an experience just passed, scarcely modified at all by oblivion as yet; then, although the remembered event may be of old standing, it seems "as though it had been yesterday." Recent memories, on the other hand, may exist as mere awareness of facts, without emotional tone, without any detail, and even become confused with imagined events, so we can truly say: "I remember that it happened, but I cannot clearly recall how it was."

The primary illusion created by poesis is a history entirely "experienced"; and in literature proper (as distinct from drama, film, or pictured story) this virtual history is in the mode typified by memory. Its form is the closed, completed form that in actuality only memories have. Literature need not be made out of the author's memories (though it may be), nor does it necessarily present events explicitly *as* somebody's memories (though it may do so), but the *mode* in which events appear is the mode of completed experience, i.e. of the past. This explains why the normal tense of literary narration is the past tense. The verb form —a purely linguistic factor—effects the "literary projection" by creating a virtual past.

This past, however, which literature engenders, has a unity that actual personal history does not have; for our accepted past is not entirely experiential. Like our apprehensions of space, of time, and of the forces that control us, our sense of the past derives from memories mixed with extraneous elements, assumptions and speculations, that present life as a chain of events rather than as a single progressive action. In fiction, however, there is nothing but virtual memory; the illusion of life must be experiential through and through. The poetically created world is not limited to the impressions of one individual, but it is limited to impressions. All its connections are *lived* connections, i.e. motivations, all causes and effects operate only as the motives for expectation, fulfillment, frustration, surprise. Natural events are simply the molds in which human experiences are cast; their occurrence has to be inherent in the story which is a *total action*. Consider, for instance, the perfectly natural storm in the ballad of Sir Patrick Spens: it is a psychologically motivated "next step" after his defiant sailing from Norway because the inhospitable Norwegians have taunted him. Nor is it introduced as mere chance, but one of his men predicts it:

> I saw the new moon late yestreen
> Wi' the auld moon in her arm;
> And if we gang to sea, master,
> I fear we'll come to harm.

In actual life we often make such reasonable predictions; and if the expected event does not occur, the prediction is soon forgotten. But in poetry nothing is forgotten except by persons in the story. If the reader forgets, he will be reminded (assuming that the story is well told); for the poet's conception includes nothing that does not serve the narrative, which is the substance of his creation. Reflections, descriptions, and gem-like lines, and even characters are just parts of *the tale,* or *what is told.*

Narrative, then, has always the semblance of memory, more purely than actual history, even the personal history that we treat as our own memory; for poetry is created, and if its events be borrowed from the artist's memory, he must replace every non-experiential factor in his actual "past" by elements of purely experiential character, just as a painter substitutes purely visual appearances for the non-visual factors in ordinary space perception. The poet makes a semblance of events that is *experience-like,* but universally accessible; an objectified, depersonalized "memory," entirely homogeneous, no matter how much is explicit and how much implicit.

The contrast between the chaotic advance of the actual present and the surveyable form of remembered life has been remarked by several artist-philosophers, notably Marcel Proust, who maintained that what we call "reality" is a product of memory rather than the object of direct encounter; the present is "real" only by being the stuff of later memories. It was a peculiarity of Proust's genius to work always with a poetic core that was a spontaneous and perfect formulation of something in actual memory. This intense, emotionally charged recollection, completely articulate in every detail, yet as sudden and immediate as a present experience, not only was the catalyst that activated his imagination, but also constituted his ideal of poetic illusion, to be achieved by the most conscious and subtle kind of story-telling.

Literature, in the strict sense, creates the illusion of life in the mode of a virtual past. "Poesis" is a wider term than literature, because there are other modes of poetic imagination than the presentation of life through language alone. Drama and its variants (pantomime, marionettes) and moving picture are essentially poetic arts in other modes that I shall discuss in a subsequent chapter; they employ words in special ways, and sometimes even dispense with them altogether. The illusion they create is virtual life, an experiential history, but not in the mnemonic projection, not a virtual Past. That mode is peculiar to "literature" in the narrow sense of verbal art—works of imagination to be heard or read.

The perfect tense is a natural device for making and sustaining an illusion of finished fact. What challenges the theorist is, rather, the occasional use of the *present* tense in narrative, and especially its normal use in lyric poetry. It is the present and the "present perfect" that require explanation. The role of these forms in the creation of virtual history sheds some interesting lights on the nature of memory; for memory has many aspects which psychologists have not discovered, but of which the poet, who constructs its image, is aware. But a poet is not a psychologist; his knowledge is not explicit but implicit in his conception of the image. The critic, analyzing the way the "remembrance" of the virtual Past is made, is the person who is in a position to discover the intricacies of real memory through the artistic devices that achieve its semblance.

There are certain ordinary, non-literary uses of the present tense that indicate its possibilities for creative purposes. Its official use is, of course, to designate action occurring at the time of speaking. Grammarians usually cite the present indicative of a verb first, and in teaching a language we teach it first, as though it were the most necessary, most useful form. Actually, it is little used in English; we rarely say "I go," "I wait," etc., but generally substitute the "progressive" form. The reason is that the pure present refers to a momentary performance, the participle with "I am" to a sustained one, an active state; an immediate action taking place is usually apparent, and does not need to be mentioned;[7] so, when we talk about present acts, we normally do so to explain our immediate behavior as part of a protracted action, and therefore use the "progressive" present: "I am going home." "I am waiting for a bus."

The most important use of the pure present is in the statement of general facts such as the laws of nature, or of relations among abstract concepts, like the propositions in an algebra book. Science and philosophy and criticism are normally written in the pure present; "$2 + 2 = 4$" is read "two plus two *equals* four," not "equaled" or "is equaling" or "will equal." The present tense in such a context is the tense of *timelessness*.[8] It is used where time is irrelevant—where abstract entities are related, general truths expressed, or mere ideas associated apart from any actual situation, as in reverie.

Perhaps it is this "timeless" character of the pure present that makes grammarians adduce it first of all the tenses; it is like a modulus of verb conjugation—a form somewhere between the infinitive, which merely names an action without asserting its occurrence at all, and the tenses which not only indicate but date it.

In literature, the pure present can create the impression of an act, yet suspend the sense of time in regard to it. This explains its normal use in lyric poetry. Many critics, assuming that the present tense must refer to the present moment, have been led by this supposed grammatical evidence to believe that lyric poetry is always the utterance of the poet's

---

[7]Except for the frequent statements—"I think . . .," "I don't believe . . .," "I feel . . ."; subjective acts being unapparent by themselves.

[8]In the literature of epistemology, the observation of this "timeless" use of the present may be found in C. I. Lewis' *Analysis of Meaning and Valuation*, p. 51.

own beliefs and actual feelings.[9] But I maintain that lyric composition is art, and therefore creative; and the use of its characteristic tense must serve the creation that is peculiar to this kind of poetry.

As already said earlier in this chapter, the semblance most frequently created in a lyric is that of a very limited event, a concentrated bit of history—the thinking of an emotional thought, a feeling about someone or something. The framework is one of occurrent ideas, not external happenings; contemplation is the substance of the lyric, which motivates and even contains the emotion presented. And the natural tense of contemplation is the present. Ideas are timeless; in a lyric they are not said to have occurred, but are virtually occurring; the relations that hold them together are timeless, too. The whole creation in a lyric is an awareness of a subjective experience, and *the tense of subjectivity is the "timeless" present*. This kind of poetry has the "closed" character of the mnemonic mode, without the historical fixity that outward events bestow on real memories; it is in the "historical projection" without chronology. Lyric writing is a specialized technique that constructs an impression or an idea as something experienced, in a sort of eternal present; in this way, instead of offering abstract propositions into which time and causation simply do not enter, the lyric poet creates a sense of concrete reality from which the time element has been canceled out, leaving a Platonic sense of "eternity."

This timelessness is really one of the striking traits of many memories. The recollection of moods and attitudes, like spring fever or pensiveness, normally has no reference to specific occasions, yet such an experience is once and for all familiar, and rises in recollection with the vividness of something very recent. Often the remotest childhood moods come back suddenly with a completely unchronological freshness; yet

---

[9]See, for example, D. G. Brinton's article, "The Epilogues of Browning: Their Artistic Significance," in *Poet Lore*, IV (1892), which lists the following conclusions:

"(1) That Browning uniformly treats the epilogue as an element, not of dramatic, but of lyric poetry.

"(2) That with him it approaches the form of the soliloquy, and is intended to bring about a direct and personal relation between himself and his reader.

"(3) That his epilogues are the only portions of his writings in which he avowedly drops the dramatic turn of his genius and expresses his own sentiments as a man."

we do not meet them as new, like the actual present, but as old possessions. Our memory of persons with whom we have lived usually has this
timeless character.

If, now, we turn from the lyric with its timeless, personal character
to narrative poetry, it is natural enough that we find the perfect and
pluperfect the normal tenses for constructing the frame of impersonal,
physical events. In simple discursive statement of historical facts, one
uses only the past tenses. But poetic statement has a different aim; its
purpose is not to inform people of what has happened and when, but
to create the illusion of things past, the semblance of events lived and
felt, like an abstracted and completed memory. Poets, therefore, exploit
the grammatical verb forms for every shade of immediacy or indirectness, continuity or finality, that is, for their power of shaping virtual
experience rather than for their literal function of naming actions and
dating them. So we encounter the present tense, even here, in its "timeless" capacity, and also in some others. One of these is the well-known
"historical present" which heightens the vividness of an action by telling
it "as though it were now." This device can be very effective, but has
been so blatantly used by journalists and novices that it has become an
obvious trick. It is interesting to note that when a real master employs
it, the present tense usually has another justification than to highlight
the action. There is a genuine "historical present" in the "Rime of the
Ancient Mariner":

> Swiftly, swiftly flew the ship,
> Yet she sailed softly too;
> Sweetly, sweetly blew the breeze—
> On me alone it blew.
> Oh! dream of joy! is this indeed
> The lighthouse top I see?
> Is this the hill? is this the kirk?
> Is this mine own countree?

The present tense does indeed intensify the sudden joy of the Mariner
as he recognizes his home port, but it does more than that: it ends the
voyage, as "now" always ends one's subjective history. The story culminates in the Mariner's return as the past culminates in the present.
Note how the landing (described in the past tense) makes a cadence

that ends with another "historical present," even overflowing into a future
tense, to reinforce the effect:

> I saw a third—I heard his voice:
> It is the hermit good!
> He singeth loud his godly hymns
> That he makes in the wood.
> He'll shrieve my soul, he'll wash away
> The albatross's blood.

The most interesting use, however, of the present tense in narratives
that really move in the past, is a use that has never, to my knowledge,
been recognized as a technical achievement at all. Perhaps literary critics
have missed it because they are inclined to think of a poem as something the poet *says* rather than something the poet *makes,* and what he
says is not enhanced by this subtle play of tenses; I mean the mingling
of past and present constructions that is commonly found in ballads,
especially in the opening and closing stanzas. It is a grammatically inconsistent practice, but so widespread that it obviously has an artistic
mission. It does not make the impression of a solecism, nor disorient the
reader with regard to the time of the action. Usually it passes unnoticed.
In old traditional ballads the diction is often so colloquial that one might
ascribe the inaccuracy of tense to popular carelessness; but one could
hardly allow it on such grounds in the excellent ballads written by modern
poets—"The Rime of the Ancient Mariner," "The Lady of Shalott," or
Goethe's "Erlkönig," in all of which it occurs, and is usually not even
remarked. It is one of the balladist's devices, and was used as naturally
by recent as by ancient poets when the ballad spirit was upon them.

To adduce some examples from the store of anonymous English poetry:
in "The Queen's Marie,"[10] the first three stanzas mix present and past
tenses; stanzas four and five are in the past; six mixes the tenses again;
seven and eight are in the present; after that the connected action begins, Marie is got up from her childbed to ride with the queen, enters
Edinburgh, is accused and condemned. All this connected action, the
work of one day, is told in the past tense, to the end of the story.

In "Sir Patrick Spens," the first stanza is in the present, the second

---

[10]Most, if not all, such old ballads are known in many versions. The version
here referred to is that given in *The Oxford Book of Ballads.*

in the past, the third begins in the present perfect and ends in the progressive pure perfect ("was walking"). With the reception of the letter,
the adventure begins, and the narrative proceeds in the past tense until
the disaster is over; the last three stanzas, which are an aftermath, are
in the present again.

If now we turn to "The Rime of the Ancient Mariner," we find the
same mixture of tenses. The first stanza is in the pure present; the second
must be discounted, since it is direct discourse; the third, fourth, and
fifth are mixed. Then begins the real story, in direct discourse, and told
in the past except for two stanzas (the ones which employ a genuine "historical present") until the tale is told and the Mariner speaks of what
is present. Only at the very end, the impersonal narrative is resumed,
and in those two closing stanzas the tenses are mixed again:

> The mariner, whose eye is bright,
> Whose beard with age is hoar,
> Is gone; and now the Wedding-Guest
> Turned from the bridegroom's door.
>
> He went like one that hath been stunned,
> And is of sense forlorn;
> A sadder and a wiser man
> He rose the morrow morn.

Even the use of "hath" and "is" in the simile, though formally correct,
is unusual, as the tense in such a relative clause usually conforms to
that of the main clause. The strictly accurate form is here used in its
strictly accurate sense, which is *timeless*, since the reference is not to
any particular "one" who *had* been stunned. This touch of timelessness
is exactly what the poet wanted.

In Tennyson's famous ballad, "The Lady of Shalott," the first seven
stanzas, which tell about the place, the lady, her life and her song, the
curse, the mirror, and the web, are in the present tense. In the eighth
stanza—the last one of Part II—the perfect is introduced almost imperceptibly. After that, the action proceeds from a definite occasion (Lance-
lot's riding by) to the end, and is told consistently in the past tense.

The principle governing such usage seems to be, that everything
needed to create the context of the story is presented as a dateless condition. This is true to the nature of memory; all our relevant knowledge

is implicit in the recollection of a past event, but is not itself "remembered" as of that time. It is the active historical environment, not the history itself; and in poetry, where the semblance of lived history is created, and its framework of implicit knowledge has also to be created by explicit telling, the sense of the difference between events and their motivating circumstances is often given through the play of tenses, that makes the time sense indefinite for everything but the action itself.

This is, of course, not a rule, but a device which may or may not be used. There are ballads in which the present tense never occurs (e.g. "Clerk Saunders"), and some where it is used in midst of the narrative to indicate a skip in the action. In "Binnorie" (thematically, I venture to say, one of the oldest legends in all our lore), the story is told in the past tense to the point where the princess lies dead beside the weir, and the harper comes by:

> And when he look'd that lady on,
> He sigh'd and made a heavy moan.
> He's made a harp of her breast-bane,
> Whose sound wad melt a heart of stane.
> He's ta'en three locks o' her yellow hair,
> And wi' them strung his harp sae rare.
> He went into her father's hall,
> And there was the court assembled all.

Thus the narrative proceeds again, in its natural form.

One of the most unusual and brilliant manipulations of tense in narrative poetry occurs in Goethe's "Erlkönig": This ballad is, throughout, a masterpiece of rhetorical structure for poetic effect.[11] There are only

---

[11] An almost incredible tension is set up and constantly heightened by *questions* on all levels of speech and experience; first the poet's impersonal question:
> Wer reitet so spät durch Nacht und Wind?

The brief narrative introduction is the answer. Then the father's inquiry:
> "Mein Sohn, was birgst du so bang dein Gesicht?"

to which the child replies with another question:
> "Siehst, Vater, du den Erlkönig nicht?
> Den Erlenkönig, mit Kron' und Schweif?"

The father throws in a single line of reassuring reply:
> "Mein Sohn, es ist ein Nebelstreif."

Then comes the soft lure of the Alder King, and the child's more urgent question:
> "Mein Vater, mein Vater, und hörest du nicht

four lines of impersonal statement before the dialogue takes over entirely, and those four lines are in the present tense. The poem ends, similarly, with four lines of narrative, all in the present, except the very last:

> Dem Vater grauset's, er reitet geschwind,
> Er hält in den Armen das ächzende Kind.
> Erreicht den Hof mit Mühe und Not;
> In seinen Armen das Kind war tot.

> (The father is shaken, he rides apace,
> The child is moaning in his embrace;
> He reaches the house, in fear and dread;
> The child within his arms was dead.)

Here the sudden incursion of the *past* tense closes the adventure and the poem, with the power of a full cadence—the "perfect" tense, accomplished fact.

The pure present there serves two effects at once—its character of being "out of time" helps to create the unreal atmosphere in which all the questions and visions arise, and its immediacy—the force of the "historical present"—heightens the action. Furthermore, of course, it prepares the effect of the time shift in the closing line.

The normal function of the past tense is to create the "historical projection," i.e. the appearance of events in the mnemonic mode, like a reality lived and remembered. People tacitly acknowledge this office of the "per-

---

> Was Erlenkönig mir leise verspricht?"

Soon the ghost himself speaks in the interrogative mood:

> "Willst, feiner Knabe, du mit mir gehn?"

And the child, again:

> "Mein Vater, mein Vater, und siehst du nicht dort
> Erlkönigs Töchter am düstern Ort?"

In this way the whole spook is created out of uncertainties, so the final declarative:

> "Ich liebe dich, mich reizt deine schöne Gestalt;
> Und bist du nicht willig, so brauch' ich Gewalt!"

comes with a terrible force, that elicits the cry:

> "Mein Vater, Mein Vater, jetzt fasst er mich an!"

and makes the very crisis seem like a solution, just because it is fact, and breaks the tension of so much questioning:

> "Erlkönig hat mir ein Leids getan!'

This is supreme composition, from the first word to the last.

fect" (note how its technical name bespeaks its formulating and defining power), by avoiding it when they tell the mere plot of a literary work. In outlining the action of a story, poem, or film, we habitually use the present tense, for we are not *composing* the action into any artistic form. The unwritten rule that such paraphrases are properly reported in the present springs from a genuine poetic feeling; the past tense would make that bare statement of plot pretend to literary status, and as literature it would be atrociously bad. So we keep our synopses in the "timeless present" to indicate that we are exhibiting materials, not presenting elements, of art.

Legend and myth and fairy tale are not in themselves literature; they are not art at all, but fantasies; as such, however, they are the natural materials of art. By their nature they are not bound to any particular words, nor even to language, but may be told or painted, acted or danced, without suffering distortion or degradation.[12] But literature proper is the use of language to create virtual history, or life, in the mnemonic mode—the semblance of memory, though a depersonalized memory. A legend presented as story is as new a creation as any work whereof the plot has just been invented; for apart from the telling, the action or "plot" is not a "work," it creates no complete and organized illusion of something lived, but is to literature what an armature or a roughly shaped block is to sculpture—a first shape, a source of ideas.

The chief exhibit of the artistic use of tense, throughout my long discussion, has been the art of ancient ballad makers, from whom some modern poets have learned their trade; so it is surprising, not to say disconcerting, to find that some recognized experts on the popular ballad maintain stoutly that it is not literary art at all, but belongs to the primitive matrix of spontaneous fantasy. Frank Sidgwick, for instance, in his little book *The Ballad*, makes this point emphatically. "A ballad," he says, "is, and always has been, so far from being a literary form that it is, in its essentials, not literary, and . . . has no single form. It is a *genre* not only older than the Epic, older than Tragedy, but older than

---

[12]This circumstance was pointed out to me by the illustrator Helen Sewell, who has given much thought to the relations between literature and painting, and the rights of both to the wellsprings of popular lore.

literature, older than the alphabet. It is *lore,* and belongs to the illiterate."[18]

So far, so good; if "literature" is taken in its strictest sense, as an art of letters, then, of course, the poetry of illiterate societies is not "literature." But when Professor Sidgwick says that the ballad is *not poetry,* I must disagree. The fact that every ballad has several versions, and therefore no *single* form, does not mean that it has *no* form. Myths are "lore"; they have no meter, no characteristic phrases, and are just as often recorded in vase paintings and bas-reliefs as in words. A ballad, however, is a composition; and although it is protean, not bound to one completely determinate form, it is essentially poetic. Like all personally transmitted works—folk song, litany, and dance (even today), the living ballad has an *open* form; it can survive much variation, because the conception of it is not completely verbalized, although the major decisions in its progress are all made. Like a figured bass, it invites elaboration.

The essentially poetic nature of the folk ballad is well attested by a practice which developed as soon as such popular compositions were written down—the custom of furnishing a running paraphrase by means of marginal glosses. This paraphrase is kept in the present tense, and expresses the proto-poetic fantasy, the pure plot, which might just as well be embodied in a play, a tale, a frieze, a tapestry series, or an opera. The ballad, on the other hand, normally uses the tense of true narrative; it creates a poetic illusion in the literary mode, though its verbalization is pre-literate. What makes it memorable is not the plot as such, but the poem—the created piece of virtual history, which is a non-discursive expressive form.

The often repeated assertion—on which Professor Sidgwick insists— that a ballad has no author, that it is a group product, "emotion crystallized in a crowd," seems to me to be without foundation. No one has ever known a crowd to invent a song, although successive members may elaborate one, adding stanzas or proposing parodies, once its poetic theme, rhyme scheme, and tune have been proposed (the meter is usually dictated by the tune). The idea comes from one person; and a serious song, such as a "spiritual," is usually presented in a complete form, however simple. The crowd adopts it; and if the song finds favor, and is handed

[18]*The Ballad,* pp. 7–8.

on, its authorship is soon obscured, though the composer may have local fame as one frequently inspired.[14]

The concept of the "folk" as a perfect democracy of talent is a pseudo-ethnological fiction which arises, I believe, from the anonymity of folk art. But, to return to the ballad, it is highly improbable that no one invented such a poem as "The Wife of Usher's Well." No matter how many versions there may be, someone composed the tale originally in meter and rhyme, and furnished the "poetic core" of all variants that may be gathered under its title.

Is this "open form" an essential characteristic of the true ballad? If the "true ballad" is an ethnological concept, yes; but if one regards it as a poetic category, no. Writing down the words of a ballad does not destroy it, though its sociological function may be altered or even destroyed. Theoretically, all its versions could be written down, none made pre-eminent, except in practice, by popular favor, once everybody has access to all of them. The fact is, of course, that editors and publishers mediate between the public and the work, and standardize the versions of their choice; the ethnic effects of literacy cannot be evaded.

Since any poem known by heart may be written down, the ballad, though not "literature" in its pristine state, was destined to *become* a literary form; and many versions of orally remembered ballads were artistically interesting, well balanced and even subtle. As soon as they appeared in print they furnished the literate and literary world with a highly characteristic form. This new form, however, is not for singing; it is not even for recitation, but—like most full-fledged "literature"—for reading.

Professor Sidgwick's stout insistence that the ballad is not poetry may rest not on any misunderstanding of the ballad form (which would be most unlikely in a person of his qualifications), but on what I would consider a too narrow conception of poetic art: the identification of this

[14]There is an interesting study by Elsa Mahler of the Russian dirge as a species of peasant poetry. The metrical form, the figures of speech, and other rubrics are traditional; but every woman is expected to be able to extemporize the dirge for her dead (this is a feminine office). Naturally, talent and imagination differ widely; but each dirge, which is certainly pure "folk poetry," is always the work of one poet. Since custom demands a new poem for every occasion, there is no cause to write down even the best. See Elsa Mahler, *Die russiche Totenklage, ihre rituelle u. dichterische Deutung*.

art with its own highest development, which is "literary" in the strict sense, a making of completely fixed, invariable, verbal structures—fixed by being written down *ab initio*, by their authors. Such poems are to folk poetry what so-called "art songs" are to folk song; but folk song, the simple air with variable text and any sort, or no sort, of accompaniment, is still music, and nothing but music; and the traditional ballad with its numerous versions, some crude and some formally beautiful, is still poetry in the "literary" mode of virtual memory.

Perhaps the strict view of "literature" as reading matter springs from an unavowed but quite justified protest against a popular theory, held also by many aestheticians, that the printed word is an enemy of poetic experience—that all poetry and (some say) even all prose should really be read aloud, and that silent reading is only a poor substitute for hearing the spoken word. Perhaps the notion that literature begins only with letters is simply a bit of over-compensation in opposition to this fairly widespread but superficial doctrine. The art of printing, according to the "oral" theory of poetry, has deprived us of much literary pleasure, for our ability to preserve innumerable works from oblivion has been bought at the price of our real experience of them. Words, like music, are essentially something for physical hearing.[15]

If Professor Sidgwick's principle of dating "literature" from the advent of literacy is indeed a revolt against such a theory, I can only assent in spirit even while I criticize his own definition of poetry. The treatment of poetry as physical sound comparable to music rests, I believe, on an utter misconception of what a writer creates, and what is the role of sound in that creation. There is poetry that profits by, or even demands, actual speech[16] (E. E. Cummings, for instance, gains tremendously by being read aloud; where words are used impressionistically and not intended to be dwelt upon and examined for a literal meaning, recitation is an asset, for it does not allow one to stop, but forces one to pass over the problematic word and receive only the impression it is

---

[15]The expression of this view by Calvin S. Brown, Jr., in his *Music and Literature: A Comparison of the Arts* has already been quoted and discussed in Chap. 9, pp. 134–135.

[16]Many people assume that very sonorous or musical poetry, especially, loses its beauty if it is not spoken. But such poetry is, in fact, the easiest to "hear" inwardly.

designed to make). But much poetry and nearly all prose should be read somewhat faster than the normal rate of speech.[17] Fast speaking does not meet this demand, because it becomes precipitous. Silent reading actually *is* faster, but does not appear so, because it is not hurried at the quicker tempo, whereas physical enunciation is. The images want to pass more swiftly than the spoken word. And furthermore, in prose fiction as well as in a good many poems, the voice of a speaker tends to intrude on the created world, turning formal lyric address, such as:

> I tell you, hopeless grief is passionless

into genuine speech, addressed by the poet's proxy—the speaker—to another real person, the listener.[18] A novel that centers chiefly in the creation of virtual personalities almost always suffers, when read aloud, by the peripheral presence of the reader (fairy tales, adventure stories, and mediaeval romances are not greatly influenced in this way).

The surest sign that writing and reading do not sap the life of poetic art is the historical fact that the true development of such art—the emergence of its special forms, both in poetry and prose—takes place in a culture only after writing is established. It is the literate poet who

---

[17]This view is corroborated in the words of H. W. Boynton, who wrote, nearly half a century ago: "Outside of poetry there are few forms of literature which are not as well or better off without the interposition of the voice. The reason appears to be that a printed page empowers the ear with a faculty of rapid hearing. The inward ear may receive an impression quite as surely as the outward ear, and far more rapidly. Printed words represent sound rather than form to most people. . . ." ("Pace in Reading," in *Journalism and Literature, and Other Essays*, p. 62.)

[18]The confusion becomes even more disastrous where the direct address is put into the mouth of a character, and presupposes a respondent not accounted for in the poem, e.g.:

> "Nay, but you, who do not love her,
> Is she not pure gold, my mistress?"

or:

> "Let us go then, you and I,
> When the evening is spread out against the sky
> Like a patient etherised upon a table."

One recent critic, Morris Weitz, has proposed as an obvious interpretation, that Prufrock—a fictitious person, an element in the poetic whole—takes the reader into his confidence, that we are to see *ourselves* walking with him down half-deserted streets, and that the poem does not create, but reveals, "Prufrock's and our own indecisiveness"! (See *Philosophy of the Arts*, p. 96.)

explores the many technical means of which his art permits, invents new stylistic elements, and extends his designs to encompass more and more material. Only in writing could prose become an artistic medium at all. This and all other special forms have grown up, I believe, by the exploitation of alternative techniques; every means of creating the poetic illusion produced its own kind of composition. To trace this evolution of the great literary forms, each on the strength of its pre-eminent devices, is the readiest way to demonstrate that all "creative writing" is poesis, and so far as it works with words alone, creates the same illusion: virtual memory, or history in the mode of an experienced Past.

Chapter sixteen

THE GREAT LITERARY FORMS

All artistic conventions are devices for creating forms that express some idea of vitality or emotion. Any element in a work of art may contribute to the illusory dimension in which such forms are presented, or to their appearance, their harmonization, their organic unity and clarity; it may serve many such aims at once. Everything, therefore, that belongs to a work is expressive; and all artifice is functional. To suppose that a good poet used a particular vocabulary simply because it was considered the proper language for poetry in his day, is an unhistorical explanation. The important question is, why poets in his day used such words—what sort of semblance they were making, and by what means, i.e. what those words were doing in literature.

The poetic vocabulary of an age consists of the ways of speaking which poets are exploiting at that time. Let one man introduce a new turn of phrase, a new image, or a new rhythmic device to (say) expand an action, or to hurry it, or to dwell on it, and other poets will of course be struck by his technique. The weaker ones will imitate it; but his true peers will use analogous solutions for their own problems, and develop other devices in harmony and combination with it. We do not know, for instance, who was the first poet to employ a line of only one or two beats, halting the flow of a stanza which then continues with a slowed cadence; but the practice is common in Elizabethan poetry, and serves more than one purpose. Herrick uses it to deepen a feeling or a thought, as in his poem "To Daffodils"; Donne uses it to beget a sense of stiffness and coolness:

> Though she were true, when you met her,
> And last till you write your letter,
>   Yet she
>   Will be
> False, ere I come, to two or three.

Fletcher lets the short line serve as a response, a formal assent, like a bow:

> Cynthia, to thy power and thee
> We obey.

All the uses of that little instrument, one by one, are exploited—not only to slow a rhythm, but also to halt it with a note of finality:

> Forbear therefore,
> And lull asleep
> Thy woes, and weep
> No more.

It serves as a pause, as an accent, as an echo, as a closing chord, and undoubtedly a little research would reveal various other functions.

The two-beat line is an Elizabethan convention. Even the printers recognized its value and developed a proper way of centering it, to help the inner ear with an emphasis for the eye.[1] Yet the easy assumption that poets used it as pure stock in trade, in order to make their poems conform to a fashion, is given the lie as soon as one looks at the variety of ends that were achieved with it. To scholars classifying literary works it may be simply an earmark of poetry in a particular style; but in the hands of the poets who established that style, it was, in each occurrence, an expressive element. The "fashion" developed from the versatility of the device, and its power to do things which those particular poets wanted to do.

Structure, diction, imagery, the use of names, allusions, are all creative devices that someone's imagination has seized upon in making the image of life that was to express his "Idea." In an age when poetry is alive and progressive, there is a unity of interest that leads many writers to explore the same predominant feelings, so there comes to be a certain solidarity of style that is entirely genuine with each contributor. Devices then become traditions, yet they serve many different poetic purposes. They are technical assets, not imitative practices; they are used by good poets until their possibilities are exhausted, or until another invention makes them ineffectual, superfluous, and consequently banal.

The effect of artistic elements on one another, and therefore of each

---

[1] In literature that is offered for silent reading, the typographer's task becomes an artistic one, closely akin to performance.

creative means on some or all others, has often been remarked, but never, to my knowledge, seriously studied. Yet it is the principle of artistic construction that leads to the evolution of special forms within one great general field of art—forms as distinct as the ballad, the romance, the novel, the literary essay, the short story, the catechism, the dialogue.

There are critics, and especially teachers of rhetoric and poetics, who judge the excellence of a work according to the number of well-known virtues they can find in it (somewhat as dogs in a show are judged by "points") : word-music, wealth of imagery, sensuousness, emotional intensity, economy, story interest, "obliquity," irony, depth of thought, realism, dramatic characterization, power, and whatever else is usually praised and recommended as a literary value.[2] There are differences of opinion as to which is the chief value: imagery or musicality in lyrics, character or plot in novels, realism or "depth" in the short story, irony or intensity of feeling or economy or what not in everything. But whichever trait is taken as the *sine qua non* of literature, or of the particular genre in question, a work is thought to be always enriched by the presence of further assets, and the complete lack of any major virtue is regarded as a "limitation."[3] Thus a poem full of sensuous imagery is, on principle, deemed better than one without, an economical statement always better than a wordy circumlocution, and so forth.

What these critics (some of whom are serious theorists) fail to see is that such "values" are not the stuff of literature at all, but devices for making the true elements that constitute the poetic illusion. Their use is properly relative to the poet's creative purpose; he may need many of them or few, exploit them to the utmost or change freely from one to the other; as some workmen have a favorite tool that serves them almost everywhere, while others choose a different implement for every special task. The cardinal principle is that every artifice employed must be employed to a poetic purpose, not because it is fun, or the fashion, or a new experiment, to use it.[4] Consequently one technical asset may make

---

[2]An excellent example of this practice may be found in Stephen Pepper's *The Basis of Criticism in the Arts,* chap. vi, pp. 115–120, the "mechanist's" evaluation. Professor Pepper does not indicate anywhere that he finds it objectionable.

[3]This practice is not restricted to literary criticism; a German music critic regards Mozart's genius as "limited" because he has no love of outdoor life.

[4]Genuinely new practices or means, such as great artists sometimes introduce,

another, or even many others, unnecessary; and also, since two practices that might both be valuable in the same work may yet be incompatible, one may have to be sacrificed.

If one bears steadily in mind that everything a poet writes is a stroke in the creation of a piece of virtual history, one may view the evolution of every literary genre as the exploitation of some pre-eminent technical principle and its influence—positive or negative—on the poetic value of all other available practices and materials. As the employment of narrative makes simple versification and simple diction sufficient, and therefore excellent, the folk ballad, governed by a story, has none of the intensity of thought and feeling that may be found in the lyric folk song.[5] Instead of concentration it has scope; the usual structure, which is a series of events succeeding each other in a single causal chain, makes the poem move fast through many stanzas; and in the interest of keeping the story clear, the stanzas are usually constructed in regularly alternating verse lengths and alternating rhymes. Everything is designed to get on with the story. That eliminates many favorite poetic means: descriptions, comparisons, protestations of feeling, and with these the turns of phrase and metrical variations that enrich a more contemplative poetry.

One simple progressive action, however, is not the only pattern in which a narrative can unfold. With trained and growing skill the storytellers elaborated their histories to embrace a wider scene, more complicated events, even parallel adventures that occasionally touched upon each other, involving more than one set of agents; the resultant form was the "romance." Its larger design required stronger means of sustaining the illusion of events and keeping their forms and movements clear than the simple rhymed quatrain and pithy statement which the ballad supplied. This brought the well-known but usually incidental art of description into a new and prominent role. It has been often said that the troubadours (and their imitators) introduced their detailed accounts of

---

and perhaps point out with enthusiasm, are not "experiments"; for the artist does not use them just to see what will happen; he starts with a new conception that sets him a task for which he knows they will serve, and merely shows how they solve his problem in an eminently suitable way. Cf. Picasso's statement, quoted on p. 122.

[5]A poetic form more common in Germany, Scandinavia, and Russia than in England or in the story-loving Latin countries.

weapons and costumes, tournaments, banquets and funerals for the sheer pleasure of sensuous imagination. But no matter how delightful these ingredients are, they could no more be inserted into a poem for their own sakes than an extra pound of sugar could happily be poured into a cake batter just because sugar is so nice. They are, in fact, powerful formal elements; they hold back the narrative and cause the events to appear spread out as in a third dimension, instead of racing to a conclusion like the adventures of Sir Patrick Spens or Thomas the Rhymer. If the troubadour's audience reveled in his descriptions and called on him to expand them, his artistic sense demanded other literary elements that would motivate and support a riot of images. The story, slowed and broadened by imagery and detail to allow its complex actions to intertwine, produced a new structural factor, the constant relations of characters to each other. In folk poetry, the actors appear and disappear as they are needed. The king sits in Dunfermline Town, but after he has written his "braid letter" he vanishes. He has no gesture to make in praise or sorrow for the hero when the disaster is completed. The agents in mediaeval romances, however, remain in the background when they are not needed, because there is a background. Instead of the implicit natural setting of sea, moor, fairyland, or graveyard willows, the romance has an explicit social setting: the king's court, the military encampment, the hall. It is in such human environments that actions naturally intersect, and histories are woven together.

The king who sits in Dunfermline Town may disappear when Sir Patrick goes to sea, but the king who sits in Camelot remains seated until he has something else to do. Yet there is no more of him than the story requires for its continuity and the creation of its sustained human background. The characters of romance, as everybody knows, are strictly personages, not personalities. Their importance derives from their status. Textbooks of literary history usually point out that the troubadours and minnesingers had not yet learned to develop individual characters. It seems more likely, however, that they had no desire to make their characters "live" as men and women, because what was really to "live" was the social world, the world of the poem, dominated by spectacular actions; and this romantic life would not have been helped at all by a greater individuation of characters. Personages were exactly what was needed:

royalty, clergy, knights always in armor, ladies always beautiful. These are not products of wishful thinking or naiveté—they are the needed human elements in a special kind of poetical work.

The real novelty and power of that genre lies in the description of *how* things are done; and this long dwelling on each action gives even the most familiar events—journeying, love-making, dying—a new form. It is like painting suddenly in three dimensions instead of two. The descriptive technique arrests one movement of history while another flows on; this throws the whole virtual experience into a subtle distortion, and produces the appearance of existences and happenings in the background, events which are not being "followed," but may emerge into full focus again at any time.[6] The fact that such arrests of action are not always "lifelike," not always made where overt action halts naturally, has made many people believe the expansive, colorful details to be superadded decorations, and laugh at the "unrealistic" moments of delay they cause in the progress of the story. But such descriptive expansions are just what give the true romance its vitality. It is this special use of sensuous images and itemized procedures, rather than the fact that there are genuine contemporary courses of action, that produces the effect of a fabric, instead of a thread, of history.

Because the descriptive treatment of events is here the major poetic device, even the narrative interest has to be held in check. Not only the characters but also their adventures tend to be typical: the quest, the mission, the contest, the rescue, the pledge redeemed. Tournaments and receptions of strangers and royal death scenes or nuptials fill the world of chivalry. Dragon killings, crusades and love ordeals give its life dramatic form; but in essence it is spectacular.

The mediaeval romance has an abundance of poetic resources. The narrative frame is such that more story elements may be developed almost anywhere; that is why the quest—for the Grail, or for dark towers and captive ladies, or for a white unicorn—is a favorite motif. It can accommodate subsidiary adventures. Besides the narrative structure, there are persons of every degree; there is the Church with all its legend; visions, warnings, promises. Above all, the mediaeval poet had the love-theme to lend fire and glamor to almost every canto.

---

[6]Compare the analysis of incommensurable tensions in consciousness, pp. 112–113.

With such a wealth of technical means, the poem did not really need the hypnotic powers of rhythmic speech to hold its auditors under its spell. There were plenty of other means to sustain the poetic illusion and to develop its expressive form. Versification, therefore, became a noticeable convention; especially after books succeeded to singers as the means of presentation, tradition rather than necessity kept the old verse forms alive. Such a state is the old age of a tradition, wherein it properly dies. Meter and rhyme died out of the chivalrous romance as its living (and therefore unnoticed) conventions became rich and assured enough to dispense with purely auditory helps.

Prose fiction arose when its poetic requirements were fulfilled; but between it and "poetry" in the strict sense the differences are primarily technical.[7] As David Daiches has written, in a recent book: "In prose fiction the disposition of the action carries the greater load, while in poetry it is the use of the resources of language in relation to each other that bears the major burden. *Both aim at achieving the same kind of end.*"[8]

Prose fiction is the favorite literary form of our own society. The short story, the German "Novelle," the fantasy (satiric or prophetic) and above all the novel are our staple poetic diet. The modern novel plays the part in our intellectual life which the romance played in that of the Middle Ages: it portrays the contemporary scene. The troubadour's recitation, with its picturesque plan, inviting a use of personages and establishments, was modeled on actualities and stressed the most immediate interests of an age when the growth of a social order out of the tribal and colonial chaos of Europe was still a modern achievement. Similarly, the novel is peculiarly suited to formulate our modern life by taking our most pervasive interest for its theme—the evaluation and the hazards of personality. This central topic normally entails an envisagement of the social order from the standpoint of individual life; so the creation of "characters," or genuine persons, leads as naturally to representation of our contemporary world as the personages of an older literature led to the world picture of that time. Our interest in personality

---

[7] On the difference of function that technical means, for example, poetic imagery, may undergo in the development of new forms, cf. C. Day Lewis, *The Poetic Image*, pp. 86–87.

[8] *A Study of Literature*, p. 139.

is what makes our world different and most of its problems relatively new. The source of this change of interests is, of course, historical: economic, religious, political, all in one. But whatever has caused it, the new vision of reality that emerges is not yet in full focus, and therefore is emotionally confusing. Unfamiliar feelings make us afraid of ourselves and each other; their elusive presence haunts our minds, and challenges the artistic imagination to realize them in perceptible forms.

The novel is an answer to that challenge. It creates a virtual experience of relatively large scope; its form is elastic, and allows of practically limitless complication or simplification, because its structural resources are immensely varied and rich. It may employ swift, factual narrative, or the most indirect half-statements, glowing descriptions, or no description at all; it may be the history of a single soul, or a lusty crowd of buccaneers, a whole society, or even a gathering of the living and the dead (as in Sartre's *Les jeux sont faits*). It is a recent genre, still evolving, still seizing on everything that is characteristic of the "modern" scene to supply its thematic materials, to motivate and develop its illusion of life.

Yet it is fiction, poesis, and its import is formulated feeling, not sociological or psychological theory; its aim is, as Professor Daiches declared, simply the aim of all literature, and for that matter of all art. Its critical evaluation, therefore, should be in all respects a literary judgment. Since, however, the setting of the story is usually an image of the time and place in which its readers live, it is all too easy for them to become entirely absorbed in the author's representations, judge them as fair or false, and treat the book as his commentary on actual problems and confession of his own feelings. Most literary critics today tend to praise or blame a contemporary novel as a document, instead of a work of fiction with a poetic aim to achieve. Its fictitious character is treated as a rhetorical ruse to make the reader listen to a whole statement, which he would be inclined to interrupt and dispute were it presented in straightforward discourse. Often a novel is viewed as an example from individual human life to illustrate a general social condition, and is measured entirely by its relevance to actual problems, political, psychiatric, or moral. Koestler's *Darkness at Noon* and Mann's *Dr. Faustus* owe their enthusiastic reception by the educated public mainly if not wholly to their por-

trayal and evaluation of contemporary culture. In the flood of discussion
Kafka and Sartre have evoked, one hears hardly a word about their
literary powers but only about their alleged personal feelings and moral
attitudes, their hopes and fears for the actual world, their criticism of life.
But most of this "criticism" is not artistic envisagement of life itself,
such as one finds in Joyce, Proust, Turgenev, Thackeray, Goethe; it is
reasoned opinion, more or less fictionalized, and it is received as such
—as the author's comment, wise or splenetic or desperate, as it may be,
on our postwar civilization.

There is no reason why such commentary should not exist in fiction; the only artistic demand is that if it is to exist it must be necessary to the work. In Tolstoi's *The Death of Ivan Ilyich* the heartlessness
of a "refined" society and the emptiness of that unemotional life are the
theme of the story; the story itself, however, does not simply show up
this society, with the author's comments, but uses it to make the setting
for Ivan's intense human experience, the longing for life and love, which
grows as his illness slowly weans him from the world of sham, destroys
his power as a personage, and leaves him nothing but his needs as a
person, until he breaks into the scream of protest that stops only with
death.

The difficulty which many people encounter in judging prose fiction
as good or bad fiction lies largely in the medium—discursive language,
not even formalized by meter or rhyme—just the same discursive language we use for conversation; it is hard not to be deceived into sup-
posing the author intends, by his use of words, just what we intend by
ours—to inform, comment, inquire, confess, in short: to talk to people.[9]
But a novelist intends to create a virtual experience, wholly formed, and

[9] Cf. the opinions of A. C. Ward expressed in his *Foundations of English
Prose*, p. 28: "The demand made of the novel in the twentieth century is that
it shall portray life as fully as possible in literature; that it shall inform us about
many important matters; and that it shall illuminate us with increased knowledge
and wisdom."

Also Winfield Rogers, "Form in the Art-Novel" (*Helicon*, II, 1939), p. 3:
"The artist is attempting to convey ·. summation of the way life is grouped, at
a particular moment or period, a summation, of course, which may give way to
others in the future. . . . All aspects of technique are means by which the novelist
attempts to convey his attitude or philosophy and are the natural expression of
philosophy."

wholly expressive of something more fundamental than any "modern" problem: human feeling, the nature of human life itself.

The novel, although it is our most exuberant, characteristic, and popular literary production, is a relatively recent phenomenon, and its artistic form is still evolving, still surprising critics with unprecedented effects and completely new conceptions of structure and technical means.[10] So perhaps it is natural that they are still inclined to concern themselves primarily with its representational features: references to actual events, portrayal of persons in the author's environment (private or public), comments on the passing scene, and revelations of his own personality, through one fictitious character or even through a group of *personae* who are regarded as symbols of separate, sometimes conflicting "selves" in his own Self. Such features, at least, may always be found and talked about, even if their uses for poetic creation are quite unapparent to the critic.

Yet a more knowing sort of criticism is well under way; and putting together the truly literary observations on novels and novel writing since Flaubert and Henry James gave this new genre recognition as a genuine art form, one can see its artistic aims, and the attendant problems of attaining a completely virtual, vital (i.e. organic) form, emerging with the advance of the art itself. De Quincey still treats only of poetry as real "literature," but remarks with surprise that even "the commonest novel, by moving in alliance with human fears and hopes" belongs somehow to "the literature of power"—a literature which sets forth human aims and emotions directly, not for discursive understanding but for "the heart, i.e. the great *intuitive* [or non-discursive] organ."[11]

Forty years later Henry James explicitly declared the novel a work of art, and moreover, a kind of history; though the relation of this "history" to genuine history, the memory or recovery of actual events, eluded him, so he resorted to a flat denial that there was any difference, and

---

[10]Edith Wharton, in 1924, began her book, *The Writing of Fiction*, with the words: "To treat of the practice of fiction is to deal with the newest, most fluid and least formulated of the arts."

[11]Thomas De Quincey, "Alexander Pope." First published in *North British Review*, August, 1848, reprinted in his *Literary Criticism*, 1908. See p. 96. The parenthetical gloss is De Quincey's.

at the same time remarked that fictional history had its own premises.

"The only reason for the existence of a novel is that it does attempt to represent life. . . . and the analogy between the art of the painter and the art of the novelist is, so far as I am able to see, complete. Their inspiration is the same, their process (allowing for the different quality of the vehicle) is the same, their success is the same. . . . as the picture is reality, so the novel is history. That is the only general description (which does it justice) that we may give of the novel."[12]

James felt that somehow this "history" was objective and bound the novelist to its faithful pursuit. He did not recognize that his comparison of the writer's work with the painter's contained at once the justification of his claim, and its limitation: the novel is history *as the picture is reality*. He did not understand in what sense the picture is reality, so he could only put on record his conviction that the novel must be *treated* exactly like history. Speaking of Anthony Trollope, he said: "In a digression, a parenthesis or an aside, he concedes to the reader that he and this trusting friend are only 'making believe.' He admits that the events he narrates have not really happened, and that he can give his narrative any turn the reader may like best. Such a betrayal of a sacred office seems to me, I confess, a terrible crime; . . . and it shocks me every whit as much in Trollope as it would have shocked me in Gibbon or Macaulay. It implies that the novelist is less occupied in looking for the truth (the truth, of course I mean, that he assumes, the premises that we must grant him, whatever they may be) than the historian, and in doing so it deprives him at a stroke of all his standing room. To represent and illustrate the past, the actions of men, is the task of either writer. . . ."

Yes, but with a profound difference; for the novelist explores a virtual past, a past of his own creation, and "the truth that he assumes" has its roots in that created history. The trouble with Trollope's admissions (where they do trouble us) is that they blast the poetic illusion, they make his stories *appear* to be untrue; instead of presenting us with a virtual past, he invites us to share his own actual experience of indulging in irresponsible fancies. No wonder that James the artist, recognizing

---

[12]"The Art of Fiction," in *American Critical Essays*, edited by Norman Foerster. See p. 158.

the novel as a work of art, was shocked at such a ruinous conception of the author's business.

The prose fiction writer, like any other poet, fabricates an illusion of life entirely lived and felt, and presents it in the "literary" perspective which I have called the "mnemonic mode"—like memory, only depersonalized, objectified. His first task is to make that illusion convincing, i.e. make it, however far it may be from actuality, seem real. James, despite his troubled reflection on the novel as history, knew that the *appearance* of history was its true measure; and in the same essay that recorded his horror of Trollope's attitude, he went on, somewhat later, to say: ". . . the air of reality (solidity of specification) seems to me to be the supreme virtue of a novel—the merit on which all its other merits (including that conscious moral purpose of which Mr. Besant speaks) helplessly and submissively depend. If it be not there they are all as nothing, and if these be there, they owe their effect to the success with which the author has produced the illusion of life."[13]

To produce this illusion of life, writers have employed many and various means, beginning with the obvious trick of professing to write actual memoirs or history. If you can get people to take your fiction as fact, it seems that "the air of reality" must have been achieved. Yet oddly enough, newspaper reports, which usually (according to their editors) have "foundation in fact," quite commonly lack just that air of immediate and important reality which Augusto Centeno calls "livingness" —the *sense of life* rather than the familiar contents of it.[14] The claim to historical truth (such as Defoe made for *The Journal of the Plague Year*) or to some foreign authorship (*Sonnets from the Portuguese* or the poems of Ossian) is not an integral part of the work, which could produce a genuinely *literary* illusion, but is a pretense that is supposed to arouse the reader's non-literary interest, i.e. "sell" him the piece, or to absolve the author from responsibility for its shortcomings, or perhaps to shield a Victorian poetess from any suspicion that she is indelicately revealing her own sentiments.

---

[13]*Op. cit.*, pp. 168–169.

[14]See his Introduction to *The Intent of the Artist*, p. 11: "Livingness . . . is a sense of life, deep and intense, arising out of spiritual relationships and. to be apprehended only by the intuition. What rhythm is to time, it may be suggested, is the relation livingness bears to life."

The "livingness" of a story is really much surer, and often greater, than that of actual experience. Life itself may, at times, be quite mechanical and unperceived by those who live it; but the perception of a reader must never fall into abeyance. People in the book may be dull and dreary, but not the book itself. Virtual events, however subdued, have character and savor, distinct appearance and feeling-tone, or they simply cease to exist. We sometimes praise a novel for approaching the vividness of actual events; usually, however, it exceeds them in vividness. A slavish transcript of actual life is dim beside the word-created experiences of virtual life, as a plaster mask made directly from a living subject is a dead counterfeit compared to even the most "conservative" portrait sculpture.[15] In a review of an autobiographical story—Carlton Brown's *Brainstorm*—the reviewer described the book as "not quite a novel, although some of it, particularly the lines written in a hospital for the mentally diseased, has the intensity and participation of fiction."[16] What is this "participation" that characterizes fiction, and sometimes occurs in actuality? The quality of being completely felt—"livingness," s Centeno says, or in the words of Henry James, "felt life."

Where the establishing of the primary illusion entails a semblance of so-called "real life" there must be, of course, a constant safeguard against the possibility of confusing the work with its model, identifying the central character with oneself and consequently letting the events in the novel stand for one's own experiences, by chance actual, or otherwise merely imagined. DeWitt Parker said the poet's business is "to make us dream an interesting dream";[17] I say the poet's business is to keep us from bringing in our dreams, so that we may see his poetic abstractions—essential forms of history—composed into transparent symbols of feeling itself.

The second major concern of literature, therefore, correlative with having to give a work "the air of reality," is the problem of *keeping it fiction*. Many people recognize the devices whereby a writer attains lifelikeness; but few are aware of the means that sustain the difference between art and life—the simplification and manipulation of life's image

---

[15]See the comparison in W. R. Valentiner's *Origins of Modern Sculpture* between a "realistic" sculpture and a life mask, p. 34 (plates 20, 21, 22).

[16]Lorine Pruette in the New York *Herald Tribune*, December 31, 1944.

[17]*The Analysis of Art*, p. 70.

that makes it essentially different from its prototype. Style is determined in large measure by the ways in which authors handle these two basic requirements. C. E. Montague, in a chatty but thoughtful book called *A Writer's Notes on his Trade,* remarks on the odd phenomenon that in fiction past happenings seem to gain authenticity by being retailed at second- or third-hand—told by some character who may even claim to have the story from another: "I'm only tellin' ye what 'e told me."[18] In actual life such hearsay is certainly no voucher for truth. Why should it add to the value of virtual events?

Because it projects them at once into the experiential mode, and assures their essentially literary form. A person telling about an event naturally gives it a "slant," because he must have an interest in it to motivate his speaking of it. What the story gains by being merely reported is not authenticity, but poetic transformation; recall and hearsay turn fact into fiction (wherefore, in actual life, a story becomes less convincing with each retelling). The presentation of past events in a novel by direct discourse from one of the characters is a simple technique that almost always works; it allows a long and scattered history to be gathered and foreshortened, without making it a mere preparation for the presented action, for it becomes an ingredient in that action itself.

The success of this method to assure some sort of orientation in the virtual "world" of the story has led, I think, to the convention (for it is nothing more) of limiting the events to one character's impressions and evaluations: the "unified point of view" which is the angle of vision, or experience, of someone in the story. The character in question is not telling a tale, but is experiencing the events, so that they all take on the appearance they would have had for that person. Filtering them all through one mind assures, of course, their conception in terms of personal feeling and encounter, and gives to the whole work—action, setting, speech, and all—the natural unity of a perspective. Edith Wharton named this method as nothing less than a principle of fiction writing.

"The impression produced by a landscape, a street or a house," she said in *The Writing of Fiction,* "should always, to the novelist, be an event in the history of a soul, and the use of the 'descriptive passage,' and its style, should be determined by the fact that it must depict only

---

[18]See pp. 39 ff.

what the intelligence concerned would have noticed, and always in terms within the register of that intelligence."[19]

"Applied to the novel this may seem a hard saying, since the longer passage of time and more crowded field of action presuppose, on the part of the visualizing character, a state of omniscience and omnipresence likely to shake the reader's sense of probability. The difficulty is most often met by shifting the point of vision from one character to another, in such a way as to comprehend the whole history and yet preserve the unity of impression."[20]

It is customary to contrast with this method the unfolding of a story from a point of view that originates beyond any of the characters themselves. Van Meter Ames, in his *Aesthetics of the Novel* (a book which perpetuates too many misconceptions that encumber aesthetics, from art as daydream to art as social ethics), says of the latter way: "The ordinary method has been that of the omniscient author who constantly intrudes upon the story to tell the reader what he needs to know. The artificiality of this procedure tends to destroy the story's illusion, and unless the author be exceedingly interesting in his own person his intrusion is unwelcome."[21] It seems to me that a very interesting author would be even more objectionable than a dull one, as he would interrupt our concentration on his story more effectively. But the question is really a vain one, for it arises out of a misconception, namely, that the author is a person connected with the story at all. Professor Ames criticizes Conrad's shifting of the point of view in *Almayer's Folly*, where, he says, "Conrad was the omniscient author. As far as the story is told from the angle of Almayer the reader gets a consistent impression, and it seems as if Conrad had somehow got the tale from Almayer. But when the point of view is needlessly shifted to the thoughts of Almayer's Malay wife and other characters, the unified effect is lost, the illusion of reality is impaired. The reader begins to wonder if all these people had told Conrad their secrets."[22]

Now, there is no Mr. Conrad in the story, to whom anyone could

---

[19]*Op. cit.*, p. 85.

[20]*Ibid.*, p. 87. A couple of pages later she remarks, however, that all uses of the principle are simply conventions.

[21]*Aesthetics of the Novel*, p. 179.

[22]*Loc. cit.*

have told anything; the trouble is not that the author is represented as omniscient, but that a particular reader wishes to go beyond the story and pretend it really happened, and "Conrad had somehow got the tale from Almayer" or from some other person in the book. But Conrad, who is not in it, need not and could not have "got" it at all; and I cannot find a single passage where his personality suddenly intrudes on the virtual world. The pretense that fiction is based on actual memory or hearsay belongs to the beginning of the novelist's art, when stories had previously always been told, not written, and a deliberately composed prose narrative seemed to require some semblance of the story-teller's setting.[23] The shift begot a transitional form in which the new kind of presentation still simulates the old; as the earliest Greek stone columns simulated tree trunks, and our first electric lamps were made to look as much like candles or kerosene lamps as possible.

This transfer from story-telling to story-writing was undoubtedly, too, the source of the old-fashioned trick of using expressions like "my heroine," "dear reader," "I cannot begin to tell . . .," which is a real intrusion by the author on the virtual world of his characters. Dickens, whose realism was revolutionary, may have resorted to it sometimes to offset that extreme verisimilitude, and assure the fictional character of his work; but it is, even for that purpose, an unfortunate device, robbing Peter to pay Paul. The shadowy story-teller and hypothetical listener are too slightly formulated not to become identical with the real author sitting at his desk and a real reader sitting in his chair. The realism of the story loses its excessive power as people become used to a technique that once seemed violent, but the direct address never stops flirting with actuality, and soon, instead of just keeping the related events in the realm of fiction, it begets the impression which Trollope made on James—that the story is not serious, but is a mere fancy whereby the author entertains himself or his company.

The events in a novel are purely virtual events, "known" only to equally virtual people; the "omniscient author" is as much a chimaera

---

[23]This heritage explains, I think, the fact on which Professor Daiches comments with some puzzlement: "In the early days of the English novel, writers used every possible device to persuade their readers that what they were telling them had really happened." (*A Study of Literature*, p. 91.)

as the author who sees or judges through the mind of his hero.[24] Even a story told in the first person, if it is a piece of literature, is completely transformed by the poetic imagination, so that the person called "I" is simply a character so called. Every event may have its model in the author's actual memory, and every character be a portrait; but a portrait is not the sitter—not even a self-portrait. In the same way, actually observed events, recorded perhaps in journals or letters, are not literary elements but literary materials. "Observation is the tool of imagination," as David Daiches has said, "and imagination is that which can see potential significance in the most casual seeming events."[25] But imagination always creates; it never records.

In a later passage, Professor Daiches illustrates his tenet with Joyce's *Portrait of the Artist as a Young Man:* "It is fiction," he says, "in the sense that the selection and arrangement of the incidents produce an artistically patterned work, a totality in which there is nothing superfluous, in which every detail is artistically as well as biographically relevant. Joyce, in fact, has given us one of the few examples in English literature of autobiography successfully employed as a mode of fiction."[26]

The fewness of such examples bears out Edith Wharton's opinion, that "the autobiographical gift does not seem very closely related to that of fiction."[27] The reason is, I think, that many people do have a limited literary talent, and where the skeleton of a story is ready-made for them and the point of view automatically given, as in their own life history, they can handle it poetically with fair success; but these are the people who "have only one book in them." They have the autobiographical gift, but not the fecund imagination of a real novelist, to whom his own life is only one theme among many. The barely fictionalized self-

---

[24]The fallacy of regarding the author and the reader as given with the story seems to me to underlie Mrs. Wharton's moralistic attitude, too, which is expressed in her generally admirable book, *The Writing of Fiction*, p. 27: "In one form or another there must be some sort of rational response to the reader's unconscious but insistent inner question: 'What am I being told this story for? What judgment on life does it contain for me?'" A story that seems "true to life" may elicit such a judgment from the reader; but it can *contain* one only for the people in its world.

[25]*The Novel and the Modern World*, p. 85.

[26]*Ibid.*, p. 101.

[27]*Op. cit.*, p. 77.

story then bears the marks of its origin: for the incidents are not consistently projected into the mode of memory. They are variously tinged with that modality, depending on whether they spring from real memory, available records, or invention filling the gaps of recollection. In the hands of a true novelist, on the contrary, his own story is entirely raw material, and the end product entirely fiction. Mrs. Wharton points this out in speaking of Tolstoi's *The Kreutzer Sonata:*

"There is a gulf between such a book and 'Adolphe.' Tolstoy's tale, though almost avowedly the study of his own tortured soul, is as objective as Othello. The magic transposition has taken place; in reading the story we do not feel ourselves to be in a resuscitated *real world* (a sort of Tussaud Museum of wax figures with actual clothes on), but in that other world which is the image of life transposed in the brain of the artist, a world wherein the creative breath has made all things new."[28]

The moral of this lengthy critique is that prose fiction is exactly as high and pure a creation as lyric poetry, or as drama (which will be considered in the next chapter), and although its material is discursive language, not even modified and distinguished from ordinary speech by the conventions of verse, yet the product is not discourse, but the illusion of life directly lived, a world in which thinking and conversation may occur. For the purpose of creating this virtual history the prose writer chooses his words as precisely as the verse writer, and spins out his apparently casual lines just as carefully. A name or a turn of phrase in a story may be the means of creating a setting or a situation at one stroke. Consider, for instance, the peculiar romance achieved in Kipling's *Jungle Books,* especially in the tales of "Mowgli," which makes them appeal not to the very young children who normally like stories of talking animals, but to children in their teens, and even adults. The fantastic "reality" is achieved mainly with language: the animals speak an archaic English, call each other "thou," use the subjunctive ("for we be lonely in the Jungle without thee, Little Brother") and the pure present instead of the usual progressive form ("I go now" instead of "I am going"); their speeches, consequently, have the flavor of a translation, which gives them a subtle air of being "in translation" from the animal language. The scattering of Hindu words helps to make it a jungle language. The char-

---

[28]*Op. cit.,* p. 79.

acters have Hindu names, too, which attach them to a strange land, and the strangeness is enhanced by a purely poetic device: exaggerated description, in very few words, of an already exotic scene. Yet those same names give the scene a bona fide geographical location; even as they make it extraordinary, they save it from being "fairyland," and give the stories a semblance of being close to nature—closer, indeed, than most people's actual life appears to be.

These juvenile stories are most skillful poetic creations. I have cited them because their magic is fairly easy to analyze, and the analysis reveals what may, in fact, be found in any well-told story—that the whole fabric of illusory events takes its appearance and emotional value entirely from the way the statements which actually compose the story are worded, the way the sentences flow, stop, repeat, stand alone, etc., the concentrations and expansions of statement, the charged or denuded words. The ways of telling make the place, the action, the characters in fiction; and nothing, in my opinion, could be more hopelessly mistaken than the distinction between poetry and prose made by F. W. Bateson:

"The structure of prose is, in the widest sense of the word, *logical;* its statements are always ultimately reducible to a syllogistic form. A passage of prose, *any* passage, not even excluding so-called 'poetic' prose, resolves itself under analysis into a series of explanations, definitions, and conclusions. It is by these means that the book progresses. They are the framework into which the content of the prose—its subject-matter—must somehow be fitted. . . .

"The structure of poetry, on the other hand, is ultimately determined by its technique. . . ."[29]

"The words of prose are inconspicuous because they form part of a logical structure. They are counters. . . . And so a word in prose has no value in itself. . . .

"The words of poetry are more conspicuous, more *solid,* because they are part of a structure which they themselves create."[30]

If Mr. Bateson had not thrown in his remark about "so-called 'poetic'

---

[29]*English Poetry and the English Language,* p. 20.

[30]*Ibid.*, p. 23. A similar identification of prose with discursive statement is made by A. C. Ward, in *Foundations of English Prose* (see especially pp. 20–22), and by S. Alexander in "Poetry and Prose in the Arts," though neither of those writers makes it as unreservedly as Bateson.

prose," one might believe that he was pointing out the difference between language used in discourse and language used in art. But apparently he holds that all verse, simply as such, is creative—even "Mary had a little lamb"; and all prose, simply as such, tenders explanations, definitions, and conclusions—even "The morning stars sang together."

The difference between poetry and prose fiction is purely a difference of devices and their effects. Both literary forms set up the poetic illusion, i.e. create a virtual history in which all events are experiences—longings and thrills, reflections, vows, marriages, murders. The illusion is effected by the use of words, whether that use be the devious weaving of lines found in a Horatian ode, or the rapid, even colloquial sentences of prose narrative—"that careful artifice which is the real carelessness of art."[31]

Literature is a supple, elastic art, which takes its motifs from all the corners of the earth and all aspects of life. It creates places and happenings, thoughts, actions, persons. The novel centers on the development of persons; to such an extent, indeed, that people often lose sight of every other element in it, and will praise as great art any work that presents an interesting character.[32] But a novel, to be vital, needs more than character study; it requires an illusion of a world, of history perceived and felt—"a corner of life seen through a temperament," as Zola said.

Clive Bell, stepping out of his usual role of purely visual aesthete, once wrote a little book about Marcel Proust in which he studied not his own aesthetic emotion, but the secret of a literary creation. Here, where he was rid of all responsibility for the difficult emotion, he looked deeply into the work itself to see what makes it so strange and yet so powerful; and long conversance with other arts than the poetic let him perceive its artistic elements unobscured by too many principles of literary criticism. Above all, he judges fiction entirely as art.

"His psychology," he says of Proust, "can hardly be overpraised, but it is the easiest thing in the world to overpraise psychology. Psychology is not the most important thing in the literary or any other art. On the contrary, the supreme masterpieces derive their splendor, their supernat-

---

Wharton, *op. cit.*, p. 48.

[32]Cf. Arnold Bennett, "Is the Novel Decaying?" (In *Things That Have Interested Me*, Third Series, p. 193): "The foundation of good fiction is character-creating, and nothing else."

ural power, not from flashes of insight, nor yet from characterization, nor from an understanding of the human heart even, but from form— I use the word in its richest sense, I mean the thing that artists create, their expression. Whether you call it "significant form' or something else, the supreme quality in art is formal; it has to do with order, sequence, movement and shape. . . ."[33]

Bell, in contemplating that form, had lit upon the source of both its oddity and its power of revealing a new sort of truth. "Proust tries our patience so long as we expect his story to move forward: that not being the direction in which it is intended to move. . . . It is in states, not action, that he deals. The movement is that of an expanding flower or insect. . . . Proust does not get forward, we complain. Why should he? Is there no other line of development in the universe?"[34]

Proust's most notable trait is his feeling for time; time is not something he mentions, but something he creates for one's direct perception. It is a secondary illusion in his writings, as space is in music, and as the most careful descriptions of "musical space" unconsciously echo the principles of plastic space conception, so Bell's account of Proust's poetic time-illusion leans on a musical simile, and presents time as a plenum wherein shapes and motions exist.

"Time is the stuff of which *A la recherche du temps perdu* is composed: the characters exist in time, and were the sense of time abstracted would cease to exist. In time they develop; their relations, colour and extension are all temporal. Thus they grow; situations unfold themselves not like flowers even but like tunes. . . ."

"Proust deals with time as modern painters deal with space. The painter will not allow scientifically attained spatial relations and laws of perspective to restrict his imagination."[35]

"*A la recherche du temps perdu* is a shape in time; it is not an arabesque on time. It is constructed in three dimensions. . . ."

In another place, the ingenuous critic speaks of Proust's handling of facts, which are the poet's "models" as objects are the painter's or sculptor's; and all unconsciously he speaks of them as "objects," and his

---

[33]*Proust*, p. 67.
[34]*Ibid.*, p. 16.
[35]*Ibid.*, pp. 55–56.

comment on Proust's method is a striking parallel to Cézanne's on his own work.

"It was the contemplation, the realization, of facts which provoked the poet in him. He kept his eye on the object much as the great impressionists had done, he observed, he analyzed, he rendered; but what he saw was not what the writers of his generation saw, but the object, the fact, in its emotional significance."[36]

Finally, after uncovering all these practices and effects that touch subtly on the other arts, Mr. Bell pays tribute to Proust's creation of the poetic illusion itself: "So acute was his sense of that invented world and at the same time so critical, so vivid and historical his manner of rendering it, that reading his fiction one has a sense of reading memoirs."[37]

Prose fiction is so great a topic that one could go on indefinitely analyzing its techniques and achievements; but in a single book dealing with all the arts, there must be a stop. There is simply not room to discuss the historical novel, the symbolical fantasy (such as Kafka writes in novel form), the fictionalized biography (e.g. Mörike's *Mozart auf der Reise nach Prag*), the novel of propaganda and of satire. But one great literary order must yet be considered: Non-fiction.

This category includes the critical essay, which serves to set forth the author's opinions and define his attitudes; philosophy, the analysis of ideas; history, presenting the ascertainable facts of an actual past in their causal unity; biography, or personal history; reports; and all kinds of exposition.

What all these species of composition have in common is their relation to actuality. The author does not use given events, conditions, proposals and theories merely as motifs to develop a fiction; he does not create persons and happenings as he needs them, but draws every item, even to the smallest detail, from life. Such writing is in essence not poetry (all poetry is fictive; "non-fiction" is "non-poetic"). Yet, whenever it is well done, it meets a standard which is essentially literary, i.e. an artistic standard.

Discursive writing—that is the proper designation for this whole category—is a highly important form of so-called "applied art." One usually

---

[36]*Ibid.*, p. 26.
[37]*Ibid.*, p. 79.

thinks primarily of textiles, ceramics, furniture, and commercial signs under that rubric; but discursive writing is really its purest example, and sets forth its relations, both positive and negative, to "liberal" or freely creative art more clearly than any other instance. So, in keeping with the practical rule of treating a problem that belongs to several arts only in connection with the one which exhibits it most perfectly, I have reserved the theoretical discussion of "applied art" for this appropriate even if somewhat unexpected context.

In the first discussion of "semblance" I pointed out that semblance is not necessarily deceptive; only, when a perfectly normal semblance—the visual appearance of a pot, for instance—is so strikingly revealed that all one's interest in the object centers on its visual aspect, the object itself seems like a sheer vision. The beholder becomes as much aware of its form as he would if it were nothing but a form, i.e. an illusion.

Literal, logical thought has a characteristic form, which is known as "discursive," because it is the form of discourse. Language is the prime instrument of thought, and the product bears the stamp of the fashioning tool. A writer with literary imagination perceives even this familiar form as a vehicle of feeling—the feeling that naturally inheres in studious thinking, the growing intensity of a problem as it becomes more and more complex, and at the same time more definite and "thinkable," until the demand for the answer is urgent, touched with impatience; the holding back of assent as the explanation is prepared; the cadential feeling of solution, and the expansion of consciousness in new knowledge. If all these phases merge in one configured passage, the thought, however hard, is natural; and the height of discursive style is the embodiment of such a feeling pattern, modeled, word by word, on the progressing argument. The argument is the writer's motif, and absolutely nothing else may enter in. As soon as he leads feeling away from the motivating thought to (say) mystical or moral reaction, he is not supporting the process of understanding.

A subtle leading away from the literal statement in a discourse is the basis of what is commonly called "rhetoric." In rhetorical writing the discourse is a motif more or less freely used; the writer's aim is to make the conclusion of the represented argument look acceptable rather than to make the argument entirely visible. Good discourse seeks above all to be transparent, not as a symbol of feeling, but as a vehicle of sense; the artistic form is strictly bound to the literal function. That is why such writing is not poetry; the writer is not free to create whatever semblance of intellectual or imaginative experience his motif, a discursive thought, puts into the reach of his imagination, but is committed to the envisagement of one living experience—the intellectual experience of following this discourse. The feeling presented has to be actually appropriate to the matter represented, the "model"; and the excellence of an expositional style depends on two factors instead of one—the unity and vividness of the feeling presented (which is the only criterion for "free" art), and the sustained relation of this feeling to the actual progress of the discourse represented.

There are not many "applied" arts as closely bound to actuality as discursive writing. Another that comes to mind is scientific drawing. In some old botany books one finds tinted drawings of plants, with enlarged details of their minute parts, as beautiful as Dürer's flowers and animals, but meticulously faithful to a scientific ideal. The beauty of those illustrations is in the spacing of the items, the proportion of the field to the figures, the toning of the tints, the choice of color—always pale and unobtrusive, but quite varied—of the backgrounds. The simplicity and clearness of forms shown, which have to be botanically accurate and elaborate, are made into an artistic convention rather than an artistic limitation. Such drawing is art, though it serves science; as religious architecture or sculpture is art though it serves faith and exaltation.

It is a fatal mistake to think of "applied art" as an addition of artistic fancies to objects that are essentially common and banal. This is, unhappily, the most popular idea, which dominates so-called "commercial art." The best schools of design are gradually blasting it; but even their members have not always realized the precise relation between art and artifact, which is that the artifact is taken as the essential motif of the art work; created appearance is a "true" appearance (in the ordinary sense of "true," i. e. "factual"), the object presents itself to the eye for what it is, and arrests one's vision by its semblance of organic unity just as a decorative design does.

In architecture this principle is known as "functionalism." It has sometimes been regarded as the supreme principle of the builder's art. I think that is a mistake; architecture is essentially a creative art.[38] But a great deal of "applied art" belongs to it, for furniture and furnishings are part of architecture. The "ethnic domain" is, indeed, so closely related to specific functions that only architecture itself can make the abstraction of it for our perception; and the passage from freely creative art to applied art in this realm should properly be almost invisible.

Similarly, the passage from fiction, in which the thematic material is completely transformed and not "given" as an actuality at all, to true exposition, wherein the discursive use of language is emphasized so that the actual discourse becomes apparent, may at times be a fluid transition. Plato's dialogues are such "didactic fiction"; so are many "utopias," allegories, and prophetic fantasies. Formally composed prayers, creeds, and manifestoes are all poetically treated actual discourse.

All species of literature may, in fact, intersect, because their separateness is never absolute. They arise from the power of different devices. In the foregoing chapters I began the analysis of literary forms with that of the lyric, because lyric poetry employs the smallest amount of material to create its poetic elements, and consequently exploits those materials to the utmost. Intellectually, the larger designs may be successively built up by adding more powerful means of creation—narrative, action and even contemporaneous actions, extensive description, character, realistic setting, conversation, and what not. But historically this has not been the process of producing the various types of literature. The oldest form was probably that in which all the separate developments were implicit—the epic.

The epic is really, like the true ballad, pre-literary poetry; and it is the great matrix of all poetic genres. All devices of the art occur in it sooner or later—but never all of them at once. There are lyric verses, romantic quests, descriptions of ordinary life, self-contained incidents that read like a ballad. In the Greek epics one finds political conflicts, personal histories, characters growing with their actions; in the Edda there are riddles and proverbs, in the Kalevala cosmological fantasies; and in all epics, invocations and praises of the gods. The epic is a hodge-

---

[38]See above, Chap. 6, especially p. 93.

podge of literary creations, vaguely yet grandly spanned by a story— the all-inclusive story of the world.

It was probably the discovery that different poetic practices had different effects, causing various moods and movements in successive parts of the epic, that gave rise to the special literary forms. Each separate means of poetic creation could be exploited and gave rise to a genre of smaller scope but more organized form. At the same time, lesser beginnings may have been made in song, e.g. in dirges and paeans, magic utterances, spells and mystical recitations. We know little of literary beginnings. But we know that the great poetic tradition, in all languages, has been achieved with the development of writing, and in fact only with the free use of letters; the art of words is not essentially an oratorical art, inadequately recorded by visual symbols and somewhat degraded in the process, but is truly and fairly named "literature."

Chapter seventeen

THE DRAMATIC ILLUSION

Most theoretical treatments of literature draw their material and evidence as much from drama as from lyric and narrative works. A serious analysis of literary art with only an occasional, passing mention of Shakespeare may have seemed to many readers a curious innovation. The reason for it, however, is simple enough, and has been suggested above: Shakespeare is essentially a dramatist, and drama is not, in the strict sense, "literature."

Yet it is a poetic art, because it creates the primary illusion of all poetry—virtual history. Its substance is an image of human life—ends, means, gains and losses, fulfillment and decline and death. It is a fabric of illusory experience, and that is the essential product of poesis. But drama is not merely a distinct literary form; it is a special poetic mode, as different from genuine literature as sculpture from pictorial art, or either of these from architecture. That is to say, it makes its own basic abstraction, which gives it a way of its own in making the semblance of history.

Literature projects the image of life in the mode of virtual memory; language is its essential material; the sound and meaning of words, their familiar or unusual use and order, even their presentation on the printed page, create the illusion of life as a realm of events—completed, lived, as words formulate them—events that compose a Past. But drama presents the poetic illusion in a different light: not finished realities, or "events," but immediate, visible responses of human beings, make its semblance of life. Its basic abstraction is the act, which springs from the past, but is directed toward the future, and is always great with things to come.

In using common words, such as "event" or "act," as analytic terms, one runs the danger of suggesting far less general concepts, and indeed a variety of them, all equally inadequate to the purpose in hand. "Event," in the foregoing chapters, was used in the sense given it by Whitehead, to cover all space-time occurrence, even the persistence of objects, the repetitious rhythms of life, the occasion of a thought as well as of an earthquake. Similarly, by "act" I mean any sort of human response, physical or mental. The word is commonly used, of course, in more specialized senses. It may mean one of the major divisions of a play—Act I, Act II, etc.; or it may refer to overt behavior, rushing about, laying hands on someone, taking or surrendering an object, and so forth; or it may mean a piece of dissembling, as when one says of a person that he feels one way and acts another. In the general sense here employed, however, all *reactions* are acts, visible or invisible; so in drama, any illusion of physical or mental activity is here called an "act," and the total structure of acts is *a virtual history in the mode of dramatic action.*

An act, whether instinctive or deliberate, is normally oriented toward the future. Drama, though it implies past actions (the "situation"), moves not toward the present, as narrative does, but toward something beyond; it deals essentially with commitments and consequences. Persons, too, in drama are purely agents—whether consciously or blindly, makers of the future. This future, which is made before our eyes, gives importance to the very beginnings of dramatic acts, i.e. to the motives from which the acts arise, and the situations in which they develop; the making of it is the principle that unifies and organizes the continuum of stage action. It has been said repeatedly that the theater creates a perpetual present moment[1]; but it is only a present filled with its own future that is really dramatic. A sheer immediacy, an imperishable direct experience without the ominous forward movement of consequential action, would not be so. As literature creates a virtual past, drama creates a virtual future. The literary mode is the mode of Memory; the dramatic is the mode of Destiny.

---

[1]For example, R. E. Jones in *The Dramatic Imagination*, p. 40, says: "This is drama; this is theatre—*to be aware of the Now.*" And Thornton Wilder, in "Some Thoughts on Playwriting," lists as one of the "four fundamental conditions of the drama" that "its action takes place in a perpetual present time."—"On the stage it is always now." (*The Intent of the Artist*, p. 83.)

The future, like the past, is a conceptual structure, and expectation, even more obviously than memory, is a product of imagination.[2] The "now" created by poetic composition is always under the aegis of some historical vision which transcends it; and its poignancy derives not from any comparison with actuality, but from the fact that the two great realms of envisagement—past and future—intersect in the present, which consequently has not the pure imaginative form of either memory or prophecy, but a peculiar appearance of its own which we designate as "immediacy" or "now."

In actual life the impending future is very vaguely felt. Each separate act is forward-looking—we put on a kettle expecting it to boil, hand someone a bill and expect to be given change, board a bus with casual confidence that we shall leave it again at an intended point, or board an airplane with somewhat more conscious interest in our prospective exit from its inside. But we do not usually have any idea of the future as a total experience which is coming because of our past and present acts; such a sense of destiny arises only in unusual moments under peculiar emotional stress.

In drama, however, this sense of destiny is paramount. It is what makes the present action seem like an integral part of the future, howbeit that future has not unfolded yet. The reason is that on the stage, every thought expressed in conversation, every feeling betrayed by voice or look, is determined by the total action of which it is a part—perhaps an embryonic part, the first hint of the motive that will soon gather force. Even before one has any idea of what the conflict is to be (i.e. before the "exposition" has been given), one feels the tension developing. This tension between past and future, the theatrical "present moment," is what gives to acts, situations, and even such constituent elements as gestures and attitudes and tones, the peculiar intensity known as "dramatic quality."

In a little-known volume, bearing the modest, impersonal title: *Essays by Divers Hands* (a volume of "Transactions" of the Royal Society of

---

[2]Compare the observations of Georg Mehlis, quoted on p. 263 n. Mehlis mistook the nature of the "distancing" effect of memory and expectation, which he thought rested on people's tendency to leave out the unpleasant, and a consequent "aesthetic improvement" of the facts; but despite this error he noted truly the transformational power of both projections.

Literature in England),[3] there is a very thoughtful philosophical essay by Charles Morgan, called "The Nature of Dramatic Illusion," in which he seems to me to have both stated and answered the question of what is created in the full-fledged work of dramatic art—the enacted play.

"With every development of dramatic technique," he wrote there, "and every departure from classical structure, the need increases for a new discussion which . . . shall establish for the stage not indeed a formal rule but an aesthetic discipline, elastic, reasoned, and acceptable to it in modern circumstances.

"It is my purpose, then, to discover the principle from which such a discipline might arise. This principle I call the principle of illusion."[4]

"Illusion, as I conceive it, is form in suspense. . . . In a play form is not valuable *in itself;* only the suspense of form has value. In a play, form is not and cannot be valuable in itself, because until the play is over form does not exist. . . .

"A play's performance occupies two or three hours. Until the end its form is latent in it. . . .

"This suspense of form, by which is meant the incompleteness of a known completion, is to be clearly distinguished from common suspense —suspense of plot—the ignorance of what will happen, . . . for suspense of plot is a structural accident, and suspense of form is, as I understand it, essential to the dramatic form itself. . . .

"What form is chosen . . . matters less than that while the drama moves *a* form is being fulfilled."[5]

"Fulfilled" is here the key word to the idea of dramatic form. Everything, of course, has a form of some sort: the famous million monkeys playing a million typewriters for a million years, turning out chance combinations of letters, would be rendering countless phonetic forms (though some of these might not encourage pronunciation); similarly, the most aimless conglomerate of events, acts, utterances, or what not, would *produce* a form when taken together; but before such collections were complete (which would be simply when, for any reason, one stopped collecting), no one could imagine their form. There has to be a sense of

[3]N. S. Vol. 12, ed. by R. W. Macan, 1933. The article in question covers pp. 61–77.

[4]*Ibid.*, p. 61.

[5]*Ibid.*, pp. 70–72.

the whole, some anticipation of what may or even must come, if the production of new elements is to give the impression that "a form is being fulfilled."

Dramatic action is a semblance of action so constructed that a whole, indivisible piece of virtual history is implicit in it, as a yet unrealized form, long before the presentation is completed. This constant illusion of an imminent future, this vivid appearance of a growing situation before anything startling has occurred, is "form in suspense." It is a human destiny that unfolds before us, its unity is apparent from the opening words or even silent action, because on the stage we see acts in their entirety, as we do not see them in the real world except in restrospect, that is, by constructive reflection. In the theatre they occur in simplified and completed form, with visible motives, directions, and ends. Since stage action is not, like genuine action, embedded in a welter of irrelevant doings and divided interests, and characters on the stage have no unknown complexities (however complex they may be), it is possible there to see a person's feelings grow into passions, and those passions issue in words and deeds.

We know, in fact, so little about the personalities before us at the opening of a play that their every move and word, even their dress and walk, are distinct items for our perception. Because we are not involved with them as with real people, we can view each smallest act in its context, as a symptom of character and condition. We do not have to find what is significant; the selection has been made—whatever is there is significant, and it is not too much to be surveyed *in toto*. A character stands before us as a coherent whole. It is with characters as with their situations: both become visible on the stage, transparent and complete, as their analogues in the world are not.[6]

---

[6]A German critic, Peter Richard Rohden, saw this difference in our understanding of illusory and actual persons, respectively, as something of a paradox. "What," he wrote, "distinguishes a character on stage from a 'real' person? Obviously the fact that the former stands before us as a fully articulated whole. Our fellowmen we always perceive only in fragmentary fashion, and our power of self-observation is usually reduced, by vanity and cupidity, to zero. What we call 'dramatic illusion' is, therefore, the paradoxical phenomenon that we know more about the mental processes of a Hamlet than about our own inner life. For the poet-actor Shakespeare shows not only the deed, but also its motives, and indeed more perfectly than we ever see them together in actual life." (See "Das Schauspielerische Erlebnis," in Ewald Geissler's collection of essays, *Der Schauspieler* p. 36.)

But what really assures the artistic unity Morgan called "form in suspense," is the illusion of Destiny itself that is given in drama, and that arises chiefly from the way the dramatist handles circumstance. Before a play has progressed by many lines, one is aware not only of vague conditions of life in general, but of a special situation. Like the distribution of figures on a chessboard, the combination of characters makes a strategic pattern. In actual life we usually recognize a distinct situation only when it has reached, or nearly reached, a crisis; but in the theater we see the whole setup of human relationships and conflicting interests long before any abnormal event has occurred that would, in actual life, have brought it into focus. Where in the real world we would witness some extraordinary act and gradually understand the circumstances that lie behind it, in the theater we perceive an ominous situation and see that some far-reaching action must grow out of it. This creates the peculiar tension between the given present and its yet unrealized consequent, "form in suspense," the essential dramatic illusion. This illusion of a visible future is created in every play—not only in very good plays, but in everything we recognize as a play, and not as dance, pageantry, or other non-dramatic "theater art."[7] It is the primary illusion of poetry, or virtual history, in the mode peculiar to drama. The future appears as already an entity, embryonic in the present. That is Destiny.

Destiny is, of course, always a virtual phenomenon—there is no such thing in cold fact. It is a pure semblance. But what it "resembles" (or, in the Aristotelian language which has lately been revived, what it "imitates") is nonetheless an aspect of real experience, and, indeed, a fundamental one, which distinguishes human life from animal existence: the sense of past and future as parts of one continuum, and therefore of life as a single reality.

This wide awareness, which we owe to our peculiarly human talent of symbolic expression, is rooted, however, in the elementary rhythms which we share with all other organisms, and the Destiny which dramatic art creates bears the stamp of organic process—of predeterminate func-

---

[7] On this point Mr. Morgan might not agree with me. Having stated that "form in suspense" is the dramatic illusion itself, and the suspense of form something "without which drama is not," he speaks elsewhere of the dramatic illusion as a rare experience, "the highest reward of playgoing." I do not know whether he uses two concepts or only one, somewhat different from mine.

tion, tendency, growth, and completion. The abstraction of those vital forms by means of art has already been considered in Chapter 4, with reference to primitive design. In every art it is differently achieved; but in each one, I think, it is equally subtle—not a simple reference to natural instances of that form, but a genuinely abstractive handling of its reflection in non-living or even non-physical structures. Literally, "organic process" is a biological concept; "life," "growth," "development," "decline," "death"—all these are strictly biological terms. They are applicable only to organisms. In art they are lifted out of their literal context, and forthwith, in place of organic processes, we have dynamic forms: instead of metabolism, rhythmic progression, instead of stimulus and response, completeness, instead of maturation, fulfillment, instead of procreation, the repetition of the whole in the parts—what Henry James calls "reflection" in the parts,[8] and Heinrich Schenker "diminution,"[9] and Francis Fergusson "analogy."[10] And in lieu of a law of development, such as biology sets up, in art we have destiny, the implicit future.

The purpose of abstracting vital forms from their natural exemplifications is, of course, to make them available for unhampered artistic use. The illusion of growth, for instance, may be made in any medium, and in numberless ways: lengthening or flowing lines, that represent no live creatures at all; rhythmically rising steps even though they divide or diminish; increasing complexity of musical chords, or insistent repetitions; a centrifugal dance; poetic lines of gradually deepening seriousness; there is no need of "imitating" anything literally alive in order to convey the appearance of life. Vital forms may be reflected in any elements of a work, with or without representation of living things.

In drama the *situation* has its own "organic" character, that is to say, it develops, or grows, as the play proceeds. That is because all happenings, to be dramatic, must be conceived in terms of acts, and acts belong only to life; they have motives rather than causes, and in turn motivate further and further acts, which compose integrated *actions*. A situation is a complex of impending acts. It changes from moment to moment, or rather, from move to move, as the directly imminent acts

---

[8]*The Art of Fiction*, p. 170.
[9]Cf. Chap. 8, p. 129.
[10]*The Idea of a Theater*, p. 104.

are realized and the future beyond them becomes distinct and fraught with excitement. In this way, the *situation* in which characters act differs from their "environment"—a term with which it is sometimes confused, through the influence of the social sciences that invaded the theater a generation ago and bred a teeming, if shortlived progeny of sociological plays, with a few real dramas among them. The environment wherein characters have developed, and whereby they are stunted or hardened, refined or falsely veneered, is almost always implicit (*almost* always, i.e. except where it becomes a conscious factor of interest to someone in the play). The situation, on the other hand, is always explicit. Even in a vague romantic world like that of Pelléas and Mélisande, removed from all actual history, and so ungeographical that the environment is really just castle walls and a forest, without population (the chorus of women in the death-scene simply springs up *ex nihilo*—there were no inhabitants in the background before, as there are in Shakespeare's castles), the situation that elicits the action is clear.

The situation is, indeed, part of the action; it is conceived entirely by the dramatist, and is given by him to the actors to understand and enact, just as he gives them the words to be spoken. The situation is a created element in the play; it grows to its climax, often branching out into elaborate detail in the course of its development, and in the end it is resolved by the closing of the action.

Where "environment" enters into drama at all, it enters as an idea entertained by persons in the play, such as the slum visitors and reformers of the "radical" problem play. They themselves, however, do not appear in an environment, because that sociological abstraction has no meaning for the theater. They appear in a setting. "Environment" is an invisible constant, but "setting" is something immediate, something sensuously or poetically present. The playwright may utilize a setting as Strindberg did in his earlier plays, to establish the feeling of everyday life, or he may put it to the opposite purpose of removing the scene from all familiar associations, as Wagner sought to do by his extravagant stage demands. The setting is a highly variable factor, which the poets of former ages used to entrust to those who put their plays on the boards; a practice which harbors dangers, but also speaks of a healthy faith in the power of the script to guide the theatrical imagination that is to project it. There is a grand freedom given with the simple indication: "Thebes."

Drama is more variable, more tolerant of choices made by performing artists, than any other art and mode. For this reason, the "commanding form," which is established by the playwright, must be clear and powerful. It has to govern the crisscross of many imaginative minds, and hold them all—the director, the actors, the designers of sets and lights and costumes—to one essential conception, an unmistakable "poetic core." But the poet must give his interpreters scope, too; for drama is essentially an enacted poem, and if the acting can only duplicate what the lines already effect, there will be unintended redundancy, and an apparent clutter of superfluous elements that makes the total form impure and opaque (such failures of clear conception, not the use of materials "belonging" to other arts, nor bold secondary illusions, are the source of impurity in a work; if the commanding form is organic and its realization economical, the most abnormal materials will be assimilated, the most intense effects of abstracted space, time, or power will become part of the pure dramatic work).

If drama is not made of words as a piece of literature is, how can the poet, who composes only the "lines," be said to create the commanding form? "Lines" in a play are only the stuff of speeches; and speeches are only some of the acts that make drama.

They are, however, acts of a special sort. Speech is a highly specialized activity in human life, and its image in all modes of poetry, therefore, has peculiar and powerful uses. Verbal utterance is the overt issue of a greater emotional, mental. and bodily response, and its preparation in feeling and awareness or in the mounting intensity of thought is implicit in the words spoken. Speech is like a quintessence of action. Edith Wharton described its relation to the rest of our activities very aptly, when she indicated its use in her own poetic medium, prose fiction: "The use of dialogue in fiction . . . should be reserved for the culminating moments, and regarded as the spray into which the great wave of narrative breaks in curving toward the watcher on the shore."[11]

Mrs. Wharton's metaphor of the wave is more apt than her literal statement, because one naturally thinks of "culminating moments" as

---

[11] *The Writing of Fiction,* p. 73.

rare moments, high points of the story, whereas the culmination of thought and feeling in speech is a frequent occurrence, like the culmination and breaking of each wave in a constant surf.

If, moreover, one contemplates the metaphor a little more deeply, it conveys a further relation of speech to the poetic elements that surround it, namely: that it is always of the same nature as they, subject to the basic abstraction of the mode in which it is used. In narrative it is an event, like all the events that compose the virtual Past—the private events that culminate in "direct discourse," the public events that intersect in the speaker's experience, and those which the speech, as a new event, engenders. In drama speech is an act, an utterance, motivated by visible and invisible other acts, and like them shaping the oncoming Future.

A playwright who writes only the lines uttered in a play marks a long series of culminating moments in the flow of the action. Of course he indicates the major non-verbal acts, but that may be done with the fewest possible words: *enter So-and-so, exit So-and-so,* or such laconic directions as: *dies, they fight, excursions and alarums.* Modern playwrights sometimes write pages of instructions to the actors, even describing the heroine's figure and face, or the style of some character's motions and postures (Strindberg tells the leading actor in *Miss Julia* to look like a half-educated man!). Such "stage directions" are really literary treatments of the story—what Clayton Hamilton called, "the sort of stage-directions which, though interesting to the reader, are of no avail whatever to the actor,"[12] because they do not partake of the dramatic form. Ibsen prefaced his opening scenes with minute descriptions of persons and set; but his greatest interpreters have always made free with them. The lines of the play are the only guide a good director or actor needs. What makes the play the author's work is that the lines are really the highlights of a perpetual, progressive action, and determine what can be done with the piece on stage.

Since every utterance is the end of a process which began inside the speaker's body, an enacted utterance is part of a virtual act, apparently springing at the moment from thought and feeling; so the actor has to

---

[12] *The Theory of the Theatre,* p. 307. A few paragraphs later he remarked on Granville-Barker's plays: "Barker's printed stage-directions are little novels in themselves."

create the illusion of an inward activity issuing in spontaneous speech, if his words are to make a dramatic and not a rhetorical effect. As a very interesting German writer, Ferdinand Gregori, expressed it, "Gesture is older than words, and in the actor's dramatic creation, too, it must be their herald. Whether it is visible to the audience or not, it must always be the pacemaker. Anyone who starts with the words and then hunts for the appropriate gesture to accompany them, lies to the face of art and nature both."[13]

The need of preparing every utterance by some elements of expression and bearing that foreshadow it, has led many theorists and almost all naive spectators to the belief that an actor must actually undergo the emotive experiences he renders—that he must "live" his part, and produce speech and gesture from a genuine passion. Of course the stage-occurrence is not his own life, but (according to this view) he must pretend to be the individual he represents, until he actually feels the emotions he is to register. Oddly enough, people who hold this belief do not ask whether the actor must also actually have the motives and desires of his alter ego—that is, whether he must really intend or at least wish to kill his antagonist, or to divulge a secret.

The imputation of bona fide feelings and emotions to the actor on stage would be only a negligible popular error, were it not part and parcel of a broader fallacy—the confusion of theatrical representation with "make-believe," or pretense, which has always led both playwrights and directors to misconceive the relation of the audience to the play, and saddled them with the gratuitous and silly problem of the spectator's credulity. The classic expression of this concern is, of course, Castelvetro's warning in his *Poetics*, published in 1570: "The time of the representation and that of the action presented must be exactly coincident. There is no possibility of making the spectators believe that many days and nights have passed, when they themselves obviously know that only a few hours have actually elapsed; they refuse to be so deceived."[14] Corneille, a generation later, still accepted the principle, though he complained that to limit a dramatic action quite strictly to one room and the

---

[13]"Die Vorbildung des Schauspielers," in Ewald Geissler's collection *Der Schauspieler*. See p. 46.

[14]Reprinted in *The Great Critics, An Anthology of Literary Criticism*, edited by J. H. Smith and E. W. Parks. See p. 523.

time span of a theater visit often "is so awkward, not to say impossible, that some enlargement of place must of necessity be found, as also of time."[15]

An art principle that cannot be fully and wholeheartedly applied, but requires compromises and evasions, should be immediately suspect; yet the principle of making the spectators believe that they are witnessing actual happenings has been accepted down to our own day,[16] and though most theorists have seen its error, it still crops up in contemporary criticism, and—worse yet—in theater practice. We have fairly well recovered from the epidemic of naturalism, the stagecraft that sought to dispense with all artifice, and consequently borrowed living material from the actual world—"drugstore clerks drafted to impersonate themselves in real drugstores transferred bodily to the stage," as Robert Edmond Jones described this sort of dramaturgy. Now it is true that real art *can* be made with such devices; no device in itself is taboo, not even putting stage-beggars in clothes begged from real beggars (Edward Sothern, in his autobiography, recalls his acquisition of one such unalluring treasure). But the theory that a play is a game of "make-believe" designed by the poet, carried on by the actors, and supported by an audience willing to pretend that the stage history is actual, which still persists, and with it its practical counterpart—the principle of deluding the audience, aiding the public "make-believe" by making the play seem as real as possible—is another story.

The whole conception of theater as delusion is closely linked with the belief that the audience should be made to share the emotions of the protagonists. The readiest way to effect this is to extend the stage action

---

[15]*Ibid.*, p. 531. From *A Discourse on the Three Unities.*

[16]Strindberg, for instance, was convinced that the spectators in the theater let themselves be deluded, tricked into believing or making-believe that what they saw was actual life going on in their presence, and he was seriously afraid of what popular education, and the general enlightenment it was expected to bring, would do to people's credulity. In the famous preface to *Miss Julia* he observes that "the theater has always served as a grammar school to young people, women, and those who have acquired a little knowledge, all of whom retain the capacity for deceiving themselves and being deceived," but that "in our time, when the rudimentary, incomplete thought-processes operating through our fancy seem to be developing into reflection, research, and analysis, the theater might stand on the verge of being abandoned as a decaying form, for the enjoyment of which we lack the requisite conditions."

beyond the stage in the tensest moments, to make the spectators feel themselves actually present as witnesses of the scene. But the result is artistically disastrous, since each person becomes aware not only of his own presence, but of other people's too, and of the house, the stage, the entertainment in progress. Rosamond Gilder reported such an experience in her comment on Orson Welles' staging of *Native Son*; describing the scene wherein Bigger Thomas is cornered by his pursuers, she said: "Here flashing lights, gun-play, shouting and shooting converge on the stage from balcony and boxes. The theatrical illusion, far from being increased, is shattered, and the scene becomes nothing more than a nineteen-forty-one version of Eliza crossing the ice."[17]

I, too, remember vividly to this day the terrible shock of such a recall to actuality: as a young child I saw Maude Adams in *Peter Pan*. It was my first visit to the theater, and the illusion was absolute and overwhelming, like something supernatural. At the highest point of the action (Tinkerbell had drunk Peter's poisoned medicine to save him from doing so, and was dying) Peter turned to the spectators and asked them to attest their belief in fairies. Instantly the illusion was gone; there were hundreds of children, sitting in rows, clapping and even calling, while Miss Adams, dressed up as Peter Pan, spoke to us like a teacher coaching us in a play in which she herself was taking the title role. I did not understand, of course, what had happened; but an acute misery obliterated the rest of the scene, and was not entirely dispelled until the curtain rose on a new set.

The central fallacy in such play production, and in the concept of drama that it assumes, is the total disregard of what Edward Bullough, in an essay that has become deservedly famous,[18] called "psychical Distance." All appreciation of art—painting, architecture, music, dance, whatever the piece may be—requires a certain detachment, which has been variously called the "attitude of contemplation," the "aesthetic attitude," or the "objectivity" of the beholder. As I pointed out in an early chapter of this book,[19] it is part of the artist's business to make his work elicit this attitude instead of requiring the percipient to bring an ideal

---

[17]"Glamor and Purpose," in *Theatre Arts*, May, 1941, pp. 327–335.

[18]" 'Psychical Distance' as a Factor in Art and an Aesthetic Principle," *British Journal of Psychology*, June, 1912.

[19]See Chap. 4.

frame of mind with him. What the artist establishes by deliberate stylistic devices is not really the beholder's attitude—that is a by-product
—but a relation between the work and its public (including himself).
Bullough terms this relationship "Distance," and points out quite rightly
that "objectivity," "detachment," and "attitudes" are complete or incomplete, i.e. perfect or imperfect, but do not admit of degrees. "Distance, on the contrary, admits naturally of degrees, and differs not only
according to the nature of the *object,* which may impose a greater or
smaller degree of Distance, but varies also according to the *individual's
capacity* for maintaining a greater or lesser degree."[20]

He describes (rather than defines) his concept, not without resort to
metaphor, yet clearly enough to make it a philosophical asset:

"Distance . . . is obtained by separating the object and its appeal
from one's own self, by putting it out of gear with practical needs and
ends. . . . But it does not mean that the relation between the self and
the object is broken to the extent of becoming 'impersonal'. . . . On the
contrary, it describes a *personal* relation, often highly emotionally colored,
but *of a peculiar character.* Its peculiarity lies in that the personal character of the relation has been, so to speak, filtered. It has been cleared
of the practical, concrete nature of its appeal. . . . One of the best-
known examples is to be found in our attitude towards the events and
characters of the drama. . . ."[21]

This relation "of a peculiar character" is, I believe, our natural relation to a symbol that embodies an idea and presents it for our contemplation, not for practical action, but "cleared of the practical, concrete
nature of its appeal." It is for the sake of this remove that art deals
entirely in illusions, which, because of their lack of "practical, concrete
nature," are readily distanced as symbolic forms. But delusion—even the
quasi-delusion of "make-believe"—aims at the opposite effect, the greatest
possible nearness. To seek delusion, belief, and "audience participation"
in the theater is to deny that drama is art.

There are those who do deny it. There are very serious critics who
see its essential value to society not in the sort of revelation that is proper

---

[20]*Op. cit.,* p. 94.

[21]*Op. cit.,* p. 91. The attitude referred to is, of course, the famous "aesthetic
attitude," here treated as an index to the proper degree of distance.

to art, but in its function as a form of ritual. Francis Fergusson and T. S. Eliot have treated drama in this vein,[22] and several German critics have found in the custom of hand clapping a last vestige of the audience participation that is really the public's lost birthright.[23] There are others who regard the theater not as a temple, but primarily as an amusement hall, and demand of drama that it shall please, delude us for a while, and incidentally teach morals and "knowledge of man." Brander Matthews extended the demand for amusement—any or every sort of amusement—to all the arts; but as his renown rests entirely on his dramatic criticism and teaching, his view of "art" is really a view of the theater casually extended to all other realms. "The primary purpose of all the arts is to entertain," said Matthews, "even if every art has also to achieve its own secondary aim. Some of these entertainments make their appeal to the intellect, some to the emotions, and some only to the nerves, to our relish for sheer excitement and for brute sensation; but each of them in its own way seeks, first of all, to entertain. They are, every one of them, to be included in the show business."[24]

Here we have certainly two extremes of dramatic theory; and the theory I hold—that drama is art, a poetic art in a special mode, with its own version of the poetic illusion to govern every detail of the performed piece—this theory does not lie anywhere between these extremes. Drama is neither ritual nor show business, though it may occur in the frame of either one; it is poetry, which is neither a kind of circus nor a kind of church.

Perhaps the greatest snare in the course of our thinking about theater is its free trafficking with the standard materials of all the other arts. People are so used to defining each art by its characteristic medium that when paint is used in the theater they class the result as "the painter's

---

[22]Cf. Francis Fergusson, *The Idea of a Theater*. A book so full of ideas, scholarship and discernment that even in taking issue with it I would recommend it to every reader.

T. S. Eliot, in "A Dialogue on Dramatic Poetry," (in *Selected Essays, 1917–1932*), p. 35, lets "E." say, "The only dramatic satisfaction that I find now is in a High Mass well performed."

[23]E.g., Theodor Wiesengrund-Adorno, "Applaus," *Die Musik*, 23 (1930–31), p. 476; also A. E. Günther, "Der Schauspieler und wir," in Geissler's *Der Schauspieler*, p. 144.

[24]*A Book About the Theater*, p. 6.

art," and because the set requires building, they regard the designer of it as an architect. Drama, consequently, has so often been described as a synthesis of several or even all arts that its autonomy, its status as a special mode of a great single art, is always in jeopardy. It has been treated as essentially dance, by confusion with pantomimic dances that have a dramatic plot; it has been conceived as tableau and pageantry heightened by speech and action (Gordon Craig held that the designer of its visual aspects was its real creator), and as poetic recitation accompanied by gestures, sometimes by dance-gestures. This last view is traditional in India, where it is supported by the obvious epic sources of Hindu plays (as usual, finding the source of a phenomenon is supposed to reveal its "real" nature). Hindu aestheticians, therefore, regard drama as literature, and judge it by literary standards.[25] Nietzsche found its origin in "the spirit of music" and consequently regarded its true nature as musical. Thornton Wilder describes it as an exalted form of narrative: "The theater," he writes, "carries the art of narration to a higher power than the novel or the epic poem. . . . The dramatist must be by instinct a story-teller."[26]

But story-telling, narration, is something quite different from story-enactment in a theater. Many first-rate story-tellers cannot make a play, and the highest developments of narration, such as the modern novel and short story, show devices of their own that have no meaning for the stage. They project a history in retrospect, whereas drama is history coming. Even as performed arts, narration and dramatization are distinct. The ancient rhapsodist, for all his gesticulations and inflections, was not an actor, and today, too, people who are known as good readers of poetry or prose need not therefore have any aptitude for the theater.

The concept of drama as literature embellished with concurrent appeals to the sense of sight is belied most convincingly in the very society where it enjoys its traditional vogue; the fact that in India the classic

---

[25]Cf. Sylvain Lévi, *Le théâtre indien*, p. 257: "They [Indian theorists] are wont to consider drama as the juxtaposition of two arts, which simultaneously pursue their respective ends, namely poetry and mimetic dance. . . . Dance and mummery, stagecraft and scenery combine to heighten the illusion and pleasure by appealing to several senses. Representation, therefore, surpasses reading by a quantitative difference of emotion; there is no qualitative difference between them." See also A. B. Smith, *The Sanskrit Drama*, pp. 294–295.
[26]"Some Thoughts on Playwrighting," p. 86.

drama survived as a popular art for centuries after both the Sanskrit and the various Prakrits in which it was composed had become dead languages, understood only by scholars, proves that the stage action was no mere accompaniment, but was instinctively developed by the actors to the point of self-sufficiency, making the precise word meanings of the speeches dispensable; that this drama is, in fact, what Cocteau called "a poetry of the theater," as well as "poetry in the theater."

As for dance, though it probably preceded drama on the boards, and though it uses dramatic plots after its own fashion, it does not give rise to drama—not even to true pantomime. Any direct dramatic action tends to suspend the balletic illusion. The fact that Greek drama arose amidst ritual dancing has led several art historians to consider it as a dance episode; but the dance was, in fact, only a perfect framework for the development of an entirely new art; the minute the two antagonists stepped out of the choric ensemble and addressed not the deity, nor the congregation, but each other, they created a poetic illusion, and drama was born in midst of the religious rite. The choric dance itself was assimilated to the world of the virtual history they presented.

Once we recognize that drama is neither dance nor literature, nor a democracy of various arts functioning together, but is poetry in the mode of action, the relations of all its elements to each other and to the whole work become clear: the primacy of the script, which furnishes the commanding form; the use of the stage, with or without representational scenery, to delimit the "world" in which the virtual action exists; the need of making the scene a "place," so that often the designer produces a plastic illusion that is secondary here, but primary in the art of architecture;[27] the use of music and sometimes of dance to keep the fictitious history apart from actuality and insure its artistic abstraction;[28] the nature of dramatic time, which is "musical" instead of practical time,

---

[27]Cf. Jones, *op. cit.*, p. 75: "The energy of a particular play, its emotional content, its aura, so to speak, has its own definite physical dimensions. It extends just so far in space and no farther. The walls of the setting must be placed at precisely this point."

George Beiswanger, in a little article entitled "Opera for the Eye" (*Theatre Arts*, January, 1943, p. 59), makes a similar remark: "Each opera has its own ideal dimensions, and their illusion must be created whether the actual stage be large or small."

[28]Schiller, in his famous preface to *Die Braut von Messina*, called the Greek chorus, which he revived in this play, "a living wall" to preserve the Distance of the work.

and sometimes becomes strikingly evident—another secondary illusion in poetry, but the primary one of music. The guiding principle in the use of so many transient borrowed illusions is the making of an *appearance*, not under normal circumstances, like a pretense or social convention, but under the circumstances of the play. Its total emotional tone is like the "palette" of a picture, and controls the intensity of color and light, the sober or fantastic character of the sets, the requirements such as overture, interludes, and what not.

Above all, that emotional tone guides the style of the actors. The actors are the chief interpreters—normally, the only indispensable ones —of the poet's incomplete but commanding creations. An actor does not express his emotions, but those of a fictitious person. He does not undergo and vent emotions; he conceives them, to the smallest detail, and enacts them.

Some of the Hindu critics, although they subordinate and even deprecate dramatic art in favor of the literary elements it involves, understand much better than their Western colleagues the various aspects of emotion in the theater, which our writers so freely and banefully confuse: the feelings experienced by the actor, those experienced by the spectators, those presented as undergone by characters in the play, and finally the feeling that shines through the play itself—the vital feeling of the piece. This last they call *rasa;* it is a state of emotional knowledge, which comes only to those who have long studied and contemplated poetry. It is supposed to be of supernatural origin, because it is not like mundane feeling and emotion, but is detached, more of the spirit than of the viscera, pure and uplifting.[29]

Rasa is, indeed, that comprehension of the directly experienced or "inward" life that all art conveys. The supernatural status attributed to its perception shows the mystification that beset the ancient theorists when they were confronted with the power of a symbol which they did not recognize as such. Audiences who can dispense with the helps that the box stage, representational setting and costumes, and sundry stage properties lend to our poetic imagination have probably a better understanding of drama as art than we who require a potpourri of means. In Indian, Chinese, and Japanese drama—but most consistently in the Far Eastern—not only events and emotions, but even *things* are enacted. Stage

[29]Sylvain Lévi, *op. cit.*, p. 295.

properties exist, but their use is symbolic rather than naturalistic. Even the simulation of feeling may be sacrificed to enhance the formal value, the emotional effect of the play as a whole. Objects involved in the action are simply implied by gesture.[30] In India, some stage properties do occur —carts, dragons, even elephants—and are elaborately made of paper, bamboo, lacquer, etc.; others are left to the imagination. The deciding factor seems to be whether the action turns on the non-human element, or not. A king who quite incidentally mounts a chariot merely indicates its existence by an act, but in *The Little Clay Cart* the cart is really put upon the stage. European spectators at Chinese plays always find it surprising and offensive that attendants in ordinary dress come and go on the stage; but to the initiated audience the stagehand's untheatrical dress seems to be enough to make his presence as irrelevant as to us the intrusion of an usher who leads people to a seat in our line of vision.

On the Japanese stage, an actor may step out of his part by giving a signal and address the audience, then by another formal sign resume his role.

A public that enjoys such pure acting gives itself up to the dramatic illusion without any need for sensuous delusion. But sensuous satisfaction it does want: gorgeous robes and curtains, a rich display of colors, and always music (of a sort that Westerners often find no asset). These elements make the play dramatically convincing precisely by holding it aloof from actuality; they assure the spectator's "psychical Distance" instead of inviting him to consider the action as a piece of natural behavior. For in the theater, where a virtual future unfolds before us, the import of every little act is heightened, because even the smallest act is oriented toward that future. What we see, therefore, is not behavior, but the self-realization of people in action and passion; and as every act has exaggerated importance, so the emotional responses of persons in a play are intensified. Even indifference is a concentrated and significant attitude.

As every act and utterance set down in the poet's script serves to create a perceptible destiny, so all plastic, choreographic, or musical ele-

---

[30]See Jack Chen, *The Chinese Theater;* A. E. Zucker, *The Chinese Theater;* Noël Peri, *Cinq nô: Drames lyriques japonais.* The last-named gives the most detailed account of this technique.

ments that are added to his play in the theater must support and enhance that creation. The dramatic illusion is poetic, and where it is primary—that is to say, where the work is a drama—it transmutes all borrowings from other arts into poetic elements. As Mr. Jones says in *The Dramatic Imagination,* "In the last analysis the designing of stage scenery is not the problem of an architect or a painter or a sculptor or even a musician, but of a poet."[31] It is the painter (or architect, or sculptor) turned poet who understands the commanding form which the author has composed by writing the lines of the play, and who carries this form to the further state of visibility, and it is the actor-poet who takes the whole work—words, setting, happenings, all—through the final phase of its creation, where words become utterances and the visible scene is fused into the occurrence of the virtual life.

Histrionic imagination is the same fundamental talent in the playwright, the leading actors, the performers of even the smallest parts in so far as they are genuine actors, the scene and light designer, the costumer, the light controller, the composer or selector of incidental music, the ballet master, and the director who surveys the whole to his satisfaction or despair. The work on which they are engaged is one thing—an apparition of Destiny.

"From the Greeks to Ibsen the actor has represented, by elocution as well as by movement, human character and human destiny. . . . When drama takes on the abstract character of music or pure dance it ceases to be drama. . . .

"The dramatist . . . is a writer, a poet, before he is a musician or a choreographer. Wagner of course showed that many dramatic elements can be embodied in orchestral music; silent movies showed how much can be done with the visual element alone; but if you add Wagner to Eisenstein and multiply by ten you still do not have a Shakespeare or an Ibsen. This does not say that drama is better than music, dancing, or the visual arts. It is different.

"The defenders of the arts of the theater must be infected by the commodities of the theater if they can forget that all 'theater arts' are means to one end: the correct presentation of a poem."[32]

---

[31]P. 77.

[32]From E. R. Bentley, "The Drama at Ebb," *Kenyon Review,* VII, 2 (Spring, 1945), 169–184.

Chapter eighteen

THE GREAT DRAMATIC FORMS:
THE COMIC RHYTHM

Of all the arts, the most exposed to non-artistic interpretation and criticism are prose fiction and the drama. As the novel has suffered from being treated as a psycho-biographical document, drama has suffered from moralism. In the theater, most people—and especially the most competent spectators—feel that the vision of destiny is the essence of the work, the thing that unfolds before their eyes. In critical retrospect they forget that this visibly growing future, this destiny to which the persons in the play are committed, is the artistic form the poet set out to make, and that the value of the play lies in this creation. As critics, they treat the form as a device for conveying a social and moral content; almost all drama analysis and comment is concerned with the moral struggle involved in the action, the justice of the outcome, the "case" of society against the tragic hero or the comic villain, and the moral significance of the various characters.

It is true that tragedy usually—perhaps even always—presents a moral struggle, and that comedy very commonly castigates foibles and vices. But neither a great moral issue, nor folly inviting embarrassment and laughter, in itself furnishes an artistic principle; neither ethics nor common sense produces any image of organic form. Drama, however, always exhibits such form; it does so by creating the semblance of a history, and composing its elements into a rhythmic single structure. The moral content is thematic material, which, like everything that enters into a work of art, has to serve to make the primary illusion and articulate the pattern of "felt life" the artist intends.

"The tragic theme" and "the comic theme"—guilt and expiation, vanity and exposure—are not the essence of drama, not even the determinants of its major forms, tragedy and comedy; they are means of dramatic construction, and as such they are, of course, not indispensable, however widespread their use. But they are to European drama what the representation of objects is to painting: sources of the Great Tradition. Morality, the concept of deed and desert, or "what is coming to the doer," is as obvious a subject for the art of creating a virtual future as the depiction of objects is for the art of creating virtual space. The reason for the existence of these two major themes, and for their particular respective contents, will be apparent as soon as we consider the nature of the two great forms, comic drama and tragic.

It is commonly assumed that comedy and tragedy have the same fundamental form, but differ in point of view—in the attitude the poet and his interpreters take, and the spectators are invited to take, toward the action.[1] But the difference really goes deeper than surface treatment (i. e. relative levity or pathos). It is structural and radical. Drama abstracts from reality the fundamental forms of consciousness: the first reflection of natural activity in sensation, awareness, and expectation, which belongs to all higher creatures and might be called, therefore, the pure sense of life; and beyond that, the reflection of an activity which is at once more elaborate, and more integrated, having a beginning, efflorescence, and end—the personal sense of life, or self-realization. The latter probably belongs only to human beings, and to them in varying measure.

The pure sense of life is the underlying feeling of comedy, developed in countless different ways. To give a general phenomenon one name is not to make all its manifestations one thing, but only to bring them conceptually under one head. Art does not generalize and classify; art sets forth the individuality of forms which discourse, being essentially general, has to suppress. The sense of life is always new, infinitely complex, therefore infinitely variable in its possible expressions. This sense, or "enjoyment" as Alexander would call it,[2] is the realization in direct

---

[1]Cf., for instance, the letters of Athene Seyler and Stephen Haggard, published under the title: *The Craft of Comedy*. Miss Seyler writes: ". . . comedy is simply a point of view. It is a comment on life from outside, an observation on human nature. . . . Comedy seems to be the standing outside a character or situation and pointing out one's delight in certain aspects of it. For this reason it demands the cooperation of . . . the audience and is in essence the same as recounting a good story over the dining-table." (P. 9.)

[2]S. Alexander, *Space, Time and Deity*. See Vol. I, p. 12.

feeling of what sets organic nature apart from inorganic: self-preservation, self-restoration, functional tendency, purpose. Life is teleological,
the rest of nature is, apparently, mechanical; to maintain the pattern
of vitality in a non-living universe is the most elementary instinctual
purpose. An organism tends to keep its equilibrium amid the bombard-
ment of aimless forces that beset it, to regain equilibrium when it has
been disturbed, and to pursue a sequence of actions dictated by the need
of keeping all its interdependent parts constantly renewed, their structure intact. Only organisms have needs; lifeless objects whirl or slide
or tumble about, are shattered and scattered, stuck together, piled up,
without showing any impulse to return to some pre-eminent condition
and function. But living things strive to persist in a particular chemical
balance, to maintain a particular temperature, to repeat particular functions, and to develop along particular lines, achieving a growth that seems
to be preformed in their earliest, rudimentary, protoplasmic structure.

That is the basic biological pattern which all living things share: the
round of conditioned and conditioning organic processes that produces
the life rhythm. When this rhythm is disturbed, all activities in the total
complex are modified by the break; the organism as a whole is out of
balance. But, within a wide range of conditions, it struggles to retrieve
its original dynamic form by overcoming and removing the obstacle, or
if this proves impossible, it develops a slight variation of its typical form
and activity and carries on life with a new balance of functions—in other
words, it adapts itself to the situation. A tree, for instance, that is bereft
of the sunshine it needs by the encroachment of other trees, tends to
grow tall and thin until it can spread its own branches in the light. A
fish that has most of its tail bitten off partly overcomes the disturbance
of its locomotion patterns by growing new tissue, replacing some of the
tail, and partly adapts to its new condition by modifying the normal uses
of its fins, swimming effectively without trying to correct the list of its
whole body in the water, as it did at first.

But the impulse to survive is not spent only in defense and accom-
modation; it appears also in the varying power of organisms to seize on
opportunities. Consider how chimney swifts, which used to nest in
crevasses among rocks, have exploited the products of human architecture, and how unfailingly mice find the warmth and other delights of

our kitchens. All creatures live by opportunities, in a world fraught with disasters. That is the biological pattern in most general terms.

This pattern, moreover, does not develop sporadically in midst of mechanical systems; when or where it began on the earth we do not know, but in the present phase of this planet's constitution there appears to be no "spontaneous generation." It takes life to produce further life. Every organism, therefore, is historically linked with other organisms. A single cell may die, or it may divide and lose its identity in the reorganization of what was formerly its protoplasm round two nuclei instead of one. Its existence as one maturing cell is a phase in a continuum of biological process that varies its rhythm at definite points of growth, starting over with multiplied instances of the immature form. Every individual in this progression that dies (i.e. meets with disaster) instead of dividing is an offshoot from the continuous process, an end, but not a break in the communal biography.

There are species of such elementary life that are diffused in air and water, and some that cohere in visible colonies; above all, there are genetically related organic structures that tend to interact, modify each other, vary in special ways, and together—often by hundreds, thousands, millions together—produce a single higher organism. In such higher organisms, propagation no longer occurs by binary fission, and consequently the individual is not a passing phase in an endless metabolic process; death, which is an accident in amoeboid existence, becomes the lot of every individual—no accident, but a phase of the life pattern itself. The only "immortal" portion of such a complex organism is a class of cells which, during its lifetime, forms new individuals.

In relatively low forms of individualized life, for instance the cryptogams, new specimens may spring entirely from one parent, so that the entire ancestry of an organism forms a single line. But the main evolutionary trend has been toward a more complex form of heredity: two cells of complementary structure, and from different individuals, fuse and grow into a common offspring. This elaborate process entails the division of the race into two sexes, and radically affects the needs and instincts of its members. For the jellyfish, the desire for continuity is enough; it seeks food and avoids destructive influence. Its rhythm is the endless metabolic cycle of cellular growth, punctuated by fissions and rearrangements, but ageless except for the stages of each passing individuation, and in principle deathless. The higher organisms, however, that do not give themselves up by division into new units of life, are all doomed to die; death is inherent in a form of life that achieves complete individuation. The only vestige in them of the endless protoplasmic life passing through organism after organism is their production of the "immortal" cells, ova or spermatozoa; this small fraction of them still enjoys the longer life of the stock.

The sex impulse, which presumably belongs only to bisexual creatures (whatever equivalents it may have in other procreative processes), is closely intertwined with the life impulse; in a mature organism it is part and parcel of the whole vital impetus. But it is a specialized part, because the activities that maintain the individual's life are varied and adaptable to many circumstances, but procreation requires specific actions. This specialization is reflected in the emotional life of all the higher animals; sexual excitement is the most intense and at the same time the most elaborately patterned experience, having its own rhythm that engages the whole creature, its rise and crisis and cadence, in a much higher degree than any other emotive response. Consequently the whole development of feeling, sensibility, and temperament is wont to radiate from that source of vital consciousness, sexual action and passion.

Mankind has its rhythm of animal existence, too—the strain of maintaining a vital balance amid the alien and impartial chances of the world, complicated and heightened by passional desires. The pure sense of life springs from that basic rhythm, and varies from the composed well-being of sleep to the intensity of spasm, rage, or ecstasy. But the process of living is incomparably more complex for human beings than for even the highest animals; man's world is, above all, intricate and puzzling. The powers of language and imagination have set it utterly apart from that of other creatures. In human society an individual is not, like a member of a herd or a hive, exposed only to others that visibly or tangibly surround him, but is consciously bound to people who are absent, perhaps far away, at the moment. Even the dead may still play into his life. His awareness of events is far greater than the scope of his physical perceptions. Symbolic construction has made this vastly involved and extended world: and mental adroitness is his chief asset for exploiting it. The pattern of his vital feeling, therefore, reflects his deep emotional relation to those symbolic structures that are his realities, and his instinctual life modified in almost every way by thought—a brainy opportunism in face of an essentially dreadful universe.

This human life-feeling is the essence of comedy. It is at once religious and ribald, knowing and defiant, social and freakishly individual. The illusion of life which the comic poet creates is the oncoming future fraught with dangers and opportunities, that is, with physical or social events occurring by chance and building up the coincidences with which individuals cope according to their lights. This ineluctable future—ineluctable because its countless factors are beyond human knowledge and control—is Fortune. Destiny in the guise of Fortune is the fabric of comedy; it is developed by comic action, which is the upset and recovery of the protagonist's equilibrium, his contest with the world and his triumph by wit, luck, personal power, or even humorous, or ironical, or philosophical acceptance of mischance. Whatever the theme—serious and lyrical as in *The Tempest,* coarse slapstick as in the *Schwänke* of Hans Sachs, or clever and polite social satire—the immediate sense of life is the underlying feeling of comedy, and dictates its rhythmically structured unity, that is to say its organic form.

Comedy is an art form that arises naturally wherever people are gathered to celebrate life, in spring festivals, triumphs, birthdays, weddings, or initiations. For it expresses the elementary strains and resolutions of animate nature, the animal drives that persist even in human nature, the delight man takes in his special mental gifts that make him the lord of creation; it is an image of human vitality holding its own in the world amid the surprises of unplanned coincidence. The most obvious occasions for the performance of comedies are thanks or challenges to fortune. What justifies the term "Comedy" is not that the ancient ritual procession, the Comus, honoring the god of that name, was the source of this great art form—for comedy has arisen in many parts of the world, where the Greek god with his particular worship was unknown —but that the Comus was a fertility rite, and the god it celebrated a fertility god, a symbol of perpetual rebirth, eternal life.

Tragedy has a different basic feeling, and therefore a different form; that is why it has also quite different thematic material, and why character development, great moral conflicts, and sacrifice are its usual actions. *It is also what makes tragedy sad,* as the rhythm of sheer vitality makes comedy happy. To understand this fundamental difference, we must turn once more to the biological reflections above, and carry them a little further.

In the higher forms of life, an organism is not split up into other organisms so as to let its career as an individual properly end without death and decay; each separate body, on the higher levels, having completed its growth, and normally having reproduced, becomes decadent and finally dies. Its life has a definite beginning, ascent, turning point, descent, and close (barring accidental destruction of life, such as simple cells may also suffer); and the close is inevitably death. Animals—even highly developed ones—instinctively seek to avoid death when they are suddenly confronted with it, and presumably do not realize its coming if and when they die naturally. But human beings, because of their semantically enlarged horizon, are aware of individual history as a passage from birth to death. Human life, therefore, has a different subjective pattern from animal existence; as "felt life" (to borrow Henry James' phrase once more) it has a different dimension. Youth, maturity, and age are not merely states in which a creature may happen to be, but are stages through which persons must pass. Life is a voyage, and at the end of it is death.

The power to conceive of life as a single span enables one also to think of its conduct as a single undertaking, and of a person as a unified and developed being, a personality. Youth, then, is all potentiality, not only for physical growth and procreation, but also for mental and moral growth. Bodily development is largely unconscious and involuntary, and the instincts that aid it are bent simply upon maintaining the vital rhythms from moment to moment, evading destruction, letting the organism grow in its highly specialized fashion. Its maturation, procreative drive, then a fairly long period of "holding its own" without further increase, and finally the gradual loss of impetus and elasticity—these processes form one organic evolution and dissolution. The extraordinary activity of man's brain, however, does not automatically parallel his biological career. It outruns the order of animal interests, sometimes confusing his instincts, sometimes exaggerating them (as simple sexual passion, for instance, is heightened by imagination into romantic passion and eternal devotion), and gives his life a new pattern dominated by his foreknowledge of death. Instead of simply passing through the natural succession of his individualized existence, he ponders its uniqueness, its brevity and limitations, the life impulses that make it, and the fact that in the end the organic unity will be broken, the self will disintegrate and be no more.

There are many ways of accepting death; the commonest one is to deny its finality, to imagine a continued existence "beyond" it—by resurrection, reincarnation, or departure of the soul from the body, and usually from the familiar world, to a deathless existence in hades, nirvana, heaven or hell. But no matter how people contrive to become reconciled to their mortality, it puts its stamp on their conception of life: since the instinctive struggle to go on living is bound to meet defeat in the end, they look for *as much life as possible* between birth and death—for adventure, variety and intensity of experience, and the sense of growth that increase of personality and social status can give long after physical growth has stopped. The known limitation of life gives form to it and makes it appear not merely as a process, but as a career. This career of the individual is variously conceived as a "calling," the attainment of an ideal, the soul's pilgrimage, "life's ordeal," or self-realization. The last of these designations is, perhaps, the most illuminating in the present context, because it contains the notion of a limited potential personality given at birth and "realized," or systematically developed, in the course of the subject's total activity. His career, then, appears to be preformed in him; his successive adventures in the world are so many challenges to fulfill his individual destiny.

Destiny viewed in this way, as a future shaped essentially in advance and only incidentally by chance happenings, is Fate; and Fate is the "virtual future" created in tragedy. The "tragic rhythm of action," as Professor Fergusson calls it, is the rhythm of man's life at its highest powers in the limits of his unique, death-bound career. Tragedy is the image of Fate, as comedy is of Fortune. Their basic structures are different; comedy is essentially contingent, episodic, and ethnic; it expresses the continuous balance of sheer vitality that belongs to society and is exemplified briefly in each individual; tragedy is a fulfillment, and its form therefore is closed, final and passional. Tragedy is a mature art form, that has not arisen in all parts of the world, not even in all great civilizations. Its conception requires a sense of individuality which some religions and some cultures—even high cultures—do not generate.

But that is a matter for later discussion, in connection with the tragic theater as such. At present I wish only to point out the radical nature of the difference between the two types of drama, comedy and tragedy; a difference which is, however, not one of opposites—the two forms are perfectly capable of various combinations, incorporating elements of one in the other. The matrix of the work is always either tragic or comic; but within its frame the two often interplay.

Where tragedy is generally known and accepted, comedy usually does not reach its highest development. The serious mood is reserved for the tragic stage. Yet comedy may be serious; there is heroic drama, romantic drama, political drama, all in the comic pattern, yet entirely serious; the "history" is usually exalted comedy. It presents an incident in the undying life of a society that meets good and evil fortunes on countless occasions but never concludes its quest. After the story comes more life, more destiny prepared by the world and the race. So far as the story goes, the protagonists "live happily ever after"—on earth or in heaven. That fairy-tale formula is tacitly understood at the close of a comedy. It is implicit in the episodic structure.

Dante called his great poem a comedy, though it is entirely serious—visionary, religious, and sometimes terrible. The name *Divina Commedia,* which later generations attached to it, fits it, even if not too literally since it is not actually a drama as the title suggests.[3] Something analogous to the comedy pattern, together with the tones of high seriousness that European poets have generally struck only in tragedy, yields a work that invites the paradoxical name.

------

[3]Professor Fergusson and Mr. T. S. Eliot both treat *The Divine Comedy* as an example of genuine drama. The former even speaks of "the drama of Sophocles and Shakespeare, the *Divina Commedia* of Dante—in which the idea of a theater has been briefly realized." (*The Idea of a Theater,* p. 227.) But between drama and dramatic narrative there is a world of difference. If everything these two eminent critics say of great drama holds also for Dante's poem, this does not mean that the poem is a drama, but that the critics have reached a generalization applying to more than drama.

Paradoxical, however, only to our ears, because our religious feeling is essentially tragic, inspired by the contemplation of death. In Asia the designation "Divine Comedy" would fit numberless plays; especially in India triumphant gods, divine lovers united after various trials (as in the perennially popular romance of Rama and Sita), are the favorite themes of a theater that knows no "tragic rhythm." The classical Sanskrit drama was heroic comedy—high poetry, noble action, themes almost always taken from the myths—a serious, religiously conceived drama, yet in the "comic" pattern, which is not a complete organic development reaching a foregone, inevitable conclusion, but is episodic, restoring a lost balance, and implying a new future.[4] The reason for this consistently "comic" image of life in India is obvious enough: both Hindu and Buddhist regard life as an episode in the much longer career of the soul which has to accomplish many incarnations before it reaches its goal, nirvana. Its struggles in the world do not exhaust it; in fact they are scarcely worth recording except in entertainment theater, "comedy" in our sense—satire, farce, and dialogue. The characters whose fortunes are seriously interesting are the eternal gods; and for them there is no death, no limit of potentialities, hence no fate to be fulfilled. There is only the balanced rhythm of sentience and emotion, upholding itself amid the changes of material nature.

The personages in the nataka (the Sanskrit heroic drama) do not undergo any character development; they are good or evil, as the case may be, in the last act as they were in the first. This is essentially a comedy trait. Because the comic rhythm is that of vital continuity, the protagonists do not change in the course of the play, as they normally do in tragedy. In the latter there is development, in the former developments. The comic hero plays against obstacles presented either by nature (which includes mythical monsters such as dragons, and also "forces," personified like the "Night Queen," or impersonal like floods, fires, and pests), or by society; that is, his fight is with obstacles and enemies, which his strength, wisdom, virtue, or other assets let him overcome.[5] It

[4]Cf. Sylvain Lévi, *Le théâtre indien*, p. 32: "The heroic comedy (nataka) is the consummate type of Indian drama; all dramatic elements can find their place in it."

[5]In Chinese drama, even exalted heroes often conquer their enemies by ruse rather than by valor; see Zucker, *The Chinese Theater*, especially p. 82.

is a fight with the uncongenial world, which he shapes to his own fortunes. Where the basic feeling of dramatic art always has the comic
rhythm, comedy enjoys a much fuller development than it does where
tragedy usurps its highest honors. In the great cultures of Asia it has
run through all moods, from the lightest to the most solemn, and through
all forms—the one-act skit, the farce, the comedy of manners, even to
dramas of Wagnerian proportions.

In the European tradition the heroic comedy has had a sporadic existence; the Spanish *Comedia* was perhaps its only popular and extended
development.[6] Where it reaches something like the exalted character of
the nataka, our comedy has generally been taken for tragedy, simply
because of its dignity, or "sublimity," which we associate only with
tragedy. Corneille and Racine considered their dramas tragedies, yet the
rhythm of tragedy—the growth and full realization of a personality—is
not in them; the Fate their personages meet is really misfortune, and
they meet it heroically. This sad yet non-tragic character of the French
classical drama has been noted by several critics. C. V. Deane, for instance, in his book, *Dramatic Theory and the Rhymed Heroic Play,* says
of Corneille: "In his tragedies the incidents are so disposed as to bring
out to the full the conflict between an overmastering will and the forces
of Fate, but the interest centres in the dauntless endurance of the individual, and there is little attempt to envisage or suggest the universal
moral problem inherent in the nature of Tragedy, nor do his chief characters submit to ordinary morality; each is a law unto himself by virtue
of his particular kind of heroism."[7] Earlier in the book he had already remarked on the fact that the creation of human personalities
was not the aim of these playwrights;[8] and in a comment on Otway's
translation of Racine's *Bérénice* he really exposed—perhaps without real-
izing it himself—the true nature of their tragedies, for he said that Otway

---

[6]Brander Matthews describes the *Comedia* as "often not a comedy at all in
our English understanding of the term, but rather a play of intrigue, peopled with
hot-blooded heroes. . . ." (Introduction to Lope De Vega Carpio's *The New Art
of Writing Plays.*)

[7]*Dramatic Theory and the Rhymed Heroic Play,* p. 33.

[8]*Ibid.,* p. 14: "It is true that during the course of its history the heroic play seldom succeeded in creating characters which were credible as human beings; this,
however, was really foreign to its purpose."

was able "to reproduce the spirit of the original," though he was not scrupulously true to the French text. "Even Otway, however, adapts rather than translates," he observed, "and the tilt toward the happy ending in his version betrays an acquiescence in the stereotyped poetic justice which the English playwrights (appreciably influenced by Corneille's practice) deemed inseparable from the interplay of heroism and honor." (P. 19.)

How could a translator-editor bring a tragic play to a happy ending and still "reproduce the spirit of the original"? Only by virtue of the non-tragic structure, the fundamentally comic movement of the piece. These stately Gallic classics are really heroic comedies. They are classed as tragedies because of their sublime tone, which is associated, in our European tradition, with tragic action,[9] but (as Sylvain Lévi pointed out)[10] they are really similar in spirit and form to the nataka. Corneille's and Racine's heroic characters are godlike in their rationality; like the divine beings of Kalidasa and Bhavabhuti, they undergo no real *agon*, no great moral struggle or conflict of passions. Their morality (however extraordinary) is perfect, their principles clear and coherent, and the action derives from the changes of fortune that they meet. Fortune can bring sad or happy occasions, and a different course of events need not violate "the spirit of the original." But there is no question of how the heroes will meet circumstances; they will meet them rationally; reason, the highest virtue of the human soul, will be victorious. This reason does not grow, through inner struggles against passional obstacles, from an

---

[9] The strength of this association is so great that some critics actually treat "sublimity" as the necessary and sufficient condition for tragedy. Racine himself said: "It is enough that its action be great, its actors heroic, that the passions be excited in it; and that the whole give the experience of majestic sadness in which the whole pleasure of tragedy resides." (Quoted by Fergusson, *op. cit.*, p. 43.)

The same criteria are evidently applied by Professor Zucker when he writes: "Tragedy is not found in the Chinese drama. The plays abound in sad situations, but there is none that by its nobility or sublimity would deserve to be called tragic." (*Op. cit.*, p. 37.) Jack Chen, on the other hand, in his book *The Chinese Theater*, says that during the Ching dynasty "Historical tragedy was greatly in vogue. *The Bloodstained Fan* dealing with the last days of the Mings and *The Palace of Eternal Life* . . . are perennially popular even today." (P. 20.) The last-named play, which deals with the death of Lady Yang, is certainly a genuine tragedy.

[10] See *Le théâtre indien*, p. 425.

original spark to full enlightenment, as "the tragic rhythm of action" would demand, but is perfect from the outset.[11]

Romantic drama such as Schiller's *Wilhelm Tell* illustrates the same principle. It is another species of serious heroic comedy. Tell appears as an exemplary personage in the beginning of the play, as citizen, husband, father, friend and patriot; when an extreme political and social crisis develops, he rises to the occasion, overcomes the enemy, frees his country, and returns to the peace, dignity and harmonious joy of his home. The balance of life is restored. As a personage he is impressive; as a personality he is very simple. He has the standard emotions—righteous indignation, paternal love, patriotic fervor, pride, anxiety, etc.—under their obvious conditions. Nothing in the action requires him to be more than a man of high courage, independent spirit, and such other virtues as the mountaineers of Switzerland boasted, to oppose the arrogance and vanity of foreign oppressors. But this ideal male he was from the start, and the Gessler episode merely gives him opportunity to show his indomitable skill and daring.

Such are the serious products of comic art; they are also its rarer examples. The natural vein of comedy is humorous—so much so that "comic" has become synonymous with "funny." Because the word "comic" is here used in a somewhat technical sense (contrasting "the comic rhythm" with "the tragic rhythm"), it may be well to say "comical" where the popular sense is intended. There are all degrees of humor in comedy, from the quick repartee that elicits a smile by its cleverness without being intrinsically funny at all, to the absurdity that sets young and old, simple or sophisticate, shouting with merriment. Humor has its place in all the arts, but in comic drama is has its home. Comedy may be frivolous, farcical, ribald, ludicrous to any degree, and still be true art. Laughter springs from its very structure.

---

[11]Cf. Fergusson's analysis of *Bérénice:* "The scenes of dialogue correspond to the agons; but the polite exchange between Arsace and Antiochus, in the first act, is far from the terrible conflict between Oedipus and Tiresias, wherein the moral beings of the antagonists are at stake. . . . [In *Bérénice*] the moral being is unmistakable and impossible to lose while the stage life continues at all . . . the very possibility of the interchange depends upon the authority of reason, which secures the moral being in any contingency. . . . But if the moral being is *ex hypothesi* secure, . . . there cannot be a pathos in the Sophoclean sense at all." (*Op. cit.*, p. 52.)

There is a close relation between humor and the "sense of life," and several people have tried to analyze it in order to find the basis of that characteristically human function, laughter; the chief weakness in their attempts has been, I think, that they have all started with the question: What sort of thing makes us laugh? Certainly laughter is often evoked by ideas, cognitions, fancies; it accompanies specific emotions such as disdain, and sometimes the feeling of pleasure; but we also laugh when we are tickled (which may not be pleasurable at all), and in hysterics. Those predominantly physiological causes bear no direct relation to humor; neither, for that matter, do some kinds of pleasure. Humor is one of the causes of laughter.

Marcel Pagnol, who published his theory of laughter in a little book entitled *Notes sur le rire,* remarks that his predecessors—he names particularly Bergson, Fabre, and Mélinand—all sought the source of laughter in funny things or situations, i.e. in nature, whereas it really lies in the subject who laughs. Laughter always—without exception—betokens a sudden sense of superiority. "Laughter is a song of triumph," he says. "It expresses the laugher's sudden discovery of his own momentary superiority over the person he laughs at." This, he maintains, "explains all bursts of laughter in all times and all countries," and lets us dispense with all classifications of laughter by different kinds or causes: "One cannot classify or arrange in categories the radii of a circle."[12]

Yet he proceeds directly to divide laughter into "positive" and "negative" kinds, according to its social or antisocial inspiration. This indicates that we are still dealing with *ludicrous situations,* though these situations always involve the person to whom they are ludicrous, so it may be said that "the source of the comical is in the laugher."[13] The situation, moreover, is something the subject must discover, that is, laughter requires a conceptual element; on that M. Pagnol agrees with Bergson, Mélinand, and Fabre. Whether, according to Bergson's much-debated view, we see living beings following the law of mechanism, or see absurdity in midst of plausibility as Mélinand says, or, as Fabre has it, create a

---

[12]*Notes sur le rire*, p. 41. His argumentation is, unfortunately, not as good as his ideas, and finally leads him to include the song of the nightingale and the rooster's crow as forms of laughter.

[13]*Ibid.*, p. 17.

confusion only to dispel it suddenly, we feel our own superiority in de-
tecting the irrational element; more particularly, we feel superior to
those who perform mechanical actions, introduce absurdities, or make
confusions. Therefore M. Pagnol claims that his definition of the laughable applies to all these supposedly typical situations.

It probably does; but it is still too narrow. *What is laughable* does
not explain the nature of laughter, any more than what is rational explains the nature of reason. The ultimate source of laughter is physiological, and the various situations in which it arises are simply its normal
or abnormal stimuli.

Laughter, or the tendency to laugh (the reaction may stop short of
the actual respiratory spasm, and affect only the facial muscles, or even
meet with complete inhibition) seems to arise from a surge of vital feeling. This surge may be quite small, just so it be sudden enough to be
felt distinctly; but it may also be great, and not particularly swift, and
reach a marked climax, at which point we laugh or smile with joy. Laughter is not a simple overt act, as the single word suggests; it is the spectacular end of a complex process. As speech is the culmination of a mental
activity, laughter is a culmination of feeling—the crest of a wave of felt
vitality.

A sudden sense of superiority entails such a "lift" of vital feeling. But
the "lift" may occur without self-flattery, too; we need not be making
fun of anyone. A baby will laugh uproariously at a toy that is made to
appear suddenly, again and again, over the edge of the crib or the back
of a chair. It would take artful interpretation to demonstrate that this
fulfillment of his tense expectation makes him feel superior. Superior to
whom? The doll? A baby of eight or nine months is not socialized enough
yet to think: "There, I knew you were coming!" and believe that the
doll couldn't fool him. Such self-applause requires language, and enough
experience to estimate probabilities. The baby laughs because his wish
is gratified; not because he believes the doll obeyed his wishing, but
simply because the suspense is broken, and his energies are released. The
sudden pleasure raises his general feeling tone, so he laughs.

In so-called "gallows humor"—the harsh laugh in distress—the "lift"
of vital feeling is simply a flash of self-assertion. Something similar probably causes the mirthless laughter of hysterics: in the disorganized re-

sponse of a hysterical person, the sense of vitality breaks through fear and depression spasmodically, so that it causes explosive laughter, sometimes alternating with sobs and tears.

Laughter is, indeed, a more elementary thing than humor. We often laugh without finding any person, object, or situation funny. People laugh for joy in active sport, in dancing, in greeting friends; in returning a smile, one acknowledges another person's worth instead of flaunting one's own superiority and finding him funny.

But all these causes of laughter or its reduced form, smiling, which operate directly on us, belong to actual life. In comedy the spectator's laugh has only one legitimate source: his appreciation of humor in the piece. He does not laugh with the characters, not even at them, but at their acts—at their situations, their doings, their expressions, often at their dismay. M. Pagnol holds that we laugh at the characters directly, and regards that as a corroboration of his theory: our pleasure in the comic theater lies in watching people to whom we feel superior.[14]

There is, however, one serious defect in that view, namely that it supposes the spectator to be aware of himself as a being in the same "world" as the characters. To compare them, even subconsciously, to himself he must give up his psychical Distance and feel himself copresent with them, as one reads an anecdotal news item as something apart from one's own life but still in the actual world, and is moved to say: "How could she do such a thing! Imagine being so foolish!" If he experiences such a reaction in the theater, it is something quite aside from his perception of the play as a poetic fabrication; he has lost, for the moment, his Distance, and feels himself inside the picture.

Humor, then, would be a by-product of comedy, not a structural element in it. And if laughter were elicited thus by the way, it should not make any difference to the value of the work where it occurred; a stage accident, a bad actor who made every amateur actor in the audience feel superior, should serve as well as any clever line or funny situation in the play to amuse the audience. We do, in fact, laugh at such failures; but we do not praise the comedy for that entertainment. In a good play the "laughs" are poetic elements. Its humor as well as its pathos belongs

---

[14]*Ibid.*, p. 92. There is further discussion of this problem at the end of the present chapter.

to the virtual life, and the delight we take in it is delight in something created for our perception, not a direct stimulus to our own feelings. It is true that the comical figures are often buffoons, simpletons, clowns; but such characters are almost always sympathetic, and although they are knocked around and abused, they are indestructible, and eternally self-confident and good-humored.

The buffoon is, in fact, an important comic personage, especially in folk theater. He is essentially a folk character, that has persisted through the more sophisticated and literary stages of comedy as Harlequin, Pierrot, the Persian Karaguez, the Elizabethan jester or fool, the *Vidusaka* of Sanskrit drama; but in the humbler theatrical forms that entertained the poor and especially the peasantry everywhere before the movies came, the buffoon had a more vigorous existence as Hans Wurst, as Punch of the puppet show, the clown of pantomime, the Turkish Karagöz (borrowed from Persian tradition) who belongs only to the shadow play.[15] These anciently popular personages show what the buffoon really is: the indomitable living creature fending for itself, tumbling and stumbling (as the clown physically illustrates) from one situation into another, getting into scrape after scrape and getting out again, with or without a thrashing. He is the personified *élan vital;* his chance adventures and misadventures, without much plot, though often with bizarre complications, his absurd expectations and disappointments, in fact his whole improvised existence has the rhythm of primitive, savage, if not animalian life, coping with a world that is forever taking new uncalculated turns, frustrating, but exciting. He is neither a good man nor a bad one, but is genuinely amoral,—now triumphant, now worsted and rueful, but in his ruefulness and dismay he is funny, because his energy is really unimpaired and each failure prepares the situation for a new fantastic move.[16] The most forthright of these infantilists is the English Punch, who carries out every impulse by force and speed of action—chastises his wife, throws his child out of the window, beats the policeman, and finally spears the devil and carries him out triumphantly on a pitchfork. Punch is not a real buffoon, he is too successful; his appeal is probably a sub-

---

[15]See N. N. Martinovitch, *The Turkish Theater, passim.*

[16]Falstaff is a perfect example of the buffoon raised to a human "character" in comedy.

jective one, to people's repressed desires for general vengeance, revolt, and destruction. He is psychologically interesting, but really a degenerated and stereotyped figure, and as such he has little artistic value because he has no further poetic progeny. What has caused his persistence in a single, mainly vulgar, and not particularly witty role, I do not know, nor is this the place to investigate it; but when he first appeared in England as Punchinello, borrowed from the Italian marionettes, he was still the pure comic protagonist. According to a statement of R. M. Wheeler in the *Encyclopaedia Britannica,* which we may, presumably, take as authority, "The older Punchinello was far less restricted in his actions and circumstances than his modern successor. He fought with allegorical figures representing want and weariness as well as with his wife and with the police, was on intimate terms with the patriarchs and the seven champions of Christendom, sat on the lap of the queen of Sheba, had kings and dukes for his companions, and cheated the Inquisition as well as the common hangman."

The high company this original Punch keeps is quite in accordance with the dignified settings in which he makes his appearance. From the same article we learn that the earliest recorded appearances of Punch in England were in a puppet play of the Creation of the World, and in another representing the Deluge. To the modern, solemn religious mind, scriptural stories may seem a strange context for such a secular character, and perhaps this apparent incongruity has led to the widespread belief that the clown in modern comedy derives from the devil of mediaeval miracle plays.[17] The devil is, of course, quite at home in sacred realms. It is not impossible that this relation between devil and fool (in his various forms as clown, jester, freak) really holds; yet if it does, that is a historical accident, due to the peculiar Christian conception that identifies the devil with the flesh, and sin with lust. Such a conception brings the spirit of life and the father of all evil, which are usually poles apart, very close together. For there is no denying that the Fool is a red-blooded fellow; he is, in fact, close to the animal world; in French tradition he wears a cockscomb on his cap, and Punchinello's nose is probably the residue of a beak. He is all motion, whim, and impulse—the "libido" itself.

---

[17]See the article "Clown" (unsigned) in the *Encyclopaedia Britannica.*

But he is probably older than the Christian devil, and does not need any connection with that worthy to let him into religious precincts. He has always been close to the gods. If we view him as the representative of mankind in its struggle with the world, it is clear at once why his antics and impertinences are often an integral part of religious rites— why, for instance, the clowning orders in Pueblo society were held in high honor:[18] the clown is Life, he is the Will, he is the Brain, and by the same token he is nature's fool. From the primitive exuberant religions that celebrate fertility and growth he tends ever to come into the ascetic cults, and tumble and juggle in all innocence before the Virgin.

In comedy the stock figure of the buffoon is an obvious device for building up the comic rhythm, i.e. the image of Fortune. But in the development of the art he does not remain the central figure that he was in the folk theater; the lilt and balance of life which he introduced, once it has been grasped, is rendered in more subtle poetic inventions involving plausible characters, and an *intrigue* (as the French call it) that makes for a coherent, over-all, dramatic action. Sometimes he remains as a jester, servant, or other subsidiary character whose comments, silly or witty or shrewd, serve to point the essentially comic pattern of the action, where the verisimilitude and complexity of the stage-life threaten to obscure its basic form. Those points are normally "laughs"; and that brings us to the aesthetic problem of the joke in comedy.

Because comedy abstracts, and reincarnates for our perception, the motion and rhythm of living, it enhances our vital feeling, much as the presentation of space in painting enhances our awareness of visual space. The virtual life on the stage is not diffuse and only half felt, as actual life usually is: virtual life, always moving visibly into the future, is intensified, speeded up, exaggerated; the exhibition of vitality rises to a breaking point, to mirth and laughter. We laugh in the theater at small incidents and drolleries which would hardly rate a chuckle off-stage. It is not for such psychological reasons as that we go there to be amused, nor that we are bound by rules of politeness to hide our hilarity, but these trifles at which we laugh are really funnier *where they occur* than they would

---

[18]On the secret societies of clowns, see F. H. Cushing, *Zuni Creation Myths* (Report of the Bureau of American Ethnology, 1892), concerning the order of "Koyemshi" ("Mudheads").

be elsewhere; they are *employed* in the play, not merely brought in casually. They occur where the tension of dialogue or other action reaches a high point. As thought breaks into speech—as the wave breaks into foam—vitality breaks into humor.

Humor is the brilliance of drama, a sudden heightening of the vital rhythm. A good comedy, therefore, builds up to every laugh; a performance that has been filled up with jokes at the indiscretion of the comedian or of his writer may draw a long series of laughs, yet leave the spectator without any clear impression of a very funny play. The laughs, moreover, are likely to be of a peculiar sameness, almost perfunctory, the formal recognition of a timely "gag."

The amoral character of the comic protagonist goes through the whole range of what may be called the comedy of laughter. Even the most civilized products of this art—plays that George Meredith would honor with the name of "comedy," because they provoke "thoughtful laughter" —do not present moral distinctions and issues, but only the ways of wisdom and of folly. Aristophanes, Menander, Molière—practically the only authors this most exacting of critics admitted as truly comic poets —are not moralists, yet they do not flaunt or deprecate morality; they have, literally, "no use" for moral principles—that is, they do not use them. Meredith, like practically all his contemporaries, labored under the belief that poetry must teach society lessons, and that comedy was valuable for what it revealed concerning the social order.[19] He tried hard to hold its exposé of foibles and vindication of common sense to an ethical standard, yet in his very efforts to justify its amoral personages he only admitted their amoral nature, and their simple relish for life, as when he

---

[19]His well-known little work is called *An Essay on Comedy, and the Uses of the Comic Spirit*. These uses are entirely non-artistic. Praising the virtues of "good sense" (which is whatever has survival value in the eyes of society), he says: "The French have a school of stately comedy to which they can fly for renovation whenever they have fallen away from it; and their having such a school is the main reason why, as John Stuart Mill pointed out, they know men and women more accurately than we do." (Pp. 13–14.) And a few pages later: "The *Femmes Savantes* is a capital instance of the uses of comedy in teaching the world to understand what ails it. The French had felt the burden of this new nonsense [the fad of academic learning, new after the fad of excessive nicety and precision in speech, that had marked the *Precieuses*]; but they had to see the comedy several times before they were consoled in their suffering by seeing the cause of it exposed." (Pp. 19–20.)

said: "The heroines of comedy are like women of the world, not necessarily heartless from being clear-sighted. . . . Comedy is an exhibition
of their battle with men, and that of men with them. . . ."

There it is, in a nutshell: the contest of men and women—the most
universal contest, humanized, in fact civilized, yet still the primitive
joyful challenge, the self-preservation and self-assertion whose progress
is the comic rhythm.

This rhythm is capable of the most diverse presentations. That is
why the art of comedy grows, in every culture, from casual beginnings
—miming, clowning, sometimes erotic dancing—to some special and distinctive dramatic art, and sometimes to many forms of it within one
culture, yet never seems to repeat its works. It may produce a tradition
of dignified drama, springing from solemn ritual, even funereal, its emotional movement too slow to culminate in humor at any point; then other
means have to be found to lend it glamor and intensity. The purest heroic
comedy is likely to have no humorous passages at all, but to employ the
jester only in an ornamental way reminiscent of tragedy, and in fact to
use many techniques of tragedy. It may even seem to transcend the
amoral comic pattern by presenting virtuous heroes and heroines. But
their virtue is a formal affair, a social asset; as Deane remarked of the
French classic heroes,[20] they do not submit to ordinary morality; their
morality is "heroism," which is essentially strength, will, and endurance
in face of the world. Neither have the divinities of oriental drama any
"ordinary morality"; they are perfect in virtue when they slay and when
they spare, their goodness is glory, and their will is law. They are Super-
man, the Hero, and the basic pattern of their conquest over enemies whose
only wickedness is resistance, is the amoral life pattern of fencing with
the devil—man against death.

Humor, then, is not the essence of comedy, but only one of its most
useful and natural elements. It is also its most problematical element,
because it elicits from the spectators what appears to be a direct emotional response to persons on the stage, in no wise different from their
response to actual people: amusement, laughter.

The phenomenon of laughter in the theater brings into sharp focus the
whole question of the distinction between emotion symbolically presented,

---

[20]Cf. *supra*, p. 336.

and emotion directly stimulated; it is, indeed, a *pons asinorum* of the theory that this distinction is radical, because it presents us with what is probably the most difficult example. The audience's laugh at a good play is, of course, self-expressive, and betokens a "lift" of vital feeling in each laughing person. Yet it has a different character from laughter in conversation, or in the street when the wind carries off a hat with the "hair-do" attached, or in the "laugh house" at an amusement park where the willing victims meet distorting mirrors and things that say "boo." All these laughs of daily life are direct responses to separate stimuli; they may be as sporadic as the jokes bandied in a lively company, or may be strung along purposely like the expected and yet unforeseen events in the "laugh house," yet they remain so many personal encounters that seem funny only if one is in the mood for them. Sometimes we reject witticisms and are bored with tricks and clowning.

It is different in the theater: the play possesses us and breaks our mood. It does not change it, but simply abrogates it. Even if we come in a jovial mood, this does not notably increase our appreciation of humor in the play; for the humor in a good comedy does not strike us directly. What strikes us directly is the dramatic illusion, the stage action as it evolves; and the joke, instead of being as funny as our personal response would make it, seems as funny as its occurrence in the total action makes it. A very mild joke in just the right place may score a big laugh. The action culminates in a witticism, an absurdity, a surprise; the spectators laugh. But after their outburst there is not the letdown that follows an ordinary laugh, because the play moves on without the breathing spell we usually give our own thought and feeling after a joke. The action carries over from one laugh to another, sometimes fairly far spaced; people are laughing *at the play*, not at a string of jokes.

Humor in comedy (as, indeed, in all humorous art) belongs to the work, not to our actual surroundings; and if it is borrowed from the actual world, its appearance in the work is what really makes it funny. Political or topical allusions in a play amuse us because they are *used*, not because they refer to something intrinsically very comical. This device of playing with things from actual life is so sure to bring laughs that the average comic writer and improvising comedian overdoes it to the point of artistic ruin; hence the constant flood of "shows" that have immense popularity but no dramatic core, so they do not outlive the hour of their passing allusions.

Real comedy sets up in the audience a sense of general exhilaration, because it presents the very image of "livingness" and the perception of it is exciting. Whatever the story may be, it takes the form of a temporary triumph over the surrounding world, complicated, and thus stretched out, by an involved succession of coincidences. This illusion of life, the stage-life, has a rhythm of feeling which is not transmitted to us by separate successive stimulations, but rather by our perception of its entire *Gestalt*—a whole world moving into its own future. The "livingness" of the human world is abstracted, composed, and presented to us; with it the high points of the composition that are illuminated by humor. They belong to the life we see, and our laugh belongs to the theatrical exhilaration, which is universally human and impersonal.[21] It is not what the joke happens to mean to us that measures our laughter, but what the joke does in the play.

For this reason we tend to laugh at things in the theater that we might not find funny in actuality. The technique of comedy often has to clear the way for its humor by forestalling any backsliding into "the world of anxious interest and selfish solicitude." It does this by various devices—absurd coincidences, stereotyped expressions of feeling (like the clown's wails of dismay), a quickened pace of action, and other unrealistic effects which serve to emphasize the comic structure. As Professor Fergusson said, "when we understand a comic convention we see the play with godlike omniscience. . . . When Scaramouche gets a beating, we do not feel the blows, but the idea of a beating, at that moment, strikes us as funny. If the beating is too realistic, if it breaks the light rhythm of thought, the fun is gone, and the comedy destroyed."[22]

That "light rhythm of thought" is the rhythm of life; and the reason it is "light" is that all creatures love life, and the symbolization of its impetus and flow makes us really aware of it. The conflict with the world whereby a living being maintains its own complex organic unity is a delightful encounter; the world is as promising and alluring as it is dangerous and opposed. The feeling of comedy is a feeling of heightened

---

[21]The reader is referred to the Hindu view mentioned in Chap. 17, p. 323.
[22]*Op. cit.*, pp. 178–179.

vitality, challenged wit and will, engaged in the great game with Chance. The real antagonist is the World. Since the personal antagonist in the play is really that great challenger, he is rarely a complete villain; he is interesting, entertaining, his defeat is a hilarious success but not his destruction. There is no permanent defeat and permanent human triumph except in tragedy; for nature must go on if life goes on, and the world that presents all obstacles also supplies the zest of life. In comedy, therefore, there is a general trivialization of the human battle. Its dangers are not real disasters, but embarrassment and loss of face. That is why comedy is "light" compared to tragedy, which exhibits an exactly opposite tendency to general exaggeration of issues and personalities.

The same impulse that drove people, even in prehistoric times, to enact fertility rites and celebrate all phases of their biological existence, sustains their eternal interest in comedy. It is in the nature of comedy to be erotic, risqué, and sensuous if not sensual, impious, and even wicked. This assures it a spontaneous emotional interest, yet a dangerous one: for it is easy and tempting to command an audience by direct stimulation of feeling and fantasy, not by artistic power. But where the formulation of feeling is really achieved, it probably reflects the whole development of mankind and man's world, for feeling is the intaglio image of reality. The sense of precariousness that is the typical tension of light comedy was undoubtedly developed in the eternal struggle with chance that every farmer knows only too well—with weather, blights, beasts, birds and beetles. The embarrassments, perplexities and mounting panic which characterize that favorite genre, comedy of manners, may still reflect the toils of ritual and taboo that complicated the caveman's existence. Even the element of aggressiveness in comic action serves to develop a fundamental trait of the comic rhythm—the deep cruelty of it, as all life feeds on life. There is no biological truth that feeling does not reflect, and that good comedy, therefore, will not be prone to reveal.

But the fact that the rhythm of comedy is the basic rhythm of life does not mean that biological existence is the "deeper meaning" of all its themes, and that to understand the play is to interpret all the characters as symbols and the story as a parable, a disguised rite of spring or fertility magic, performed four hundred and fifty times on Broadway. The stock characters are probably symbolic both in origin and in appeal.

There are such independently symbolic factors, or residues of them, in all the arts,[23] but their value for art lies in the degree to which their significance can be "swallowed" by the single symbol, the art work. Not the derivation of personages and situations, but of the rhythm of "felt life" that the poet puts upon them, seems to me to be of artistic importance: the essential comic feeling, which is the sentient aspect of organic unity, growth, and self-preservation.

---

[23]E.g., the symbolization of the zodiac in some sacred architecture, of our bodily orientation in the picture plane, or of walking measure, a primitive measure of actual time, in music. But a study of such non-artistic symbolic functions would require a monograph.

Chapter nineteen

THE GREAT DRAMATIC FORMS:
THE TRAGIC RHYTHM

As comedy presents the vital rhythm of self-preservation, tragedy exhibits that of self-consummation.

The lilting advance of the eternal life process, indefinitely maintained or temporarily lost and restored, is the great general vital pattern that we exemplify from day to day. But creatures that are destined, sooner or later, to die—that is, all individuals that do not pass alive into new generations, like jellyfish and algae—hold the balance of life only precariously, in the frame of a total movement that is quite different; the movement from birth to death. Unlike the simple metabolic process, the deathward advance of their individual lives has a series of stations that are not repeated; growth, maturity, decline. That is the tragic rhythm.

Tragedy is a cadential form. Its crisis is always the turn toward an absolute close. This form reflects the basic structure of personal life, and therewith of feeling when life is viewed as a whole. It is that attitude —"the tragic sense of life," as Unamuno called it—that is objectified and brought before our eyes in tragedy. But in drama it is not presented as Unamuno presents it, namely by an intellectual realization of impending death which we are constitutionally unable to accept and therefore counter with an irrational belief in our personal immortality, in "immortalizing" rites and supernatural grace.[1] Irrationalism is not insight,

---

[1] See his *The Tragic Sense of Life, passim.* Unamuno's feelings are strong and natural; his aphorisms are often poetic and memorable. With his philosophical assertions, however, one cannot take issue, because he prides himself on being inconsistent, on the ground that "life is irrational," "truth is not logical," etc. Consistency of statements he regards as a mark of their falsity. Like some exasperating ladies, who claim "a woman's right to be inconsistent," he cannot, therefore, be worsted in argument, but—also like them—he cannot be taken seriously.

but despair, a direct recognition of instincts, needs, and therewithal of one's mental impotence. A "belief" that defies intellectual convictions is a frantically defended lie. That defense may constitute a great tragic theme, but it is not itself a poetic expression of "the tragic sense of life"; it is actual, pathetic expression, springing from an emotional conflict.

Tragedy dramatizes human life as potentiality and fulfillment. Its virtual future, or Destiny, is therefore quite different from that created in comedy. Comic Destiny is Fortune—what the world will bring, and the man will take or miss, encounter or escape; tragic Destiny is what the man brings, and the world will demand of him. That is his Fate.

What he brings is his potentiality: his mental, moral and even physical powers, his powers to act and suffer. Tragic action is the realization of all his possibilities, which he unfolds and exhausts in the course of the drama. His human nature is his Fate. Destiny conceived as Fate is, therefore, not capricious, like Fortune, but is predetermined. Outward events are merely the occasions for its realization.

"His human nature," however, does not refer to his *generally* human character; I do not mean to say that a tragic hero is to be regarded as primarily a symbol for mankind. What the poet creates is a personality; and the more individual and powerful that personality is, the more extraordinary and overwhelming will be the action. Since the protagonist is the chief agent, his relation to the action is obvious; and since the course of the action is the "fable" or "plot" of the play, it is also obvious that creating the characters is not something apart from building the plot, but is an integral portion of it. The agents are prime elements in the action; but the action is the play itself, and artistic elements are always for the sake of the whole. That was, I think, what prompted Aristotle to say: "Tragedy is essentially an imitation[2] not of persons but of action and life, of happiness and misery. All human happiness or misery takes the form of action; the end for which we live is a certain kind of activity, not a quality. Character gives us qualities, but it is in our actions —what we do—that we are happy or the reverse. In a play accordingly they do not act in order to portray the Characters; they include the

---

[2]"Imitation" is used by Aristotle in much the same sense in which I use "semblance." I have avoided his word because it stresses similitude to actuality rather than abstraction from actuality.

Characters for the sake of the action. So that it is the action in it, i.e. its Fable or Plot, that is the end and purpose of the tragedy; and the end is everywhere the chief thing."[3] This "end" is the work as such. The protagonist and all characters that support him are introduced that we may see the fulfillment of his Fate, which is simply the complete realization of his individual "human nature."

The idea of personal Fate was mythically conceived long before the relation of life history to character was discursively understood. The mythical tradition of Greece treated the fate of its "heroes"—the personalities springing from certain great, highly individualized families—as a mysterious power inherent in the world rather than in the man and his ancestry; it was conceived as a private incubus bestowed on him at birth by a vengeful deity, or even through a curse pronounced by a human being. Sometimes no such specific cause of his peculiar destiny is given at all; but an oracle foretells what he is bound to do. It is interesting to note that this conception of Fate usually centers in the mysterious predictability of *acts* someone is to perform. The occasions of the acts are not foretold; the world will provide them.

For the development of tragedy, such determination of the overt acts without circumstances and motives furnished an ideal starting point, for it constrained the poets to invent characters whose actions would issue naturally in the required fateful deeds. The oracular prophecy, then, became an intensifying symbol of the necessity that was really given with the agent's personality; the "fable" being just one possible way the world might elicit his complete self-realization in endeavor and error and discovery, passion and punishment, to the limit of his powers. The prime example of this passage from the mythical idea of Fate to the dramatic creation of Fate as the protagonist's natural, personal destiny is, of course, the *Oedipus Tyrannus* of Sophocles. With that tremendous piece of self-assertion, self-divination and self-exhaustion, the "Great Tradition" of tragedy was born in Europe.

There is another mythical conception of Fate that is not a forerunner of tragedy, but possibly of some kinds of comedy: that is the idea of Fate as the will of supernatural powers, perhaps long decreed, perhaps spontaneous and arbitrary. It is the "Fate" of the true fatalist, who takes

---

[3]*De Poetica,* chap. 6, II (1450a), translation by W. R. Roberts.

no great care of his life because he deems it entirely in the hand of Allah (or some other God), who will slay or spare at his pleasure no matter what one does. That is quite a different notion from the "oracular" Fate of Greek mythology; the will of a god who gives and takes away, casts down or raises up, for inscrutable reasons of his own, is Kismet, and that is really a myth of Fortune.[4] Kismet is what a person encounters, not what he is. Both conceptions often exist side by side. The Scotsman who has to "dree his weird" believes nonetheless that his fortunes from moment to moment are in the hands of Providence. Macbeth's Weird Sisters were perfectly acceptable to a Christian audience. Even in the ancient lore of our fairy tales, the Sleeping Beauty is destined to prick herself—that is, she has a personal destiny. In Greek tradition, on the other hand, where the notion of "oracular Fate" was so generally entertained that the Oracle was a public institution, Fate as the momentary decree of a ruling Power is represented in the myth of the Norns, who spin the threads of human lives and cut them where they list; the Three Fates are as despotic and capricious as Allah, and what they spin is, really, Kismet.

Tragedy can arise and flourish only where people are aware of individual life as an end in itself, and as a measure of other things. In tribal cultures where the individual is still so closely linked with his family that not only society but even he himself regards his existence as a communal value, which may be sacrificed at any time for communal ends, the development of personality is not a consciously appreciated life pattern. Similarly, where men believe that Karma, or the tally of their deeds, may be held over for recompense or expiation in another earthly life, their current incarnation cannot be seen as a self-sufficient whole in which their entire potentialities are to be realized. Therefore genuine tragedy—drama exhibiting "the tragic rhythm of action," as Professor Fergusson has called it[5]—is a specialized form of art, with problems and devices of its own.

---

[4] Cf. N. N. Martinovitch, *The Turkish Theatre*, p. 36: "According to Islamic speculation, man has almost no influence on the development of his own fate. Allah is sovereign, doing as he likes and accounting to no one. And the screen of the haial [the comic shadow theater] is the dramatization of this speculative concept of the world."

[5] In *The Idea of a Theater*, especially p. 18.

The word "rhythm," which I have used freely with respect to drama, may seem a question-begging word, borrowed from the realm of physiology —where indeed the basic vital functions are generally rhythmic—and carried over somewhat glibly to the realm of conscious acts, which, for the most part—and certainly the most interesting part—are not repetitive. But it is precisely the *rhythm* of dramatic action that makes drama "a poetry of the theater," and not an imitation (in the usual, not the Aristotelian sense) or make-believe of practical life. As Hebbel said, "In the hand of the poet, Becoming must always be a passage from *form* to *form* [von *Gestalt* zu *Gestalt*], it must never appear, like amorphous clay, chaotic and confused in our sight, but must seem somehow like a perfected thing."[6] The analysis and definition of rhythmic structure, given in Chapter 8 with reference to musical forms,[7] may be applied without distortion or strain to the organization of elements in any play that achieves "living" form.

A dramatic act is a commitment. It creates a situation in which the agent or agents must necessarily make a further move; that is, it motivates a subsequent act (or acts). The situation, which is the completion of a given act, is already the impetus to another—as, in running, the footfall that catches our weight at the end of one bound already sends us forward to land on the other foot. The bounds need not be alike, but proportional, which means that the impetus of any specially great leap must have been prepared and gathered somewhere, and any sudden diminution be balanced by some motion that carries off the driving force. Dramatic acts are analogously connected with each other so that each one directly or indirectly motivates what follows it.[8] In this way a genuine rhythm of action is set up, which is not simple like that of a physical repetitive process (e.g. running, breathing), but more often intricate, even deceptive, and, of course, not given primarily to one particular sense, but to the imagination through whatever sense we employ to perceive and evaluate action; the same general rhythm of action appears in a play

---

[6]Friedrich Hebbel, *Tagebücher,* collected in Bernhard Münz's *Hebbel als Denker* (1913). See p. 182.

[7]See pp. 126–129.

[8]An act may be said to motivate further acts indirectly if it does so through a total situation it helps to create; the small acts of psychological import that merely create personality are of this sort.

whether we read it or hear it read, enact it ourselves or see it performed. That rhythm is the "commanding form" of the play; it springs from the poet's original conception of the "fable," and dictates the major divisions of the work, the light or heavy style of its presentation, the intensity of the highest feeling and most violent act, the great or small number of characters, and the degrees of their development. The total action is a cumulative form; and because it is constructed by a rhythmic treatment of its elements, it appears to *grow* from its beginnings. That is the playwright's creation of "organic form."

The tragic rhythm, which is the pattern of a life that grows, flourishes, and declines, is abstracted by being transferred from that natural activity to the sphere of a characteristically human action, where it is exemplified in mental and emotional growth, maturation, and the final relinquishment of power. In that relinquishment lies the hero's true "heroism"—the vision of life as accomplished, that is, life in its entirety, the sense of fulfillment that lifts him above his defeat.

A remarkable expression of this idea of tragedy may be found in the same book from which I borrowed, a few paragraphs above, the phrase, "the tragic rhythm of action." Speaking of Hamlet, Professor Fergusson observes: "In Act V . . . he feels that his role, all but the very last episode, has been played. . . . He is content, now, to let the fated end come as it will. . . . One could say that he feels the poetic rightness of his own death. . . .

"However one may interpret it, when his death comes it 'feels right,' the only possible end for the play. . . . We are certainly intended to feel that Hamlet, however darkly and uncertainly he worked, had discerned the way to be obedient to his deepest values, and accomplished some sort of purgatorial progress for himself and Denmark."[9]

"The second scene of Act V," the critique continues, "with the duel between Hamlet and Laertes, shows the denouements of all the intrigues in the play. . . . But these events, which literally end the narratives in the play, and bring Claudius' regime to its temporal end, tell us nothing new but the fact: that the sentence, which fate or providence pronounced long since, has now been executed. It is the pageantry, the

---

[9] *Op. cit.*, pp. 132–133. "To be obedient to his deepest values" is nothing else than to realize his own potentialities, fulfill his true destiny.

ceremonial mummery, in short the virtual character of this last scene which makes us feel it as the final epiphany. . . ."[10]

Tragic drama is so designed that the protagonist grows mentally, emotionally, or morally, by the demand of the action, which he himself initiated, to the complete exhaustion of his powers, the limit of his possible development. He spends himself in the course of the one dramatic action. This is, of course, a tremendous foreshortening of life; instead of undergoing the physical and psychical, many-sided, long process of an actual biography, the tragic hero lives and matures in some particular respect; his entire being is concentrated in one aim, one passion, one conflict and ultimate defeat. For this reason the prime agent of tragedy is heroic; his character, the unfolding situation, the scene, even though ostensibly familiar and humble, are all exaggerated, charged with more feeling than comparable actualities would possess.[11] This intensification is necessary to achieve and sustain the "form in suspense" that is even more important in tragic drama than in comic, because the comic denouement, not marking an absolute close, needs only to restore a balance, but the tragic ending must recapitulate the whole action to be a visible fulfillment of a destiny that was implicit in the beginning. This device, which may be called "dramatic exaggeration," is reminiscent of "epic exaggeration," and may have been adopted quite unconsciously with the epic themes of ancient tragedy. But that does not mean that it is an accidental factor, a purely historical legacy from an older poetic tradition; inherited conventions do not maintain themselves long in any art unless they serve its own purposes. They may have their old *raison d'être* in new art forms, or take on entirely new functions, but as sheer trappings—traditional requirements—they would be discarded by the first genius who found no use for them.

Drama is not psychology, nor (though the critical literature tends to make it seem so) is it moral philosophy. It offers no discourse on the hero's or heroine's native endowments, to let us estimate at any stage

---

[10]*Op. cit.*, p. 138.

[11]As Robert Edmond Jones has put it: "Great drama does not deal with cautious people. Its heroes are tyrants, outcasts, wanderers. From Prometheus, the first of them all, the thief who stole the divine fire from heaven, these protagonists are all passionate, excessive, violent, terrible. 'Doom eager,' the Icelandic saga calls them." *The Dramatic Imagination*, p. 42.

in the action how near they must be to exhaustion. The action itself must reveal the limit of the protagonist's powers and mark the end of his self-realization. And so, indeed, it does: the turning point of the play is the situation he cannot resolve, where he makes his "tragic error" or exhibits his "tragic weakness." He is led by his own action and its repercussions in the world to respond with more and more competence, more and more daring to a constantly gathering challenge; so his character "grows," i.e. he unfolds his will and knowledge and passion, as the situation grows. His career is not change of personality, but maturation. When he reaches his limit of mental and emotional development, the crisis occurs; then comes the defeat, either by death or, as in many modern tragedies, by hopelessness that is the equivalent of death, a "death of the soul," that ends the career.

It has been reiterated so often that the hero of tragedy is a strong man with one weakness, a good man with one fault, that a whole ethics of tragedy has grown up around the significance of that single flaw. Chapters upon chapters—even books—have been written on the required mixture of good and evil in his character, to make him command pity and yet make his downfall not repugnant to "our moral sense." Critics and philosophers, from Aristotle to Croce, have written about the spectator's acceptance of the hero's fate as a recognition of the moral order he has defied or ignored, the triumph of justice the hero himself is supposed to accept in his final "conciliation" or "epiphany." The restoration of the great moral order through suffering is looked upon as the Fate he has to fulfill. He must be imperfect to break the moral law, but fundamentally good, i.e. striving for perfection, in order to achieve his moral salvation in sacrifice, renunciation, death.

All this concern with the philosophical and ethical significance of the hero's sufferings, however, leads away from the *artistic* significance of the play, to discursive ideas about life, character, and the world. At once we are faced with the usual dilemma of the critic who sees art as a representation of actual life, and an art form as a *Weltanschauung*: not every work of the genre can really be said to express the *Weltanschauung* that is supposed to characterize it, nor to give us the same general picture of the world, such as the "moral order" in which justice is inevitably done or the amoral "cosmic order" in which man is a plaything of forces beyond his control. Then the critic may come to the despairing conclusion that the genre cannot be defined, but is really just a name that changes its essential meaning from age to age. No less an authority than Ashley Thorndike decided that tragedy is really indefinable; one can trace the historical evolution of each conception, but not the defining attribute that runs through them all and brings them justly under one name. The only features that he found common to all tragedies were representation of "painful and destructive actions," and "criticism of life."[12] Either of these could, of course, occur in other art forms, too. A. C. Bradley, in his excellent *Shakespearean Tragedy,* points out that Shakespeare did not, like the Greek tragedians, postulate a superhuman power determining men's actions and accidents, nor a special Nemesis, invoked by past crimes, belonging to certain families or persons; he claims, in fact, to find no representation of Fate in Shakespeare.[13] Even justice, he holds, is not illustrated there, because the disasters men bring upon themselves are not proportioned to their sins; but something one might call a "moral order," an order not of right and wrong, but at least of good and evil. Accident plays its part, but in the main the agents ride for the fall they take.[14] Edgar Stoll, exactly to the contrary, maintains that the action in Shakespeare's tragedies "does not at bottom develop out of character."[15] One could go on almost indefinitely in citing examples of contradiction or exception to the various standards of tragic action, especially the fatalistic standard.

---

[12]"Any precise and exact definition is sure to lack in comprehensiveness and veracity. . . . We seem forced to reject the possibility of any exact limitation for the dramatic species, to include as tragedies all plays presenting painful or destructive actions, to accept the leading elements of a literary tradition derived from the Greeks as indicating the common bonds between such plays in the past, but to admit that this tradition, while still powerful, is variable, uncertain, and unauthoritative." (*Tragedy,* p. 12.) At the end of the book he sets up, as the only common standard, "an unselfish, a social, a moral inquiry into life." (P. 376.)

[13]In a footnote on p. 30 he writes: "I have raised no objection to the use of the idea of fate, because it occurs so often both in conversation and in books about Shakespeare's tragedies that I must suppose it to be natural to many readers. Yet I doubt whether it would be so if Greek tragedy had never been written; and I must in candour confess that to me it does not often occur while I am reading, or when I have just read, a tragedy of Shakespeare."

[14]The discussion of justice (Lecture I, "The Substance of Tragedy," p. 5) is noteworthy especially for his recognition of the *irrelevance of the concept* to dramatic art.

[15]*Shakespeare and Other Masters,* p. 31.

The fallacy which leads to this crisscross of interpretations and opinions is the familiar one of confusing what the poet creates with what he represents. It is the fallacy of looking, not for the artistic function of everything he represents and the way he represents it, but for something that his representations are supposed to illustrate or suggest—something that belongs to life, not the play. If, then, tragedy is called an image of Fate, it is expected to illustrate the workings of Fate. But that is not necessary; it may just as well illustrate the workings of villainy, neurosis, faith, social justice, or anything else the poet finds usable to motivate a large, integral action. The myth of Fate often used in Greek tragedies was an obvious motif, as in later plays romantic love defying circumstance, or the vast consequences of a transgression. But one should not expect a major art form to be bound to a single motif, no matter in how many variations or even disguises; to reduce the many themes that may be found in tragedy, from Aeschylus to O'Neill, all to "the workings of Fate," and the many *Weltanschauungen* that may be read out of (or into) it to so many recognitions of a supernatural order, a moral order, or a pure causal order, leads only to endless sleuthing after deeper meanings, symbolic substitutions, and far-reaching implications that no playgoer could possible infer, so they would be useless in the theater.

Fate in tragedy is the created form, the virtual future as an accomplished whole. It is not the expression of a belief at all. Macbeth's fate is the structure of his tragedy, not an instance of how things happen in the world. That virtual future has the form of a completely individualized, and therefore mortal, life—a measured life, to be exhausted in a small span of time. But growth, efflorescence, and exhaustion—the prototype of Fate—is not what the play is about; it is only what the movement of the action is like. The play is about somebody's desires, acts, conflict, and defeat; however his acts are motivated, however his deeds undo him, the total action is his dramatic fate. Tragic action has the rhythm of natural life and death, but it does not refer to or illustrate them; it abstracts their dynamic form, and imprints it on entirely different matters, in a different time span—the whole self-realization may take place in days or hours instead of the decades of biological consummation—so the "tragic rhythm" stands clear of any natural occasion, and becomes a perceptible form.

The kind of art theory that measures the value of drama by the way it represents life, or by the poet's implied beliefs about life, not only leads criticism away from poetry into philosophy, religion, or social science, but also causes people to think of the protagonist as an ordinary fellow man whom they are to approve or condemn and, in either case, pity. This attitude, which is undoubtedly derived—whether rightly or mistakenly—from Aristotle, has given rise to the many moral demands on the hero's character: he must be admirable but not perfect, must command the spectators' sympathy even if he incurs their censure; they must feel his fate as their own, etc.[16]

In truth, I believe, the hero of tragedy must *interest* us all the time, but not as a person of our own acquaintance. His tragic error, crime, or other flaw is not introduced for moral reasons, but for structural purposes: it marks his limit of power. His potentialities appear on stage only as successful acts; as soon as his avowed or otherwise obvious intentions fail, or his acts recoil on him and bring him pain, his power has reached its height, he is at the end of his career. In this, of course, drama is utterly different from life. The moral failure in drama is not a normal incident, something to be lived down, presumably neither the doer's first transgression nor his last; the act that constitutes the protagonist's tragic error or guilt is the high-water mark of his life, and now the tide recedes. His "imperfection" is an artistic element: that is why a single flaw will do.

All persistent practices in art have a creative function. They may serve several ends, but the chief one is the shaping of the work. This holds not only for character traits which make a dramatic personage credible or sympathetic, but also for another much-discussed device in drama—so-called "comic relief," the introduction of trivial or humorous interludes in midst of serious, ominous, tragic action. The term "comic relief" in-

---

[16]Thorndike regarded tragedy as the highest art form, because, as he put it, "it brings home to us the images of our own sorrows, and chastens the spirit through the outpouring of our sympathies, even our horror and despair, for the misfortune of our fellows." (*Op. cit.*, p. 19.) Shortly before, he conceded that it might also give us—among other pleasures—"aesthetic delight in a masterpiece." (P. 17.)

dicates the supposed purpose of that practice: to give the audience a respite from too much emotional tension, let them have entertainment as well as "pity and fear." Here again traditional criticism rests too confidently, I think, on Aristotle's observations, which—after all—were not the insights of a playwright, but the reflections of a scientifically inclined man interested in psychology. Aristotle considered the comic interlude as a concession to human weakness; and "comic relief" has been its name ever since.

The humorous interludes in tragedy are merely moments when the comic spirit rises to the point of hilarity. Such moments may result from all sorts of poetic exigencies; the famous drunken porter in *Macbeth* makes a macabre contrast to the situation behind the door he beats upon, and is obviously introduced to heighten rather than relieve the tense secrecy of the murder.

But the most important fact about these famous touches of "comic relief" is that they always occur in plays which have a vein of comedy throughout, kept for the most part below the level of laughter. This vein may be tapped for special effects, even for a whole scene, to slow and subdue the action or to heighten it with grotesque reflection. In those heroic tragedies that are lowered by the incursion of farce, and not structurally affected by its omission, there is no integral, implicit comedy —no everyday life—in the "world" of the play, to which the clowning naturally belongs and from which it may be derived without disorganization of the whole.[17] In *Macbeth* (and, indeed, all Shakespearean plays) there is a large, social, everyday life of soldiers, grooms, gossips, courtiers and commoners, that provides an essentially comic substructure for the heroic action. Most of the time this lower stratum is subdued, giving an impression of realism without any obvious byplay; but this realism carries the fundamental comic rhythm from which grotesque interludes may arise with perfect dramatic logic.

The fact that the two great rhythms, comic and tragic, are radically distinct does not mean that they are each other's opposites, or even incompatible forms. Tragedy can rest squarely on a comic substructure,

---

[17]Thorndike points out that *Tamburlaine* is of this genre: "Originally," he says, "the play contained comic scenes, omitted in the published form and evidently of no value in structure or conception." (*Op. cit.*, p. 90.)

See also J. B. Moore, *The Comic and the Realistic in English Drama.*

and yet be pure tragedy.[18] This is natural enough, for life—from which all felt rhythms spring—contains both, in every mortal organism. Society is continuous though its members, even the strongest and fairest, live out their lives and die; and even while each individual fulfills the tragic pattern it participates also in the comic continuity.[19] The poet's task is, of course, not to copy life, but to organize and articulate a symbol for the "sense of life"; and in the symbol one rhythm always governs the dynamic form, though another may go through the whole piece in a contrapuntal fashion. The master of this practice is Shakespeare.

Did the stark individual Fate of the purest Greek tragedy rule out, by its intense deathward movement, the comic feeling of the eternally full and undulating stream of life? Or was the richness that the comic-tragic counterpoint creates in other poetic traditions supplied to Aeschylus and Sophocles by the choric dance which framed and embellished the play? The satyr play at the end of the long, tragic presentation may well have been necessary, to assure its truth to the structure of subjective reality by an exuberant celebration of life.

There is yet another factor in drama that is commonly, and I think mistakenly, treated as a concession to popular taste: the use of spectacle, pageantry, brilliant show. Many critics apparently believe that a playwright makes provision for spectacular effects quite apart from his own poetic judgment and intent, simply to lure the audience into the theater. Thorndike, in fact, asserts that the use of spectacle bespeaks "the double purpose, hardly separable from the drama and particularly manifest in the Elizabethan dramatists, the two desires, to please their audiences and to create literature."[20] Brander Matthews said bluntly that not only theater, but all art whatever is "show business," whatever it may be besides.

---

[18]A striking example is J. M. Barrie's little tragedy dating from the first World War, *The Old Lady Shows her Medals*. Despite the consistently comic treatment one expects the inevitable (and wordless) last scene.

[19]There is also a genre known as "tragicomedy" (the Germans call it *Schauspiel*, distinguishing it from both *Lustspiel* and *Trauerspiel*), which is a comic pattern playing with the tragic; its plot-structure is *averted tragedy*, temporizing with the sense of fate, which usually inspires a tragic diction, little or no exuberance (humor), and often falls into melodrama. A study of its few artistic successes, and their precise relations to pure comedy and pure tragedy, might raise interesting problems.

[20]*Op. cit.*, p. 98.

[21]*A Book About the Theater*, pp. 8–9. Cf. *supra*, p. 320.

Art, and especially dramatic art, is full of compromises, for one possible effect is usually bought at the expense of another; not all ideas and devices that occur to the poet are co-possible. Every decision involves a rejection. And furthermore, the stage, the available funds, the capabilities of the actors, may all have to be considered. But no artist can make concessions to what he considers bad taste without ruining his work. He simply cannot think as an artist and accept inexpressive forms or admit an element that has no organic function in the whole. If, therefore, he wishes to present spectacular scenes, he must start with an idea that demands spectacular presentation.

Every play has its intended audience, and in that audience there is one pre-eminent member: the author. If the play is intended for, say, an Elizabethan audience, that honorary member will be an Elizabethan theater-goer, sharing the best Elizabethan taste, and sometimes setting its fashion. Our dramatic critics write as though the poets of the past were all present-day people making concessions to interests that have long spent themselves. But the poets who provided stage spectacles had spectacular ideas, and worked with them until their expressive possibilities were exhausted.

The element of pure show has an important function in dramatic art, for it tends to raise feeling, whatever the feeling is. It does this even in actual life: a splendid hall, an ornate table arrangement, a company in full dress, make a feast seem bigger and the gathering more illustrious than a plain table in a cafeteria, refectory, or gymnasium, with the guests in street dress. A splendid funeral, passing in procession behind chanting priests, is more solemn than a drab one, though perhaps no one at the spectacular service feels more sad than at the colorless one. In the theater, the element of show is a means of heightening the atmosphere, whether of gaiety or terror or woe; so it is, first of all, a ready auxiliary.

But in tragedy it has a more specialized and essential function, too. Tragedy, which expresses the consciousness of life and death, must make life seem worth while, rich, beautiful, to make death awesome. The splendid exaggerations of the stage serve tragic feeling by heightening the lure of the world. The beautiful world, as well as the emotional tone of the action, is magnified by the element of spectacle—by lighting and color, setting and grouping, music, dance, "excursions and alarums." Some playwrights avail themselves freely of this help; others dispense with it almost entirely (never quite; the theater is spectacular at any time), because they have other poetic means of giving virtual life the glory that death takes away, or despair—the "death of the soul"—corrupts.

Spectacle is a powerful ingredient in several arts. Consider what playing fountains can do for a courtyard or a square, and how a ceremonial procession brings the interior of a cathedral to visible life! Architectural design may be marvelously altered by a supplement of fortuitous spectacle. The Galata bridge over the Golden Horn in the middle of Istanbul, with thousands of people and vehicles passing over it, coming from steep hillsides on either hand, looks as though it were hung from the mosque-crowned heights above; without the pageantry of its teeming cosmopolitan traffic it shrinks to a flat thoroughfare across the river, between its actual bridgeheads. An esplanade without the movement of water below it would be utterly unimpressive; flooded with moonlight, which picks out the surface movement of the water, or standing immovable against a towering surf, it may become veritably an architect's dream.

But pure show, not assimilated to any art, does not constitute a "work." Acrobatics, tennis playing, some beautiful occupational rhythms such as hauling nets, swinging hammers, or the evolutions of boats in a race, are fascinating, aesthetically thrilling, so they hold the spectator in a joyful trance; but they are not art. For a work of art, this trance is only one requisite. Spectacle, however beautiful, is always an *element* in art. It may well be a major element, as it was in Noverre's ballets, and in the court masques, but even these largely spectacular products are rated as "works" because they had something else that motivated the display: an imaginative core, a "commanding form." A circus could be a work of art if it had some central feeling and some primary, unfailing illusion. As it is, the circus sometimes contains genuine little "works" —a riding act that is really an equestrian dance, a piece of clowning that rises to genuine comedy. But on the whole the circus is a "show," not a work of art, though it is a work of skill, planning and fitting, and sometimes copes with problems that arise also in the arts. What it lacks is the first requisite for art—a conception of feeling, something to express.

Because a dramatic work has such a core, everything in it is poesis. It is, therefore, neither a hybrid product pieced together at the demand of many interests, nor a synthesis of all the arts—not even of a more modest "several." It may have use for paint and plaster, wood and brick, but not for painting, sculpture, or architecture; it has use for music, but not for even a fragment of a concert program; it may require dancing, but such dancing is not self-contained—it intensifies a scene, often abstracts a quintessence of its feeling, the image of sheer powers arising as a secondary illusion in the midst of the virtual history.

Drama is a great form, which not only invites expression of elemental human feeling, but also permits a degree of articulation, complexity, detail within detail, in short: organic development, that smaller poetic forms cannot exhibit without confusion. To say that such works express "a concept of feeling" is misleading unless one bears in mind that it is the whole life of feeling—call it "felt life," "subjectivity," "direct experience," or what you will—which finds its articulate expression in art, and, I believe, only in art. So great and fully elaborated a form as (say) a Shakespearean tragedy may formulate the characteristic mode of perception and response, sensibility and emotion and their sympathetic overtones, that constitutes a whole personality. Here we see the process of art expression "writ large," as Plato would say; for the smallest work does the same thing as the greatest, on its own scale: it reveals the patterns of possible sentience, vitality, and mentality, objectifying our subjective being—the most intimate "Reality" that we know. This function, and not the recording of contemporary scenes, politics, or even moral attitudes, is what relates art to life; and the big unfolding of feeling in the organic, personal pattern of a human life, rising, growing, accomplishing destiny and meeting doom—that is tragedy.

PART III

THE POWER
OF THE SYMBOL

Chapter twenty

EXPRESSIVENESS

A work of art is a single, indivisible symbol, although a highly articulated one; it is not, like a discourse (which may also be regarded as a single symbolic form), composite, analyzable into more elementary symbols—sentences, clauses, phrases, words, and even separately meaningful parts of words: roots, prefixes, suffixes, etc.; selected, arranged and permutable according to publicly known "laws of language." For language, spoken or written, is a *symbolism,* a system of symbols; a work of art is always a prime symbol. It may, indeed, be analyzed, in that its articulation may be traced and various elements in it distinguished; but it can never be constructed by a process of synthesis of elements, because no such elements exist outside it. They only occur in a total form; as the convex and concave surfaces of a shell may be noted as characterizing its form, but a shell cannot be synthetically composed of "the concave" and "the convex." There are no such factors before there is a shell.

So far I have dealt systematically with the making of art symbols, every one of which is a "work." Now that the principles of their creation and articulation have been discussed with respect to each of the traditional great dimensions: plastic art, music, dance, poetry (there may, of course, be others, even other "primary illusions," certainly other modes of the ones mentioned), it is time to come to grips with some of the major philosophical problems which this theory of art raises. In the first part of the book, that was not possible; one cannot completely elucidate general statements before their uses are clear. But in the end there is an epistemological challenge to be met. There are many psychological questions, too, that naturally arise, some of which might lead right to the heart of anthropology and even biology. Such issues I shall reserve for a subsequent work. But, although this book is not a Psychology of Art, it may touch on psychological matters, because some characteristic responses of the artist to themes and materials, or of a percipient to a work, show up the nature of art; and to evade such issues on the ground that they belong to psychology (as Clive Bell rejected the problem of what caused his "aesthetic emotion") is to block the progress of systematic thought by the artificial barriers of pseudo-scientific pigeon-holes. A problem belongs to the discipline in which it logically arises and for which its solution is of consequence.

The central questions, however, are logical and epistemological:

(1) How can a work of art which does not involve temporal sequence—a picture, a statue, a house—express any aspect of vital experience, which is always progressive? What community of logical form can there be between such a symbol and the morphology of feeling?

(2) How is the import of a work known to anyone but the artist?

(3) What is the measure of good art? Consequently: What is "good taste" in art?

(4) What is beauty, and how is it related to art?

(5) What is the public importance of art?

I will try to answer these questions in their order.

Plastic art, like all other art, exhibits an interplay of what artists in every realm call "tensions." The relations of masses, the distribution of accents, direction of lines, indeed all elements of composition set up *space-tensions* in the primary virtual space. Every choice the artist makes —the depth of color, the technique—smooth or bold, delicately suggestive like Japanese drawings, full and luminous like stained glass, chiaroscuro, or what not—every such choice is controlled by the total organization of the image he wants to call forth. Not juxtaposed parts, but interacting elements make it up. Their persistent contrast affords space-tensions; but what unites them—the singleness of quality that pervades any good work—is space-resolution. Balance and rhythm, the recession and fusion of supporting elements which takes place so naturally and perfectly that one does not even know what makes the decision between design and background, every device that integrates and simplifies vision, creates the complement to space-tensions, space-resolutions. If that complement were not steadily apparent, the whole system of tensions would go unperceived; and that means it would not exist, for "space-tension" is an attribute belonging only to virtual space, where *esse est percipi*. In actual, common space there is no such thing.[1]

Sentient beings react to their world by constantly changing their total condition. When a creature's attention shifts from one center of interest to another, not only the organs immediately involved (the two eyes seeing a new object, the two ears receiving and "placing" a sound, etc.) but hundreds of fibers in the body are affected. Every smallest shift of awareness calls out a readjustment, and under ordinary circumstances such readjustments pass easily one into another. Underneath this variable process of what one might call "waking life," constantly influenced by things outside the creature's skin, is another sequence of changes, more simply rhythmic, the system of vital functions. Whether that sequence reflects the functions of outward awareness all the time, or only when the latter rise above some particular degree of disturbance, I do not know; but certainly, major excitements from outside throw the entire system —voluntary and involuntary muscles, heart, skin and glands as well as eyes and limbs—into unusual activity.

The same thing may occur, at least in human beings, not from outward causes, but from crises in the continual (if not continuous) process of ideation. We know little of the mental life of animals, and fortunately it does not concern us here; but certainly in human life the intellectual and imaginative functions have a controlling share of influence on waking activity. In sleep they have probably almost a monopoly (not quite, at least in adults; for we do *learn* not to fall out of bed—that is, to draw back from the edge of the mattress—and to control our viscera even in sleep).

---

[1] It may be argued, of course, that actual space exists only by virtue of physical tensions, the differentiations of the electromagnetic field into objects and physical events. But tensions of that sort are not experienced *as such;* on the "molar" level, whereon a comparison between actual and virtual experience lies, actual space is homogeneous and static.

This mental activity and sensitivity is what chiefly determines the way a person meets his surrounding world. Pure sensation—now pain, now pleasure—would have no unity, and would change the receptivity of the body for future pains and pleasures only in rudimentary ways. It is sensation remembered and anticipated, feared or sought or even imagined and eschewed that is important in human life. It is perception molded by imagination that gives us the outward world we know. And it is the continuity of thought that systematizes our emotional reactions into attitudes with distinct feeling tones, and sets a certain scope for an individual's passions. In other words: by virtue of our thought and imagination we have not only feelings, but a *life of feeling*.

That life of feeling is a stream of tensions and resolutions. Probably all emotion, all feeling tone, mood, and even personal "sense of life" or "sense of identity" is a specialized and intricate, but definite interplay of tensions—actual, nervous and muscular tensions taking place in a human organism. This concept of what is quite properly called "inner life" has already been discussed in Chapter 8; and its image in the "flow" of composed sound is not hard to find. But the fact that music is a temporal, progressive phenomenon easily misleads one into thinking of its passage as a *duplication* of psychophysical events, a *string of events* which parallels the passage of emotive life, rather than as a symbolic projection which need not share the conditions of what it symbolizes, i.e. need not present its import in temporal order because that import is something temporal. The symbolic power of music lies in the fact that it creates a pattern of tensions and resolutions. As its substance—its primary illusion—is a virtual (scientifically quite unrealistic) Time, the fabric of musical tensions is temporal. But the same sort of pattern confronts us in a non-temporal projection in the plastic arts. The abstraction effected by the symbol is probably no greater there, but it is more evident. Painting, sculpture, architecture, and all kindred arts do the same thing as music.

In a book I have already had several occasions to cite—Francis Fergusson's *The Idea of a Theater*—there is a passage that shows how readily artistic understanding may dispense with temporal presentation and find its way with the timeless image: speaking of the structure of Wagner's *Tristan und Isolde*, Professor Fergusson says, "Wagner has so arranged the incidents of the story as always to show on stage passionate moments. These successive moments constitute a sequence, or rhythm of feeling, or (if one thinks of them together, instead of in the temporal succession in which we get them) a spectrum of emotions generated by absolute passion . . ."[2]

That spectrum of emotions is the organizing "idea" in the non-temporal arts. The life of feeling is shown in timeless projection. Only art, which creates its elements instead of taking them from the world, can exhibit tension and resolution simultaneously, through the illusion of "space-tensions" and "space-resolutions."

But, although a work of art may abstract from the temporal character of experience, what it renders in its own logical projection must be true in design to the structure of experience. That is why art seems essentially organic; for all vital tension patterns are organic patterns. It must be remembered, of course, that a work of art is not an actual organism, but presents only the appearance of life, growth, and functional unity. Its material constitution is either inorganic, like stone, dead organic matter like wood or paper, or not a "thing" at all. Music is a disturbance of the air. Poetry is the same, unless it is a trail of ink. But just because the created appearance is all that has organic structure, a work of art shows us the *appearance* of life; and the semblance of functional unity is indispensable if the illusory tension pattern is to connote felt tensions, human experience. Technically, this means that every element must seem at once distinct, i.e. itself, and also continuous with a greater, self-sustained form (cf. Hildebrand's analysis of pictorial space, chapter 5); this integral relationship is, I think, what produces the oft-remarked quality of "livingness" in all successful works. And because art is a symbolic presentation and not a copy of feeling, there can be as much knowledge of feeling projected into the timeless articulated form of a painting, or a stained glass window, or a subtly proportioned Greek temple, as into the flowing forms of music, dance, or recitation.

If feeling and emotion are really complexes of tension, then every affective experience should be a uniquely determined process of this sort; then every work of art, being an image of such a complex, should express a particular feeling unambiguously; instead of being the "unconsummated

---

[2] P. 79.

symbol" postulated in *Philosophy in a New Key*, it might have, indeed, a single reference. I suspect that this is the case, and that the different emotional values ascribed to a work of art lie on a more intellectual plane than its essential import: for what a work of art sets forth—the course of sentience, feeling, emotion, and the *élan vital* itself—has no counterpart in any vocabulary. Its elements, therefore, are discursively known to us only as they figure in typical situations and actions; we name them for associated conditions. But the same progress of excitation may occur in entirely different circumstances, in situations that build up to disaster and in others that dissolve without practical consequences. The same feeling may be an ingredient in sorrow and in the joys of love. A work of art expressing such an ambiguously associated affect will be called "cheerful" by one interpreter and "wistful" or even "sad" by another. But what it conveys is really just one nameless passage of "felt life," knowable through its incarnation in the art symbol even if the beholder has never felt it in his own flesh.

Even the artist need not have experienced in actual life every emotion he can express. It may be through manipulation of his created elements that he discovers new possibilities of feeling, strange moods, perhaps greater concentrations of passion than his own temperament could ever produce, or than his fortunes have yet called forth. For, although a work of art reveals the character of subjectivity, it is itself objective; its purpose is to objectify the life of feeling. As an abstracted form it can be handled quite apart from its sources and yield dynamic patterns that surprise even the artist. All alien influences on his work are such contributions to his human knowledge (I do not say "psychological" knowledge, because psychology is a science, and only discursive knowledge can belong to it). Byzantine art, Negro art, Hindu or Chinese or Polynesian art become important for our own artistic life just in so far as our artists grasp the feelings of those exotic works.

That brings us to the second major question, which is epistemological: How can the import of an art symbol (i.e. a work of art) be known to anyone but its creator?

By the most elementary intellectual process—barring from the "intellectual" category that recognition of *things* as practical entities which

Coleridge called "primary imagination," and which we probably share with the higher animals—the basic intellectual act of *intuition*.

The word "intuition," used in the context of philosophical art theory, naturally brings to mind two great names—Bergson and Croce. But if one thinks of intuition in the ways they have made familiar, it sounds paradoxical to speak of "intellectual intuition," because—whatever differences their doctrines may show—one point where they agree is the non-intellectual nature of intuition. Croce explicitly claims to have "freed intuitive knowledge from any suggestion of intellectualism";[3] Bergson's opposition of intuition, the direct revelation of reality, and intellect, the falsification of reality for practical purposes, is too well known to require any restatement here.[4] But intuition as Bergson conceived it is so close to mystical experience that it really eludes philosophical analysis; it is simply a sudden illumination, infallible knowledge, rare, and incommensurable with the rest of mental life. Croce has a more usable notion, namely immediate awareness, which is always of an individual thing, event, image, feeling—without any judgment as to its metaphysical status, i.e. whether it be fact or fancy.[5] But here the act of intuition is not, as Bergson would have it, a blind "taking possession" or emotional experience of "reality"; it is, for Croce, an act of perception whereby the content is *formed,* which means, for him, *turned into form.*[6] This is a difficult concept, though not without justification; I will not elaborate or criticize it here, as it would lead far into his metaphysics. It is, I think, essentially the same concept as Kant's of the *data* of experience, which are already formed by the activity of perception—already made perceptual, which is the lowest form of being intelligible. Croce's lack of precision in the use of such words as "fact," "activity," "matter," gives his *Aesthetic* a more

---

[3]*Aesthetic as Science of Expression and General Linguistic,* p. 5.

[4]Any reader who is not familiar with it may find its classic statement in Bergson's little book, *Introduction to Metaphysics.*

[5]*Op. cit.,* p. 4: "Intuition is the undifferentiated unity of the perception of the real and of the simple image of the possible. In our intuitions we do not oppose ourselves as empirical beings to external reality, but we simply objectify our impressions, whatever they be."

[6]*Ibid.,* pp. 15–16: "In the aesthetic fact, expressive activity is not added to the fact of the impressions, but these latter are formed and elaborated by it. . . . The aesthetic fact, therefore, is form, and form alone."

cryptic and dubious appearance than it need have, at least with respect
to art theory. Such looseness of language does, I think, invite and cover
up some logically inadmissable steps that lead to his metaphysics of
"the Spirit"; in aesthetics it produces only one confusion of great consequence—the identification of intuition and expression,[7] which finally
leads to the doctrine that a work of art is essentially something in the
artist's mind, and that its duplication in material terms is incidental.
This unfortunate conclusion has been adequately analyzed and criticized
by Bernard Bosanquet, L. A. Reid, and others;[8] it is, indeed, an error
Croce should never have fallen into, and would not, save for one basic
misconception which is common to most theorists who deal with intuition—the false conception of the relation of intuition to symbolism.

What Croce means by "intellectual" is, upon all internal evidence,
simply "discursive." The "expressive activity" whereby impressions are
"formed and elaborated" and made amenable to intuition is, I believe,
the process of elementary symbol-making; for the basic symbols of human
thought are images, which "mean" the past impressions that begot them
and also those future ones that exemplify the same form. That is a very
low level of symbolization, yet it is on this level that characteristically
human mentality begins. No human impression is only a signal from the
outer world; it always is *also* an image in which possible impressions are
formulated, that is, a symbol for the conception of *such* experience.

The notion of "such" bespeaks an elementary abstraction, or awareness of form. That is, I think, what Croce meant by the "intuition"
which is indistinguishable from "expression," when he wrote in conclusion of his first chapter: "Intuitive knowledge is expressive knowledge
. . . intuition or representation are distinguished as *form* from what is
felt and suffered, from the flux or wave of sensation, or from psychic
matter; and this form, this taking possession, is expression. To intuite
is to express; and nothing else (nothing more, but nothing less) than
to express."[9]

Formulation, representation, abstraction: these are the characteristic

<hr>

[7]Another instance of the widespread fallacy of simply identifying any two
terms that bear some constant and close relation to each other.

[8]See especially Bernard Bosanquet, *Three Lectures on Aesthetics;* Louis Arnaud
Reid, "The Problem of Artistic Production," *Journal of Philosophical Studies,* V
(1930), 533–544.   [9]*Op. cit.,* p. 11.

functions of symbols. As such they have been studied, however, mainly in connection with discursive symbols; and that is why, as Croce said, "There exists a very ancient science of intellectual knowledge, admitted by all without discussion, namely, Logic; but a science of intuitive knowledge is timidly and with difficulty asserted by but a few."[10] As long as intuition is treated apart from any objective correlate, neither its varieties nor its relations to reason, imagination, or any other non-animalian mental trait can be studied. Logicians may look to the complex and often elusive functions of language (either "natural" language or "artificial," i.e. technical) to record their cognitive experiences—conception, coordination of concepts, inference, judgment—and find some pattern of intellectual activity reflected in the patterned discourse that mediates it. But by contemplating intuitions as direct experiences, not mediated, not correlated to anything public, one cannot record or systematize them, let alone construct a "science" of intuitive knowledge, which will be "the true analogue of logic."[11] The process of formulation, as Croce presents it, is transcendental: an intuition—a purely subjective act—takes place spontaneously, and without any medium, in a mind. There are no different kinds of intuition. Consequently—since intuition is presently equated to expression—there cannot be different kinds of expression, though there are different contents. This has a far-reaching implication for art theory, namely that there are no varieties of art, no modes, no styles—no differences between music and painting and poetry and dance, but only intuitive knowledge of some unique experience.[12]

When Croce says: "Every true intuition or representation is also *expression*," he really points the way to a possible study of intuition; for by expression he means what I have called "logical expression," no matter how much he might protest the word "logical." He does not mean emotional symptoms, but formulation. There is, I think, no formulation without symbolic projection; what his "science" of non-intellectual knowledge awaited was a recognition of non-discursive symbolization. He himself observed that "as a general rule, a too restricted meaning is given to the word expression. It is generally restricted to what are called verbal expressions alone. But there exist also non-verbal expressions, such as those of line, colour and sound, and to all of these must be extended our

---

[10]*Ibid.*, p. 1.   [11]*Ibid.*, p. 14.   [12]*Ibid.*, Chap. iv, *passim*.

affirmation. . . . But be it pictorial, or verbal, or musical, . . . to no intuition can expression in one of its forms be wanting; it is, in fact, an inseparable part of intuition."[13]

It was Cassirer who furnished the propaedeutic to a study of intuition, in his great *Philosophie der symbolischen Formen;* and in studying the functions of symbols of various sorts, on various levels, one finds that they negotiate not only one kind of intuition, the envisagement of experiences as individual, intelligible forms, *this* thing, *this* event, etc. (which answers to Croce's notion), but also other kinds. All cognition of form is intuitive; all relatedness—distinctness, congruence, correspondence of forms, contrast, and synthesis in a total *Gestalt*—can be known only by direct insight, which is intuition. And not only form, but *formal significance,* or import, is seen intuitively (wherefore it is sometimes said to be "felt"), or not at all; that is the basic symbolic value which probably precedes and prepares verbal meaning.[14]

The comprehension of form itself, through its exemplification in formed perceptions or "intuitions," is spontaneous and natural *abstraction;* but the recognition of a metaphorical value of some intuitions, which springs from the perception of their forms, is spontaneous and natural *interpretation.* Both abstraction and interpretation are intuitive, and may deal with non-discursive forms. They lie at the base of all human mentality, and are the roots from which both language and art take rise.[15]

Philosophers who recognize the intuitive character of artistic appreciation seem to have, quite generally, a strong prejudice against scientific conception and logical demonstrations. They seem to find it necessary to deprecate logic in order to uphold the value and dignity of intuition, and usually make a great issue of the opposition between the two "methods of knowing." But there is, in truth, no such opposition—if only because intuition is not a "method" at all, but an event. It is, moreover, the beginning and end of logic; all discursive reasoning would be frustrated

---

[13]*Ibid.,* p. 8. This passage bespeaks the impossibility of dispensing with kinds, or different forms, of expression (intuition).

[14]A fuller discussion of the "sense of import" and the nature of language may be found in *New Key,* chap. v, *passim.*

[15]The dual nature of language, as both a record of mythic conception and the source of generalization and scientific conception, is treated at length in Cassirer's *Philosophie der symbolischen Formen,* and briefly in several essays, especially *Language and Myth.*

without it. The simple concatenation of propositions known as "syllogism" is only a device to lead a person from one intuition to another. Anyone who, convinced that all men are mortal and even granting that Socrates is a man, still does not recognize that *therefore* Socrates is mortal, is devoid of logical understanding because he does not respond with normal intuition at each station of the discourse. Even at a lower level rationality would fail if intuition did not duly take place: if that astonishingly ungifted person knew the meanings of all the words: "Socrates," "man," "is," and "a," but failed to understand the meaning of "Socrates is a man" because the order of the words did not weld their sense into a single concept for him, he could not even get as far as the "therefore" hurdle. Even people of normal intelligence faced with an inflected language like Latin or German may find themselves staring at words that will not fuse into a proposition; but when the syntactical signs (inflections, verb forms) as well as the denotations of all the words are really understood, the sentence-meaning suddenly emerges. That emergence of meaning is always a logical intuition or insight. All discourse aims at building up, cumulatively, more and more complex logical intuitions.

The import of an art symbol cannot be built up like the meaning of a discourse, but must be seen *in toto* first; that is, the "understanding" of a work of art begins with an intuition of the whole presented feeling. Contemplation then gradually reveals the complexities of the piece, and of its import. In discourse, meaning is synthetically construed by a succession of intuitions; but in art the complex whole is seen or anticipated first.[16] This creates a real epistemological impasse: artistic import, unlike verbal meaning, can only be exhibited, not demonstrated to any one to whom the art symbol is not lucid. Since there are no semantic units with assigned meanings which, by paraphrase or translation, could be

---

[16]Cf. my article "Abstraction in Science and Abstraction in Art," in *Structure, Method, and Meaning: Essays in Honor of Henry M. Sheffer*, pp. 171–182. In a review of that article (*Journal of Aesthetics*, X, 3) Professor Eliseo Vivas imputes to me the tenet that "In one case abstraction goes from part to whole and in the other from whole to part." That, of course, is nonsense; abstraction has nothing to do with wholes and parts; it is *perception*, on whatever level of abstraction it may be, that proceeds in these different ways. Abstraction in science is effected by successive *generalizations*, and in art without any such intellectual steps. Professor Vivas overlooked or forgot to mention generalization, but it happens to be the differentia between the two modes of abstraction.

conveyed by equivalent symbols, as words may be defined or translated, there is no way of further identifying the import of a work. The only way to make the feeling-content of a design, a melody, a poem, or any other art symbol public, is to present the expressive form so abstractly and forcibly that anyone with normal sensitivity for the art in question will see this form and its "emotive quality" (cf. Chap. 2, especially pp. 20–21: Baensch on emotion as a quality in a work of art).

A symbol that cannot be separated from its sense cannot really be said to refer to something outside itself. "Refer" is not the right word for its characteristic function. And where the symbol does not have an accepted reference, the use of it is not properly "communication." Yet its function *is* expression, in the logical, not the biological, sense (weeping, raging, tail-wagging) ; and in good art the expression is true, in bad art false, and in poor art unsuccessful. Where no intent or impulse to express anything enters in at all, the product—even if it be a human figure, like a tailor's dummy or a doll—is not art. A tailor's dummy could be art, and dolls can be and sometimes are.

On the subject of artistic truth and falsity I find myself in full agreement with at least one eminent aesthetician, R. G. Collingwood. This is all the more gratifying to me, and I hope to him, too, as I did not read his *Principles of Art* until my own ideas were completely formed, so the similarity of our conclusions is a mutual corroboration. With his epistemology I cannot quite agree; the ingredient of self-consciousness, and indeed the strict limitation of artistic expression to actual experience, seem to me misconceived; but more of that later, with the rest of our differences. The present problem is truth.

Art is envisagement of feeling, which involves its formulation and expression in what I call a symbol and Mr. Collingwood calls "language." (It is, of course, unfortunate that words are so differently used by different writers—he uses "symbol" only to denote what semanticists today call "artificial language," such as mathematical symbolism or the constructed languages which Carnap analyzes—but taking his words as he evidently means them, his statements about expression and envisagement ring true.) This envisagement, however, may be interfered with by emotions which are not formed and recognized, but affect the imagination of other subjective experience. Art which is thus distorted at its very source by lack of candor is bad art, and it is bad because it is not true to *what a candid envisagement would have been*. Candor is the standard: "seeing straight," the vernacular calls it. As Mr. Collingwood says, where envisagement is false one cannot really speak of either error or lie, because error arises only on the higher level of "intellect" (discursive thinking), and lying presupposes "knowing better"; but lack of candid vision takes effect on the deep level of imagination. This kind of falseness he calls, therefore, "corruption of consciousness."[17] *Bad art is corrupt art.* It is false in the most vicious way, because this falseness cannot be subsequently helped, as a lie may be exposed and retracted, and error may be found and corrected. Corrupt art can only be repudiated and destroyed.

"A bad work of art," he says, "is an activity in which the agent tries to express a given emotion, but fails. This is the difference between bad art and art falsely so called. . . . In art falsely so called there is no failure to express, because there is no attempt at expression; there is only an attempt (whether successful or not) to do something else."[18]

To these distinctions between art and non-art on the one hand, good and bad art on the other, I would add a further, though less fundamental one within the sphere of essentially good art, namely free art and hampered or *poor* art.

This arises on a level of imaginative activity corresponding to the "intellectual" level of mentality, namely the level of *art work*. Mr. Collingwood does not admit the artist's craft as such a higher development, because he maintains that art cannot be craft; art has no technique.[19] At this point I cannot bear him company. Our difference may be "verbal," but even as such it is important, because the way one uses words is not arbitrary; it reveals one's basic conceptions; so the criticism of his terminology which follows is really a criticism of what I consider his inadequate notions.

These are, in chief, his concepts of work, of means and ends, the art

---

[17]See *The Principles of Art*, p. 219.

[18]*Ibid.*, p. 282. The entire section (chap. xii, "Art as Language," §3, "Good Art and Bad Art") is relevant here, but of course too long to quote; the reader, therefore, is urgently advised to read it at its source—and, indeed, to read the entire book.

[19]*Ibid.*, p. 111: "Expression is an activity of which there can be no technique."

382 PART III *The Power of the Symbol*

medium, and the relations of various human activities to each other. In criticism, he has a tendency to what one might call "simple rejection": examining the alleged relationship of two terms such as, for instance, representation and artistic expression, finding that the proposed relation does not hold, and consequently asserting that the terms have *no relation whatever* to one another.[20] This tendency prevents him from subjecting the process of artistic creation to the detailed and fruitful sort of study which he gave to the process of imaginative envisagement, and leads him finally to regard the artist's imagination of feeling (which is all he has really analyzed) as the work of art itself. In one place he writes that "a work of art may be completely created when it has been created as a thing whose only place is in the artist's mind" (p. 130), and shortly after: "The music, the work of art, is not the collection of noises, it is the tune in the composer's head." (P. 139.) Similar statements are scattered throughout Book I. Here is the Crocean identification of expression and intuition (though Mr. Collingwood uses "knowledge"—"intuition" does not even appear in his index), and their further identification with art; the statue completely seen in imagination, the unpainted picture.

The most dubious of all his tenets, however, is that an artist cannot know what sort of work—even in the broadest lines, e.g. whether a comedy or a tragedy—he is about to create; because "If the difference between tragedy and comedy is a difference between the emotions they express, it is not a difference that can be present to the artist's mind when he is beginning his work; if it were, he would know what emotion he was going to express before he had expressed it. No artist, therefore, . . . can set out to write a comedy, a tragedy, an elegy, or the like. So far as he is an artist proper, he is just as likely to write any one of these as any other. . . ."[21]

---

[20]For instance: "Deciding what psychological reaction a work of art produces (for example, asking yourself how a certain poem 'makes you feel') has nothing whatever to do with deciding whether it is a real work of art or not." (P. 32.) There is a sense in which feeling is the surest guide to good art; the feeling of excitement about the work which bespeaks its importance *as art,* not as anything else. Or again: "The origin of perspective . . . was connected with the use of painting as an adjunct to architecture. . . . For movable pictures, perspective is mere pedantry." (Pp. 253 ff.) Its purpose in easel pictures is, indeed, not to bring out a wall-plane; but may one therefore say so glibly that it has no other purpose?

[21]*Ibid.,* p. 116. The context of this passage is the most radical treatment I have

In Book III, Mr. Collingwood seems to take many of his quixotic statements back. He grants that artists paint in order to formulate their vision and express their feelings, and that painting is part of creative seeing, a different thing from "looking at the subject without painting it" (p. 308); and also that musicians "compose for performance," and that the performers "are not only permitted but required to fill in the details" (pp. 320–321). With the best will in the world to follow his transitions, it is not always possible to reconcile such admissions with what went before; how can the performers, the audience, and even other artists "collaborate" on a piece that is "a tune in the composer's head" or any other (perhaps plastic) work "completely created . . . in the artist's mind"?

Perhaps the best way to overcome the difficulties of his critical portion (Book I) is to ask *why* he is anxious to deny craftsmanship any role in art and consequently to reject the concept of technique, and why he has to deprecate the ideal of literal expression in science and philosophy and treat language as essentially expression of feeling with a conceptual content only incidentally conveyed. Something is missing in the epistemological structure. The badness of his arguments against the "theory of technique" and the conception of "art as craft," and against all and sundry theories of linguistic forms and literal meaning, bespeaks a fear of unacceptable conclusions: and that is nothing less than a lack of philosophical candor—"corruption of consciousness"—a failing as natural and common in philosophy as in art. He himself has stated this fact: "Corruption of consciousness is not a recondite sin which overcomes only an unfortunate or accursed few; it is a constant experience in the life of any artist, and his life is a constant and, on the whole, a successful warfare against it. . . ."

"A truthful consciousness gives intellect a firm foundation on which to build; a corrupt consciousness forces intellect to build on quicksand."[22]

Let us find the evidences of sin. They are, in Book I, the distortions in which he presents the concepts he wishes to reject, for instance the reduction of all "craft" to "ways of bringing human beings into certain mental conditions," which is obviously sophistical and made only in order

---

found of art as "a fine frenzy" without plan or context.

[22]*Ibid.*, p. 284.

to identify any admission of *craft in art* with a conception of *art as craft*, and the latter, in turn, with *art as emotional stimulus*—which is the idea he really, and properly, sets out to combat. Something has fused all these concepts into one vague mass.

Secondly: on page 108 he makes the categorical statement, "The element which the technical theory calls the end (i.e. the aim of art) is defined by it as the arousing of emotion." But he has quoted no defender of something that could be called "the technical theory" to the effect that the purpose of technique is to arouse emotion, let alone proven that all its adherents would agree to this. The tenets of "the technical theory" are, in fact, what he himself has chosen to lump under that name; and again, it is *art as stimulation of feeling* that he really wants to get rid of, and "technique" is vaguely associated with that false theory.

The weakness of such untrue arguments shows up clearly in the fact that the definitions of terms which are said not to belong to art, but to other spheres, are so rigid and barren that they would be no more usable in their alleged proper places than in art. His definition of "symbol," for instance, is so narrow that it is synonymous with "artificial language"; but since linguistics and logic are said to rest upon the use of symbols, the narrow definition serves to make those disciplines seem like trivial artifices. That is philosophical malpractice. It is the same sin that positivists commit when they lump all problems of art, of which they know nothing, under "emotional reaction," which they then relegate to a "science of psychology" of which they know nothing either.

Finally, Mr. Collingwood asserts that language is not the semantic structure it is supposed to be, but has neither vocabulary nor syntax; it is pure expression, created by "consciousness"; it is art, and has no technique, no "use" (correct or incorrect), and no symbolic function— it is expression of feeling, like dance, painting, or music. All speech is poetry. Grammar and syntax and even the recognition of words are purely arbitrary inventions for cutting it up (somewhat, we may assume, like the "verses" into which mediaeval scholars divided the Holy Scripture for quick identification of any passage). But here, where a strong argument is most needed to establish so radical a doctrine, his powers of demonstration break down altogether. He is content to show that language always has something to do with feeling, that it can exist only where imagination has already grasped and formed "psychical feeling," and as this imagination is the root of art, all language is art and all art is language; which he proves by slandering grammarians ("A grammarian is not a kind of scientist . . . he is a kind of butcher"[23]) and insulting I. A. Richards (referring to his "fastidious Cambridge mouth," etc.).[24] Such writing is unworthy of a man who has true things to say. Here he is on intellectual quicksand; here is the passional rejection of some concept that is not to be entertained, the fear of some Black Beast of aesthetics.

The Black Beast of which most aestheticians who hold a theory of art as expression stand in fear, is the concept of the Art Symbol. The unavowed fact which haunts them is the fact that an expressive form is, after all, a symbolic form. As soon as one looks this fact in the face, all the major paradoxes and anomalies disappear—"significant form" that is not significant of anything,[25] poetry and music of which "we may say, if we like, that both are expressive," but should avoid trouble "by insisting that they 'express' nothing, nothing at all,"[26] Croce's theory of artistic expression requiring no medium, and Collingwood's similar concept of the "expressive act," which occurs only in the artist's head, as the work of art itself. So long as one tries to evade the symbolic form which mediates the "expression of the Idea," one cannot study the process of that expression, nor point out precisely how it differs from other activities. But as soon as one admits that "expressive form" is a special kind of symbolic form, interesting problems present themselves for solution, and some ever-threatening dangers of *mésalliance* between aesthetics and ethics or science are safely obviated. There is no danger of embracing a "vicious intellectualism" once the difference between an art symbol and a scientific symbol—or better, scientific *symbolism*—is understood: they are as different as art is from science: it is, indeed, the radical difference between their respective symbolic forms that makes art and discourse (logic, science, matter of fact) fundamentally different realms, and removes the hope (or fear, as the case may be) of some philosophers

---

[23]*Ibid.*, p. 257.

[24]*Ibid.*, p. 264.

[25]The reference is, of course, to Clive Bell's phrase.

[26]O. K. Bowsma, "The Expression Theory of Art," in Max Black's anthology, *Philosophical Analysis*. See p. 97.

that in an "age of science" art will aspire and finally graduate to the dignity of scientific thought.[27]

The first crucial problem that finds solution is, how a work of art may be at once a purely imaginative creation, intrinsically different from an artifact—not, indeed, properly a physical "thing"—yet be not only "real," but objective. The concept of the *created* thing as non-actual, i.e. illusory, but imaginatively and even sensuously present, functioning as a symbol but not as a physical datum, not only answers the immediate question, but answers it in a way which suggests the answer to its corollary, the problem of technique. To assert that art has no technique, no intimate relation to craft is, after all, a *tour de force;* and in little passages, here and there, the author of that doctrine tries to soften it by saying that although "the painted picture is not the work of art in the proper sense of that phrase," yet "its production is somehow necessarily connected with the aesthetic activity, that is, with the creation of the imaginative experience which is the work of art."[28] He proposes to show the necessity of the connection; but the demonstration is always precarious and evasive.

If, however, we regard the picture as the art symbol which expresses the imaginative experience, i.e. the artist's envisagement of feeling, then the painted picture *is* the work of art "in the proper sense of that phrase,"

---

[27]Santayana, in *Reason in Art*, p. 111, speaks of "that half-mythical world through which poets, for want of a rational education, have hitherto wandered," and hopes for a *rapprochement* between poetry and science: "A rational poet's vision would have the same moral functions which myth was asked to fulfil, and fulfilled so treacherously; it would employ the same ideal faculties which myth expressed in a confused and hasty fashion. More detail would have been added, and more variety in interpretation. . . . Such a poetry would be more deeply rooted in human experience than any casual fancy, and therefore more appealing to the heart."

"If knowledge were general and adequate the fine arts would accordingly be brought around to expressing reality. . . . Thus there would be no separation of useful from fine art." (*Ibid.*, p. 214.)

In Eugène Véron's *L'Esthetique* the same hope is expressed that art will abandon mythical imagination and become scientific. Strindberg expected the same development, but feared that public enlightenment would be the end of drama, which demands an easily deluded audience (Preface to *Miss Julia*).

The extreme statement of the servile attitude a whole generation of artists and critics took toward science may be found in a little book published in 1913 by two authors who were ranked, at that time, with the *avant-garde: The Modern Evolution of Plastic Expression,* by M. De Zayas and P. B. Haviland. Here we and we are relieved of the problem why the "proper" sense is one that has never been used; for even good artists, and such as think about art theory, say of Leonardo's "Last Supper" that it is a work of art, and not of themselves that they are "having" one when they see or think of the picture. The picture is, indeed, not the paint on the wall, but the illusion which Leonardo created by means of paint on damp plaster. The paint, unhappily, has largely disappeared; but there is enough left to sustain the illusion, so the picture is still there. If time obliterates that last faint pigmentation, the work of art will have disappeared, no matter how well anyone may know and remember its vital import—the harmonies of feeling it revealed.

The artist's work is the making of the emotive symbol; this making involves varying degrees of craftsmanship, or technique. Beyond the rudiments which everyone learns—how to use a pencil at all, how to use language at all, how to whittle a stick, chip a stone, sing a tune—he learns his craft as he needs it for his purpose, which is to create a virtual object that shall be an expressive form. But craft, or technique, is not the mechanical, routine, dictated procedure that Mr. Collingwood describes; every artist invents his technique, and develops his imagination as he does so. That is why painting and seeing are all of a piece when a person is creating a picture;[29] hearing and composing, or at a later stage of musical work, hearing and playing or singing, are indivisible acts.

Because every artist must master his craft in his own way, for his own purposes of symbolizing ideas of subjective reality, there may be *poor* art, which is not corrupt, but fails to express what he knew in too brief an intuition. It is hard to hold an envisagement without a more or less permanent symbol; and to be confronted with a *wrong* symbol can undo an inward vision. An unfamiliar tool, an inadequate musical instrument, but also a physically uncontrollable hand may contradict imagination, and, in the earliest moments of a dawning idea, may ruth-

---

find: "Art is being largely influenced and possibly absorbed by science inasmuch as it expresses a scientific phenomenon which can only be expressed through form. . . . It is trying to make form a vehicle for psychology and metaphysics." (P. 19.) But in an earlier passage they admitted, rather sadly: "We do not think that art has yet reached a stage where it can be considered as a pure scientific expression of man. . . ." (P. 13.)

[28]Collingwood, *op. cit.*, p. 305.

[29]*Ibid.*, p. 303.

lessly put it out. The result is a poor and helpless product, sincere enough, but confused and frustrated by recalcitrance of the medium or sheer lack of technical freedom.

I can see no point in defining "technique" so it means "manufacture," except as part of the campaign against the treatment of art works as "goods" and of people who value them as "consumers." This campaign is right-minded and justified enough; but it need not sweep away all relations of art to the activities which normally feed it—the crafts, and the world-wide interest in sheer entertainment. Mr. Collingwood, like Brander Matthews, speaks only of "amusement," which has an overtone of self-indulgence, triviality, and cheapness, and is easily relegated to the category of non-art;[30] but entertainment is another thing. Mozart's *Marriage of Figaro,* Shakespeare's *Tempest,* Jane Austen's *Pride and Prejudice* are excellent entertainment; they are also very good art. To admit the possible coincidence of artisanship or entertainment with artistic expression is not enough;[31] they stand, evidently, in some intimate relation. And the connection is really obvious: the crafts (including the literary and theatrical crafts) furnish the materials and techniques of artistic creation. A person who is by intuition an artist cannot shape a pot, or make up a song for a festive occasion, without feeling the artistic possibilities of the project. If the pot is ugly or the song banal, that is not because an artist made the pot for the dime store, or the song for "magic" purposes; it is because the maker was not an artist but a vulgar person, who thought the ugly pot "pretty" or the banal song "grand," or perhaps did not think of perceptual values at all, so long as his pot held twelve ounces, or his song was accepted by the program committee.

The crafts, in short, provide opportunities to make works of art; they have actually been the school of feeling (feeling becomes clear and conscious only through its symbols), as they were the incentives to articulation and the first formulators of abstractive vision. Whether art is practiced in the service of religion or of entertainment, or in the house-

---

[30]Matthews used the term for the opposite purpose—to show that all art, "from Buffalo Bill's Wild West to the 'Oedipus' of Sophocles," was really just amusement, hence a commodity, and therefore as respectable as golf and as close to the hearts of Americans as popcorn and ice cream. See *A Book About the Theater,* Chap i.

[31]Collingwood, *op. cit.,* p. 277.

hold by women potters and weavers, or passionately in forlorn attics with leaky skylights, makes no differences to its own aims, its purity, or its dignity and importance.

One further problem of artistic creation, which Mr. Collingwood disposed of in a way that is either Pickwickian or very dubious, is the problem of what he calls "kinds" of work—tragedy, comedy, elegy, sonnet —and in other arts, still life or landscape, song or string quartet, etc. Croce also claims that such "kinds" of work do not exist; but what his protest comes to is that there are no separate standards whereby to judge different "kinds" of painting, poetry and so forth, and any classification is, consequently, philosophically trivial.[32] That is true; but the futility of labeling works according to their themes, materials, size, or what not, is a different matter altogether from the supposed inability of the artist to know, at the outset, what will be the scope and general character of his work.[33]

In creating an emotive symbol, or work of art, the creator does articulate a vital import which he could not imagine apart from its expression, and consequently cannot know before he expresses it. But the act of conception which sets his work going, whether it comes suddenly like an inspiration or only after much joyless and labored fuddling, is the envisagement of the "commanding form," the fundamental feeling to be explored and expressed. *This is "the work of art in the artist's head."* As soon as he conceives this matrix of the work-to-be, he knows what must be its general structure, its proportions, its degree of elaboration; a tragedy begins with an adumbration of its particular "tragic rhythm," which determines its weightiness, its diction, its whole economy; a lyric springs from one total lyric feeling, it is not a series of little feeling-glimpses that may string out into a play or a novel for all the artist knows. A true artist is, indeed, not likely to set out with the resolve: "I want to write a lyric," but rather with the discovery: "I have an idea for a lyric." Yet even such alleged marks of the "true artist" must be taken with a grain of salt. A competent painter, accepting a commission for a portrait, a mural, or any other "kind" of work, simply trusts that, contemplating the powers of the medium, he will have a sudden insight

---

[32]*Aesthetic*, p. 35.
[33]*Supra.*, Chap. 8, *passim.*

into a feeling it can express; and working with it, he will pursue and learn and present that feeling. What he is likely to say, however, is that if he thinks about the commissioned subject long enough, he will know "what to do with it." Certainly every architect has to *find* the proper feeling to express in each building he designs. He cannot let his inner need decide whether he will plan a cottage or a cathedral.

Such opportunism and compliance would be absurd if the total import of a work of art had to be an actual emotion experienced by its author. Here again the assumption that the work is a free symbol, not an emotion (however "filtered," or, in Collingwood's phrase, "denatured"), nor a confession of emotions, saves the concept of expressive form from leading into an "aestheticism" which would rule out, on principle, some genuine pieces—even masterpieces—because they may be *theoretically* shown to have "impure" or "non-artistic" motives.[34] The great cognitive value of symbols is that they may present ideas transcending the interpretant's past experience. Now, the first person to perceive the vital import of an artistic form, the emotive possibilities of an element, the expressive value of a change in composition (perhaps through a small detail), is the artist himself. He is the first, the steadiest, and usually the most competent percipient of his work. And he is an artist not so much because of his own feelings, as by virtue of his intuitive recognition of forms symbolic of feeling, and his tendency to project emotive knowledge into such objective forms. In handling his own creation, composing a symbol of human emotion, he learns from the perceptible reality before him possibilities of subjective experience that he has not known in his personal life. His own mental scope and the growth and expansion of his personality are, therefore, deeply involved with his art.

But to say that he does not render his own emotions would be simply silly. All knowledge goes back to experience; we cannot know anything that *bears no relation* to our experience. Only, that relation may be more complex than the theory of direct personal expression assumes.

I once heard an excellent artist, who is also an articulate philosopher, say: "When I was a young child—before I went to school, I think—I already knew what my life would be like. Not, of course, that I could guess what my fortunes would be, what economic situations and what

---

[34]Cf. the discussion of "pure poetry," Chap. 14, pp. 246 ff.

political events I'd get into; but from the very beginning of my self-consciousness I knew *what anything that could happen to me would have to be like.*"

Anything an artist can envisage is "like" his own subjectivity, or is at least connected with his ways of feeling. Such connections normally occur for him through his widening knowledge of other people's art; that is, by symbolic revelation. The appreciation of new art is a development of one's own emotive possibilities; and that, of course, is an expansion of native powers, not an intellectual acceptance of novelty in a tolerant spirit. Toleration is another matter, and is in order precisely where we do *not* understand other people's expressions, because they are new, exotic, or very individual. An artist's catholicity grows with his growing artistic thought, his freedom in varying, building, and developing forms, and the progressive discovery of import through his own funded imagination. Even his own works—which stem from his inner experience—may, and happily do, outgrow the compass of his personal life, and show him, in a much greater vision, what anything that can happen to humanity must be like. Knowledge of his own subjectivity becomes part of that greater vision, though it remains at the center. His knowledge of life goes as far as his art can reach.

So much for the artist and his work, the idea and its form, conception and expression; but the work that leaves its author's keeping enters, therewith, into other people's lives, and this circumstance raises the further questions: By what standards shall they measure it? What is it to them? What is its public importance?

These are the ultimate questions in a philosophy of art, because they presuppose knowledge of the art symbol itself—its nature, its import, and its truth-value. Only at the end of a systematic study, therefore, may they be profitably raised, in expectation of some well-founded answer.

Chapter twenty-one

THE WORK AND ITS PUBLIC

So far, we have considered art almost entirely from what might be called "the studio standpoint," seeing the art work as an expression of its author's "Idea," i.e. something that takes shape as he articulates an envisagement of realities which discursive language cannot properly express. What he makes is a symbol—primarily a symbol to capture and hold his own imagination of organized feeling, the rhythms of life, the forms of emotion. In one sense, therefore, he may be said to make each piece for himself, for his own satisfaction.

In another sense, however, he makes it for other people; that is one of the differences between art and reveries. A work of art has a public —at least a hypothetical public (for instance, when a prisoner in exile composes poetry in his own tongue, not knowing whether it will ever reach an understanding ear); and its social intent, which is essential to it, sets its standard of significance. Even a person who produces a work so unfamiliar, so difficult and original that he has no hope of meeting with intuitive understanding from his fellows, works with the conviction that when they have contemplated it long enough the intuition of its import will come. He has, moreover, another article of faith, without which he probably could not work: that even while the public recoils under the shock of his confounding and estranging presentation, there will be those who do perceive, at once, the commanding organic form of the work as a whole, and suspect the great emotive vision which would be evident if they were not staggered by the excessive novelty of its projection; that consequently the most serious and competent judges will contemplate it long enough to transcend its "shocking" character and find it lucid.

The public function of the art symbol imposes on it a standard of complete objectivity. It has to be entirely given; what is left to imagination being implied, not missing. But the implication may be subtle. It is a great mistake to think an artist must constantly bear in mind the particular public that will visit the gallery or the concert hall or the bookstore where his work will make its first appearance.[1] He works for an ideal audience. Even when he paints a mural, knowing what public will use the building that houses his work, he paints for his idealization of this public, or he paints badly. A work directed *ad hominem* is as flimsy and unworthy as a philosophical argument *ad hominem;* it is the psychological compromise that Mr. Collingwood relegates to "craft" and regards as an attempt to stimulate direct emotion (which it need not be; in fact, it usually becomes too confused to be anything so rational, even in the realm of non-art). The ideal beholder is the measure of a work's objectivity; he may come into actual existence only after many years of its career.

As beholders, trying to meet the artist halfway, we see his work not from "the studio standpoint," but from the art lover's, "the audience standpoint"; and we have problems of our own concerning it. How do we know that we have understood its creator's message? How can we judge the value of this particular piece, and rate it properly among others —his and other people's? If we do not like it, is that our fault or his? Should we accept it even if we cannot find it beautiful?

Most of these questions have no direct answers, because they are not direct questions; they rest on misconceptions which are expressed in the terms they employ. Often, when a question is set right, there is no problem, or the solution is simple. Let us begin with the first query: How do we know that we have understood the artist's message?

Since the art symbol is not a discourse, the word "message" is misleading. A message is something communicated. But, as I remarked in the foregoing chapter, a work of art cannot be said, in all semantic strictness, to effect a communication between its maker and his fellows; its symbolic function, though it has much in common with that of language (wherefore Croce subsumes art under "linguistic," and Collingwood declares that art, and not discourse, "really" deserves the name of lan-

---

[1]This is, I think, the fallacy in Brander Matthews' theory that every play must be written for a given audience in a given theater, and that its shortcomings are usually due to loss by its removal from this setting. See *A Book About the Theater,* Chap. i.

guage), is a more direct traffic with intuition than we hold by discursive symbols. The study of non-discursive expression has been hampered and somewhat snarled by an unfortunate "working model," which is *comment*. The use of that model has obscured the most distinctive characteristic of art—that its import is not separable from the form (the picture, poem, dance, etc.) that expresses it. It has been generally assumed that if a work of art expresses anything, in a symbolic and not a symptomatic way, then it must be its author's comment on something. But a comment always does direct one's interest to something distinct from the words, gestures, or other signs conveying it; these are mere signs, they point to an object considered, and convey some opinion about it. So the questions arise in art criticism: what is the artist commenting on, what does he say, and how does he say it? These are, I believe, spurious questions. He is not saying anything, not even about the nature of feeling; he is *showing*. He is showing us the appearance of feeling, in a perceptible symbolic projection; but he does not refer to a public object, such as a generally known "sort" of feeling, outside his work. Only in so far as the work is objective, the feeling it exhibits becomes public; it is always bound to its symbol. The effect of this symbolization is to offer the beholder a way of conceiving emotion; and that is something more elementary than making judgments about it.

The art lover who views, hears, or reads a work from "the audience standpoint" enters into a direct relation not with the artist, but with the work. He responds to it as he would to a "natural" symbol,[2] simply finding its significance, which he is likely to think of as "the feeling in it." This "feeling" (which may range from a fleeting small experience to the subjective pattern of a whole human life) is not "communicated," but revealed; the created form "has" it, so that perception of the virtual object—say, the famous frieze from the Parthenon—is at once the perception of its amazingly integrated and intense feeling. To ask whether the sculptor wanted to convey this particular feeling is to ask whether he made what he wanted to make; and in a work so unmistakably successful the question is rather silly.

---

[2]The subject of "natural symbols" was discussed in Chap. 14, pp. 236–239, and at greater length in *New Key*, chap. v; and originally by Cassirer, *Die Philosophie der symbolischen Formen*, Vol. II, *passim*.

Once we stop worrying about understanding the sculptor, and give ourselves up purely to the work, we do not seem to be confronted with a symbol at all, but with an object of peculiar emotional value. There is an actual emotion induced by its contemplation, quite different from "the feeling in it"; this actual emotion, which has been called "the aesthetic emotion," is not expressed in the work, but belongs to the percipient; it is a psychological effect of his artistic activity, essentially the same whether the object which holds his attention be a fragile bit of poetry, a work of terrible impact and many torturing dissonances like Joyce's *Ulysses,* or the serene Parthenon frieze; the "aesthetic emotion" is really a pervasive feeling of *exhilaration,* directly inspired by the perception of good art. It is the "pleasure" that art is supposed to give. "Pleasure" is an indiscriminate word; its use has led to endless confusion, so it is best avoided altogether. But so many artists and good critics, from the ancients, through Goethe, Coleridge, and Keats, to Santayana and Herbert Read,[3] have used it that it is worth while to note its exact meaning with respect to art; since it is not likely that those men labored (or labor) under any of the misconceptions to which its commoner meanings have given rise. For my part, however, I think best to avoid both "pleasure" and "the aesthetic emotion." There is, indeed, not much to say about the feeling in question except that it is an index of good art. Other things than art can evoke it, if and only if they excite the same intuitive activity that art excites.

The direct perception of emotional forms may occur when we look at nature with "the painter's eye," think poetically of actual experiences, find a dance motif in the evolutions of circling birds, etc.—that is, when anything strikes us as *beautiful.* An object perceived in this way acquires the same air of illusion that a temple or a textile, physically as actual as birds and mountains, exhibits; that is why artists can take themes upon themes, inexhaustibly, from nature. But natural objects become expressive only to the artistic imagination, which discovers their forms. A work of art is intrinsically expressive; it is designed to abstract and present forms for perception—forms of life and feeling, activity, suffer-

---

[3] See especially George Santayana, *The Sense of Beauty,* in which beauty is defined as "pleasure objectified," and Herbert Read, *The Meaning of Art* (1931), p. 18: ". . . art is most simply and most usually defined as an attempt to create pleasing forms."

ing, selfhood—whereby we conceive these realities, which otherwise we
can but blindly undergo.

Every good work of art is beautiful; as soon as we find it so, we
have grasped its expressiveness, and until we do we have not seen it as
good art, though we may have ample intellectual reason to believe that
it is so. Beautiful works may contain elements that, taken in isolation,
are hideous; the obscenities that Ezra Pound piles one upon the other
in Cantos XIV and XV are revolting, but their function in the poem is
that of a violent dissonance. Here is a creation of Hell without its name
(which occurs only in retrospect, in Canto XVI, and then only once)
and without a single mention of torture, punishment, fire, or any other
traditional image. The passage following "Andiamo!", though in itself
not at all delightful, achieves the sense of release long before the nightmare really lets go; the *words* have let go. Such elements are the strength
of the work, which must be great to contain and transfigure them. The
emergent form, the whole, is alive and therefore beautiful, as awful
things may be—as gargoyles, and fearful African masks, and the Greek
tragedies of incest and murder are beautiful. Beauty is not identical with
the normal, and certainly not with charm and sense appeal, though all
such properties may go to the making of it. Beauty is expressive form.

The entire qualification one must have for understanding art is responsiveness. That is primarily a natural gift, related to creative talent,
yet not the same thing; like talent, where it exists in any measure it
may be heightened by experience or reduced by adverse agencies. Since
it is intuitive, it cannot be taught; but the free exercise of artistic intuition often depends on clearing the mind of intellectual prejudices and
false conceptions that inhibit people's natural responsiveness. If, for instance, a reader of poetry believes that he does not "understand" a poem
unless he can paraphrase it in prose, and that the poet's true or false
opinions are what make the poem good or bad, he will read it as a piece
of discourse, and his perception of poetic form and poetic feeling are
likely to be frustrated. He may be naturally quite sensitive and responsive to literature, but anything he identifies as "poetry" will seem incomprehensible or else fallacious to him. His intellectual attitude, fostered
by a theoretical conviction, stands in the way of his responsiveness. Simi-

larly, if academic training has caused us to think of pictures primarily as examples of schools, periods, or the classes that Croce decries ("landscapes," "portraits," "interiors," etc.), we are prone to think *about* the picture, gathering quickly all available data for intellectual judgments, and so close and clutter the paths of intuitive response.

The exhilaration of a direct aesthetic experience[4] indicates the depth of human mentality to which that experience goes. A work of art, or anything that affects us as art does, may truly be said to "do something to us," though not in the usual sense which aestheticians rightly deny —giving us emotions and moods. What it does to us is to formulate our conceptions of feeling and our conceptions of visual, factual, and audible reality together. It gives us *forms of imagination* and *forms of feeling*, inseparably; that is to say, it clarifies and organizes intuition itself. That is why it has the force of a revelation, and inspires a feeling of deep intellectual satisfaction, though it elicits no conscious intellectual work (reasoning). Aesthetic intuition seizes the greatest form, and therefore the main import, at once; there is no need of working through lesser ideas and serried implications first without a vision of the whole, as in discursive reasoning, where the total intuition of relatedness comes as the conclusion, like a prize. In art, it is the impact of the whole, the immediate revelation of vital import, that acts as the psychological lure to long contemplation.

In a work that requires an appreciable length of time for complete physical perception, such as a novel, a musical piece, a dance, or a play, the author's first task is to imply, at the very outset, the scope and vital import of the whole. If his imagination of the piece is clear, that task is usually met unconsciously; and the "lure of feeling" (to borrow a phrase from Whitehead) is established almost at once. It is true, therefore, that one has to read or witness a piece in its entirety before one can judge it, but not before one enjoys it.

---

[4]John Dewey, in *Art as Experience*, distinguishes the "artistic" attitude and experience from the "aesthetic"; his division corresponds, I think, to what I called the "studio standpoint" and the "audience standpoint" respectively—creative imagination and responsiveness. Actually, of course, we move freely from one attitude to the other; every responsive person has some creative imagination, and certainly every artist must perceive and enjoy art, if only to be his own **first** public.

The outstanding instance of what one might call "intuitive anticipation" is the excitement that seizes a real lover of drama as the curtain goes up (or, sometimes, even before). This excitement has been so often remarked that some people have sought an explanation of it outside the realm of art experience proper, and taken it as a vestige of the religious emotion that was supposedly associated with dramatic performances in past ages.[5] But to the instinctive devotee of the theater the imminent poetic experience seems quite enough to justify his anticipation without any atavistic reference to primitive religion or other tribal interests. Charles Morgan, who evidently knows it well, finds its source in the drama's artistic function alone.

"Every playgoer," he writes, in the article I have quoted before (on p. 309), "has been made aware now and then of the existence in the theatre of a supreme unity, a mysterious power, a transcendent and urgent illusion, which, so to speak, floats above the stage action and above the spectator, . . . endowing him with a vision, a sense of translation and ecstasy, alien to his common knowledge of himself. The hope of this illusion is the excitement, and the experience of it the highest reward, of playgoing. . . . Again and again we are disappointed. . . . But now and then a persistent playgoer's hope, or a part of it, is fulfilled. The order of his experience is always the same—a shock, and after the shock an inward stillness, and from that stillness an influence emerging, which transmutes him. Transmutes *him*—not his opinions. This great impact is neither a persuasion of the intellect nor a beguiling of the senses. . . . It is the enveloping movement of the whole drama upon the soul of man. We surrender and are changed."[6]

In a later passage he explains—correctly, I think—what bestows this extraordinary value on a work of art that really moves us, in the aesthetic and not the ordinary sense:

"Dramatic art has . . . a double function—first to still the preoccupied mind, to empty it of triviality, to make it receptive and meditative; then to impregnate it. Illusion is the impregnating power. It is that spiritual force in dramatic art which impregnates the silences of the spectator [reference here is to Wordsworth's "long barren silence" by

---

[5]Cf. Chap. 17, p. 320.
[6]"The Nature of Dramatic Illusion," pp. 63–64.

the fireside], enabling him to imagine, to perceive, even to become, what he could not of himself become or perceive or imagine."[7]

What Mr. Morgan says of drama may be said of any work that confronts us as a major aesthetic experience: it makes a revelation of our inner life. But it does more than that—it shapes our imagination of external reality according to the rhythmic forms of life and sentience, and so impregnates the world with aesthetic value. As Kant observed in the *Critique of Judgment,* the beauty of nature is its conformity to our understanding, and that conformity is something originally imposed on it by our intuition.[8]

Life as we see, act, and feel it is as much a product of the art we have known as of the language (or languages) which shaped our thought in infancy. Guillaume Apollinaire, in a little monograph on Cubism (the first portion largely vitiated by irresponsible use of borrowed terms, "the fourth dimension," "infinity," etc.), observed this fact in the effect of certain great painters on popular visual conception. "Without poets," he said, "without artists . . . the order which we find in nature, and which is only an effect of art, would at once vanish." And further:

"To create the illusion[9] of the typical is the social role and peculiar end of art. God knows how the pictures of Renoir and Monet were abused! Very well! But one has only to glance at some photographs of the period

---

[7]*Ibid.,* p. 70. A very similar observation is made in C. E. Montague's informal but valuable little book, *A Writer's Notes on his Trade:* "At the climax of a tragedy it seems as if the average man or woman could understand almost anything—even things which may again become incomprehensible to them next day when they try to understand how they understood them." (P. 237.) Further on, he remarks that part of the thrill of reading or seeing great tragedy is exultation "at our own strangely heightened power of being moved without being numbed and of seeing, as it seems, right into life's glowing heart with a clearness and calm not attainable in almost any other mood." (P. 237.) Only, it is not the mood, I believe, that makes such insight viable, but the *means;* it is unattainable by any other symbol. He is, furthermore, well aware of the growth of consciousness, the clarification, which aesthetic experience initiates: "When a perfect tragedy possesses your mind you seem for a moment to have your hand near to some clue to all that region of enigma. You cannot keep your hold on the clue but, for those moments verging on trance, everything has run almost clear in your mind; when the experience is over, you feel sure that what you have had was vision and not delusion." (P. 238.)

[8]*Critique of Judgment,* Introduction, VIII; in Meredith's translation (Oxford, 1911), p. 34 of the text.

[9]The meaning here is *delusion*—a cause of error—not created appearance.

to see how closely people and things conformed to the pictures of them by these great masters.

"Since of all the plastic products of an epoch, works of art have the most energy, this illusion seems to me quite natural. The energy of art imposes itself on men, and becomes for them the plastic standard of the period. . . . All the art works of an epoch end by resembling the most energetic, the most expressive, and the most typical works of the period. Dolls belong to popular art; yet they always seem to be inspired by the great art of the same period."[10]

As painting affects visual imagination, poetry (in the broad sense, including verse, prose, fiction, and drama) affects one's conception of events. There is a passage in D. H. Lawrence's *Sons and Lovers* that presents with great authenticity a person's need of *composing* dreadful events in order to make them definite, emotionally significant, before coping with them practically and morally. The situation which is the context of this passage has been developed gradually: Morel, a miner who is becoming a confirmed drunkard, has grown more and more abusive and violent toward his hard-driven and pregnant wife, until, at the moment in question, he has just laid rough hands on her, for the first time, and thrown her out of the house. The narrative reads: "For a while she could not control her consciousness; mechanically she went over the last scene, then over it again, certain phrases, certain moments coming each time like a brand red-hot down on her soul; and each time she enacted again the past hour, each time the brand came down at the same points, till the mark was burnt in, and the pain burnt out, and at last she came to herself."

Life is incoherent unless we give it form. Usually the process of formulating our own situations and our own biography is not as conscious as Mrs. Morel's struggle to conceive the outrage she had suffered; but it follows the same pattern—we "put it into words," tell it to ourselves, compose it in terms of "scenes," so that in our minds we can enact all its important moments. The basis of this imaginative work is the poetic art we have known, from the earliest nursery rhymes to the most profound, or sophisticated, or breath-taking drama and fiction.[11] What Apolli-

---

[10]*The Cubist Painters. Aesthetic Meditations* (translated by L. Abel), p. 13.

[11]A precocious young child of my acquaintance once related, at the breakfast

naire observed about the influence of Renoir and Monet on people's visualization may be said also of Wordsworth's influence on their vocabulary and Balzac's on their sense of irony.

Above all, however, art penetrates deep into personal life because in giving form to the world, it articulates human nature: sensibility, energy, passion, and mortality. More than anything else in experience, the arts mold our actual life of feeling. This creative influence is a more important relation between art and contemporary life than the fact that motifs are derived from the artist's environment.[12] Surely, art is rooted in experience; but experience, in turn, is built up in memory and preformed in imagination according to the intuitions of powerful artists, often long dead (it takes time for an influence to reach the deepest strata of mentality, and what we learn in childhood, never to lose again, always stems from an earlier age), more rarely prophets in our own generation.[13]

Artistic training is, therefore, the education of feeling, as our usual schooling in factual subjects, and logical skills such as mathematical "figuring" or simple argumentation (principles are hardly ever explained), is the education of thought. Few people realize that the real education of emotion is not the "conditioning" effected by social approval and disapproval, but the tacit, personal, illuminating contact with symbols of feeling. Art education, therefore, is neglected, left to chance, or regarded as a cultural veneer. People who are so concerned for their children's scientific enlightenment that they keep Grimm out of the library and Santa Claus out of the chimney, allow the cheapest art, the worst of bad singing, the most revolting sentimental fiction to impinge on the children's minds all day and every day, from infancy. If the rank and file of youth grows up in emotional cowardice and confusion, sociologists

---

table, a dream she had had during the night—evidently a vivid paradisal dream—and ended with the ecstatic reflection: "It was so lovely—the grass under the trees, and so many, many puppies in the grass—and all in Technicolor!"

[12]André Malraux, speaking of the sculptures of Rheims cathedral, says: "Thirteenth-century man found both his inner order and its paradigm in the outer world." (*The Creative Act*, p. 81.)

[13]Cf. Owen Barfield's remark in *Poetic Diction*, p. 143: "Oscar Wilde's *mot*—that men are made by books, rather than books by men—was certainly not pure nonsense; there is a very real sense, humiliating as it may seem, in which what we generally call *our* feelings are really Shakespeare's 'meaning.'" Also Irwin Edman's, in *Arts and the Man*, p. 29: "For many people, it is literature rather than life that teaches them what their native emotions are."

look to economic conditions or family relations for the cause of this deplorable "human weakness," but not to the ubiquitous influence of corrupt art, which steeps the average mind in a shallow sentimentalism that ruins what germs of true feeling might have developed in it. Only an occasional devotee of the arts sees the havoc, as for instance Percy Buck, who remarked, nearly thirty years ago:

"There seems to be complete indifference, at all events in England, . . . whether the emotional side of a man is developed in any way at all. The one and only conviction an Englishman has about emotion is that you should learn, as early as possible, to suppress it entirely."

". . . what exercise should be to the physical side of our lives, religion to our moral, and learning to our intellectual side, this can art be, and nothing else but art, to our emotional side."[14]

And finally:

"All planning and design, that is to say all structure, is the presentation of feeling in terms of understanding."[15]

Art does not affect the viability of life so much as its quality; that, however, it affects profoundly. In this way it is akin to religion, which also, at least in its pristine, vigorous, spontaneous phase, defines and develops human feelings. When religious imagination is the dominant force in society, art is scarcely separable from it; for a great wealth of actual emotion attends religious experience, and unspoiled, unjaded minds wrestle joyfully for its objective expression, and are carried beyond the occasion that launched their efforts, to pursue the furthest possibilities of the expressions they have found. In an age when art is said to serve religion, religion is really feeding art. Whatever is holy to people inspires artistic conception.

When the arts become "liberated," as the saying is, from religion, they simply have exhausted the religious consciousness, and draw upon other sources. They were never bound to ritual or morals or sacred myth, but flourished freely in sacred realms as long as the human spirit was concentrated there. As soon as religion becomes prosaic or perfunctory, art appears somewhere else. Today the Church tolerates utterly bad painting and sculpture, and banal music, in the belief that saccharine

---

[14]Percy C. Buck, *The Scope of Music*, p. 52.
[15]*Ibid.*, p. 76.

Virgins and barbershop harmonies are "nearer to the people" than the "distanced," visionary Madonnas to which great artists gave (and still give) their souls and skills. And so they are, those sentimental reminders of pious ideas; they are as near as the china kitten and the long-legged doll, and all that sets them apart from such worldly objects is their literal meaning. They corrupt the religious consciousness that is developed in their image, and even while they illustrate the teachings of the Church they degrade those teachings to a level of worldly feeling. Bad music, bad statues and pictures are irreligious, because everything corrupt is irreligious. Indifference to art is the most serious sign of decay in any institution; nothing bespeaks its old age more eloquently than that art, under its patronage, becomes literal and self-imitating.

Then the most impressive, living art leaves the religious context, and draws on unrestricted feeling somewhere else. It cannot do otherwise; but in so doing it loses its traditional sphere of influence, the solemn, festive populace, and runs the danger of never reaching beyond the studio where it was created. Then artists talk heroically about "art for art's sake," as though art could ever have had any but artistic aims. The trouble is merely that for the average person, their work no longer has a natural place of display. A few rich people may own pictures and statues; but big, important art has always been public, and should be so. The museum, therefore, comes into being.

The problems of exhibition in a museum are many, and the effectiveness of a work is often gravely impaired by the presence of other pieces all around it. André Malraux has pointed out this danger in his *Museum Without Walls,* in which he praised, as one hopeful remedy, the ever-improving technique of reproduction which gives art lovers the album, a private collection of masterpieces. That in turn has its drawbacks, and they are many; but the real loss which art has suffered by its secularization is common to the real museum and the "imaginary museum" of printed plates: people do not naturally and constantly see works of art. Going into a museum is not a normal, regular occurrence in the average life, like going to Church or Temple. The album lies in a rack from which it is occasionally taken to be looked at; its treasures do not loom up before one in their greatness, as altarpieces and splendid windows and statues do. The plastic arts have become estranged from their public.

All, that is, except one, which flourishes today, perhaps most vigor-
ously in America: architecture. Everyone sees great buildings, bridges,
viaducts, grain elevators, chimneys, ships, and consciously or unconsciously feels their impact on his emotional life and his *Weltanschauung*.
That is the education of the "inward eye," of the creative imagination
that guides perception.

Music, dance, and drama, meanwhile, have become entirely natural-
ized in a realm that seems, at first sight, the very opposite of the sacred
precinct where they were born; they have found acceptance as entertainment. But, as I have said before, entertainment is not essentially
frivolous, like amusement. The latter is a temporary stimulus, the "lift"
of vital feeling that normally issues in laughter. It is generally pleasant,
and sometimes erroneously sought as a cure for depression. But entertainment is any activity without direct practical aim, anything people
attend to simply because it interests them. Interest, not amusement nor
even pleasure, is its watchword. Social conversation, table talk, is entertainment. It may be the gross humor of the smoking room, the chatter
of the cocktail party, the famous breakfast conversation of Oliver Wendell
Holmes or the more famous table talk of Mohammed. Entertainment is
not in itself a value-category. It includes both pastime and the satisfaction of imperious mental needs; but, trivial or serious, it is always
work of the mind. Whitehead has defined it as "what people do with
their freedom."[16]

The degree of refinement in individuals may be gauged by what
amuses them (George Meredith held that Germans were too gross to be
amused by comedy); but their mental energy and emotional strength is
shown in what interests them—the seriousness and difficulty to which
their entertainment may go, without becoming "work," (like the great
books one reads only in school, or the concerts and plays to which one
"ought" to go for educational reasons). Shakespeare's tragedies were
written for an entertainment theater in which people sought not amusement but the exhilaration of artistic experience, overwhelming drama.

Art is as properly at home in entertainment as in religion. There is

---

[16]"Freedom" is a better word than the more common term "leisure," because
"leisure" connotes *relaxation*, whereas free activity is often the greatest stretch of
which our minds are capable.

no need of interpreting Hamlet as a modern Oedipus, or the Elizabethan stage in the light of the Athenian choric theater, to understand the power of the secular tragic drama. But the similarity to ancient ritual which Francis Fergusson and some other scholars[17] profess to find in Shakespearean tragedy, and even in that of Ibsen, does indicate, I believe, the common *artistic* purpose of all these works—the envisagement of individual existence as a whole, and of its complete development to the limits of action and passion. This envisagement, first presented in sacred art, is a necessity to people who have attained a mature self-consciousness; once the sense of tragedy dawns in us, we are haunted by it, and crave to see it clarified and composed. Few people know why tragedy is a source of deep satisfaction; they invent all sorts of psychological explanations, from emotional catharsis to a sense of superiority because the hero's misfortunes are not one's own.[18] But the real source is the joy of revelation, the vision of a world wholly significant, of life spending itself and death the signature of its completion. It is simply the joy of great art, which is the perception of created form wholly expressive, that is to say, beautiful.

Tragedy, difficult or overwhelming music, the passionately serious dancing of some modern ballets, have their place in "entertainment" because we give ourselves up to their contemplation spontaneously, eagerly, without any other intent than to hear and see and be enthralled. But we seek them from that need of art which used to be assuaged more surely and more often by sacred objects and offices.

The same need of art, and not an indiscriminate wish for amusement, is met by comedy, bright music, humorous choreography; solemnity is not necessary to expressiveness—not even to greatness. The criterion of good art is its power to command one's contemplation and reveal a feeling that one recognizes as real, with the same "click of recognition" with which an artist knows that a form is true. All the forms of feeling are important, and the joyous pulse of life needs to be made apparent quite as much as the most involved passions, if we are to value it.

One of the stock questions of the classroom, and of people who read

---

[17]Cf. Chap. 19, pp. 319–320.

[18]Lucretius subscribed to this theory, in the opening passage of *De Rerum Natura*.

books "to learn about art," is: "What makes one work of art better than another?" This is, I think, a mistaken question. Works of art are not usually comparable.[19] Only prize-juries have to evaluate them with reference to some standard, which is inevitably arbitrary and in many cases inapplicable. A competent jury does not even define a standard. If it consists of people who have developed their powers of perception by long conversance with the order of art (i.e. poetry, sculpture, music, etc.) in which their judgments are to be made, intuition will guide the verdict. There will be disagreements—not because good and bad works cannot be distinguished, but because among successful ones there is no sure principle of selection. Personal or social factors usually tip the balances; "ratings" are trivial.

This does not mean, however, that works of art cannot be criticized. Appreciation—being impressed or left cold—comes first; but the recognition of how the illusion was made and organized and how the sense of import is immediately given by a strong piece, even though the critic himself may be nonplussed by its strange feeling—that recognition is a product of analysis, reached by discursive reasoning about the work and its effects. Such findings, however, are not criteria of excellence; they are explanations of it, or contrariwise of failure. As soon as they are generalized and used as measures of achievement they become baneful. In the case, for instance, of a poem that mediates no intuition, i.e. a bad poem, a little study may trace its lack of "livingness" to the use of ready-made phrases, where their presence as familiar phrases serves no artistic purpose. The poem suggests other poems, it does not incorporate them; it is synthetic, it has no body—no organic structure—of its own. But to regard the presence of borrowed phrases, or indeed of *any* materials however shopworn, in itself as a criterion of badness is dangerous.[20] Materials are neither good nor bad, strong nor weak. Judg-

---

[19]Exceptions to this rule may be found, for instance among the several works of one author, if he uses the same main idea in a number of pieces. Herrick's poems "To Daffodils" and "To Blossoms" are essentially the same; the latter would probably be more famous than it is if the former were not a more successful treatment of the same poetic idea. Böcklin painted four versions of his "Toteninsel"; these four paintings are comparable works. Malraux, in *The Creative Art*, compares the four versions of El Greco's "Christ Driving the Money Lenders out of the Temple," to good purpose.

[20]Cf. the discussion of Tillyard's comments on the Stabat Mater, in Chap. 13, pp. 229–230.

ment, therefore, must be guided by the virtual results, the artist's success or failure, which is intuitively known or not at all.

No theory can set up criteria of expressiveness (i.e. standards of beauty).[21] If it could, we could learn to make poetry or paint pictures by rule. But because every artist must find the means of expressing his own "Idea," he can be helped only by criticism, not by precept or example; and criticism, if it is to develop his powers, must be based on his partial success—that is, the critic must see the commanding form of the disciple's work, because that is the measure of right and wrong in the work. Where there is no matrix of envisaged feeling to be articulated there is no technical problem.

Talent is essentially the native ability to handle such ideas as one has, to achieve desired effects. It seems to be closely linked with body-feeling, sensitivity, muscular control, verbal or tonal memory, as well as the one great mental requirement, aesthetic responsiveness. Because of its complex alliances now with this, now with that chance factor in the human organism, it tends to be specialized and perhaps hereditary, and to occur in all possible gradations, as everybody knows. The average person has a little talent for singing or playing music, a little talent for writing, acting, dancing, can draw a little, shape a rudimentary sculpture (at least a snow man), etc. A complete lack of some talent—utter inability to sing a tune, for instance, or to take part in a square dance—is unusual enough to be remarked. And what is known as an "average talent" for an art can be developed to a considerable extent by giving it exercise.

Genius, on the other hand, is generally supposed to admit of no degrees, but is regarded as itself a superlative degree of talent. In the various systems of psychometrics that have been invented to gauge aptitudes and talents, there is (or used to be) a certain point on the scale known as the "genius level." "A genius" is thought to do with ease what

---

[21]David Prall, in his *Aesthetic Analysis*, pointed out all sorts of philosophical difficulties in the way of an aesthetics which could yield intellectual criteria to judge of artistic "masterpieces," but he did not, apparently, find the demand itself unreasonable (see p. 26: "If we should look for a sure criterion of masterpieces, only sound aesthetics would serve to give us one"); he only despaired of its feasability. Yet later, as with a sudden insight, he says: "The difference between perceiving clearly and understanding distinctly is not the great difference that we are sometimes led to think it. And the most obvious fact about knowing works of art is that direct apprehension is the final adequate knowledge that we want." (P. 39.) What further criterion, then, should "a sound aesthetics" yield?

others achieve only by long and painful effort. For this reason, precocity is commonly taken for a sign of genius; and every year the concert stage, the radio, the screen, and sometimes even the picture gallery hail as an undoubted genius some truly amazing child, whose talent overcomes the difficulties of technique as a deer takes the pasture bars; and sometimes that child grows up to set the art world afire (Mozart was not the only one), but far more often its adult life proves to be that of a good professional artist without special distinction.

Genius is, in fact, not a degree of talent at all. Talent is special ability to express what you can conceive; but genius is the power of conception. Although some degree of talent is necessary if genius is not to be stillborn, great artists have not always had extraordinary technical ability; they have often struggled for expression, but the urgency of their ideas caused them to develop every vestige of talent until it rose to their demands. Calvocoressi reports that Musorgsky "created laboriously, clumsily, imperfectly. It was truly owing to the power of his genius that he produced immortal pages: he always did this, when his inspiration was sufficiently powerful to record itself in its own way. . . ."[22] Here the distinction between genius and talent is implicit.

Malraux, in his great *Psychology of Art*, recognizes it explicitly when he says: "Caravaggio was a firm believer in 'the real,' and the emotional tension of his style, at its best, comes from the fact that, while his talent made him cling to this realism, his genius urged him to break free from it."[23] Here talent and genius appear not only distinct, but at odds, though they seem more evenly matched than in Musorgsky. An interesting case of great talent without any notable genius is reflected in Friedrich Ludwig Schröder's criticism of his famous colleague, Iffland, whose extraordinary natural gifts had astonished Goethe, and led Schiller to predict that in him Germany would at last find a truly great actor: "Iffland," wrote Schröder, with more insight than the poets, "is not a creator. Even for his comic roles he always seeks some model that he can copy. My principle, which experience has never yet belied, is: a great actor cannot copy."[24]

---

[22]M. D. Calvocoressi: *Musorgsky, the Russian Musical Nationalist*. Quoted by J. T. Howard in his article, "Inevitability as a Criterion of Art," *Musical Quarterly*, 9 (1923), pp. 303–13.

[23]Vol. III, *The Twilight of the Absolute*, p. 226.

[24]Quoted in Manfred Barthel's *Schauspielerbriefe aus zwei Jahrhunderten*.

When, however, genius is single-mindedly served by a supreme talent, it is free to unfold, as Mozart's did, and Raphael's. But it is a mistake to think genius is complete from the beginning. Talent is much more likely to be so, wherefore the infant prodigy is a well-known phenomenon. Genius, indeed, sometimes appears only with maturity, as in Van Gogh, whose early pictures are undistinguished, and grows and deepens from work to work, like Beethoven's, Shakespeare's, or Cézanne's, long after technical mastery has reached its height.

Since genius is not superlative talent, but the power to conceive invisible realities—sentience, vitality, emotion—in a new symbolic projection that reveals something of their nature for the first time, it does admit of degrees; and a small amount of genius is not a rare endowment. Whatever its scope, it is the mark of the true artist; and though he be a craftsman by profession, it sets him above the pure craftsman, the copyist and exploiter, in the realm of art.

Art is a public possession, because the formulation of "felt life" is the heart of any culture, and molds the objective world for the people. It is their school of feeling, and their defense against outer and inner chaos. It is only when nature is organized in imagination along lines congruent with the forms of feeling that we can understand it, i.e. find it rational (this was Goethe's ideal of science, and Kant's concept of beauty). Then intellect and emotion are unopposed, life is symbolized by its setting, the world seems important and beautiful and is intuitively "grasped."

But why, if art is indeed the clarification of emotional life, is the "artistic temperament" proverbially a perturbed, unbridled, or even slightly mad temperament? Why is the artist himself not the principal beneficiary of his genius?

In a way, of course, he is; in every successful work it is primarily his problem that he has solved, his mind that he has enlightened. But he does not rest in his creations, as the lay public does; his formulations and revelations are an end product for him. His reward is the image, not the use of it, for while other people contemplate and enjoy it and incorporate his vision in their lives, he is already in pursuit of another.[25] He has no time to put his own house in order.

---

[25] Perhaps that is why people who, as the saying goes, "have only one book in them," are usually better adjusted than the boundlessly fertile genius. They compose the image of their own lives and clarify their own feelings in that image, and having found their mental security, are not hag-ridden by further visions.

One word more: for the consideration of art as a cultural heritage brings us back to a concept that was set aside in an earlier connection —the concept of art as a kind of "communication." It has its dangers because, on the analogy of language, one naturally expects "communication" to be between the artist and his audience, which· I think is a misleading notion. But there is something that may, without danger of too much literalness, be called "communication through art," namely the report which the arts make of one age or nation to the people of another. No historical record could tell us in a thousand pages as much about the Egyptian mind as one visit to a representative exhibit of Egyptian art. What would the European know of Chinese culture, with its vast reach into the past, if Chinese feeling had not been articulated in sculpture and painting? What would we know of Israel without its great literary work—quite apart from its factual record? Or of our own past, without mediaeval art? In this sense, art is a communication, but it is not personal, nor anxious to be understood.

The problems raised by the theory of the Art Symbol, and capable of solution in its light, seem inexhaustible, but books must have an end; I must leave the rest to the future,[26] perhaps to other thinkers. The theory itself, which I have here set forth, is not really one person's work. It is a step—and I think, an important one—in a philosophy of art on which many aestheticians have already labored, the theory of expressive form. Despite all shortcomings, blind leads, or mistakes that they may see in each other's doctrines, I believe that Bell, Fry, Bergson, Croce, Baensch, Collingwood, Cassirer, and I (not to forget such literary critics as Barfield and Day Lewis and others too, whom I have not named and perhaps not even read) have been and are, really, engaged on one philosophical project. It was Cassirer—though he never regarded himself as an aesthetician—who hewed the keystone of the structure, in his broad and disinterested study of symbolic forms; and I, for my part, would put that stone in place, to join and sustain what so far we have built.

---

[26]The nature of artistic abstraction, hardly touched upon here, and the unity of all the arts, is an obvious sequel to the present study, which I hope to treat in a following book.

A NOTE ON THE FILM

Here is a new art. For a few decades it seemed like nothing more than a new technical device in the sphere of drama, a new way of preserving and retailing dramatic performances. But today its development has already belied this assumption. The screen is not a stage, and what is created in the conception and realization of a film is not a play. It is too early to systematize any theory of this new art, but even in its present pristine state it exhibits—quite beyond any doubt, I think—not only a new technique, but a new poetic mode.

Much of the material for the following reflections was collected by four of my former seminar students,[1] at Columbia Teachers College, who have kindly permitted me to use their findings. I am likewise indebted to Mr. Robert W. Sowers, who (also as a member of that seminar) made a study of photography that provided at least one valuable idea, namely that photographs, no matter how posed, cut, or touched up, must *seem* *factual*, or as he called it, "authentic." I shall return later to that suggestion.

The significant points, for my purposes, that were demonstrated by the four collaborating members were (1) that the structure of a motion picture is not that of drama, and indeed lies closer to narrative than to drama; and (2) that its artistic potentialities became evident only when the moving camera was introduced.

The moving camera divorced the screen from the stage. The straightforward photographing of stage action, formerly viewed as the only artistic possibility of the film, henceforth appeared as a special technique.

---

[1] Messrs. Joseph Pattison, Louis Forsdale, William Hoth, and Mrs. Virginia E. Allen. Mr. Hoth is now Instructor in English at Cortland (New York) State Teachers College; the other three are members of the Columbia Teachers College staff.

The screen actor is not governed by the stage, nor by the conventions of the theater, he has his own realm and conventions; indeed, there may be no "actor" at all. The documentary film is a pregnant invention. The cartoon does not even involve persons merely "behaving."

The fact that the moving picture could develop to a fairly high degree as a silent art, in which speech had to be reduced and concentrated into brief, well-spaced captions, was another indication that it was not simply drama. It used pantomime, and the first aestheticians of the film considered it as essentially pantomime. But it is not pantomime; it swallowed that ancient popular art as it swallowed the photograph.

One of the most striking characteristics of this new art is that it seems to be omnivorous, able to assimilate the most diverse materials and turn them into elements of its own. With every new invention—montage, the sound track, Technicolor—its devotees have raised a cry of fear that now its "art" must be lost. Since every such novelty is, of course, promptly exploited before it is even technically perfected, and flaunted in its rawest state, as a popular sensation, in the flood of meaningless compositions that steadily supplies the show business, there is usually a tidal wave of particularly bad rubbish in association with every important advance. But the art goes on. It swallows everything: dancing, skating, drama, panorama, cartooning, music (it almost always requires music).

Therewithal it remains a poetic art. But it is not any poetic art we have known before; it makes the primary illusion—virtual history—in its own mode.

This is, essentially, *the dream mode*. I do not mean that it copies dream, or puts one into a daydream. Not at all; no more than literature invokes memory, or makes us believe that *we* are remembering. An art mode is *a mode of appearance*. Fiction is "like" memory in that it is projected to compose a finished experiential form, a "past"—not the reader's past, nor the writer's, though the latter may make a claim to it (that, as well as the use of actual memory as a model, is a literary device). Drama is "like" action in being causal, creating a total imminent experience, a personal "future" or Destiny. Cinema is "like" dream in the mode of its presentation: it creates a virtual present, an order of direct apparition. That is the mode of dream.

The most noteworthy formal characteristic of dream is that the dreamer is always at the center of it. Places shift, persons act and speak, or change or fade—facts emerge, situations grow, objects come into view with strange importance, ordinary things infinitely valuable or horrible, and they may be superseded by others that are related to them essentially by feeling, not by natural proximity. But the dreamer is always "there," his relation is, so to speak, equidistant from all events. Things may occur around him or unroll before his eyes; he may act or want to act, or suffer or contemplate; but the *immediacy* of everything in a dream is the same for him.

This aesthetic peculiarity, this relation to things perceived, characterizes the *dream mode:* it is this that the moving picture takes over, and whereby it creates a virtual present. In its relation to the images, actions, events, that constitute the story, the camera is in the place of the dreamer.

But the camera *is* not a dreamer. We are usually agents in a dream. The camera (and its complement, the sound track) is not itself in the picture. It is the mind's eye and nothing more. Neither is the picture (if it is art) likely to be dreamlike in its structure. It is a poetic composition, coherent, organic, governed by a definitely conceived feeling, not dictated by actual emotional pressures.

The basic abstraction whereby virtual history is created in the dream mode is immediacy of experience, "givenness," or as Mr. Sowers calls it, "authenticity." This is what the art of the film abstracts from actuality, from our actual dreaming.

The percipient of a moving picture sees with the camera; his standpoint moves with it, his mind is pervasively present. The camera is his eye (as the microphone is his ear—and there is no reason why a mind's eye and a mind's ear must always stay together). *He takes the place of the dreamer,* but in a perfectly objectified dream—that is, he is not in the story. The work is the appearance of a dream, a unified, continuously passing, significant *apparition.*

Conceived in this way, a good moving picture is a work of art by all the standards that apply to art as such. Sergei Eisenstein speaks of good and bad films as, respectively, "vital" and "lifeless"[2]; speaks of photo-

---

[2]*The Film Sense,* p. 17.

graphic shots as "elements,"[3] which combine into "images," which are "objectively unpresentable" (I would call them poetic impressions), but are greater elements compounded of "representations," whether by montage or symbolic acting or any other means.[4] The whole is governed by the "initial general image which originally hovered before the creative artist"[5]—the matrix, the commanding form; and it is this (not, be it remarked, the artist's emotion) that is to be evoked in the mind of the spectator.

Yet Eisenstein believed that the beholder of a film was somewhat specially called on to use his imagination, to create his own experience of the story.[6] Here we have, I think, an indication of the powerful illusion the film makes not of things going on, but of the dimension in which they go on—a *virtual* creative imagination; for it *seems* one's own creation, direct visionary experience, a "dreamt reality." Like most artists, he took the virtual experience for the most obvious fact.[7]

The fact that a motion picture is not a plastic work but a poetic presentation accounts for its power to assimilate the most diverse materials, and transform them into non-pictorial elements. Like dream, it enthralls and commingles all senses; its basic abstraction—direct apparition—is made not only by visual means, though these are paramount, but by words, which punctuate vision, and music that supports the unity of its shifting "world." It needs many, often convergent, means to create the continuity of emotion which holds it together while its visions roam through space and time.

It is noteworthy that Eisenstein draws his materials for discussion

---

[3]*Ibid.*, p. 4.
[4]*Ibid.*, p. 8.
[5]*Ibid.*, p. 31.
[6]*Ibid.*, p. 33: ". . . the spectator is drawn into a creative act in which his individuality is not subordinated to the author's individuality, but is opened up throughout the process of fusion with the author's intention, just as the individuality of a great actor is fused with the individuality of a great playwright in the creation of a classic scenic image. In fact, every spectator . . . creates an image in accordance with the representational guidance, suggested by the author, leading him to understanding and experience of the author's theme. This is the same image that was planned and created by the author, but this image is at the same time created also by the spectator himself."
[7]Compare the statement in Ernest Lindgren's *The Art of the Film*, p. 92, apropos of the moving camera: "It is the spectator's own mind that moves."

from epic rather than dramatic poetry; from Pushkin rather than Chekhov, Milton rather than Shakespeare. That brings us back to the point noted by my seminar students, that the novel lends itself more readily to screen dramatization than the drama. The fact is, I think, that a story narrated does not require as much "breaking down" to become screen apparition, because it has no framework itself of fixed *space,* as the stage has; and one of the aesthetic peculiarities of dream, which the moving picture takes over, is the nature of its space. Dream events are spatial—often intensely concerned with space—intervals, endless roads, bottomless canyons, things too high, too near, too far—but they are not oriented in any total space. The same is true of the moving picture, and distinguishes it—despite its visual character—from plastic art: *its space comes and goes.* It is always a secondary illusion.

The fact that the film is somehow related to dream, and is in fact in a similar mode, has been remarked by several people, sometimes for reasons artistic, sometimes non-artistic. R. E. Jones noted its freedom not only from spatial restriction, but from temporal as well. "Motion pictures," he said, "are our thoughts made visible and audible. They flow in a swift succession of images, precisely as our thoughts do, and their speed, with their flashbacks—like sudden uprushes of memory—and their abrupt transition from one subject to another, approximates very closely the speed of our thinking. They have the rhythm of the thought-stream and the same uncanny ability to move forward or backward in space or time. . . . They project pure thought, pure dream, pure inner life."[8]

The "dreamed reality" on the screen can move forward and backward because it is really an eternal and ubiquitous virtual present. The action of drama goes inexorably forward because it creates a future, a Destiny; the dream mode is an endless Now.

---

[8]*The Dramatic Imagination,* pp. 17–18.

BIBLIOGRAPHY

(The titles starred compose a selective reading list in the philosophy of art.)

*ADRIANI, BRUNO, *Problems of the Sculptor*. New York: Nierendorf Gallery, 1943.

AMES, VAN METER, *Aesthetics of the Novel*. Chicago: University of Chicago Press, 1928.

ARMITAGE, MERLE (ed.), *Modern Dance*. Compiled by Virginia Stewart. New York: E. Weyhe, 1935.

*BARFIELD, OWEN, *Poetic Diction: A Study in Meaning*. London: Faber & Gwyer, 1928.

BARNES, A. C., *The Art in Painting*. New York: Harcourt, Brace & Co., 1928.

BARTHEL, MANFRED, *Schauspielerbriefe aus zwei Jahrhunderten*. München: B. Funck Verlag, 1947.

BATESON, F. W., *English Poetry and the English Language: An Experiment in Literary History*. Oxford: Clarendon Press, 1934.

BEAUMONT, CYRIL W., *A Miscellany for Dancers*. London: C. W. Beaumont, 1934.

BEETHOVEN, L. VAN, *Briefe und Gespräche*. Edited by M. Hürlimann. Zürich: Atlantis Verlag, 1944.

*BELL, CLIVE, *Art*. London: Chatto & Windus, 1914.

BENNETT, ARNOLD, *Things That Have Interested Me*. Third Series. London: Chatto & Windus, 1926.

*BERGSON, HENRI, *Introduction to Metaphysics*. Translated by T. E. Hulme. New York: G. P. Putnam's Sons, 1912.

———. *Matière et mémoire*. Paris: Presses Universitaires, 1946. Translated as *Matter and Memory* by N. M. Paul and W. S. Palmer. New York: Macmillan Co., 1911.

———. *La pensée et le mouvant*. Paris: Presses Universitaires, 1946.

BEST-MAUGARD, ADOLFO, *A Method for Creative Design*. New York: A. A. Knopf, 1937.

BIRKHOFF, G. D., *Aesthetic Measure*. Cambridge (Mass.): Harvard University Press, 1933.

BLAIR, HUGH, *Lectures on Rhetoric and Belles Lettres*. London: W. Strahan, 1783.

BORODIN, GEORGE, *This Thing Called Ballet*. London: MacDonald & Co., [1945].

*BOSANQUET, BERNARD, *Three Lectures on Aesthetic*. New York: Macmillan Co., 1915.

BOURGUÈS, L., and DENÉRÉAZ, A., *La musique et la vie intérieure: Essai d'une histoire psychologique de l'art musical*. Paris: F. Alcan, 1921.

BOYNTON, H. W., *Journalism and Literature, and Other Essays*. Boston: Houghton Mifflin Co., 1904.

*BRADLEY, A. C., *Shakespearean Tragedy: Lectures on Hamlet, Othello, King Lear, Macbeth*. London: Macmillan Co., 1932.

BROWN, CALVIN, *Music and Literature: A Comparison of the Arts*. Athens (Georgia): University of Georgia Press, 1948.

BUCK, PERCY C., *The Scope of Music*. 2nd ed. London: Oxford University Press, 1927.

BUERMEYER, LAURENCE, *The Aesthetic Experience*. Merion (Penna.): Barnes Foundation, 1924.

BYNNER, WITTER, and KIANG KANG-HU, *The Jade Mountain*. New York: A. A. Knopf, 1929.

CASSIRER, ERNST, *An Essay on Man: An Introduction to a Philosophy of Human Culture*. New Haven: Yale University Press, 1944.

*———. *Language and Myth* (1925). Translated by S. K. Langer. New York: Harper & Bros., 1946.

———. *Die Philosophie der symbolischen Formen*. 3 vols. Berlin: B. Cassirer, 1923–29.

*CENTENO, AUGUSTO (ed.), *The Intent of the Artist*. Princeton: Princeton University Press, 1941.

CÉZANNE, PAUL, *Letters*. Edited by John Rewald. London: B. Cassirer, 1941.

CHEN, JACK, *The Chinese Theatre*. London: D. Dobson, 1949.

*COLLINGWOOD, R. G., *The Principles of Art*. Oxford: Clarendon Press, 1938.

*CROCE, BENEDETTO, *Aesthetic as Science of Expression and General Linguistic* (1901). Translated by Douglas Ainslie. 2nd ed. London: Macmillan Co., 1922.

CUSHING, F. H., *Zuñi Creation Myths*. (Report of the Bureau of American Ethnology.) Washington, D. C.: Government Printing Office, 1892.

DAICHES, DAVID, *The Novel and the Modern World*. Chicago: University of Chicago Press, 1939.

———. *A Study of Literature: For Readers and Critics*. Ithaca: Cornell University Press, 1948.

DANCKERT, WERNER, *Ursymbole Melodischer Gestaltung*. Kassel: Bärenreiter Verlag, 1932.

DEANE, C. V., *Dramatic Theory and the Rhymed Heroic Play*. London: Oxford University Press, 1931.

*DEWEY, JOHN, *Art as Experience*. New York: G. P. Putnam's Sons, 1934.

DUCASSE, CURT, *The Philosophy of Art*. New York: Dial Press, 1929.

DUNCAN, ISADORA, *My Life*. New York: Boni and Liveright, 1927.

DURKHEIM, ÉMILE, *Les formes élémentaires de la vie religieuse: Le système totémique en Australie*. Paris: F. Alcan, 1912.

EDMAN, IRWIN, *Arts and the Man*. New York: W. W. Norton & Co., 1939; New American Library, 1950.

*EISENSTEIN, SERGEI M., *The Film Sense*. Translated and edited by Jay Leyda. New York: Harcourt, Brace & Co., 1942.

ELIOT, T. S., *Selected Essays, 1917–1932*. New York: Harcourt, Brace & Co., 1932.

FAURÉ-FRÉMIET, PHILIPPE, *Pensée et ré-création*. Paris: F. Alcan, 1934.

*FERGUSSON, FRANCIS, *The Idea of a Theater*. Princeton: Princeton University Press, 1949.

FLACCUS, L. W., *The Spirit and Substance of Art*. 2nd ed. New York: F. S. Crofts & Co., 1931.

FREUD, SIGMUND, *Psychoanalytische Studien an Werken der Dichtung u. Kunst*. Leipzig: Internationaler Psychoanalytischer Verlag, 1924.

*———. *Die Traumdeutung*. Translated by A. A. Brill as *The Interpretation of Dreams*. New York: Macmillan Co., 1913.

*FRY, ROGER, *Vision and Design*. London: Chatto & Windus, 1925.

GEISSLER, EWALD, *Der Schauspieler*. Berlin: Bühnenvolksbundverlag, 1926.

GHYKA, MATILA C., *Essai sur le rythme*. Paris: Gallimard, 1938.

*GODDARD, JOSEPH, *The Deeper Sources of the Beauty and Expression of Music*. London: W. Reeves [1905].

GOETHE, J. WOLFGANG VON, *Maximen und Reflexionen über Kunst*. Weimar: Goethe-Gesellschaft, 1907.

*GOLDWATER, ROBERT, and TREVES, MARCO (editors), *Artists on Art*. New York: Pantheon Books, Inc., 1945.

GOURMONT, REMY DE, *Le problème du style*. Paris: Mercure, 1924.

HAMILTON, CLAYTON, *The Theory of the Theatre, and Other Principles of Dramatic Criticism*. New York: Henry Holt & Co., 1910.

*HANSLICK, EDUARD, *Vom Musikalisch-Schönen, Ein Beitrag zur Revision der Aesthetik der Tonkunst*. 9th ed. Leipzig: J. A. Barth, 1896. Translated by Gustav Cohen as *The Beautiful in Music*. 7th ed. London: Novello, 1891.

H'DOUBLER, MARGARET, *Dance: A Creative Art Experience*. New York: F. S. Crofts & Co., 1940.

HENDERSON, W. J., *What Is Good Music?* 3rd ed. New York: Charles Scribner's Sons, 1920.

HENLE, PAUL (ed.), *Structure, Method and Meaning: Essays in Honor of Henry M. Sheffer*. New York: Liberal Arts Press, 1951.

*HILDEBRAND, ADOLF, *The Problem of Form in Painting and Sculpture*. New York: G. E. Stechert & Co., 1932.

*JAMES, D. G., *Skepticism and Poetry: An Essay on the Poetic Imagination*. London: G. Allen & Unwin, 1937.

*JAMES, HENRY, *The Art of the Novel*. New York: Charles Scribner's Sons, 1934.

JEANNERET-GRIS, C. É. (Le Corbusier), *Toward a New Architecture*. With an Introduction by F. Etchells. New York: Payson & Clarke, [1927].

*JONES, R. E., *The Dramatic Imagination: Reflections and Speculations on the Art of the Theatre*. New York: Duell, Sloan & Pearce, 1941.

JUNG, C. G., *Contributions to Analytical Psychology*. Translated by H. G. and C. F. Baynes. New York: Harcourt, Brace & Co., 1928.

KANT, IMMANUEL, *Critique of Aesthetic Judgment.* Translated.by J. C. Meredith. Oxford: Clarendon Press, 1911.

KEITH, B. A., *The Sanskrit Drama in its Development, Theory and Practice.* Oxford: 1924.

KÖHLER, WOLFGANG, *Gestalt Psychology.* New York: H. Liveright, 1929

KURTH, ERNST, *Musikpsychologie.* Berlin: M. Hesse, 1931.

LABAN, RUDOLF VON, *Die Welt des Tänzers: Fünf Gedankenreigen.* Stuttgart, 1922.

LANGE, KONRAD VON, *Das Wesen der Kunst: Grundzüge einer realistichen Kunst-lehre.* Berlin: G. Grote, 1901.

LANGER, S. K., *Philosophy in a New Key.* Cambridge (Mass.): Harvard University Press, 1942; 2nd ed., 1951; New York: New American Library, 1948.

————. *The Practice of Philosophy.* New York: Henry Holt & Co., 1930.

LANGFELD, H. S., *The Aesthetic Attitude.* New York: Harcourt, Brace & Howe, 1920.

LEE, VERNON (Violet Paget), *The Beautiful.* Cambridge University Press, 1913.

LÉVI, SYLVAIN, *Le theatre indien.* Paris: 1890.

*LEWIS, CECIL DAY, *The Poetic Image.* New York: Oxford University Press, 1947.

LINDGREN, ERNEST, *The Art of the Film.* London: Allen & Unwin, 1948.

LIPPS, THEODOR, *Aesthetik.* Hamburg: L. Voss, 1903.

*MACAN, R. W. (ed.), *Essays by Diverse Hands.* Transactions of the Royal Society of Literature, N. S. Vol. XII, 1933.

MAHLER, ELSA, *Die russische Totenklage: Ihre rituelle u. dichterische Deutung.* Leipzig: Harrassowitz, 1935.

*MALRAUX, ANDRÉ, *The Psychology of Art.* Translated by Stuart Gilbert. 3 vols. New York: Pantheon Books, Inc., 1949–50.

MANN, THOMAS, *Freud, Goethe, Wagner.* New York: A. A. Knopf, 1939.

*MARTINOVITCH, N. N., *The Turkish Theatre.* New York: Theatre Arts, Inc., 1933.

MATTHEWS, BRANDER, *A Book About the Theater.* New York: Charles Scribner's Sons, 1916.

MENDELSSOHN-BARTHOLDY, FELIX, *Meisterbriefe.* Edited by Ernst Wolff. Berlin: Behr Verlag, 1907.

MEREDITH, GEORGE, *An Essay on Comedy and the Uses of the Comic Spirit.* New York: Charles Scribner's Sons, 1897.

MOHOLY-NAGY, LÁSZLÓ, *The New Vision.* Translated by D. M. Hoffmann. New York: W. W. Norton & Co., 1938.

*MONTAGUE, C. E., *A Writer's Notes on His Trade.* Garden City: Doubleday, Doran & Co., 1930.

MOORE, GEORGE, *An Anthology of Pure Poetry.* New York: Boni & Liveright, 1924.

MOORE, JOHN B., *The Comic and the Realistic in English Drama.* Chicago: University of Chicago Press, 1925.

MORRIS, CHARLES, *Signs, Language and Behavior.* New York: Prentice-Hall, Inc., 1946.

MOZART, WOLFGANG AMADEUS, *Briefe*. Edited by Albert Leitzmann. Leipzig: Insel-Verlag, 1910.

MÜNZ, BERNHARD, *Hebbel als Denker*. Munich: 1913.

*NIETZSCHE, FRIEDRICH, *Die Geburt der Tragödie aus dem Geiste der Musik*. Nietzsches *Werke*, Klassiker Ausgabe, Vol I, Leipzig: 1922. Translated by H. Zimmern as *The Birth of Tragedy*. 3rd ed. New York: Macmillan Co., 1924.

NOVERRE, J. G., *Lettres sur la danse, et sur les ballets*. Lyons: 1760.

——. *Lettres sur les arts imitateurs en général et sur la danse en particulier*. Paris: L. Collin, 1807.

ORTEGA Y GASSET, JOSÉ, *La Deshumanización del Arte*. Madrid: Revista de Occidente, 1925.

PAGNOL, MARCEL, *Notes sur le rire*. Paris: Nagel, 1947.

PARKER, DeWITT, *The Analysis of Art*. New Haven: Yale University Press, 1926.

PEPPER, STEPHEN, *The Basis of Criticism in the Arts*. Cambridge (Mass.): Harvard University Press, 1945.

PERI NOËL, *Cinq nô: Drames lyriques japonais*. Paris: Bossard, 1921.

POINCARÉ, HENRI, *Science et Méthode*. Paris: E. Flammarion, 1908. Translated by F. Maitland as *Science and Method*. London: T. Nelson & Sons, 1914.

PORTER, EVELYN, *Music Through the Dance*. London: B. T. Batsford, 1937.

*POTTLE, F. A., *The Idiom of Poetry*. Rev. ed. Ithaca: Cornell University Press, 1946.

*PRALL, DAVID, *Aesthetic Analysis*. New York: Thomas Y. Crowell Co., 1936.

PRESCOTT, F. C., *The Poetic Mind*. New York: Macmillan Co., 1922.

*RADER, MELVIN, *A Modern Book of Aesthetics*. 2nd ed. New York: Henry Holt & Co., 1952.

READ, HERBERT, *The Meaning of Art*. London: Faber & Faber, Ltd., 1931.

RICHARDS, I. A., *Practical Criticism: A Study of Literary Judgment*. London: K. Paul, Trench, Trubner & Co., 1929.

——. *Principles of Literary Criticism*. New York: Harcourt, Brace & Co., 1924.

RODIN, AUGUSTE, *Art*. Conversations collected by Paul Grell and translated by Mrs. Romely Fedden. London: n. d.

SACHS, CURT, *The Commonwealth of Art: Style in the Fine Arts, Music and the Dance*. New York: W. W. Norton & Co., 1946.

*——. *World History of the Dance*. Translated by Bessie Schönberg. New York: W. W. Norton & Co., 1937.

SAKHAROFF, ALEXANDRE, *Reflexions sur la danse et la musique*. Buenos Aires: Vian, 1943.

SANTAYANA, GEORGE, *Reason in Art*. Vol. IV of *The Life of Reason*. New York: Charles Scribner's Sons, 1905–6.

——. *The Sense of Beauty*. New York: Charles Scribner's Sons, 1896.

SCHENKER, HEINRICH, *Neue musikalische Theorien u. Phantasien*. Dritter Band: *Der Freie Satz*. Wien: 1935.

SCHILLER, FRIEDRICH, *Die Braut von Messina; oder, Die Feindlichen Brüder*. Halle: Hendel, 1887.

*————. *Briefe über die aesthetische Erziehung des Menschen.* Hall: M. Niemeyer: 1927. Translated as *Letters on the Aesthetic Education of Man* in *Literary and Philosophical Essays,* Harvard Classics, 1910.

SCHILLINGER, JOSEPH, *The Mathematical Basis of the Arts.* New York: Philosophical Library, 1948.

————. *The Schillinger System of Musical Composition.* New York: C. Fischer, Inc., 1946.

SCHUMANN, ROBERT, *Gesammelte Schriften über Musik und Musiker.* 2 vols. Leipzig: Breitkopf & Härtel, 1914.

SCHWEITZER, ALBERT, *J. S. Bach, le musicien-poète.* 2nd ed. Leipzig: Breitkopf & Härtel, 1905.

SCOTT, GEOFFREY, *The Architecture of Humanism: A Study in the History of Taste.* 2nd ed. rev. London: Constable & Co., 1924.

SEYLER, ATHENE, and HAGGARD, STEPHEN, *The Craft of Comedy.* New York: Theatre Arts, Inc., 1946.

SIDGWICK, FRANK, *The Ballad.* New York: George Doran & Co. [1914].

SMITH, J. H., and PARKS, E. W., *The Great Critics: An Anthology of Literary Criticism.* New York: W. W. Norton & Co., 1932.

SOLLAS, WILLIAM J., *Ancient Hunters and Their Modern Representatives.* 3rd ed. New York: Macmillan Co., 1924.

SONNER, RUDOLF, *Musik und Tanz; von Kulttanz zum Jazz.* Leipzig: Quelle u. Meyer, 1930.

STOLL, EDGAR, *Shakespeare and Other Masters.* Cambridge (Mass.): Harvard University Press, 1940.

*SULLIVAN, LOUIS H., *Kindergarten Chats* (1901). Rev. ed. New York: Wittenborn & Schultz, 1947.

THIESS, FRANK, *Der Tanz als Kunstwerk.* 3rd ed. Munich, 1923.

THORBURN, JOHN M., *Art and the Unconscious.* London: K. Paul, Trench, Trubner & Co., 1925.

THORNDIKE, ASHLEY, *Tragedy.* Boston: Houghton, Mifflin & Co., 1908.

*TILLYARD, E. M. W., *Poetry Direct and Oblique.* London: Chatto & Windus, 1934.

*TOVEY, DONALD FRANCIS, *Essays in Musical Analysis.* 6 vols. Oxford University Press, 1935–39.

UDINE, JEAN D' (Albert Cozanet), *L'art et le geste.* Paris: 1910.

UNAMUNO Y JUGO, MIGUEL DE, *The Tragic Sense of Life in Men and in Peoples.* Translated by J. E. C. Flitch. London: Macmillan & Co., 1921.

*VALENTINER, W. R., *Origins of Modern Sculpture.* New York: Wittenborn & Co., 1946.

VEGA CARPIO, LOPE DE, *The New Art of Writing Plays.* Translated by W. T. Brewster. New York: Dramatic Museum of Columbia University, 1914.

VÉRON, EUGÈNE, *Aesthetics.* Translated by W. H. Armstrong, London: Chapman & Hall, 1879.

VINCI, LEONARDO DA, *A Treatise on Painting.* London, 1796.

WAGNER, RICHARD, *Gesammelte Schriften u. Dichtungen.* Vol. III, *Oper und Drama.* 5th ed. Leipzig: Breitkopf & Härtel, n. d.

WARD, A. C., *Foundations of English Prose*. London: G. Bell & Sons, 1931.

WEITZ, MORRIS, *Philosophy of the Arts*. Cambridge (Mass.): Harvard University Press, 1950.

*WHARTON, EDITH, *The Writing of Fiction*. New York: Charles Scribner's Sons, 1925.

WHITEHEAD, A. N., *Symbolism, Its Meaning and Effect*. New York: Macmillan Co., 1927.

WRIGHT, FRANK LLOYD, *Selected Writings, 1894–1940*. Edited with an introduction by Frederick Gutheim. New York: Duell, Sloan & Pearce, 1941.

ZAYAS, M. DE, and HAVILAND, P. B., *A Study of the Modern Evolution of Plastic Expression*. New York: Published by "291", 1913.

ZUCKER, A. E., *The Chinese Theater*. Boston: Little, Brown & Co., 1925.